Aderonke Apata

Nigerian LGBTQ Activist and Refugee Advocate − Unauthorized

Ming Yusuf

ISBN: 9781779696083
Imprint: Telephasic Workshop
Copyright © 2024 Ming Yusuf.
All Rights Reserved.

Contents

Life as a LGBTQ Activist in Nigeria   28
Escaping Persecution: A Journey to Freedom   52

Courage in the Face of Adversity   77
Courage in the Face of Adversity   77
Connecting with Other Activists   80
Aderonke's Fight against Homophobia   92
Empowering LGBTQ Youth   104
Aderonke's Impact on LGBTQ Refugee Advocacy   117

Triumph and Legacy   131
Triumph and Legacy   131
Recognitions and Awards   134
Aderonke's Advocacy Beyond Nigeria and the UK   146
The Future of LGBTQ Activism   158

The Unauthorized Story of Aderonke Apata   171
The Unauthorized Story of Aderonke Apata   171
The Controversial Book Release   173

Bibliography   179
Uncovering New Perspectives and Insights   184
Controversial Themes and Revelations   192
Aderonke's Journey: Reflections and Amidst Rumors   201

Aderonke Apata's Impact on Global LGBTQ Rights   209
Aderonke Apata's Impact on Global LGBTQ Rights   209
Advocacy and Activism in Nigeria   213
Refugee Advocacy and LGBTQ Rights   223
Aderonke's Inspirational Story and Travel Ban   232

         The Global Legacy of Aderonke Apata   240

Aderonke Apata's Continuing Fight for Justice   251
         Aderonke Apata's Continuing Fight for Justice   251
                  Current Activism and Advocacy Efforts   253
                          Future Aspirations and Goals   263
                  The Power of Aderonke's Personal Story   272
         Aderonke's Impact on LGBTQ Rights: Looking Ahead   280

Conclusion: The Aderonke Apata Story Lives On   291
         Conclusion: The Aderonke Apata Story Lives On   291
                  Reflecting on Aderonke's Journey   292
                  The Inspired Future of LGBTQ Activism   298
                  Aderonke Apata: The Unstoppable Force   305
                                   The Call to Action   312
                  A Final Farewell to Aderonke Apata   321

                                          Index   329

The Early Years in Nigeria

Aderonke Apata's journey as a prominent LGBTQ activist began in the vibrant and complex landscape of Nigeria. Born and raised in Lagos, Aderonke's early years were marked by a rich tapestry of cultural influences, traditional values, and the stark realities of societal expectations. This section delves into the foundational experiences that shaped Aderonke's identity and activism.

1.1.1 Aderonke's Childhood in Lagos

Lagos, a bustling metropolis, is often described as the heartbeat of Nigeria. It is a city where tradition and modernity collide, creating a unique environment for its inhabitants. Aderonke grew up in a family that, like many others, adhered to traditional Nigerian values. However, the expectations placed upon her as a young girl often felt stifling. The societal norms dictated that women should be submissive and conform to heteronormative roles, which clashed with Aderonke's burgeoning sense of self.

From an early age, Aderonke exhibited a fierce spirit and an unyielding desire to express her individuality. The vibrant streets of Lagos were both a playground and a battleground for her emerging identity. As she navigated her childhood, she encountered the duality of her existence: the joy of self-discovery and the pain of societal rejection.

1.1.2 The Influence of Traditional Values

Traditional values in Nigeria are deeply rooted in cultural and religious beliefs. Family structures are often patriarchal, and gender roles are rigidly defined. For Aderonke, these values presented a significant challenge. The expectation to marry a man and fulfill domestic duties was an ever-present pressure. This cultural backdrop created an internal conflict, as Aderonke began to understand her attraction to women.

The influence of traditional values extended beyond family dynamics; it permeated educational institutions and religious settings. Schools often reinforced heteronormative ideals, while churches preached messages of condemnation towards LGBTQ identities. Aderonke's experiences in these environments contributed to her understanding of the systemic oppression faced by LGBTQ individuals in Nigeria.

1.1.3 First Encounters with Homophobia

Aderonke's first encounters with homophobia were formative and painful. As she began to express her identity, she faced ridicule and ostracism from peers. The harsh realities of homophobia manifested in bullying at school, where derogatory slurs and exclusion became part of her daily existence. These experiences were not isolated incidents but rather reflections of a broader societal disdain for LGBTQ individuals.

The impact of these early encounters was profound. Aderonke learned that being true to herself came with significant risks. The fear of violence and rejection loomed large, shaping her understanding of the world around her. This sense of danger was compounded by the legal framework in Nigeria, where homosexuality is criminalized, further legitimizing discrimination and violence against LGBTQ individuals.

1.1.4 Finding Solace in the LGBTQ Community

In the midst of adversity, Aderonke found solace in the LGBTQ community. This network became a sanctuary where she could explore her identity without fear of judgment. The bonds formed with other LGBTQ individuals provided a sense of belonging that was often absent in her broader social circles. Through shared experiences, Aderonke discovered the power of community and solidarity.

The LGBTQ community in Nigeria, while marginalized, was resilient. Activism was often clandestine, as individuals sought to create safe spaces for themselves and others. Aderonke's involvement in this community sparked her passion for activism, as she began to understand the importance of fighting for visibility and rights.

1.1.5 The Struggle for Acceptance

The struggle for acceptance was a constant theme in Aderonke's early years. While she found a sense of belonging within the LGBTQ community, the outside world remained hostile. Family acceptance was a particularly challenging hurdle. Aderonke grappled with the fear of disappointing her family, who held traditional values dear. The desire for acceptance from her loved ones clashed with her need to live authentically.

This internal conflict was exacerbated by the societal stigma surrounding homosexuality. Aderonke witnessed firsthand the devastating consequences of rejection, as friends faced violence and disownment. These experiences galvanized her resolve to advocate for change, pushing her to confront the injustices faced by LGBTQ individuals in Nigeria.

1.1.6 The Impact of Religion

Religion plays a significant role in shaping societal attitudes in Nigeria. Aderonke's experiences with religion were complex, as she navigated the teachings of faith that often condemned her identity. The church, a central institution in many Nigerian communities, preached messages of intolerance towards LGBTQ individuals. This created a profound sense of alienation for Aderonke, as she struggled to reconcile her faith with her identity.

Despite the challenges posed by religious beliefs, Aderonke sought to find a spiritual path that embraced her authenticity. She began to question the interpretations of scripture that were used to justify discrimination. This critical examination of faith became a cornerstone of her activism, as she aimed to challenge the narratives that marginalized LGBTQ individuals within religious contexts.

1.1.7 Educational Pursuits and Activism

Education was a crucial aspect of Aderonke's early life. She excelled academically, driven by a desire to create a better future for herself and her community. Her educational pursuits opened doors to new ideas and perspectives, allowing her to engage with global conversations about LGBTQ rights.

As Aderonke delved into her studies, she became increasingly aware of the intersectionality of identity and oppression. This awareness fueled her activism, as she recognized the need for comprehensive approaches to LGBTQ rights that addressed the unique challenges faced by individuals in Nigeria. Aderonke's educational journey became a catalyst for her commitment to advocacy.

1.1.8 Exploring LGBTQ Activism on a Global Scale

Aderonke's exposure to global LGBTQ activism further shaped her understanding of the movement. She began to explore the successes and challenges faced by activists in different cultural contexts. This exploration highlighted the importance of solidarity and collaboration among LGBTQ individuals worldwide.

Through online platforms and international networks, Aderonke connected with activists from diverse backgrounds. These interactions inspired her to envision a future where LGBTQ rights were universally recognized and respected. The global perspective she gained fueled her determination to effect change in Nigeria.

1.1.9 The Birth of a Rebellion

The culmination of Aderonke's experiences in Nigeria led to the birth of a rebellion—a rebellion against the oppressive structures that sought to silence her and others like her. This rebellion was not merely a personal struggle; it was a collective fight for justice and equality. Aderonke understood that her identity was intertwined with the broader movement for LGBTQ rights.

Embracing her role as an activist, Aderonke began to organize events and initiatives aimed at raising awareness about LGBTQ issues. Her passion for advocacy ignited a fire within her, propelling her to stand against discrimination and injustice. The birth of this rebellion marked the beginning of Aderonke's transformative journey as a leader in the fight for LGBTQ rights.

1.1.10 Overcoming Challenges and Embracing Identity

The early years in Nigeria were fraught with challenges, yet Aderonke's resilience shone through. She learned to embrace her identity in the face of adversity, transforming pain into power. The struggles she faced became a source of strength, motivating her to advocate for others who felt marginalized and voiceless.

Aderonke's journey was not without its setbacks, but each challenge reinforced her commitment to activism. By embracing her identity and advocating for change, she became a beacon of hope for many in the LGBTQ community. Her early experiences in Nigeria laid the groundwork for a lifetime of activism, shaping her into the formidable leader she would become.

The Early Years in Nigeria

The journey of Aderonke Apata, a renowned Nigerian LGBTQ activist, begins in the vibrant city of Lagos, Nigeria. This bustling metropolis, known for its rich cultural tapestry and economic dynamism, also harbors deep-seated traditional values that often clash with the realities of modern identities, particularly those of the LGBTQ community. Understanding Aderonke's early years is crucial to grasping the complexities of her later activism.

1.1.1 Aderonke's Childhood in Lagos

Aderonke was born into a society where cultural norms dictated strict adherence to traditional gender roles and heteronormative expectations. Growing up in Lagos, she was surrounded by the vibrant sounds of street vendors, the rhythm of local music, and the warmth of family gatherings. However, beneath this colorful exterior lay an undercurrent of homophobia that would shape her formative years.

From a young age, Aderonke exhibited traits that set her apart. Her interests and preferences often clashed with societal expectations, leading to confusion and internal conflict. The cultural narrative she was exposed to emphasized conformity, and any deviation from the norm was met with scorn. This societal pressure created a duality in Aderonke's life: one that was lived in public and another that was hidden away, deep within her heart.

1.1.2 The Influence of Traditional Values

In Nigeria, traditional values are often intertwined with religious beliefs, which further complicates the acceptance of LGBTQ identities. Aderonke's upbringing was steeped in these traditions, where family honor and societal acceptance were paramount. The teachings of various religious institutions reinforced the notion that homosexuality was not only taboo but also sinful. This environment left many young people like Aderonke grappling with their identities, often feeling isolated and misunderstood.

The clash between Aderonke's emerging identity and the traditional values surrounding her led to feelings of shame and confusion. The societal expectation to marry and have children loomed large, creating a sense of urgency to conform. As she navigated her childhood, Aderonke began to feel the weight of these expectations pressing down on her, shaping her understanding of love and acceptance.

1.1.3 First Encounters with Homophobia

Aderonke's first encounters with homophobia were jarring. As she began to understand her identity, she faced bullying and ostracism from her peers. The painful words and actions of those around her served as a harsh introduction to the realities of being an LGBTQ individual in Nigeria.

For instance, during her teenage years, Aderonke attended a school where her classmates would often mock her for her perceived differences. This bullying was not limited to verbal taunts; it extended to physical intimidation and social exclusion. Such experiences left deep emotional scars and contributed to a pervasive sense of loneliness.

This early exposure to homophobia not only shaped Aderonke's understanding of her identity but also ignited a fire within her—a desire to challenge the status quo and fight for acceptance. It was during these formative years that she began to realize the importance of community and solidarity among those who shared similar struggles.

1.1.4 Finding Solace in the LGBTQ Community

Despite the challenges she faced, Aderonke found solace in the burgeoning LGBTQ community in Lagos. This community, though small and often underground, provided a safe haven for individuals like her who were searching for acceptance and understanding. Through clandestine gatherings and online forums, Aderonke connected with others who shared her experiences and struggles.

These interactions were transformative. They allowed her to express herself freely, away from the judgmental eyes of society. In this space, Aderonke discovered the power of shared stories and the strength that comes from unity. The bonds formed in these early encounters would later serve as the foundation for her activism.

1.1.5 The Struggle for Acceptance

The struggle for acceptance is a central theme in Aderonke's early life. As she began to embrace her identity, the fear of rejection loomed large. The societal stigma surrounding LGBTQ individuals in Nigeria created an environment where acceptance was often conditional or non-existent.

Aderonke's family, steeped in traditional values, struggled to understand her identity. Conversations about her sexuality were fraught with tension, leading to feelings of isolation. This lack of familial support further fueled her determination to seek acceptance within the LGBTQ community and beyond.

The desire for acceptance became a driving force in Aderonke's life, pushing her to challenge the very norms that sought to confine her. It was this struggle that ultimately laid the groundwork for her future activism, as she sought not only to find her place in the world but also to create a space for others like her.

1.1.6 The Impact of Religion

Religion plays a significant role in shaping societal attitudes towards LGBTQ individuals in Nigeria. Aderonke's experiences were no exception. Growing up in a religious household, she was often confronted with teachings that condemned homosexuality. These teachings created an internal conflict, as Aderonke grappled with her faith and her identity.

The dichotomy between her religious upbringing and her sexual orientation led to a crisis of faith. Aderonke found herself questioning the very beliefs that had been instilled in her. This struggle was not just personal; it reflected a broader societal issue where religious doctrines were used to justify discrimination and violence against LGBTQ individuals.

As she navigated her early years, Aderonke began to seek out interpretations of faith that embraced love and acceptance. This exploration would later inform her activism, as she aimed to challenge the harmful narratives perpetuated by religious institutions.

1.1.7 Educational Pursuits and Activism

Education emerged as a powerful tool for Aderonke during her formative years. It provided her with the knowledge and critical thinking skills necessary to question societal norms and advocate for change. As she pursued her studies, Aderonke became increasingly aware of the global LGBTQ movement and the strides being made in various parts of the world.

This newfound awareness ignited a passion for activism within her. Aderonke began to engage in discussions about LGBTQ rights, drawing inspiration from international movements while remaining grounded in her Nigerian context. Her educational pursuits not only shaped her understanding of activism but also equipped her with the tools to challenge discrimination and advocate for equality.

1.1.8 Exploring LGBTQ Activism on a Global Scale

As Aderonke delved deeper into her studies, she became fascinated by the global LGBTQ rights movement. She learned about the struggles and triumphs of activists around the world, and this knowledge fueled her desire to contribute to the fight for equality in Nigeria.

Aderonke's exploration of global activism revealed the interconnectedness of struggles faced by LGBTQ individuals, regardless of geographical boundaries. She began to see her fight as part of a larger tapestry of resistance against oppression. This understanding would later inform her approach to activism, emphasizing the importance of solidarity and collaboration across borders.

1.1.9 The Birth of a Rebellion

The culmination of Aderonke's early experiences led to the birth of a rebellion within her. No longer willing to accept the status quo, she began to challenge the societal norms that had constrained her for so long. This rebellion was not just personal; it was a call to action for others who felt marginalized and oppressed.

Aderonke's journey towards activism was marked by a series of pivotal moments—each reinforcing her determination to fight for LGBTQ rights in Nigeria. She began to organize small gatherings, creating safe spaces for individuals to share their stories and experiences. These gatherings laid the groundwork for a burgeoning movement that would challenge the prevailing narratives of homophobia and discrimination.

1.1.10 Overcoming Challenges and Embracing Identity

The path to embracing her identity was fraught with challenges. Aderonke faced not only societal rejection but also internal struggles as she navigated her journey. However, through resilience and determination, she began to embrace her identity fully.

Overcoming these challenges required a profound understanding of self and a commitment to authenticity. Aderonke's early years were marked by a struggle to reconcile her identity with the expectations of society, but ultimately, she emerged as a powerful voice for change. Her journey was a testament to the strength of the human spirit and the importance of embracing one's true self.

In conclusion, Aderonke Apata's early years in Nigeria were characterized by a complex interplay of cultural, religious, and societal influences. These experiences shaped her understanding of identity and fueled her passion for activism. As she navigated the challenges of growing up in a society that often rejected her, Aderonke laid the foundation for her future work as a leading LGBTQ activist and refugee advocate, demonstrating that the struggle for acceptance and equality is a journey worth taking.

ERROR. thisXsection() returned an empty string with textbook depth = 3.
ERROR. thisXsection() returned an empty string with textbook depth = 3.
ERROR. thisXsection() returned an empty string with textbook depth = 3.

The Influence of Traditional Values

In exploring the life of Aderonke Apata, it is essential to understand the profound impact of traditional values on her upbringing and her subsequent journey as an LGBTQ activist in Nigeria. Traditional Nigerian culture, deeply rooted in communal norms and values, often emphasizes heteronormative relationships and roles, which can create a challenging environment for individuals who identify as LGBTQ.

Cultural Norms and Expectations

In many Nigerian communities, traditional values dictate the framework within which individuals are expected to live their lives. These norms are often derived from historical practices, religious beliefs, and societal expectations. For instance, marriage is viewed not merely as a personal union but as a communal obligation, where family lineage and continuity are of paramount importance. This societal framework posits that heterosexual relationships are the only acceptable form of intimacy, leaving little room for acceptance of LGBTQ identities.

The pressure to conform to these cultural expectations can lead to significant internal conflict for individuals like Aderonke. The clash between personal identity and societal norms often results in feelings of isolation and shame. The societal narrative, which glorifies traditional family structures, contributes to the stigmatization of LGBTQ individuals, making it difficult for them to navigate their identities openly.

Religious Influences

Religion also plays a crucial role in shaping traditional values in Nigeria. The country is predominantly Christian and Muslim, both of which have doctrines that generally view homosexuality as sinful. This religious backdrop reinforces the stigma surrounding LGBTQ identities, often leading to discrimination and persecution. Aderonke's experiences reflect this reality, as she encountered numerous instances where her sexual orientation was condemned by religious leaders and community members.

For example, in many churches and mosques, sermons often include messages that denounce homosexuality, framing it as a moral failing. This can create a hostile environment for LGBTQ individuals, who may feel compelled to suppress their identities to avoid ostracism. Aderonke's struggle for acceptance was further complicated by these religious doctrines, which often left her feeling alienated from both her community and her faith.

The Role of Family

Family dynamics are also significantly influenced by traditional values. In Nigeria, families often prioritize honor and reputation over individual desires, leading to a culture of silence surrounding LGBTQ issues. Aderonke's relationship with her family illustrates this tension. Her family's expectations for her to marry a man and fulfill traditional roles created a rift that made it difficult for her to embrace her true self.

The pressure to conform can lead to tragic outcomes, including rejection and violence against LGBTQ individuals. Many families, influenced by traditional values, may resort to "corrective" measures aimed at forcing their children into heterosexual norms. Aderonke's narrative highlights the painful reality faced by many LGBTQ individuals who are caught between their identities and their family's expectations.

Resistance and Rebellion

Despite the overwhelming influence of traditional values, Aderonke's journey also represents a form of resistance and rebellion against these norms. Her involvement in the LGBTQ community provided her with a sense of belonging and empowerment, allowing her to challenge the traditional narratives that sought to suppress her identity.

The emergence of LGBTQ activism in Nigeria can be seen as a direct response to these traditional values. Activists like Aderonke are not merely resisting societal norms; they are redefining what it means to be Nigerian and LGBTQ. By advocating for acceptance and equality, they challenge the status quo and pave the way for future generations to embrace their identities without fear.

Conclusion

In conclusion, the influence of traditional values on Aderonke Apata's life cannot be understated. These values shaped her experiences, informed her struggles, and ultimately fueled her activism. While traditional norms can create barriers for LGBTQ individuals, they also serve as a backdrop against which resistance and transformation occur. Aderonke's story is a testament to the power of resilience in the face of deeply entrenched societal beliefs, highlighting the ongoing struggle for acceptance and equality in Nigeria.

As Aderonke continues her advocacy, her journey serves as a beacon of hope for those navigating the complexities of identity within a traditional framework, reminding us that change is possible even in the most challenging of environments.

First Encounters with Homophobia

Aderonke Apata's journey into the world of LGBTQ activism did not begin in a vacuum; rather, it was shaped by the harsh realities of growing up in a society that often viewed her identity as an abomination. In Nigeria, a country where homosexuality is criminalized and deeply stigmatized, Aderonke's first encounters with homophobia were not merely personal challenges but reflections of a broader societal issue that permeated every aspect of life.

From a young age, Aderonke was acutely aware of the traditional values that governed her community. These values, often steeped in religious doctrine and cultural norms, dictated what was deemed acceptable behavior. The influence of these traditions created an environment where any deviation from the heterosexual norm was met with hostility. For Aderonke, this hostility manifested in various forms, from verbal abuse to social ostracism.

One of her earliest memories of homophobia occurred during her time in school. Aderonke recalls a particular incident during a physical education class, where her classmates made derogatory comments about her perceived femininity. The taunts were not only hurtful; they were a painful reminder that she was different in a world that demanded conformity. This moment marked a significant turning point in Aderonke's life, as it forced her to confront the reality of her identity in a society that would rather silence her than embrace her.

The theory of social identity provides a framework for understanding Aderonke's experiences. According to Henri Tajfel's Social Identity Theory, individuals derive a sense of self from their group memberships. In Aderonke's case, her identity as a member of the LGBTQ community was in direct conflict with the dominant cultural narrative that vilified such identities. The resulting cognitive dissonance created a profound internal struggle, as she grappled with the desire for acceptance and the reality of widespread discrimination.

$$D = \frac{(I_{in} - I_{out})}{I_{in} + I_{out}} \qquad (1)$$

Where: - D is the dissonance experienced, - I_{in} is the identity associated with acceptance (in-group), - I_{out} is the identity associated with rejection (out-group).

In Aderonke's case, the dissonance was palpable. The rejection she faced from her peers was compounded by the teachings of her religious upbringing, which condemned her identity as sinful. This duality of rejection—both from society and from her spiritual beliefs—was a heavy burden to bear.

As she navigated her teenage years, Aderonke's encounters with homophobia became more pronounced. The societal pressure to conform escalated, leading to increasingly aggressive forms of discrimination. One particularly harrowing experience involved a group of older boys who cornered her after school, hurling insults and threats. The fear she felt in that moment was a visceral reminder of the dangers that awaited those who dared to be themselves in a society that enforced rigid gender norms.

The impact of these experiences extended beyond immediate emotional pain; they contributed to a pervasive sense of isolation. Aderonke often found solace in the LGBTQ community, where she discovered a network of individuals who shared similar struggles. This community became a refuge, a place where she could express her true self without fear of retribution. However, the reality of homophobia loomed large, and the safety of these spaces was often threatened by external societal pressures.

The psychological effects of homophobia can be profound and long-lasting. Research indicates that individuals who experience discrimination based on their sexual orientation are at a higher risk for mental health issues, including anxiety and depression. Aderonke's own experiences echoed these findings, as she battled feelings of worthlessness and despair during her formative years. The internalization of societal stigma often leads to a cycle of self-doubt and self-hatred, which Aderonke had to confront head-on.

In her quest for acceptance, Aderonke began to engage with LGBTQ activism on a broader scale. Her initial encounters with homophobia fueled her determination to advocate for change, both for herself and for others who faced similar challenges. She recognized that her personal narrative was part of a larger tapestry of LGBTQ experiences in Nigeria—a narrative that demanded to be heard.

As she stepped into the role of an activist, Aderonke's early encounters with homophobia became a source of strength. They served as a catalyst for her advocacy work, driving her to confront the very systems of oppression that had sought to silence her. The resilience she developed in the face of adversity would become a defining characteristic of her activism.

In summary, Aderonke Apata's first encounters with homophobia were not merely isolated incidents; they were formative experiences that shaped her identity and her commitment to LGBTQ rights. Through her struggles, she learned the importance of community, resilience, and the power of standing up against discrimination. These early experiences laid the groundwork for her future work as an activist, as she sought to dismantle the barriers that perpetuated homophobia in Nigerian society.

Finding Solace in the LGBTQ Community

In the bustling streets of Lagos, where the vibrant colors of life often masked the shadows of intolerance, Aderonke Apata discovered a sanctuary within the LGBTQ community. This refuge became a critical lifeline, providing not only companionship but also a shared understanding of the struggles faced by individuals who dared to love differently in a society steeped in traditional values and rigid norms.

The LGBTQ community in Nigeria, despite its challenges, is a tapestry woven with resilience and solidarity. The concept of *chosen family* emerged as a fundamental pillar for many, including Aderonke. In sociological terms, the chosen family refers to a group of individuals who consciously choose to support one another, often filling the emotional and social voids left by biological families that may not accept their identities. This phenomenon is particularly significant in LGBTQ contexts, where acceptance from biological families is often scarce or non-existent.

Aderonke's early encounters with the LGBTQ community were marked by an overwhelming sense of relief and belonging. For the first time, she found herself among individuals who shared similar experiences of marginalization and discrimination. The camaraderie forged within this community was instrumental in shaping her identity and fueling her activism. As she navigated the complexities of her sexuality, the community provided a safe space for exploration and self-acceptance.

$$\text{Acceptance} = \text{Understanding} + \text{Support} \qquad (2)$$

This equation encapsulates the essence of what the LGBTQ community offered Aderonke. Understanding came from shared experiences, while support manifested through collective action and emotional backing. Together, these elements fostered a sense of belonging that was crucial for Aderonke's development as an activist.

However, the journey was not without its obstacles. The LGBTQ community in Nigeria faces rampant homophobia and discrimination, which often leads to internalized shame among its members. Aderonke herself experienced moments of doubt and fear, grappling with the societal stigma that painted her identity as deviant. Yet, it was within the community that she found the strength to confront these challenges. Support groups and social gatherings became platforms for dialogue and empowerment, where stories of resilience were shared, and strategies for coping with external pressures were developed.

One poignant example of this solidarity was the organization of underground meetings, where LGBTQ individuals would gather to share their experiences and strategize on ways to advocate for their rights. These meetings often took place in secret locations, highlighting the constant threat of persecution. The act of gathering itself became a form of resistance against the oppressive societal norms that sought to silence them. Aderonke's participation in these meetings not only reinforced her sense of belonging but also ignited her passion for activism.

Moreover, the role of art and culture within the LGBTQ community served as another avenue for solace. Aderonke found inspiration in the works of queer artists who bravely expressed their identities through poetry, music, and visual arts. This artistic expression not only provided a means of catharsis but also acted as a powerful tool for advocacy, challenging societal norms and fostering dialogue around LGBTQ issues. The intersection of art and activism became a defining aspect of Aderonke's journey, as she began to understand the importance of visibility and representation in the fight for equality.

In her quest for solace, Aderonke also engaged in online communities, which expanded her network beyond the confines of Nigeria. The digital space offered a platform for connection, allowing her to interact with LGBTQ individuals globally. This exposure to diverse perspectives and experiences enriched her understanding of the global LGBTQ movement and inspired her to take action in her own community.

As Aderonke navigated the complexities of her identity and the challenges of living in a homophobic society, the LGBTQ community emerged as a beacon of hope. It was a place where she could shed the weight of societal expectations and embrace her true self. The solidarity she found within this community not only provided her with solace but also ignited a fire within her to advocate for change.

In conclusion, finding solace in the LGBTQ community was a transformative experience for Aderonke Apata. It equipped her with the tools needed to confront adversity, inspired her activism, and fostered a profound sense of belonging. This chapter of her life laid the groundwork for her future endeavors, as she emerged not just as a member of the community but as a leader committed to advocating for the rights and dignity of LGBTQ individuals both in Nigeria and beyond.

The Struggle for Acceptance

Aderonke Apata's journey towards self-acceptance and acceptance from her community was fraught with challenges that many LGBTQ individuals face, particularly in conservative societies like Nigeria. Growing up in Lagos, Aderonke was deeply influenced by the traditional values that permeated her upbringing. In a society where heteronormativity is the norm, the existence of LGBTQ identities often faces denial and hostility. The struggle for acceptance is not merely a personal battle; it encompasses societal attitudes, familial relationships, and cultural norms.

The Weight of Traditional Values

In Nigeria, traditional values dictate much of social behavior, with rigid gender roles and expectations. The concept of masculinity and femininity is often defined narrowly, leaving little room for deviation. Aderonke's early encounters with these values shaped her understanding of identity and belonging. The societal pressure to conform to these ideals can lead to internalized homophobia, where individuals struggle to reconcile their sexual orientation with the expectations placed upon them.

$$\text{Acceptance} = \frac{\text{Self-Acceptance} + \text{Community Acceptance}}{\text{Cultural Norms}} \quad (3)$$

This equation illustrates the delicate balance between self-acceptance and the acceptance from the community, moderated by the prevailing cultural norms. In Aderonke's case, the equation often resulted in a low acceptance score due to the high cultural resistance against LGBTQ identities.

First Encounters with Homophobia

Aderonke's struggle for acceptance was exacerbated by her first encounters with homophobia. As she began to explore her identity, she faced rejection not only from peers but also from family members who adhered strictly to societal norms. This rejection manifested in various forms, from verbal abuse to ostracism, creating a hostile environment that made it difficult for her to express her true self.

Finding Solace in the LGBTQ Community

In the midst of this turmoil, Aderonke discovered the LGBTQ community, which became a refuge for her. This community provided not only a sense of belonging but also a platform for activism and self-expression. However, the struggle for acceptance within the LGBTQ community itself can also be complex, as individuals may face discrimination based on factors such as gender identity, socioeconomic status, and cultural background.

The Impact of Religion

Religion plays a significant role in shaping attitudes towards LGBTQ individuals in Nigeria. Many religious doctrines promote the idea that homosexuality is sinful, leading to further marginalization of LGBTQ individuals. Aderonke experienced this firsthand, as religious teachings often clashed with her identity. The internal conflict between her faith and her sexual orientation contributed to her struggle for acceptance, leading to feelings of guilt and shame.

The Struggle for Acceptance in Activism

As Aderonke began her activism, she encountered the additional challenge of seeking acceptance from both the LGBTQ community and the broader society. Activism often requires individuals to confront deeply ingrained prejudices and advocate for change, which can be met with resistance. Aderonke's efforts to organize events and protests were met with hostility, yet they also fostered a sense of solidarity among those who sought acceptance.

$$\text{Activism Impact} = \text{Community Engagement} \times \text{Awareness Campaigns} \quad (4)$$

This equation emphasizes the importance of community engagement and awareness campaigns in promoting acceptance. Aderonke's activism aimed to amplify LGBTQ voices and challenge the misconceptions surrounding LGBTQ identities, thereby increasing the likelihood of acceptance within the community.

The Ongoing Fight for Acceptance

Despite the challenges, Aderonke's journey illustrates the resilience of those fighting for acceptance. The struggle for acceptance is ongoing, as societal attitudes continue to evolve. Through her activism, Aderonke not only seeks acceptance for herself but also paves the way for future generations of LGBTQ individuals in Nigeria.

In conclusion, the struggle for acceptance is a multifaceted issue that encompasses personal, societal, and cultural dimensions. Aderonke Apata's story is a testament to the challenges faced by LGBTQ individuals in their quest for acceptance, highlighting the need for continued advocacy and support within both the LGBTQ community and society at large.

The Impact of Religion

Religion plays a pivotal role in shaping societal norms, values, and attitudes, particularly in countries like Nigeria, where a significant portion of the population adheres to various religious beliefs. In the context of Aderonke Apata's journey as an LGBTQ activist, the influence of religion cannot be overstated. It has been both a source of comfort and conflict, impacting her personal experiences and the broader landscape of LGBTQ rights in Nigeria.

Religious Context in Nigeria

Nigeria is a nation characterized by its religious diversity, primarily split between Islam in the north and Christianity in the south. The intertwining of religion with cultural practices has led to a complex relationship with issues of sexuality and gender identity. For many individuals, religious teachings provide a framework for understanding morality, ethics, and acceptable behavior. Unfortunately, this framework often perpetuates homophobia and discrimination against LGBTQ individuals.

The Role of Religious Institutions

Religious institutions in Nigeria have historically condemned homosexuality, framing it as a sin or moral failing. Prominent religious leaders have used their platforms to preach against LGBTQ rights, often invoking scriptural references to justify their stance. For instance, many Christian denominations reference passages from the Bible, such as Leviticus 18:22, which states, "You shall not lie with a male as with a woman; it is an abomination." Similarly, Islamic teachings often emphasize traditional gender roles and heterosexual relationships, leading to a cultural environment that marginalizes LGBTQ identities.

Internal Conflict and Personal Struggles

For Aderonke, the conflict between her identity and the religious values surrounding her was profound. Growing up in a society steeped in religious conservatism, she faced significant internal struggles. The teachings of her faith often clashed with her understanding of her sexual orientation, leading to feelings of guilt and shame. This internalized homophobia can be understood through the lens of psychological theories such as Cognitive Dissonance Theory, which posits that individuals experience discomfort when holding two conflicting beliefs.

$$D = \sqrt{(B_1 - B_2)^2} \tag{5}$$

Where D represents the level of dissonance experienced, B_1 is the belief in religious teachings against homosexuality, and B_2 is the belief in her own sexual identity. The greater the difference between these beliefs, the higher the dissonance, which can lead to emotional distress.

Community Reactions and Backlash

The backlash from religious communities toward LGBTQ individuals can be severe. Aderonke witnessed firsthand the consequences of being openly LGBTQ in a religiously charged environment. Many LGBTQ individuals in Nigeria face ostracism from their families and communities, driven by the fear of being labeled as sinful or immoral. This societal rejection is often compounded by violence and discrimination, as religious rhetoric can incite hostility toward LGBTQ individuals.

For example, in 2014, the Same-Sex Marriage (Prohibition) Act was enacted in Nigeria, which criminalized same-sex relationships and imposed harsh penalties for those who engaged in them. This law was supported by various religious groups, who argued that it aligned with their moral beliefs. The act not only legitimized discrimination but also emboldened individuals to act on their prejudices, resulting in increased violence against LGBTQ individuals.

Finding Solace in Faith

Despite the challenges posed by mainstream religious teachings, Aderonke's journey also highlights the potential for finding solace and support within faith communities that embrace LGBTQ individuals. As she navigated her identity, Aderonke sought out affirming spaces where she could reconcile her faith with her sexuality. This journey reflects a growing movement within some religious communities to adopt more inclusive interpretations of scripture.

The Intersection of Faith and Activism

Aderonke's activism is also a testament to the intersection of faith and LGBTQ rights. She has worked to engage religious leaders and communities in dialogue about acceptance and love, challenging the notion that religion must inherently oppose LGBTQ identities. By advocating for a more inclusive understanding of faith, Aderonke aims to create spaces where LGBTQ individuals can feel accepted and valued within their religious communities.

In conclusion, the impact of religion on Aderonke Apata's life and activism is multifaceted. While it has posed significant challenges and contributed to societal discrimination, it has also provided a platform for dialogue, understanding, and potential reconciliation. As Aderonke continues her fight for LGBTQ rights, she embodies the possibility of bridging the gap between faith and identity, advocating for a world where love and acceptance transcend religious boundaries.

Educational Pursuits and Activism

Aderonke Apata's educational journey played a pivotal role in shaping her activism and commitment to LGBTQ rights in Nigeria. Growing up in Lagos, she faced an educational landscape fraught with challenges, particularly as a member of the LGBTQ community. Yet, Aderonke's pursuit of knowledge became a powerful tool in her fight against discrimination and injustice.

The Importance of Education

Education is often seen as a fundamental right and a key to empowerment. In the context of LGBTQ activism, education serves multiple purposes: it raises awareness, fosters understanding, and equips individuals with the knowledge necessary to challenge oppressive systems. For Aderonke, education was not just a personal achievement; it was a means to advocate for her community.

Theories of social justice emphasize the role of education in promoting equality. According to Paulo Freire's critical pedagogy, education should be a practice of freedom, enabling individuals to question and transform their reality [?]. This perspective resonated with Aderonke, who viewed her educational pursuits as a way to combat the societal norms that marginalized LGBTQ individuals.

Challenges Faced in Education

Despite her determination, Aderonke encountered significant obstacles in her educational journey. The influence of traditional values in Nigeria often manifested in educational institutions, where homophobia was prevalent. Students who identified as LGBTQ faced bullying, discrimination, and isolation, which could severely impact their academic performance and mental health.

For instance, a study by the International Lesbian, Gay, Bisexual, Trans and Intersex Association (ILGA) highlighted that LGBTQ students in Nigeria often experienced harassment from peers and educators alike [?]. This hostile environment made it challenging for Aderonke to fully engage in her studies and express her identity.

Activism Through Education

Recognizing the power of education, Aderonke actively sought to use her academic experiences to fuel her activism. She participated in various student organizations that focused on human rights and social justice. These platforms allowed her to connect with like-minded individuals and advocate for LGBTQ rights within the educational system.

Aderonke's involvement in these organizations was not without risks. She often faced backlash from both peers and authorities, yet she persisted, believing that education could be a catalyst for change. By organizing workshops and discussions on LGBTQ issues, she aimed to raise awareness and foster a more inclusive environment for all students.

Influencing Policy and Curriculum

As Aderonke progressed in her education, she became increasingly aware of the systemic barriers that LGBTQ individuals faced within the educational system. This awareness motivated her to advocate for policy changes that would promote inclusivity and protect the rights of LGBTQ students.

One significant challenge in this arena was the lack of LGBTQ-inclusive curricula. Aderonke argued that education should reflect the diversity of society, including the experiences and contributions of LGBTQ individuals. She collaborated with educators and activists to develop educational materials that highlighted LGBTQ history and issues, aiming to create a more comprehensive and accurate representation of society.

The Role of Higher Education

Aderonke's journey eventually led her to pursue higher education, where she found a more supportive environment. Universities often serve as hubs for activism and progressive thought, providing students with opportunities to engage in meaningful discussions about social justice.

At university, Aderonke became involved in LGBTQ advocacy groups that worked to create safe spaces for students. These groups organized events, workshops, and campaigns aimed at raising awareness of LGBTQ issues on campus. Aderonke's leadership in these initiatives helped to foster a sense of community among LGBTQ students and allies.

Global Perspectives on Education and Activism

Aderonke's educational pursuits also opened doors to a global perspective on LGBTQ activism. Through international conferences and exchange programs, she connected with activists from around the world, sharing experiences and strategies for advocacy. This global network enriched her understanding of the complexities of LGBTQ rights and the various approaches to activism.

For example, during a conference in Europe, Aderonke learned about the impact of comprehensive sex education on LGBTQ youth. This knowledge inspired her to advocate for similar initiatives in Nigeria, emphasizing the importance of educating young people about sexual orientation and gender identity in a safe and supportive environment.

Conclusion: Education as a Tool for Change

Aderonke Apata's educational journey illustrates the profound connection between education and activism. Through her experiences, she demonstrated that education is not merely a personal achievement but a collective tool for social change. By advocating for inclusive educational practices and policies, Aderonke aimed to empower future generations of LGBTQ activists in Nigeria and beyond.

Her commitment to education as a means of activism underscores the importance of creating safe and inclusive spaces for all individuals, regardless of their sexual orientation or gender identity. Aderonke's story serves as a reminder that the pursuit of knowledge can be a powerful catalyst for change, enabling individuals to challenge injustice and advocate for a more equitable society.

Exploring LGBTQ Activism on a Global Scale

LGBTQ activism has evolved into a powerful global movement, transcending borders and cultural barriers. Aderonke Apata, as a prominent figure in this movement, exemplifies the interconnectedness of local struggles and global advocacy. In this section, we will explore the various dimensions of LGBTQ activism on a global scale, including its theoretical frameworks, the challenges faced by activists, and notable examples of successful initiatives.

Theoretical Frameworks

To understand the dynamics of LGBTQ activism globally, it is essential to consider several theoretical frameworks that inform the movement. One such framework is **Intersectionality**, a term coined by Kimberlé Crenshaw, which emphasizes the interconnected nature of social categorizations such as race, class, and gender. This theory posits that individuals experience oppression in varying degrees based on their intersecting identities. For LGBTQ activists, this means recognizing that issues of race, socioeconomic status, and gender identity significantly impact the experiences of community members.

Another critical framework is **Globalization Theory**, which examines how global interconnectedness shapes local realities. The dissemination of information through social media has allowed LGBTQ activists to share their stories and strategies, fostering a sense of solidarity across borders. This interconnectedness has led to the emergence of a **Global LGBTQ Rights Agenda**, advocating for universal human rights, including the right to love and express one's identity without fear of persecution.

Challenges Faced by Activists

Despite the progress made, LGBTQ activists worldwide face numerous challenges. One of the most pressing issues is the **criminalization of homosexuality** in many countries. According to a report by the International Lesbian, Gay, Bisexual, Trans and Intersex Association (ILGA), as of 2021, 69 countries still criminalize same-sex relationships, with severe penalties in some regions, including imprisonment and even death.

Additionally, activists often encounter **backlash from conservative groups** and governments. For example, in countries like Russia and Uganda, anti-LGBTQ legislation has been enacted, leading to increased violence and discrimination against LGBTQ individuals. This backlash is often fueled by cultural and religious beliefs that view homosexuality as immoral, reinforcing the stigma surrounding LGBTQ identities.

Furthermore, the COVID-19 pandemic has exacerbated existing inequalities, particularly for LGBTQ individuals in marginalized communities. Access to healthcare, mental health support, and safe spaces has been significantly hindered, highlighting the urgent need for targeted interventions.

Examples of Global Activism

Despite these challenges, there are numerous examples of successful LGBTQ activism on a global scale. One notable initiative is the **Free and Equal Campaign**, launched by the United Nations Human Rights Office in 2013. This campaign aims to promote equal rights and acceptance for LGBTQ individuals worldwide, encouraging governments to adopt non-discrimination laws and policies. The campaign has successfully raised awareness and mobilized support for LGBTQ rights in various countries, demonstrating the potential of international collaboration.

Another impactful example is the **Global Equality Fund**, which provides financial support to LGBTQ organizations working in hostile environments. This fund has enabled grassroots activists to implement programs addressing violence, discrimination, and health disparities faced by LGBTQ individuals. By providing resources and support, the Global Equality Fund empowers local activists to effect change within their communities.

The Role of Social Media

Social media has played a pivotal role in amplifying LGBTQ voices and fostering global solidarity. Platforms like Twitter, Instagram, and Facebook have become vital tools for activists to share their stories, mobilize support, and raise awareness about LGBTQ issues. Campaigns such as #LoveIsLove and #Pride have garnered international attention, uniting individuals in the fight for equality.

Moreover, social media has facilitated the documentation of human rights abuses against LGBTQ individuals, allowing activists to hold governments accountable. The use of hashtags and viral campaigns has brought global attention to local struggles, creating a sense of urgency for action.

Conclusion

Exploring LGBTQ activism on a global scale reveals a complex interplay of challenges and triumphs. Aderonke Apata's journey illustrates how local activism can resonate on a global level, inspiring others to join the fight for equality. As the movement continues to evolve, it is crucial for activists to embrace intersectionality, leverage social media, and collaborate across borders to create a more inclusive and equitable world for all LGBTQ individuals. The fight for LGBTQ rights is far from over, but the resilience and determination of activists like Aderonke serve as a beacon of hope for future generations.

$$R = \frac{V}{I} \qquad (6)$$

Where R is resistance, V is voltage, and I is current. This equation metaphorically represents the resistance faced by LGBTQ activists as they work to increase the voltage of visibility and acceptance in a world that often seeks to suppress their identities.

The Birth of a Rebellion

The journey of Aderonke Apata is not merely a narrative of personal struggle; it is a powerful testament to the birth of a rebellion against systemic oppression and societal norms. In Nigeria, where LGBTQ identities are criminalized and shunned, Aderonke's emergence as an activist signified a pivotal moment in the fight for equality. This rebellion was not born overnight; it was a gradual awakening fueled by personal experiences, collective pain, and the indomitable spirit of a community yearning for acceptance and rights.

The Catalyst for Change

Aderonke's early encounters with homophobia and discrimination were critical in shaping her resolve. The oppressive environment in Lagos, where traditional values often clashed with her identity, acted as a catalyst for her activism. The stark contrast between societal expectations and her personal truth ignited a fire within her. As she faced rejection from family and society, Aderonke began to channel her pain into a broader fight against the injustices faced by the LGBTQ community.

This transformation can be understood through the lens of social movement theory, particularly the concept of *collective identity*. According to Tilly (2004), collective identity emerges when individuals recognize shared grievances and come together to advocate for change. Aderonke's experiences resonated with many others, fostering a sense of solidarity that became the backbone of the rebellion.

Mobilizing the Community

As Aderonke began to organize events and protests, she tapped into the power of collective action. She understood that to challenge the status quo, it was essential to mobilize the community. This mobilization was not without its challenges, as fear of persecution loomed large over potential participants. However, Aderonke's courage inspired others to step forward, creating a ripple effect that galvanized the LGBTQ community in Nigeria.

One significant example of this mobilization was the organization of Pride events, which served as a platform for visibility and expression. These events were not just celebrations; they were acts of defiance against a repressive regime. By creating safe spaces for LGBTQ individuals to gather and express themselves, Aderonke and her allies laid the groundwork for a rebellion that challenged societal norms.

The Role of Digital Activism

In the age of technology, Aderonke recognized the potential of social media as a tool for activism. Platforms like Twitter and Facebook became vital in disseminating information, rallying support, and amplifying LGBTQ voices. The digital realm provided a semblance of safety, allowing activists to connect and share their stories without the immediate threat of physical violence.

Aderonke's use of social media exemplified the concept of *networked activism*, where individuals leverage online platforms to mobilize support and foster community. As she shared her journey and the struggles faced by the LGBTQ community, she tapped into a global audience, garnering attention and support from international allies. This global solidarity became instrumental in legitimizing the rebellion and highlighting the plight of LGBTQ individuals in Nigeria.

Confronting the System

The rebellion was not solely about visibility; it was also about confronting the legal and institutional barriers that perpetuated discrimination. Aderonke and her fellow activists began to challenge homophobic laws and policies, advocating for legal recognition and protections for LGBTQ individuals. This aspect of their struggle can be analyzed through the framework of *political opportunity structure*, which posits that social movements thrive when there are openings in the political landscape that can be exploited for change (Tilly & Tarrow, 2015).

One notable instance of this confrontation occurred during the campaign for the repeal of the Same-Sex Marriage Prohibition Act, which criminalized same-sex relationships in Nigeria. Aderonke's fearless advocacy brought attention to the discriminatory nature of the law, and her efforts to engage with policymakers highlighted the urgent need for reform.

The Impact of Aderonke's Rebellion

The birth of this rebellion, spearheaded by Aderonke Apata, has had profound implications for the LGBTQ movement in Nigeria and beyond. It has inspired a new generation of activists who are unafraid to challenge societal norms and fight for their rights. Aderonke's story serves as a beacon of hope for those who continue to face discrimination and persecution.

Moreover, the rebellion has sparked conversations around LGBTQ rights on a global scale, drawing attention to the need for international advocacy and support. As Aderonke continues to fight for justice, her legacy is a reminder that rebellion against oppression is not just an act of defiance; it is a declaration of existence and a call for equality.

In conclusion, the birth of Aderonke Apata's rebellion represents a significant turning point in the struggle for LGBTQ rights in Nigeria. Through her courage, determination, and unwavering commitment to justice, Aderonke has not only transformed her own life but has also ignited a movement that challenges the very foundations of discrimination and inequality. The rebellion she has fostered is a testament to the power of collective action, the importance of visibility, and the enduring spirit of those who dare to dream of a world where love knows no bounds.

Overcoming Challenges and Embracing Identity

Aderonke Apata's journey of self-discovery and acceptance unfolded amidst a backdrop of adversity and societal rejection. Growing up in Lagos, Nigeria, she faced a tumultuous environment shaped by rigid traditional values and pervasive homophobia. This section delves into the multifaceted challenges Aderonke encountered and how she navigated these obstacles to embrace her identity fully.

Confronting Societal Norms

In a society where heterosexuality is often viewed as the only acceptable orientation, Aderonke's realization of her identity as a lesbian was fraught with difficulty. The cultural norms in Nigeria dictate strict gender roles, which can lead to the marginalization of those who deviate from these expectations. Aderonke's initial encounters with her sexual orientation were marked by confusion and fear, as she grappled with the implications of being different in a society that vehemently opposed such differences.

The societal pressures were compounded by the influence of religious beliefs that demonize homosexuality. In many Nigerian communities, religious institutions play a pivotal role in shaping public opinion. Aderonke experienced firsthand the impact of these beliefs, which often manifested as verbal abuse and social ostracism. This environment created a psychological battleground where Aderonke had to confront not only her identity but also the deeply ingrained prejudices surrounding it.

Finding Community and Support

Despite the challenges, Aderonke found solace in the LGBTQ community, which provided a sanctuary where she could express herself freely. This community became instrumental in her journey toward self-acceptance. The connections she formed with other individuals who shared similar experiences fostered a sense of belonging that was crucial for her emotional well-being.

The support from the LGBTQ community was not merely social; it was also educational. Aderonke learned about the broader spectrum of sexual orientation and gender identity, which helped her contextualize her experiences within a global narrative of LGBTQ rights. This newfound knowledge empowered her to challenge the stigma and discrimination she faced, as she recognized that her struggles were part of a larger fight for equality.

The Role of Activism in Identity Formation

Activism played a pivotal role in Aderonke's journey of embracing her identity. As she became more involved in LGBTQ advocacy, she transformed her personal struggles into a collective fight for rights and recognition. This transition from a personal to a political identity allowed her to reclaim her narrative and challenge the societal norms that sought to suppress her.

Through organizing events and participating in protests, Aderonke not only asserted her identity but also inspired others to do the same. The act of standing up against discrimination became a powerful form of self-affirmation. Aderonke's activism was not just about fighting for her rights; it was about creating a space where others could also embrace their identities without fear.

Psychological Resilience and Growth

Overcoming challenges is often accompanied by psychological growth. Aderonke's journey was marked by resilience, as she learned to navigate the complexities of her identity in a hostile environment. The psychological theories of resilience suggest that individuals who face adversity can develop coping strategies that enhance their ability to thrive despite challenges.

Aderonke's resilience was evident in her ability to transform pain into purpose. She began to view her experiences not as burdens but as catalysts for change. This shift in perspective is supported by the theory of post-traumatic growth, which posits that individuals can emerge from trauma with a renewed sense of strength and purpose.

Celebrating Identity and Intersectionality

Embracing her identity also meant acknowledging the intersectionality of her experiences. Aderonke recognized that her identity as a Black lesbian woman was shaped by multiple layers of oppression, including race, gender, and sexuality. This understanding deepened her commitment to advocating for marginalized voices within the LGBTQ community.

Aderonke's journey highlights the importance of celebrating identity in all its forms. By embracing her complexity, she not only affirmed her place within the LGBTQ community but also challenged the monolithic narratives that often dominate discussions about identity. Her story serves as a testament to the power of self-acceptance and the importance of recognizing the diverse experiences within the LGBTQ spectrum.

Conclusion: A Journey of Empowerment

In conclusion, Aderonke Apata's journey of overcoming challenges and embracing her identity is a powerful narrative of resilience, community, and activism. Through her experiences, she exemplifies the struggle for self-acceptance in the face of societal rejection and the transformative power of activism. Her story is not just about personal triumph; it is a call to action for others to embrace their identities and fight for a world where everyone can live authentically and freely.

The journey of embracing one's identity is ongoing, and Aderonke continues to inspire countless individuals to stand tall in their truth. As she navigates the complexities of her identity, she reminds us that the path to self-acceptance is often fraught with challenges, but it is a journey worth undertaking.

Life as a LGBTQ Activist in Nigeria

Standing Against Discrimination

Standing against discrimination is not just an act of defiance; it is a profound commitment to justice, equality, and humanity. For Aderonke Apata, this fight became a central pillar of her activism. In a country where LGBTQ individuals face systemic discrimination, violence, and criminalization, Aderonke's courage to stand up against such injustices has become a beacon of hope for many.

Theoretical Framework

To understand the gravity of Aderonke's fight against discrimination, we must first consider the theoretical frameworks that underpin LGBTQ activism. The **Intersectionality Theory**, coined by Kimberlé Crenshaw, posits that individuals experience oppression in varying configurations and degrees of intensity based on their intersecting identities, such as race, gender, and sexual orientation. In Nigeria, where colonial-era laws still criminalize homosexuality, LGBTQ individuals face unique challenges that are compounded by their socio-economic status, ethnicity, and religion.

The Nature of Discrimination in Nigeria

Discrimination against LGBTQ individuals in Nigeria is pervasive and multi-faceted. The *Same-Sex Marriage (Prohibition) Act* of 2014 exemplifies institutionalized discrimination, prohibiting same-sex marriage and imposing penalties for those who advocate for LGBTQ rights. This law not only criminalizes love but also fosters a climate of fear and violence, as individuals are often subjected to harassment, arrest, and even physical assault.

According to a report by the International Lesbian, Gay, Bisexual, Trans and Intersex Association (ILGA), Nigeria ranks among the most dangerous countries for LGBTQ individuals. The report highlights that 70% of Nigerians believe that homosexuality should be illegal, reflecting deep-rooted cultural and religious beliefs that contribute to widespread discrimination.

Aderonke's Activism

In the face of such overwhelming adversity, Aderonke Apata emerged as a formidable force against discrimination. Her activism began with grassroots organizing and awareness campaigns aimed at educating the public about LGBTQ rights. Aderonke utilized various platforms, including social media and community events, to amplify the voices of marginalized individuals and challenge harmful stereotypes.

Example: The Lagos Pride March

One of Aderonke's notable initiatives was the organization of the Lagos Pride March. This event aimed to celebrate diversity and promote acceptance within Nigerian society. Despite the risks involved, Aderonke and her team mobilized hundreds of participants, showcasing their resilience and determination to stand against discrimination. The march not only raised awareness but also fostered solidarity among LGBTQ individuals and allies, demonstrating the power of collective action.

Confronting Discrimination Head-On

Aderonke's approach to standing against discrimination involved confronting it head-on. She advocated for the decriminalization of homosexuality and fought against discriminatory laws through legal challenges and public campaigns. Her efforts included collaborating with local and international human rights organizations, which provided crucial support and resources in the fight for equality.

Legal Challenges

Aderonke's legal battles exemplify her commitment to justice. She participated in landmark cases that challenged the constitutionality of anti-LGBTQ laws in Nigeria. By leveraging both national and international legal frameworks, Aderonke sought to hold the Nigerian government accountable for its discriminatory practices. Her work underscored the importance of legal advocacy in dismantling systemic discrimination.

The Role of Media and Public Perception

Media representation plays a critical role in shaping public perception of LGBTQ issues. Aderonke recognized the power of storytelling in her activism. By sharing her personal experiences and those of others in the LGBTQ community, she humanized the struggle against discrimination. Documentaries, interviews, and social media campaigns helped to challenge negative stereotypes and foster empathy among the broader public.

Example: Social Media Campaigns

Aderonke launched several social media campaigns that highlighted the stories of LGBTQ individuals in Nigeria. These campaigns aimed to counteract the prevailing narratives that demonize LGBTQ identities. By utilizing hashtags such as #LoveIsLove and #EndHomophobia, Aderonke engaged a global audience, garnering support and solidarity from allies around the world.

Challenges and Resilience

Despite her relentless efforts, Aderonke faced numerous challenges in her fight against discrimination. Threats to her safety, harassment from authorities, and backlash from conservative groups were constant realities. However, her resilience became a source of inspiration for many. Aderonke's ability to navigate these challenges while maintaining her commitment to activism is a testament to her strength and determination.

Conclusion

Aderonke Apata's fight against discrimination is a powerful narrative of courage and resilience. By standing firm against systemic injustices, she has not only championed LGBTQ rights in Nigeria but has also inspired a global movement for equality. Her story serves as a reminder that the fight against discrimination is ongoing and that every voice matters in the quest for justice and acceptance. As Aderonke continues her advocacy, she embodies the spirit of defiance against oppression, encouraging others to join the fight for a more inclusive world.

Organizing LGBTQ Events and Protests

Aderonke Apata's journey as an LGBTQ activist in Nigeria was marked by her relentless commitment to organizing events and protests that brought visibility to the struggles faced by the community. The act of organizing is not merely about logistics; it involves strategic planning, community engagement, and a deep understanding of the socio-political landscape. In a country where LGBTQ identities are criminalized, the stakes are extraordinarily high, making the organization of events a courageous act of defiance.

Theoretical Framework

The organization of LGBTQ events and protests can be understood through the lens of social movement theory, particularly the Resource Mobilization Theory (RMT) and the Political Process Model (PPM). RMT posits that the success of social movements depends on the resources available to them, including financial support, human capital, and organizational infrastructure. In contrast, PPM emphasizes the importance of political opportunities and the mobilization of collective identities.

In the context of Nigeria, Aderonke faced numerous challenges, including limited resources, government repression, and societal stigma. However, she utilized her networks to mobilize resources effectively. For instance, collaborations with international NGOs provided financial backing and technical support, allowing her to organize events that would otherwise be impossible.

Challenges Faced

Organizing LGBTQ events in Nigeria is fraught with challenges. The legal framework criminalizing same-sex relationships creates an atmosphere of fear and uncertainty. Aderonke and her team had to navigate potential police crackdowns, societal backlash, and the threat of violence. For example, during the planning of a pride event, they had to ensure that participants were aware of safety protocols and had escape routes in case of a police raid.

Moreover, societal stigma often leads to internalized homophobia, making it difficult for individuals to participate openly. Many potential allies were hesitant to join for fear of being outed or facing repercussions in their personal and professional lives. Aderonke addressed this by creating safe spaces for dialogue, allowing individuals to express their fears and concerns while fostering a sense of community.

Event Examples

One of the most significant events organized by Aderonke was the *LGBTQ Pride March in Lagos*. This event aimed to celebrate LGBTQ identities and raise awareness about the issues facing the community. The planning process involved extensive outreach to local LGBTQ organizations, allies, and even sympathetic media outlets to garner support and visibility. Aderonke's team utilized social media platforms to create buzz and encourage participation, emphasizing the importance of solidarity and collective action.

The march itself was a testament to resilience. Despite the threat of violence, hundreds of individuals gathered, waving rainbow flags and chanting slogans demanding equality. The event was met with both support and opposition, with counter-protests organized by conservative groups. This dichotomy highlighted the polarized nature of LGBTQ rights in Nigeria, where the struggle for acceptance often leads to confrontation.

Another notable event was the *Annual LGBTQ Film Festival*, which showcased films that explored LGBTQ themes and narratives. This festival not only provided a platform for artists but also served as an educational tool for the broader public. Aderonke believed that art has the power to challenge stereotypes and foster empathy. By inviting filmmakers and activists to discuss their work, the festival created a space for dialogue and understanding.

Impact and Outcomes

The impact of these events extended beyond immediate visibility. They fostered a sense of community among LGBTQ individuals in Nigeria, providing a platform for networking and support. For many participants, these gatherings were their first experience of being in a space where they could express their identities freely. Aderonke's ability to create such spaces was instrumental in building a resilient LGBTQ community.

Furthermore, the media coverage of these events played a crucial role in raising awareness both locally and internationally. Coverage of the pride march, for instance, drew attention to the harsh realities faced by LGBTQ individuals in Nigeria, prompting international advocacy and support. Aderonke leveraged this visibility to connect with global allies, emphasizing the need for international pressure on the Nigerian government to respect LGBTQ rights.

Conclusion

Organizing LGBTQ events and protests in Nigeria is a complex endeavor that requires courage, strategy, and resilience. Aderonke Apata's efforts to create these spaces not only challenged the status quo but also inspired a new generation of activists. Through her work, she demonstrated that even in the face of adversity, the power of collective action can lead to meaningful change. The legacy of these events continues to resonate, reminding us of the importance of visibility and solidarity in the ongoing fight for LGBTQ rights in Nigeria and beyond.

Confronting Police Brutality and Arrests

The struggle for LGBTQ rights in Nigeria has been marked by a significant challenge: the brutal response from law enforcement agencies. Aderonke Apata's activism took shape against a backdrop of systemic violence and discrimination, where police brutality became a grim reality for many in the LGBTQ community. The Nigerian government, driven by a mix of cultural conservatism and religious zealotry, has often sanctioned violence against those who dare to defy societal norms.

The Nature of Police Brutality

Police brutality against LGBTQ individuals in Nigeria is not merely a series of isolated incidents; it is a manifestation of institutionalized homophobia. According to a report by the International Lesbian, Gay, Bisexual, Trans and Intersex Association (ILGA), the Nigerian police are known for their harassment, physical violence, and unlawful arrests of LGBTQ individuals. This systemic oppression is rooted in the same legal frameworks that criminalize same-sex relationships, such as the Same-Sex Marriage (Prohibition) Act of 2014, which imposes severe penalties on LGBTQ individuals, including imprisonment.

The theory of institutionalized homophobia posits that societal norms and laws create an environment where violence against marginalized communities is not only tolerated but often encouraged. This theory is exemplified in the actions of law enforcement, where officers may feel empowered to act violently against LGBTQ individuals without fear of repercussions.

Aderonke's Experiences

Aderonke's own experiences with police brutality are a testament to the harsh realities faced by LGBTQ activists in Nigeria. During one protest aimed at advocating for LGBTQ rights, Aderonke and fellow activists were met with aggressive police tactics. Eyewitness accounts described the police using excessive force, including physical assault and intimidation, to disperse the crowd. Aderonke herself was detained, enduring hours of questioning and harassment, a tactic commonly employed to instill fear within the LGBTQ community.

This experience not only fueled Aderonke's resolve to fight against police brutality but also highlighted the urgent need for legal reforms and protections for LGBTQ individuals. The psychological impact of such encounters is profound, often leading to trauma and a sense of helplessness among victims.

Legal and Social Implications

The legal implications of police brutality extend beyond individual cases; they reflect a broader societal problem. The Nigerian legal system offers little recourse for victims of police violence. Reports of abuse are frequently met with indifference or outright dismissal by authorities, perpetuating a cycle of violence and fear. Aderonke and other activists have argued that the lack of accountability for police actions emboldens further abuses.

Socially, the stigma surrounding LGBTQ identities compounds the issue. Many victims of police brutality are reluctant to report incidents due to fears of further victimization or rejection from their communities. This silence serves to reinforce the power dynamics that allow such brutality to persist.

Activism Against Police Brutality

In response to these challenges, Aderonke has mobilized efforts to confront police brutality head-on. Collaborating with local and international organizations, she has advocated for the establishment of legal aid clinics to support victims of police violence. These clinics provide crucial resources, including legal representation and psychological support, helping individuals navigate the trauma of their experiences.

Moreover, Aderonke has utilized social media as a powerful tool for raising awareness. By sharing personal stories and testimonies from victims, she has helped to shine a light on the pervasive issue of police brutality. Campaigns aimed at educating the public about the rights of LGBTQ individuals have gained traction, fostering a culture of resistance against state-sanctioned violence.

Case Studies and Examples

Several notable cases exemplify the brutal realities faced by LGBTQ individuals at the hands of Nigerian police. In 2018, a group of LGBTQ activists was arrested during a community event in Lagos. Reports indicated that the police not only detained the activists but also subjected them to physical and sexual violence while in custody. Aderonke's advocacy efforts following this incident included organizing protests, engaging with human rights organizations, and lobbying for international support to pressure the Nigerian government to address these abuses.

Another case involved the unlawful arrest of a transgender woman, who was brutally beaten by police officers after being outed in public. Aderonke rallied support for the victim, highlighting the need for immediate intervention and legal protection for LGBTQ individuals. These cases are not just statistics; they represent the lives and stories of individuals who have faced unimaginable adversity.

Conclusion

Confronting police brutality and arrests is a critical aspect of Aderonke Apata's activism. Through her efforts, she not only seeks justice for victims but also works towards a broader societal change that challenges the systemic oppression of LGBTQ individuals in Nigeria. The fight against police brutality is intertwined with the fight for LGBTQ rights, and Aderonke's unwavering commitment serves as a beacon of hope for many. As she continues to confront these injustices, her story inspires a new generation of activists to stand firm in the face of adversity, demanding a future where all individuals, regardless of their sexual orientation, can live freely and without fear.

Growing Support from International Allies

In the complex landscape of LGBTQ activism in Nigeria, the emergence of international allies has played a pivotal role in amplifying the voices of marginalized communities and fostering a more inclusive environment. This support has manifested through various forms, including financial aid, advocacy, and the sharing of resources and strategies.

Theoretical Framework

The theory of transnational advocacy networks (TANs) provides a lens through which to understand the dynamics of international support for local LGBTQ movements. According to Keck and Sikkink (1998), TANs consist of a diverse array of actors, including non-governmental organizations (NGOs), social movements, and international institutions, which collaborate across borders to promote shared values and goals. This framework is particularly relevant to LGBTQ activism, as it highlights how local struggles can be connected to global human rights discourses.

International Organizations and NGOs

International organizations such as Amnesty International, Human Rights Watch, and ILGA (International Lesbian, Gay, Bisexual, Trans and Intersex Association) have been instrumental in providing support to Nigerian LGBTQ activists. These organizations often issue reports documenting human rights abuses, which can lead to increased international scrutiny and pressure on the Nigerian government. For instance, Amnesty International's 2019 report on the crackdown against LGBTQ individuals in Nigeria not only raised awareness but also galvanized international advocacy efforts.

$$\text{Advocacy Impact} = \text{Visibility} \times \text{Pressure} \times \text{Mobilization} \qquad (7)$$

In this equation, "Visibility" refers to the awareness raised through media coverage and reports, "Pressure" signifies the diplomatic and economic consequences faced by the Nigerian government, and "Mobilization" denotes the collective action taken by international allies in solidarity with local activists.

Grassroots Collaborations

The collaboration between Nigerian activists and international allies has also led to grassroots initiatives aimed at empowering local communities. For example, training programs organized by international NGOs have equipped Nigerian activists with essential skills in advocacy, legal rights, and digital security. These initiatives not only enhance the capacity of local activists but also foster a sense of solidarity and shared purpose.

Challenges and Critiques

Despite the growing support from international allies, challenges remain. Some critics argue that foreign intervention can sometimes overshadow local voices, leading to a form of neocolonialism where international actors dictate the terms of activism. This concern is particularly salient in the context of Nigeria, where cultural and social dynamics differ significantly from those in Western countries. The imposition of external values can alienate potential allies within the local community, as seen in instances where international campaigns have faced backlash for perceived insensitivity to Nigerian cultural contexts.

Case Studies of Successful Collaborations

One notable example of successful collaboration is the partnership between Aderonke Apata and international LGBTQ organizations during the campaign for the repeal of Nigeria's Same-Sex Marriage Prohibition Act. Through strategic alliances, Aderonke was able to mobilize international attention and resources, leading to increased pressure on Nigerian lawmakers. This collaboration not only highlighted the urgent need for legal reform but also showcased the power of collective action.

Another case study involves the use of social media platforms to connect Nigerian activists with global allies. The hashtag campaigns, such as #FreeNigeriaLGBTQ, have drawn significant international attention, resulting in global protests and demonstrations in solidarity with Nigerian LGBTQ individuals. This digital activism exemplifies how international support can transcend geographical boundaries and create a unified front against oppression.

Conclusion

The growing support from international allies has been a crucial factor in the fight for LGBTQ rights in Nigeria. While challenges persist, the collaboration between local activists and global organizations has the potential to create a more equitable and just society. As Aderonke Apata and her peers continue to navigate the complexities of activism, the solidarity and support from international allies will remain an essential component of their struggle for acceptance and equality.

Navigating the Legal Battle for LGBTQ Rights

The journey for LGBTQ rights in Nigeria is fraught with legal challenges that reflect the deeply entrenched societal norms and governmental policies that discriminate against sexual minorities. This section delves into the complexities of navigating the legal landscape for LGBTQ individuals in Nigeria, exploring the barriers they face, the strategies employed by activists, and the broader implications of legal reforms.

Understanding the Legal Framework

The legal framework governing LGBTQ rights in Nigeria is primarily shaped by colonial-era laws, particularly the Same-Sex Marriage (Prohibition) Act of 2014, which criminalizes same-sex relationships and imposes severe penalties, including imprisonment. This law not only reinforces societal stigma but also emboldens state-sanctioned violence against LGBTQ individuals. The legal environment is characterized by a lack of protections against discrimination based on sexual orientation or gender identity, leaving LGBTQ individuals vulnerable to abuses.

The Role of Activism in Legal Reform

Activism plays a crucial role in challenging the legal status quo. LGBTQ activists in Nigeria have employed various strategies to navigate the legal landscape, focusing on raising awareness, mobilizing support, and advocating for legal reforms. Organizations such as *The Initiative for Equal Rights (TIERs)* and *Queer Alliance Nigeria* have been at the forefront of this struggle, utilizing both local and international platforms to highlight human rights violations and push for legal changes.

Challenges in Legal Advocacy

Navigating the legal battle for LGBTQ rights in Nigeria presents numerous challenges:

- **Hostile Environment:** Activists often operate in a hostile environment where advocacy for LGBTQ rights is met with fierce opposition from both the government and conservative societal factions. This hostility can manifest in physical violence, harassment, and even assassination attempts against prominent activists.

- **Limited Legal Recourse:** The absence of protective laws means that LGBTQ individuals have limited avenues for seeking justice when their rights are violated. Many cases of discrimination or violence go unreported due to fear of further victimization.

- **Judicial Bias:** The judiciary in Nigeria is often influenced by societal prejudices against LGBTQ individuals, resulting in biased rulings that fail to uphold human rights. This bias complicates legal advocacy efforts, as activists must contend with a legal system that is not only unwelcoming but actively hostile.

Strategic Litigation and International Pressure

Despite these challenges, strategic litigation has emerged as a powerful tool for advocating for LGBTQ rights. Activists have sought to challenge discriminatory laws through the courts, aiming to set legal precedents that affirm the rights of LGBTQ individuals. For example, in 2019, a landmark case was brought before the Nigerian courts challenging the constitutionality of the Same-Sex Marriage (Prohibition) Act. Although the case was ultimately dismissed, it highlighted the potential for legal challenges to create dialogue around LGBTQ rights in Nigeria.

International pressure also plays a vital role in advancing the legal battle for LGBTQ rights. Advocacy from global organizations such as *Human Rights Watch* and *Amnesty International* has helped to shine a spotlight on the abuses faced by

LGBTQ individuals in Nigeria, urging the Nigerian government to uphold its international human rights obligations. This external pressure can sometimes lead to incremental changes in policy, as the government seeks to improve its international standing.

The Intersection of Culture and Law

Navigating the legal battle for LGBTQ rights in Nigeria cannot be divorced from the cultural context. The interplay between cultural beliefs and legal frameworks creates a complex landscape where advocacy must be sensitive to local customs and values. Activists often find themselves balancing the need for legal reform with the necessity of engaging with cultural narratives that frame LGBTQ identities as foreign or immoral.

Conclusion: The Path Forward

The legal battle for LGBTQ rights in Nigeria is ongoing and multifaceted. While significant challenges remain, the resilience of activists and the growing visibility of LGBTQ issues present opportunities for change. Continued advocacy, strategic litigation, and international solidarity are essential in navigating this complex legal landscape. As Aderonke Apata and her fellow activists demonstrate, the fight for justice is not merely a legal battle; it is a struggle for dignity, recognition, and the right to exist freely.

$$\text{Legal Rights} = \text{Activism} + \text{Cultural Engagement} + \text{International Pressure} \quad (8)$$

The Fight for Marriage Equality

The struggle for marriage equality is a significant facet of Aderonke Apata's activism, embodying the broader fight for LGBTQ rights in Nigeria and beyond. At its core, marriage equality refers to the legal recognition of same-sex marriages, allowing couples of the same sex to enjoy the same legal rights, responsibilities, and benefits as heterosexual couples. This fight is not merely about the act of marrying; it encompasses issues of love, recognition, dignity, and equality before the law.

Theoretical Framework

The theoretical underpinnings of the fight for marriage equality can be analyzed through several lenses, including human rights theory, feminist theory, and queer theory. From a human rights perspective, the denial of marriage equality constitutes a violation of fundamental rights, including the right to love, the right to family life, and the right to non-discrimination.

$$\text{Human Rights} \supset \text{Marriage Equality} \qquad (9)$$

Feminist theory adds another layer of complexity, as it examines how traditional marriage institutions often perpetuate gender norms and inequality. Advocates argue that marriage equality challenges these norms, promoting a more inclusive understanding of partnership that transcends gender binaries.

$$\text{Marriage Equality} \equiv \text{Gender Equality} \qquad (10)$$

Queer theory further critiques the institution of marriage itself, questioning whether it should be a goal for LGBTQ activists or whether alternative forms of relationships should be prioritized. This perspective encourages a broader discussion on the nature of love and commitment beyond legal definitions.

Challenges Faced

In Nigeria, the fight for marriage equality is fraught with challenges. The Same-Sex Marriage (Prohibition) Act, enacted in 2014, criminalizes same-sex unions and imposes severe penalties on individuals who engage in or support such relationships. This legal framework not only stifles personal freedoms but also fosters a culture of homophobia and violence against LGBTQ individuals.

$$\text{Legal Framework} \rightarrow \text{Social Stigma} \rightarrow \text{Violence} \qquad (11)$$

Activists like Aderonke have faced significant backlash for their advocacy, including threats, harassment, and even violence. Despite these risks, Aderonke has remained steadfast in her commitment to fight for marriage equality, believing that love should not be constrained by legal limitations.

Strategies for Advocacy

To combat these challenges, Aderonke and her allies have employed various strategies in their fight for marriage equality:

- **Public Awareness Campaigns:** Educating the public about the importance of marriage equality and challenging misconceptions about LGBTQ relationships.

- **Legal Challenges:** Working with legal experts to challenge discriminatory laws in court, advocating for legislative reforms that recognize same-sex relationships.

- **International Support:** Building coalitions with international human rights organizations to apply pressure on the Nigerian government and raise awareness on a global stage.

- **Community Mobilization:** Organizing grassroots movements to empower LGBTQ individuals and allies to advocate for their rights and build a supportive community.

Examples of Progress

While the road to marriage equality in Nigeria remains long and arduous, there have been notable examples of progress in other regions that serve as inspiration. Countries like South Africa, which legalized same-sex marriage in 2006, have demonstrated that change is possible through persistent advocacy and public support. The South African Constitutional Court's ruling on marriage equality was grounded in a commitment to human dignity and equality, principles that resonate deeply within the LGBTQ movement.

$$\text{Marriage Equality (South Africa)} \rightarrow \text{Inspiration for Nigeria} \quad (12)$$

Moreover, international developments, such as the Obergefell v. Hodges case in the United States, which legalized same-sex marriage nationwide in 2015, have provided a framework for activists worldwide. These cases highlight the power of collective action and the importance of legal recognition in the fight for equality.

Conclusion

The fight for marriage equality is an essential component of Aderonke Apata's broader activism, representing a quest for recognition, dignity, and equal rights for LGBTQ individuals. While the challenges in Nigeria are significant, the resilience and determination of activists like Aderonke serve as a beacon of hope. As the movement continues to evolve, the fight for marriage equality remains a crucial goal, one that embodies the fundamental belief that love knows no bounds and should be celebrated, not criminalized.

In conclusion, the journey towards marriage equality may be fraught with obstacles, but it is driven by an unwavering commitment to justice and equality.

Aderonke's activism not only challenges the status quo in Nigeria but also inspires a global movement towards a more inclusive future.

$$\text{Love} \rightarrow \text{Marriage Equality} \rightarrow \text{Justice} \qquad (13)$$

Building LGBTQ Safe Spaces

Creating safe spaces for LGBTQ individuals is a critical aspect of fostering an inclusive society. Safe spaces are environments where LGBTQ individuals can feel secure, accepted, and free to express their identities without fear of discrimination, harassment, or violence. This section will explore the theoretical underpinnings of safe spaces, the challenges faced in establishing them, and practical examples of successful initiatives.

Theoretical Framework

The concept of safe spaces is grounded in several theoretical frameworks, including intersectionality, queer theory, and social justice. Intersectionality, as proposed by Crenshaw (1989), emphasizes the interconnectedness of social identities and the unique experiences of individuals who occupy multiple marginalized identities. This framework is essential for understanding the diverse needs of LGBTQ individuals, particularly those who also belong to other marginalized groups based on race, class, gender, or ability.

Queer theory further challenges normative assumptions about gender and sexuality, advocating for the deconstruction of binary classifications and the celebration of fluidity in identity. In this context, safe spaces serve as sites of resistance against heteronormative standards and allow for the exploration of diverse sexual and gender identities.

Social justice theory underscores the importance of equity and inclusion in all societal structures. Safe spaces are not merely physical locations; they are also about creating a culture of respect, understanding, and support. They facilitate dialogue and education, empowering individuals to advocate for their rights and the rights of others.

Challenges in Establishing Safe Spaces

Despite the importance of safe spaces, there are significant challenges in their establishment and maintenance:

- **Societal Stigma:** In many cultures, LGBTQ identities are still stigmatized, leading to resistance against the creation of safe spaces. This stigma can manifest in hostility from community members, making it difficult to secure support for LGBTQ initiatives.

- **Funding and Resources:** Establishing safe spaces often requires financial resources for facilities, programming, and staff. Many LGBTQ organizations struggle to secure adequate funding, which can limit their ability to create and sustain safe environments.

- **Safety Concerns:** Even within supposedly safe spaces, individuals may still face threats from outside forces. Ensuring the physical safety of participants is paramount, and organizations must develop strategies to mitigate risks.

- **Inclusivity:** Safe spaces must be genuinely inclusive, recognizing the diverse identities within the LGBTQ community. This includes addressing the needs of people of color, transgender individuals, and those with disabilities, among others. Failure to do so can lead to feelings of exclusion within the very spaces meant to provide support.

Examples of Successful Safe Spaces

Numerous initiatives around the world have successfully created safe spaces for LGBTQ individuals. Here are a few notable examples:

- **Community Centers:** Many cities have established LGBTQ community centers that serve as safe havens for individuals seeking support, resources, and social connections. For instance, the *Los Angeles LGBT Center* provides a range of services, including mental health support, legal assistance, and social activities, all within a welcoming environment.

- **Safe Schools Initiatives:** Programs aimed at creating safe schools for LGBTQ youth have emerged globally. The *GSA Network* in the United States, for example, empowers students to form Gay-Straight Alliances (GSAs) that promote inclusivity and provide a supportive environment for LGBTQ students. These alliances have been shown to reduce bullying and improve mental health outcomes for participants.

- **Online Safe Spaces:** In the digital age, online platforms have become vital for creating safe spaces, especially for individuals in hostile environments. Websites and social media groups dedicated to LGBTQ support allow individuals to connect, share experiences, and access resources. The *Trevor Project* provides crisis intervention and suicide prevention services through its online platform, offering a lifeline for LGBTQ youth in distress.

- **Art and Cultural Spaces:** Art can be a powerful medium for creating safe spaces. Initiatives like the *Queer Arts Festival* in Vancouver celebrate LGBTQ artists and provide a platform for expression in a supportive environment. These cultural spaces foster community, promote visibility, and challenge societal norms.

The Importance of Safe Spaces

The establishment of safe spaces is crucial for several reasons:

- **Mental Health:** Safe spaces provide vital support for mental health, allowing individuals to express their feelings and experiences without judgment. Studies have shown that LGBTQ individuals who have access to supportive environments experience lower rates of depression and anxiety.

- **Community Building:** Safe spaces foster a sense of belonging and community among LGBTQ individuals. They provide opportunities for networking, collaboration, and collective action, empowering individuals to advocate for their rights and the rights of others.

- **Education and Awareness:** Safe spaces serve as educational hubs, promoting awareness of LGBTQ issues and fostering understanding among allies. Workshops, discussions, and events held in these spaces can challenge stereotypes and encourage acceptance.

- **Empowerment:** By providing a platform for marginalized voices, safe spaces empower individuals to share their stories and advocate for change. This empowerment is essential for building resilience and fostering activism within the LGBTQ community.

In conclusion, building LGBTQ safe spaces is an essential component of fostering inclusivity and acceptance. By understanding the theoretical frameworks, addressing the challenges, and drawing inspiration from successful examples, activists like Aderonke Apata can continue to advocate for environments where all individuals can thrive without fear of discrimination. The ongoing work to create and sustain these spaces is vital for the future of LGBTQ rights and the well-being of individuals within the community.

Providing Resources for LGBTQ Youth

The journey towards acceptance and empowerment for LGBTQ youth is often fraught with challenges, stemming from societal stigma, discrimination, and a lack of understanding. Recognizing these challenges, Aderonke Apata has been a pivotal figure in providing resources tailored specifically for LGBTQ youth, ensuring they have access to the support and guidance necessary to navigate their identities in a complex world.

Understanding the Challenges

LGBTQ youth frequently face significant hurdles that can impact their mental health and overall well-being. According to the *Trevor Project*, LGBTQ youth are more than twice as likely to experience bullying and harassment compared to their heterosexual peers. This systemic discrimination can lead to feelings of isolation, depression, and anxiety. The *Youth Risk Behavior Surveillance System* (YRBSS) reports that LGBTQ youth are at a higher risk of suicidal ideation and attempts, emphasizing the urgent need for targeted resources and support systems.

Creating Safe Spaces

One of the primary resources that Aderonke has championed is the creation of safe spaces for LGBTQ youth. These environments are crucial for fostering a sense of belonging and acceptance. Safe spaces can take various forms, including community centers, support groups, and online forums. For instance, the *LGBTQ Youth Resource Center* in Lagos provides a sanctuary for young individuals to express themselves freely, engage with peers, and access mental health services.

Educational Initiatives

Education plays a vital role in equipping LGBTQ youth with the knowledge and skills they need to advocate for themselves. Aderonke has worked tirelessly to develop educational initiatives that focus on LGBTQ history, rights, and health. Workshops and seminars are organized to educate young people about their rights and the resources available to them. For example, the *Empowerment Through Knowledge* program, launched by Aderonke, includes sessions on sexual health, mental health awareness, and legal rights, empowering youth to make informed decisions about their lives.

Mentorship Programs

Mentorship is another critical resource that Aderonke has prioritized. By connecting LGBTQ youth with mentors who have navigated similar challenges, these programs provide guidance and support. The *LGBTQ Mentorship Initiative* pairs young individuals with established activists and professionals, fostering relationships that encourage personal growth and resilience. Mentors can offer insights into overcoming obstacles and navigating societal pressures, ultimately helping mentees build confidence in their identities.

Mental Health Resources

Mental health is a significant concern for LGBTQ youth, and Aderonke has advocated for accessible mental health resources. Collaborating with mental health professionals, she has facilitated workshops that address the unique mental health challenges faced by LGBTQ individuals. The *Mental Health Matters* campaign promotes awareness and provides resources for counseling and therapy, ensuring that youth have access to professional support.

Utilizing Technology

In the digital age, technology plays a crucial role in connecting LGBTQ youth with resources. Aderonke has harnessed the power of social media and online platforms to disseminate information and create communities. Initiatives such as the *LGBTQ Youth Online Resource Hub* offer a wealth of information, from educational materials to forums where youth can share their experiences and seek advice. This digital approach allows for greater accessibility, particularly for those in rural or conservative areas where in-person resources may be limited.

Advocacy for Policy Change

Aderonke's commitment to providing resources for LGBTQ youth extends beyond direct support. She actively engages in advocacy for policy changes that protect and empower young people. By lobbying for inclusive educational policies, anti-bullying legislation, and mental health support within schools, Aderonke works to create an environment where LGBTQ youth can thrive.

Case Studies and Success Stories

Several success stories highlight the impact of Aderonke's initiatives. For example, the story of *Chijioke*, a young gay man who found solace and support through the

LGBTQ Youth Resource Center, illustrates the transformative power of community resources. After attending workshops and participating in mentorship programs, Chijioke became an advocate for LGBTQ rights himself, demonstrating the ripple effect of empowerment.

Similarly, the *Youth Empowerment Project*, launched by Aderonke, has successfully reached over 500 LGBTQ youth in Nigeria, providing them with the resources they need to navigate their identities and advocate for their rights.

Conclusion

In conclusion, the provision of resources for LGBTQ youth is a cornerstone of Aderonke Apata's advocacy work. By creating safe spaces, offering educational initiatives, establishing mentorship programs, and promoting mental health resources, Aderonke has made significant strides in supporting the next generation of LGBTQ activists. Her work not only addresses immediate needs but also lays the groundwork for a more inclusive future, where LGBTQ youth can thrive without fear of discrimination or violence. The ongoing commitment to these resources is essential in the fight for equality and acceptance, ensuring that every young person has the opportunity to live authentically and proudly.

The Power of Social Media

In the contemporary landscape of activism, social media has emerged as a formidable tool for mobilization, awareness, and advocacy. For Aderonke Apata, the power of social media was not just a platform; it was a lifeline that connected her to a broader community and amplified her voice in the fight for LGBTQ rights in Nigeria. This section delves into the multifaceted role of social media in Aderonke's activism, exploring its theoretical underpinnings, the challenges it presents, and illustrative examples that highlight its impact.

Theoretical Framework

The influence of social media on activism can be understood through several theoretical lenses. One prominent theory is the **Networked Publics Theory**, which posits that social media transforms traditional public spheres into networked spaces where individuals can connect, share information, and mobilize for collective action. According to [?], networked publics are characterized by their ability to facilitate participation and engagement in ways that were previously unattainable. This theory underscores how social media platforms serve as digital arenas for marginalized voices, allowing activists like Aderonke to reach audiences far beyond their immediate geographic limitations.

Additionally, the **Framing Theory** is crucial in understanding how social media shapes public perception of LGBTQ issues. Framing involves the presentation of information in a way that emphasizes certain aspects over others, thus influencing how audiences interpret and respond to messages. Aderonke effectively utilized social media to frame LGBTQ rights as a fundamental human rights issue, challenging prevailing narratives that often marginalized or demonized LGBTQ individuals. Through compelling storytelling and strategic messaging, she was able to shift public discourse and garner support for the movement.

Challenges of Social Media Activism

Despite its potential, social media activism is fraught with challenges. One significant issue is the prevalence of **online harassment** and **cyberbullying**, particularly against LGBTQ individuals. Aderonke herself faced backlash and threats online, which highlighted the risks associated with being a visible activist in a hostile environment. According to [?], such harassment can lead to mental health challenges and may deter individuals from participating in online activism.

Moreover, the phenomenon of **slacktivism** poses a challenge to the effectiveness of social media activism. Slacktivism refers to the notion that individuals may feel they are contributing to a cause simply by liking or sharing posts without engaging in more substantive actions. While social media can raise awareness, it is essential for activists to encourage followers to move beyond superficial engagement and participate in tangible actions, such as attending protests or donating to organizations.

Examples of Social Media Impact

Aderonke's use of social media exemplifies its power in mobilizing support and raising awareness. One notable campaign was the #FreeAderonke initiative, which gained traction on platforms like Twitter and Instagram. This campaign sought to highlight the injustices faced by LGBTQ individuals in Nigeria, particularly those who were victims of police brutality and discrimination. By sharing personal stories, statistics, and calls to action, Aderonke was able to rally international support and put pressure on Nigerian authorities.

Another powerful example is the use of social media during Pride Month. Aderonke leveraged platforms like Facebook and Twitter to share educational content about LGBTQ history and rights, while also promoting events and safe spaces for LGBTQ individuals. This not only fostered a sense of community but also educated allies and supporters about the struggles faced by LGBTQ people in Nigeria.

In addition, Aderonke's advocacy extended to creating online forums where LGBTQ youth could connect and share their experiences. These digital safe spaces provided a crucial support network for individuals who often felt isolated and marginalized in their offline lives. The impact of such initiatives cannot be overstated; they empower individuals to express their identities and seek support in a society that often stigmatizes them.

Conclusion

The power of social media in Aderonke Apata's activism illustrates its dual potential as a tool for empowerment and a battleground for resistance. While challenges such as online harassment and slacktivism persist, the ability to connect, mobilize, and educate through social media remains unparalleled. Aderonke's journey exemplifies how digital platforms can serve as catalysts for change, enabling activists to forge connections, amplify their messages, and advocate for justice on both local and global scales. As the landscape of activism continues to evolve, the role of social media will undoubtedly remain a critical component in the ongoing fight for LGBTQ rights.

Aderonke's Impact on Nigerian LGBTQ Activism

Aderonke Apata has emerged as a pivotal figure in the landscape of LGBTQ activism in Nigeria, a nation where societal norms and government policies often clash violently with the rights and identities of LGBTQ individuals. Her journey from a marginalized identity to a leading voice for equality encapsulates the struggles and triumphs of many within the LGBTQ community in Nigeria.

Challenging Systemic Oppression

At the heart of Aderonke's activism is a staunch opposition to systemic oppression faced by LGBTQ individuals in Nigeria. The Nigerian legal framework, particularly the Same-Sex Marriage (Prohibition) Act of 2014, enforces a hostile environment for LGBTQ individuals, making same-sex relationships punishable by law. Aderonke's advocacy has focused on dismantling these oppressive structures through grassroots mobilization and international awareness campaigns.

One theoretical framework that can be applied to understand Aderonke's impact is the concept of *intersectionality*, coined by Kimberlé Crenshaw. This framework emphasizes the interconnected nature of social categorizations such as race, class, and sexual orientation, which can lead to overlapping systems of discrimination. Aderonke's activism illustrates how LGBTQ individuals in Nigeria face compounded discrimination not only due to their sexual orientation but also due to their socio-economic status and cultural background.

Creating Safe Spaces

Aderonke has been instrumental in creating safe spaces for LGBTQ individuals in Nigeria. These spaces serve as vital havens for community building, support, and empowerment. For example, she has organized numerous events that foster dialogue and solidarity among LGBTQ individuals, allowing them to share their experiences and challenges in a supportive environment. These gatherings have not only provided emotional support but have also educated attendees about their rights and available resources.

The establishment of these safe spaces is crucial in a context where public expressions of LGBTQ identity can lead to violence and ostracism. Aderonke's work has encouraged the formation of local LGBTQ organizations, which play a critical role in advocacy and education. By mobilizing community members, she has helped to shift the narrative surrounding LGBTQ identities in Nigeria, fostering a sense of pride and resilience among individuals who have long been marginalized.

International Advocacy and Solidarity

Aderonke's impact extends beyond local activism; she has forged international alliances that amplify the voices of Nigerian LGBTQ individuals on global platforms. By participating in international conferences and collaborating with global organizations, she has brought attention to the plight of LGBTQ individuals in Nigeria, advocating for their rights on a larger scale.

Her ability to connect local struggles with global movements exemplifies the power of solidarity in activism. For instance, Aderonke has worked alongside organizations such as Amnesty International and Human Rights Watch to highlight human rights abuses faced by LGBTQ individuals in Nigeria. These partnerships have been instrumental in pressuring the Nigerian government to reconsider its stance on LGBTQ rights, though significant challenges remain.

Utilizing Social Media as a Tool for Change

In the digital age, social media has become a powerful tool for activism, and Aderonke has adeptly harnessed its potential to raise awareness and mobilize support. Platforms like Twitter and Instagram have allowed her to share her story and the stories of others, creating a sense of community and urgency around LGBTQ issues in Nigeria.

Through her online presence, Aderonke has been able to challenge homophobic narratives and promote messages of acceptance and love. This has not only reached a national audience but has also resonated with international supporters, creating a global movement advocating for LGBTQ rights in Nigeria. The use of hashtags, online campaigns, and virtual events has enabled Aderonke to galvanize support, raising funds and awareness for critical initiatives.

Addressing Mental Health and Well-being

Another significant aspect of Aderonke's impact is her focus on the mental health and well-being of LGBTQ individuals in Nigeria. The stigma and discrimination faced by this community often lead to mental health challenges, including anxiety, depression, and suicidal ideation. Aderonke has prioritized mental health awareness in her activism, advocating for accessible mental health resources and support systems.

By collaborating with mental health professionals and organizations, she has facilitated workshops and support groups aimed at addressing these issues. This holistic approach to activism acknowledges that the fight for rights is intertwined with the overall well-being of individuals, and Aderonke's work has been pivotal in promoting this understanding within the LGBTQ community.

Legacy and Future Directions

Aderonke Apata's impact on Nigerian LGBTQ activism is profound and multifaceted. Her courage in the face of adversity, commitment to creating safe spaces, and ability to leverage international platforms have made her a beacon of hope for many. However, challenges remain, and the fight for LGBTQ rights in Nigeria is far from over.

Looking ahead, Aderonke's legacy will likely inspire a new generation of activists who continue to challenge oppressive systems and advocate for equality. The road to justice is long, but with leaders like Aderonke at the forefront, the movement for LGBTQ rights in Nigeria is gaining momentum. Her story exemplifies resilience, courage, and the enduring power of community, reminding us that change is possible, even in the most challenging circumstances.

In conclusion, Aderonke's impact on Nigerian LGBTQ activism is not just a testament to her individual efforts but a reflection of a broader movement towards acceptance and equality. As she continues her work, the hope for a more inclusive and just society for LGBTQ individuals in Nigeria remains alive, fueled by the passion and dedication of activists like Aderonke Apata.

Escaping Persecution: A Journey to Freedom

Forced Out of Nigeria

In the vibrant yet tumultuous landscape of Nigeria, Aderonke Apata's journey as an LGBTQ activist was fraught with peril. The country, known for its rich cultural heritage and diversity, paradoxically harbored some of the harshest anti-LGBTQ laws in the world. The Nigerian Criminal Code, along with the Same-Sex Marriage (Prohibition) Act of 2014, criminalizes same-sex relationships and imposes severe penalties, including imprisonment and, in some cases, violence against those who dare to express their identity. This legal framework created an environment of fear and oppression, compelling many, including Aderonke, to navigate the treacherous waters of persecution.

The Reality of Persecution

Aderonke's activism began to attract attention, both positive and negative. While she garnered support from the LGBTQ community and allies, she also became a target for those who opposed her stance. The threats escalated, transforming from verbal harassment into physical violence. For Aderonke, the turning point came when she faced imminent danger from local authorities who sought to silence her. The police, often complicit in acts of violence against LGBTQ individuals, began to surveil her movements and activities.

This environment of hostility forced Aderonke to make a life-altering decision. The concept of *forced migration* became her reality, as she was no longer safe in her homeland. According to the United Nations High Commissioner for Refugees (UNHCR), forced migration occurs when individuals are compelled to leave their country due to persecution, conflict, or violence. Aderonke's situation exemplified this phenomenon, as she faced the dual threats of state-sponsored violence and societal discrimination.

The Decision to Leave

The decision to leave Nigeria was not made lightly. Aderonke weighed the risks and consequences, knowing that her life depended on her choice. The emotional toll of leaving behind family, friends, and a community she had fought tirelessly for was immense. Yet, the prospect of continued persecution loomed larger. The fear of arrest, violence, and even death became unbearable.

In her reflections, Aderonke often cited the psychological impact of such forced displacement. The phenomenon known as *refugee trauma* encompasses the emotional and psychological scars left by persecution and the subsequent upheaval of one's life. Aderonke's narrative is a testament to this trauma, as she grappled with feelings of loss, fear, and uncertainty about her future.

The Journey to Asylum

With a heavy heart, Aderonke embarked on her journey to seek asylum in the United Kingdom. The journey itself was fraught with challenges. She had to navigate a complex web of borders and bureaucracies, often relying on the kindness of strangers and the support of fellow activists. Each step was a reminder of what she had left behind, but also of the hope that lay ahead.

Upon arrival in the UK, Aderonke faced the daunting asylum process. The UK has a relatively robust framework for asylum seekers, yet the experience can be harrowing. The initial reception centers are often overcrowded, and the legal processes can be confusing and lengthy. Aderonke's experience was no different. She encountered bureaucratic hurdles and faced discrimination, not just as a refugee but as a member of the LGBTQ community.

The Intersection of Identity and Asylum

In the context of Aderonke's story, the intersectionality of identity played a crucial role in her asylum journey. The concept of intersectionality, coined by scholar Kimberlé Crenshaw, refers to how various social identities—such as race, gender, and sexual orientation—interact and contribute to unique experiences of oppression. Aderonke's identity as a Black lesbian refugee placed her at the crossroads of multiple forms of discrimination, complicating her quest for safety and acceptance.

The asylum process in the UK required Aderonke to articulate her experiences of persecution in Nigeria, a task that was both painful and empowering. She had to recount her story of survival, detailing the threats she faced and the reasons for her flight. This act of storytelling not only served as a means of seeking refuge but also as a powerful assertion of her identity and resilience.

Conclusion

Ultimately, Aderonke Apata's forced migration from Nigeria was a catalyst for her evolution as an activist on a global scale. Her journey underscores the urgent need for comprehensive policies that protect LGBTQ individuals from persecution and violence. As she navigated the complexities of seeking asylum, Aderonke became a voice for countless others who faced similar fates, turning her personal ordeal into a powerful narrative of hope and resilience. Through her activism, she continues to challenge the systemic injustices that force individuals into exile, advocating for a world where everyone can live authentically and without fear.

The plight of Aderonke and others like her serves as a stark reminder of the ongoing struggles faced by LGBTQ individuals in many parts of the world. As we reflect on her journey, we must recognize the importance of solidarity, advocacy, and the relentless pursuit of justice for all marginalized communities.

Seeking Asylum in the United Kingdom

The journey of seeking asylum in the United Kingdom is fraught with complexity, particularly for individuals like Aderonke Apata, who fled Nigeria due to systemic persecution based on sexual orientation. This section explores the multifaceted nature of the asylum process, the challenges faced by LGBTQ individuals, and the broader implications of seeking refuge in a foreign land.

Understanding the Asylum Process

The asylum process in the UK is governed by international and domestic laws that aim to protect individuals fleeing persecution. The 1951 Refugee Convention defines a refugee as someone who, "owing to a well-founded fear of being persecuted for reasons of race, religion, nationality, membership of a particular social group or political opinion, is outside the country of his nationality and is unable or, owing to such fear, is unwilling to return to it."

In Aderonke's case, her identity as a member of the LGBTQ community positioned her within the category of a "particular social group." However, navigating the asylum system requires not only meeting the legal definition but also providing credible evidence of the persecution faced.

Challenges Faced by LGBTQ Asylum Seekers

LGBTQ asylum seekers often confront unique challenges that complicate their claims:

- **Cultural Stigma:** Many LGBTQ individuals come from backgrounds where their identities are stigmatized. This stigma can deter them from openly discussing their experiences, making it difficult to present a compelling case for asylum.

- **Fear of Repercussions:** The fear of being outed can lead to reluctance in sharing personal stories with authorities, which is crucial for validating their claims. This fear is exacerbated in environments where LGBTQ identities are criminalized or socially ostracized.

- **Legal Barriers:** The asylum process can be lengthy and complicated, with legal jargon that may be difficult for individuals without legal representation to navigate. Many asylum seekers lack access to legal resources, which can hinder their ability to present their cases effectively.

- **Mental Health Issues:** The trauma of fleeing persecution, combined with the stress of navigating the asylum process, can lead to significant mental health challenges. Many LGBTQ asylum seekers face depression, anxiety, and post-traumatic stress disorder (PTSD).

Aderonke's Experience

Upon arriving in the UK, Aderonke faced the daunting task of articulating her experiences to immigration authorities. The initial asylum interview is critical; it serves as the first opportunity for applicants to present their case. Aderonke had to recount her experiences of persecution in Nigeria, including threats, violence, and societal rejection due to her sexual orientation.

The interview process is not merely a formality; it is a rigorous examination of an individual's credibility. As Aderonke navigated this process, she encountered several obstacles:

- **Inconsistencies in Testimony:** Any perceived inconsistency in Aderonke's narrative could be used against her, creating a high-pressure environment where the stakes were incredibly high.

- **Lack of Documentation:** Unlike traditional refugees, LGBTQ asylum seekers may not have documentation of their persecution, such as police reports or medical records, to substantiate their claims. Aderonke's reliance on personal testimony underscored the vulnerability of her situation.

- **Support Networks:** Finding community support was crucial for Aderonke. Organizations such as Stonewall and the UK Lesbian and Gay Immigration Group (UKLGIG) played pivotal roles in providing resources and legal assistance, helping her navigate the complexities of the asylum process.

The Asylum Decision

The outcome of Aderonke's asylum application hinged on the Home Office's assessment of her credibility and the evidence provided. A successful claim would not only grant her protection but also access to resources that would aid in her integration into British society.

The decision-making process can be unpredictable, with factors such as political climate, public sentiment towards LGBTQ rights, and even the individual caseworker's biases influencing outcomes. For Aderonke, the stakes were high; a negative decision could lead to deportation back to Nigeria, where she faced severe risks.

Implications of Asylum for LGBTQ Individuals

The implications of seeking asylum extend beyond individual cases. Aderonke's experience highlights broader systemic issues within the asylum process:

- **Policy Advocacy:** The need for policy reforms to ensure that LGBTQ asylum seekers receive fair treatment and consideration within the asylum system is paramount. Advocacy groups continue to push for changes that recognize the unique challenges faced by this community.

- **Public Awareness:** Raising awareness about the plight of LGBTQ asylum seekers can foster greater understanding and empathy, leading to more supportive environments in host countries.

- **International Obligations:** Countries must uphold their obligations under international law to protect those fleeing persecution, ensuring that no one is returned to a situation where they face harm due to their identity.

Conclusion

Seeking asylum in the United Kingdom is a critical juncture for many LGBTQ individuals fleeing persecution. Aderonke Apata's journey exemplifies the complexities and challenges faced by those who seek refuge, underscoring the importance of robust support systems, legal advocacy, and public awareness in creating a more just and equitable asylum process. Her story serves as a reminder of the resilience of the human spirit and the ongoing fight for dignity and acceptance in the face of adversity.

The Challenges of the Asylum Process

The journey of seeking asylum is often fraught with challenges, and for Aderonke Apata, this process was no exception. As a Nigerian LGBTQ activist who faced persecution due to her sexual orientation, the asylum process in the United Kingdom presented a myriad of obstacles that tested her resolve and resilience.

Understanding the Asylum Process

The asylum process is designed to protect individuals who have fled their home countries due to persecution based on race, religion, nationality, political opinion, or membership in a particular social group. In Aderonke's case, she belonged to the latter category, as her identity as a lesbian in Nigeria subjected her to severe discrimination and violence. The legal framework governing asylum can be complex, involving various stages that include initial application, interviews, and potential appeals.

Initial Application and Documentation

One of the foremost challenges Aderonke faced was the requirement for substantial documentation to support her asylum claim. Applicants must provide evidence of their persecution, which can be difficult to obtain, especially when fleeing a hostile environment. Aderonke had to gather personal testimonies, medical records, and any police reports that could corroborate her experiences. This task was not only emotionally taxing but also logistically challenging, as many LGBTQ individuals in Nigeria live in fear of being outed, making it risky to document their experiences.

Credibility Assessments

Once Aderonke submitted her application, she underwent a credibility assessment during her asylum interview. This process involves the asylum officer evaluating the consistency and plausibility of her narrative. The burden of proof lies heavily on the applicant, often leading to a sense of anxiety and pressure. For Aderonke, articulating her experiences of homophobia and violence while under scrutiny was daunting, as any perceived inconsistency could jeopardize her case.

Cultural and Linguistic Barriers

Cultural and linguistic barriers also posed significant challenges. Although English is widely spoken in Nigeria, nuances in dialect and cultural references can lead to misunderstandings during interviews. Aderonke had to navigate these barriers while ensuring that her story was communicated effectively to the authorities. Additionally, the emotional weight of recounting traumatic experiences can hinder clear communication, further complicating the assessment of her claim.

Legal Representation and Resources

Access to legal representation is crucial in the asylum process, yet many applicants, including Aderonke, face difficulties in securing adequate legal support. The complexity of immigration law requires expertise that can be financially burdensome. Aderonke's limited resources meant she had to rely on pro bono services, which often come with their own challenges, such as limited availability and high caseloads for attorneys. This lack of support can result in inadequate preparation for interviews and hearings, increasing the likelihood of unfavorable outcomes.

Psychological Impact

The psychological toll of the asylum process cannot be understated. The uncertainty of the outcome, combined with the stress of recounting traumatic experiences, can lead to significant mental health challenges. Aderonke, like many asylum seekers, faced anxiety, depression, and feelings of isolation during this period. The lack of support networks in a new country can exacerbate these feelings, making it difficult for individuals to cope with the emotional strain of their circumstances.

Delays and Uncertainty

Delays in the asylum process are common and can prolong the suffering of applicants. Aderonke experienced significant waiting periods, during which she was left in limbo, unsure of her future. These delays can be attributed to various factors, including backlog in the asylum system, the need for further evidence, or changes in immigration policies. The uncertainty of when a decision will be made can lead to increased stress and anxiety, impacting an individual's ability to rebuild their life in a new country.

Potential for Rejection and Appeals

The reality of the asylum process is that many applications are initially rejected. Aderonke faced the possibility of her claim being denied, which would have forced her to return to Nigeria, where she faced persecution. The appeals process can be lengthy and complicated, requiring additional evidence and legal support. Many asylum seekers find themselves trapped in a cycle of appeals, further prolonging their uncertainty and distress.

Conclusion

In summary, the challenges faced by Aderonke Apata during the asylum process highlight the systemic issues within immigration systems that can hinder the protection of vulnerable populations. From documentation and credibility assessments to cultural barriers and psychological impacts, the journey to safety is fraught with obstacles. Aderonke's experience serves as a poignant reminder of the resilience of individuals who fight for their rights and the importance of creating supportive systems for those seeking refuge from persecution.

Facing Discrimination in the UK

Upon arriving in the United Kingdom, Aderonke Apata encountered a new set of challenges that starkly contrasted with her previous experiences in Nigeria. While the UK is often viewed as a haven for LGBTQ rights, the reality for many refugees, particularly those from marginalized backgrounds, can be fraught with discrimination and systemic barriers.

Understanding the Landscape of Discrimination

Discrimination against LGBTQ individuals in the UK, particularly among refugees and asylum seekers, can manifest in various forms. It is crucial to understand the theoretical framework surrounding discrimination, which can be examined through the lens of intersectionality, a concept developed by Kimberlé Crenshaw. Intersectionality posits that individuals experience overlapping systems of oppression based on their identities, including race, gender, sexuality, and socioeconomic status. For Aderonke, her identity as a Black Nigerian lesbian placed her at the intersection of multiple forms of discrimination.

Experiences of Discrimination

Aderonke's initial experiences in the UK included not only the trauma of displacement but also the harsh realities of being a queer refugee. Despite the legal protections afforded by the Equality Act 2010, which prohibits discrimination based on sexual orientation, many LGBTQ refugees still face hostility and prejudice. Aderonke encountered discrimination in various settings, including housing, healthcare, and social services.

For instance, upon seeking accommodation, Aderonke faced challenges in finding safe housing. Many landlords exhibited biases against her queer identity, leading to rejections based on her sexual orientation. This situation is not uncommon; studies have shown that LGBTQ refugees often experience higher rates of homelessness compared to their heterosexual counterparts. According to the UK's National LGBT Survey, nearly 30% of LGBTQ individuals reported experiencing discrimination in housing.

Healthcare Discrimination

Healthcare is another critical area where discrimination can significantly impact the well-being of LGBTQ refugees. Aderonke experienced difficulties accessing healthcare services due to a lack of understanding and sensitivity among healthcare providers regarding LGBTQ issues. The National Health Service (NHS) has made strides in promoting inclusivity; however, many LGBTQ refugees report feeling marginalized within the healthcare system. Aderonke's experiences highlight a broader issue: the necessity for cultural competency training among healthcare professionals to better serve diverse populations.

The Role of Social Services

Social services, intended to provide support to those in need, can also perpetuate discrimination. Aderonke faced bureaucratic hurdles when navigating the asylum process, which often left her feeling dehumanized and stigmatized. The Home Office's approach to asylum claims has been criticized for its lack of sensitivity to the unique challenges faced by LGBTQ individuals. Reports indicate that many LGBTQ asylum seekers face skepticism regarding their claims, often being subjected to invasive questioning that disregards their lived experiences.

Community and Support Systems

Despite these challenges, Aderonke found solace in LGBTQ community organizations that provided vital support. Groups such as *Stonewall* and *The Refugee Council* have been instrumental in advocating for the rights of LGBTQ refugees. These organizations offer resources, including legal assistance and mental health support, which are crucial for individuals facing discrimination.

Aderonke's involvement with these organizations not only helped her navigate her own struggles but also allowed her to contribute to a larger movement advocating for systemic change. By sharing her story, she raised awareness about the unique challenges LGBTQ refugees face, fostering solidarity and collective action within the community.

Conclusion

Facing discrimination in the UK was a multifaceted experience for Aderonke Apata, shaped by her intersectional identity as a Black Nigerian lesbian. While the UK offers legal protections for LGBTQ individuals, the lived realities of many refugees highlight the ongoing need for advocacy, support, and systemic reform. Aderonke's journey illustrates the importance of resilience and community in the fight against discrimination, emphasizing that the struggle for equality extends beyond borders and identities.

In the words of Aderonke, "We must continue to fight, not just for ourselves but for all those who come after us. Discrimination may be a battle we face, but it is a battle we can win together."

Raising Awareness of LGBTQ Refugees

Raising awareness of LGBTQ refugees is a critical aspect of Aderonke Apata's advocacy work, as it addresses the unique challenges faced by individuals fleeing persecution based on their sexual orientation or gender identity. The plight of LGBTQ refugees is often compounded by societal stigma, legal barriers, and a lack of understanding among the broader public. This section delves into the theoretical frameworks surrounding refugee advocacy, the specific problems encountered by LGBTQ refugees, and the impactful examples of awareness campaigns spearheaded by Aderonke and her allies.

Theoretical Frameworks

The advocacy for LGBTQ refugees can be understood through several theoretical lenses, including human rights theory, intersectionality, and social justice frameworks.

Human Rights Theory posits that all individuals possess inherent rights, including the right to seek asylum from persecution. According to the Universal Declaration of Human Rights (UDHR), Article 14 states, "Everyone has the right to seek and to enjoy in other countries asylum from persecution." This principle underscores the necessity of recognizing sexual orientation and gender identity as valid grounds for persecution, thus legitimizing the claims of LGBTQ refugees.

Intersectionality, a term coined by Kimberlé Crenshaw, provides insight into how various social identities—such as race, gender, and sexual orientation—intersect to create unique experiences of discrimination and privilege. LGBTQ refugees often navigate multiple layers of marginalization, which can complicate their asylum claims and access to resources. Understanding this intersectionality is essential in crafting effective advocacy strategies that consider the diverse backgrounds and experiences of LGBTQ refugees.

Social Justice Frameworks emphasize the importance of equity and inclusion in addressing systemic injustices. Aderonke's advocacy aligns with this framework by focusing on amplifying the voices of marginalized communities and ensuring that LGBTQ refugees receive the support and recognition they deserve.

Challenges Faced by LGBTQ Refugees

LGBTQ refugees encounter a myriad of challenges that hinder their ability to secure safety and stability in their host countries.

Legal Barriers often pose significant obstacles. Many countries lack explicit protections for LGBTQ individuals within their asylum laws, leading to inconsistent application of refugee status determinations. For example, in some jurisdictions, asylum claims based on sexual orientation may be dismissed unless the applicant can provide explicit evidence of persecution, which can be difficult to obtain.

Social Stigma also plays a crucial role in the experiences of LGBTQ refugees. Upon arrival in a new country, many face discrimination not only from the broader society but also within refugee support systems. This can lead to feelings of isolation and reluctance to seek help. For instance, LGBTQ refugees may avoid shelters or support groups due to fear of homophobia or transphobia, which can exacerbate their vulnerability.

Mental Health Issues are prevalent among LGBTQ refugees, stemming from the trauma of persecution and the stress of displacement. A study conducted by the International Organization for Migration (IOM) found that LGBTQ individuals in refugee camps reported higher rates of anxiety and depression compared to their heterosexual counterparts. This highlights the urgent need for targeted mental health support services that are culturally competent and affirming of LGBTQ identities.

Awareness Campaigns and Initiatives

Aderonke Apata's efforts to raise awareness of LGBTQ refugees have taken many forms, from grassroots campaigns to international advocacy.

Storytelling and Personal Narratives have proven to be powerful tools in humanizing the experiences of LGBTQ refugees. By sharing her own story and those of others, Aderonke has been able to connect with wider audiences and foster empathy. For example, her participation in public speaking events and panel discussions has allowed her to articulate the specific challenges faced by LGBTQ refugees, thereby educating audiences about the necessity of inclusive asylum policies.

Collaborations with Organizations such as the United Nations High Commissioner for Refugees (UNHCR) have amplified Aderonke's message. Through partnerships, she has been able to contribute to reports and recommendations aimed at improving the treatment of LGBTQ refugees globally. These collaborations have also facilitated the development of training programs for refugee support workers, ensuring they are equipped to address the needs of LGBTQ individuals effectively.

Social Media Campaigns have also played a crucial role in raising awareness. Aderonke has utilized platforms like Twitter and Instagram to share information, resources, and personal stories, reaching a global audience. Campaigns such as #LGBTQRefugeesMatter have garnered significant attention, mobilizing support and prompting discussions about the need for inclusive policies.

Conclusion

Raising awareness of LGBTQ refugees is an essential component of Aderonke Apata's advocacy work. By employing theoretical frameworks that emphasize human rights, intersectionality, and social justice, she has effectively highlighted the unique challenges faced by LGBTQ individuals in search of safety. Through storytelling, collaboration, and social media campaigns, Aderonke continues to educate the public and advocate for policy changes that recognize and support the rights of LGBTQ refugees. Her efforts not only illuminate the struggles of this marginalized group but also inspire collective action towards a more inclusive and equitable world.

Helping Others Navigate the Asylum System

In the tumultuous journey of seeking refuge, navigating the asylum system can be as daunting as the circumstances that forced individuals to flee their home countries. Aderonke Apata, having faced the harrowing realities of persecution herself, dedicated a significant portion of her activism to aiding others in traversing this complex landscape. The asylum process is often riddled with legal jargon, bureaucratic hurdles, and emotional turmoil, making it essential for advocates like Aderonke to step in and provide guidance.

Understanding the Asylum Process

The asylum process can be broken down into several critical stages, each presenting unique challenges for applicants. Typically, the process includes:

    1. **Filing an Application**: Asylum seekers must submit their application within a specific timeframe, usually within one year of arrival in the host country. This is crucial, as missing this deadline can lead to automatic denial of the application.

    2. **Interview Process**: Applicants are required to attend an interview where they must present their case. This is often a nerve-wracking experience, as the outcome hinges on the applicant's ability to convey their experiences convincingly.

    3. **Decision Phase**: After the interview, the asylum office will render a decision. This can take weeks or even months, during which applicants often live in uncertainty.

4. **Appeal Process**: If an application is denied, there is a possibility to appeal the decision. This stage can be particularly complex, requiring a deep understanding of legal frameworks and the ability to present compelling arguments.

Barriers Faced by Asylum Seekers

Aderonke recognized that many asylum seekers face barriers that complicate their ability to navigate this system effectively. These barriers include:

- **Language Proficiency**: Many asylum seekers arrive with limited proficiency in the host country's language, making it difficult to understand legal documents and communicate effectively during interviews.

- **Cultural Differences**: Different cultural backgrounds can lead to misunderstandings in how applicants present their cases or respond to questions during the interview process.

- **Psychological Trauma**: The trauma of persecution can significantly affect an individual's mental health, making it challenging to recount their experiences clearly and coherently.

- **Legal Complexity**: The asylum process involves intricate legal frameworks that can be overwhelming for those unfamiliar with the law, necessitating the support of knowledgeable advocates.

Aderonke's Advocacy Efforts

To address these challenges, Aderonke employed several strategies to assist asylum seekers:

1. **Workshops and Training**: Aderonke organized workshops aimed at educating asylum seekers about the asylum process. These sessions covered topics such as how to prepare for interviews, the importance of documentation, and understanding legal rights.

2. **One-on-One Support**: Aderonke provided personalized assistance to individuals, helping them gather necessary documentation, practice their interview responses, and understand the legal terminology involved in their cases.

3. **Building Partnerships**: Recognizing the importance of collaboration, Aderonke worked closely with legal aid organizations and other NGOs to ensure that asylum seekers had access to professional legal representation. This network of support was crucial in navigating the complexities of the asylum system.

4. **Advocacy for Policy Change**: Beyond direct support, Aderonke also engaged in advocacy efforts aimed at reforming the asylum process itself. She

highlighted the need for more accessible resources and clearer guidelines for asylum seekers, particularly those from marginalized communities.

Real-Life Examples

Aderonke's impact can be seen in the stories of individuals she helped:

- **Case Study: Amara**: A young LGBTQ individual from Nigeria, Amara faced persecution due to her sexual orientation. With Aderonke's guidance, she successfully navigated the asylum process, securing legal representation and preparing for her interview. Amara's application was approved, allowing her to start a new life free from fear.

- **Case Study: Tunde**: Tunde, a gay man who fled Nigeria after being threatened with violence, struggled with the language barrier. Aderonke arranged for translation services and conducted mock interviews with him, which significantly boosted his confidence. Tunde's asylum claim was ultimately successful, a testament to the effectiveness of Aderonke's support.

Conclusion

Helping others navigate the asylum system is not merely about providing information; it is about empowering individuals to reclaim their narratives and assert their rights. Aderonke Apata's unwavering commitment to this cause exemplifies the transformative power of advocacy. By demystifying the asylum process and offering tailored support, she not only assists individuals in their immediate quest for safety but also inspires a broader movement toward justice and equality for LGBTQ individuals worldwide. The legacy of her work continues to resonate, reminding us that the fight for asylum rights is an integral part of the larger struggle for human rights.

Aderonke's Efforts in Refugee Advocacy

Aderonke Apata's journey as a refugee advocate is a testament to her resilience and dedication to the LGBTQ community, particularly those fleeing persecution due to their sexual orientation or gender identity. Her advocacy work has been instrumental in raising awareness about the unique challenges faced by LGBTQ refugees, especially those from Nigeria, where homosexuality is criminalized and heavily stigmatized.

Understanding the Refugee Experience

The refugee experience for LGBTQ individuals is fraught with complexities that often go unrecognized. According to the United Nations High Commissioner for Refugees (UNHCR), a refugee is defined as someone who has fled their country due to a well-founded fear of persecution based on race, religion, nationality, membership in a particular social group, or political opinion. LGBTQ individuals fall under the category of a particular social group, yet their struggles are often compounded by societal discrimination, lack of understanding, and inadequate legal protections.

The intersectionality of identity plays a critical role in the refugee experience. LGBTQ refugees often face not only the trauma of fleeing their home countries but also the challenges of adapting to new environments that may not be welcoming. This dual burden can lead to heightened vulnerability, making it essential for advocates like Aderonke to address these specific needs.

Advocacy Initiatives

Aderonke has launched numerous initiatives aimed at supporting LGBTQ refugees. One of her key efforts has been to create safe spaces where LGBTQ refugees can gather, share their experiences, and access resources. These safe spaces serve as a sanctuary, providing emotional support and practical assistance, such as legal advice and housing resources.

In her role, Aderonke has collaborated with various organizations, including local NGOs and international bodies, to amplify the voices of LGBTQ refugees. She has participated in campaigns that seek to educate the public about the plight of these individuals, using social media platforms to disseminate information and mobilize support. Her efforts have included:

- **Workshops and Training Sessions:** Aderonke has facilitated workshops aimed at educating both LGBTQ refugees and the wider community about their rights. These sessions cover topics such as navigating the asylum process, understanding legal protections, and mental health resources available to LGBTQ individuals.

- **Legal Assistance Programs:** Recognizing the complexities of the asylum process, Aderonke has worked to connect LGBTQ refugees with legal professionals who specialize in immigration and asylum law. This initiative has proven crucial in helping individuals present their cases effectively and understand their rights within the legal framework.

- **Public Awareness Campaigns:** Aderonke has spearheaded campaigns that highlight the stories of LGBTQ refugees, humanizing their experiences and fostering empathy within the broader community. By sharing personal narratives, she aims to dismantle stereotypes and combat the stigma surrounding LGBTQ individuals seeking refuge.

Challenges Faced

Despite her tireless efforts, Aderonke has encountered numerous challenges in her advocacy work. One significant issue is the pervasive discrimination that LGBTQ refugees face within host countries. Even in more accepting societies, these individuals often struggle with isolation and fear of being outed, which can hinder their ability to seek help.

Moreover, the asylum process itself can be daunting and fraught with obstacles. Many LGBTQ refugees report feeling unsafe in detention centers or during interviews with immigration officials, where they may be subjected to invasive questioning about their sexual orientation or gender identity. Aderonke's advocacy has highlighted the need for sensitivity training among immigration officials to ensure that LGBTQ refugees are treated with dignity and respect.

Success Stories

Aderonke's advocacy has led to several notable successes. For instance, her collaboration with local organizations has resulted in the establishment of dedicated legal aid clinics for LGBTQ refugees, significantly improving their chances of securing asylum. Additionally, her public awareness campaigns have garnered media attention, leading to increased support from the general public and policymakers.

One particularly inspiring story is that of a Nigerian gay man who, after fleeing to the UK, found solace and support through Aderonke's initiatives. With her guidance, he successfully navigated the asylum process and is now actively involved in advocacy work himself, helping others in similar situations. This ripple effect exemplifies the power of advocacy and the importance of community support.

Theoretical Frameworks in Advocacy

Aderonke's approach to refugee advocacy can be understood through several theoretical frameworks:

- **Intersectionality:** This framework emphasizes the interconnected nature of social categorizations such as race, class, and sexual orientation, which can create overlapping systems of discrimination. Aderonke's work recognizes that LGBTQ refugees often face compounded challenges due to their intersecting identities.

- **Social Justice Theory:** Aderonke's advocacy aligns with the principles of social justice, which seeks to address systemic inequalities and promote equitable treatment for all individuals. Her efforts aim to dismantle the barriers that LGBTQ refugees face and ensure they have access to the same rights and opportunities as their heterosexual counterparts.

- **Human Rights Framework:** Aderonke's work is grounded in the belief that all individuals are entitled to fundamental human rights, regardless of their sexual orientation or gender identity. By advocating for LGBTQ refugees, she seeks to uphold these rights and challenge the injustices they endure.

Conclusion

Aderonke Apata's efforts in refugee advocacy exemplify her unwavering commitment to the LGBTQ community. Through her initiatives, she has not only provided critical support to LGBTQ refugees but has also raised awareness of their unique struggles. By addressing the intersectionality of identity, advocating for systemic change, and sharing powerful narratives, Aderonke continues to inspire hope and resilience in the face of adversity. Her work serves as a reminder of the importance of compassion and solidarity in the fight for justice, ensuring that the voices of LGBTQ refugees are heard and valued.

Speaking Out on Global LGBTQ Issues

Aderonke Apata's activism transcended the borders of Nigeria, positioning her as a prominent voice in the global discourse on LGBTQ rights. Her journey as a refugee not only highlighted the dire circumstances faced by LGBTQ individuals in oppressive regimes but also underscored the need for a unified global response to these issues. Through her advocacy, Aderonke sought to illuminate the intersectionality of LGBTQ rights with human rights, emphasizing that the struggle for equality is a universal endeavor.

One of the key theories underpinning Aderonke's approach is the **Intersectionality Theory**, which posits that individuals experience overlapping systems of discrimination based on various identities, including race, gender, and sexual orientation. This framework allows for a nuanced understanding of the challenges faced by LGBTQ individuals, particularly those from marginalized communities. Aderonke's activism exemplified this theory, as she often spoke about the compounded discrimination experienced by LGBTQ refugees, who face not only homophobia but also xenophobia and racism in their host countries.

In her speeches at international conferences, Aderonke frequently addressed the **global refugee crisis**, highlighting how LGBTQ individuals are disproportionately affected. For instance, she pointed to the harrowing statistics released by organizations such as the United Nations High Commissioner for Refugees (UNHCR), which reported that LGBTQ refugees are at a heightened risk of violence and discrimination. Aderonke emphasized the need for nations to adopt inclusive asylum policies that recognize the unique vulnerabilities of LGBTQ individuals.

Moreover, Aderonke's advocacy extended to addressing the **legal frameworks** that perpetuate discrimination against LGBTQ individuals worldwide. She often cited the example of the Anti-Homosexuality Act in Uganda, which, if passed, would impose severe penalties on LGBTQ individuals. Aderonke argued that such laws not only violate human rights but also foster an environment of fear and violence. By speaking out against these injustices, she called for international pressure on governments to repeal discriminatory laws and implement protections for LGBTQ individuals.

Aderonke also recognized the importance of **collaboration among activists** across borders. She actively sought partnerships with global LGBTQ organizations, such as ILGA (International Lesbian, Gay, Bisexual, Trans and Intersex Association) and Human Rights Campaign, to amplify her message. During her participation in international forums, she shared her experiences and strategies for mobilizing communities, thus fostering a spirit of solidarity among activists worldwide. This collective action is crucial in the fight for LGBTQ rights, as it creates a unified front against oppression.

In her speeches and writings, Aderonke often invoked the concept of **global citizenship**, urging individuals to recognize their responsibility in advocating for human rights beyond their national borders. She framed the struggle for LGBTQ rights as part of a larger human rights movement, emphasizing that the fight for equality is interconnected with the struggles against racism, sexism, and other forms of discrimination. This holistic approach resonated with many, inspiring a new generation of activists to engage in global advocacy.

One poignant example of Aderonke's impact can be seen in her involvement with the **Global Pride Movement**. In 2020, she participated in a virtual event that brought together LGBTQ activists from around the world to celebrate Pride while addressing the challenges posed by the COVID-19 pandemic. During this event, she highlighted the increased vulnerability of LGBTQ individuals during crises, advocating for inclusive support systems that address their unique needs.

Aderonke's advocacy also extended to raising awareness about the plight of LGBTQ individuals in conflict zones. She often referenced the situation in Syria, where LGBTQ individuals face persecution from both government forces and militant groups. By sharing personal stories of individuals affected by the conflict, Aderonke humanized the statistics and called for international intervention to protect vulnerable populations.

In conclusion, Aderonke Apata's commitment to speaking out on global LGBTQ issues has left an indelible mark on the movement for equality. Through her intersectional approach, emphasis on collaboration, and advocacy for global citizenship, she has inspired countless individuals to join the fight for LGBTQ rights. Her voice continues to resonate, reminding us that the struggle for justice knows no borders and that solidarity is essential in the pursuit of a more equitable world.

Fighting for LGBTQ Rights on an International Scale

Aderonke Apata's journey as an LGBTQ activist transcends borders, embodying a global struggle for equality and human rights. The fight for LGBTQ rights on an international scale is not merely a matter of local legislation but a complex interplay of cultural, political, and social factors that vary dramatically from one region to another. This section explores the theoretical frameworks, challenges, and significant examples of Aderonke's advocacy in the global arena.

Theoretical Frameworks

To understand the international fight for LGBTQ rights, we can draw on several key theoretical frameworks:

- **Intersectionality:** Coined by Kimberlé Crenshaw, this theory posits that individuals experience overlapping systems of discrimination or disadvantage. In the context of LGBTQ rights, intersectionality highlights how race, gender, socioeconomic status, and nationality impact the experiences of LGBTQ individuals. Aderonke's activism exemplifies this, as she advocates for the rights of LGBTQ refugees who often face compounded challenges due to their identities.

- **Social Movement Theory:** This framework studies the dynamics of collective action and the factors that mobilize individuals towards social change. Aderonke's work reflects the principles of social movement theory, as she organizes protests and engages in grassroots activism, rallying support from both local and international communities.
- **Human Rights Framework:** This approach emphasizes the universal rights of all individuals, regardless of sexual orientation or gender identity. Aderonke's advocacy is rooted in this framework, as she appeals to international human rights norms to challenge discriminatory laws and practices.

Challenges in Advocacy

Fighting for LGBTQ rights internationally is fraught with challenges, including:

- **Cultural Resistance:** In many countries, deeply ingrained cultural beliefs and norms oppose LGBTQ rights. Activists like Aderonke face significant pushback, as homophobic sentiments are often reinforced by traditional values and religious doctrines.
- **Legal Barriers:** Many nations have laws that criminalize same-sex relationships or discriminate against LGBTQ individuals. Aderonke's efforts to challenge these laws often involve navigating complex legal systems and advocating for legislative reforms.
- **Political Repression:** In regions where LGBTQ rights are viewed as a threat to national identity or morality, activists may face harassment, imprisonment, or violence. Aderonke's own experiences of persecution in Nigeria underscore the risks faced by LGBTQ advocates in hostile environments.

Examples of International Advocacy

Aderonke has played a pivotal role in several international initiatives aimed at advancing LGBTQ rights:

- **United Nations Advocacy:** Aderonke has participated in UN meetings and forums, where she has presented testimonies about the plight of LGBTQ individuals, particularly refugees. Her advocacy has contributed to the inclusion of LGBTQ issues in broader human rights discussions, emphasizing the need for international protections.

- **Collaborative Campaigns:** By collaborating with international LGBTQ organizations, Aderonke has helped to amplify the voices of marginalized LGBTQ communities. Initiatives such as the *Global Equality Fund* have benefitted from her insights, promoting funding and resources for grassroots LGBTQ organizations in Nigeria and beyond.

- **Social Media Mobilization:** Aderonke leverages social media platforms to raise awareness about LGBTQ issues globally. Campaigns like *#LoveIsLove* have gained traction, allowing activists to share their stories and connect with allies worldwide. This digital activism has proven essential in bypassing traditional media censorship and reaching a broader audience.

Case Studies

To illustrate the impact of Aderonke's international advocacy, we can examine specific case studies:

- **The 2018 UN Human Rights Council:** Aderonke participated in a panel discussion addressing the rights of LGBTQ refugees. Her powerful testimony about the dangers faced by LGBTQ individuals in Nigeria led to increased scrutiny of Nigerian policies by international bodies, prompting calls for action from member states.

- **The Campaign Against Anti-LGBTQ Legislation in Uganda:** Aderonke joined forces with Ugandan activists to combat the proposed Anti-Homosexuality Bill. Through coordinated efforts, they were able to mobilize international pressure, resulting in the bill being shelved temporarily. This case exemplifies the power of transnational solidarity in the fight for LGBTQ rights.

- **The Refugee Crisis and LGBTQ Inclusion:** Aderonke's work with organizations like *Rainbow Railroad* has focused on ensuring that LGBTQ refugees are included in humanitarian responses to crises. By advocating for specific provisions for LGBTQ individuals, she has helped to shape policies that recognize their unique vulnerabilities.

Conclusion

Aderonke Apata's commitment to fighting for LGBTQ rights on an international scale illustrates the interconnected nature of global activism. By employing various theoretical frameworks and navigating complex challenges, she has made significant strides in advocating for equality and justice. Her work not only impacts the lives of LGBTQ individuals in Nigeria but also resonates with activists and allies around the world, inspiring a collective movement towards a more inclusive future.

In the words of Aderonke, "The fight for our rights is not just a local battle; it is a global call for justice and humanity." Her ongoing efforts remind us that while the road to equality may be long and fraught with obstacles, the pursuit of justice knows no borders.

Aderonke's Continued Impact as a Refugee Advocate

Aderonke Apata's journey from Nigeria to the United Kingdom is not merely a tale of escape; it is a powerful narrative of resilience and advocacy that continues to shape the landscape of refugee rights, particularly for LGBTQ individuals. Her experience as a refugee has informed her activism, allowing her to address the unique challenges faced by LGBTQ refugees, a population often marginalized within both the LGBTQ community and broader refugee discourse.

Understanding the Refugee Experience

The refugee experience is fraught with complexities, particularly for LGBTQ individuals fleeing persecution. According to the United Nations High Commissioner for Refugees (UNHCR), LGBTQ refugees face heightened risks of violence, discrimination, and exclusion in both their home countries and host nations. Aderonke's advocacy work highlights the need for policies that recognize these unique vulnerabilities.

The theoretical framework surrounding refugee studies often emphasizes the concept of *intersectionality*, which posits that individuals experience multiple, overlapping identities that can compound their experiences of discrimination and marginalization. For LGBTQ refugees, factors such as race, gender, and socioeconomic status can significantly influence their experiences and access to resources. Aderonke's work embodies this intersectional approach, advocating for a more nuanced understanding of refugee rights that includes sexual orientation and gender identity as critical components.

Advocacy Initiatives

Aderonke has engaged in various initiatives aimed at improving the lives of LGBTQ refugees. One notable example is her involvement with organizations that provide legal assistance and support services tailored specifically for LGBTQ individuals navigating the asylum process. This includes workshops on legal rights, mental health support, and community-building events that foster solidarity among LGBTQ refugees.

Furthermore, Aderonke has been instrumental in raising awareness about the plight of LGBTQ refugees through public speaking engagements and media appearances. By sharing her personal story, she humanizes the statistics and challenges that often seem abstract to the general public. Her eloquence and passion have led to increased media coverage and public discourse surrounding LGBTQ refugee issues, contributing to a growing recognition of the need for targeted interventions.

Collaboration with International Organizations

Recognizing that systemic change requires collective action, Aderonke has collaborated with various international organizations, such as the International Refugee Assistance Project (IRAP) and OutRight Action International. These partnerships have facilitated the development of comprehensive advocacy strategies that address the legal and social barriers faced by LGBTQ refugees.

For instance, Aderonke has participated in lobbying efforts aimed at influencing policy changes within the UK government, advocating for the inclusion of LGBTQ-specific provisions in asylum legislation. Such efforts are crucial, as the legal framework often fails to adequately protect LGBTQ individuals, leaving them vulnerable to deportation and further persecution.

The Role of Community Support

Aderonke's impact as a refugee advocate extends beyond formal organizations; she has also emphasized the importance of community support in fostering resilience among LGBTQ refugees. By establishing safe spaces and support networks, she has helped create environments where individuals can share their experiences and access essential resources.

The concept of *community resilience* is particularly relevant here, as it underscores the capacity of communities to withstand and recover from adversities. Aderonke's initiatives have empowered LGBTQ refugees to rebuild their lives, fostering a sense of belonging and hope amidst the challenges they face.

Challenges and Ongoing Struggles

Despite her significant contributions, Aderonke acknowledges the ongoing struggles within the refugee advocacy landscape. The intersectional challenges faced by LGBTQ refugees are compounded by societal stigma, discrimination, and the often bureaucratic nature of the asylum process. Aderonke's advocacy work continues to confront these barriers, pushing for reforms that prioritize the needs of LGBTQ individuals.

Moreover, the rise of anti-immigrant sentiment in various parts of the world presents additional hurdles. Aderonke's commitment to combating these narratives is evident in her public speeches, where she emphasizes the humanity of refugees and the contributions they make to society.

A Vision for the Future

Looking ahead, Aderonke envisions a world where LGBTQ refugees are not only protected but celebrated. Her advocacy is rooted in the belief that everyone deserves the right to live authentically, free from fear of persecution. This vision aligns with the broader goals of the LGBTQ rights movement, which seeks to dismantle systemic oppression and promote equality for all.

In conclusion, Aderonke Apata's continued impact as a refugee advocate is marked by her unwavering dedication to improving the lives of LGBTQ refugees. Through her advocacy, she has highlighted the urgent need for policies that address the unique challenges faced by this vulnerable population, fostering a more inclusive and equitable society. Her work serves as a powerful reminder that the fight for justice is ongoing and that every voice matters in the pursuit of equality.

Courage in the Face of Adversity

Courage in the Face of Adversity

Courage in the Face of Adversity

In the relentless pursuit of justice and equality, Aderonke Apata embodies the spirit of courage that rises above adversity. Her journey as a Nigerian LGBTQ activist is a testament to the power of resilience, a quality that not only defines her character but also serves as a beacon of hope for countless others facing similar struggles. This chapter delves into the multifaceted nature of courage in activism, illustrating how Aderonke's experiences reflect broader themes within the LGBTQ rights movement.

Defining Courage in Activism

Courage in activism can be understood through various lenses, including psychological, sociological, and political perspectives. Psychologically, courage is often defined as the ability to confront fear, pain, or adversity despite the risks involved. As noted by [?], true courage is not the absence of fear but the determination to act in spite of it. This notion resonates deeply within the LGBTQ community, where many individuals face societal rejection, discrimination, and violence.

Sociologically, the concept of courage can also be examined through the framework of collective action. Activists, like Aderonke, often find strength in solidarity, drawing courage from their communities. This collective bravery is essential in challenging oppressive systems and advocating for change. The political dimension of courage highlights the importance of standing up against unjust laws and policies. Aderonke's efforts to confront the Nigerian government's anti-LGBTQ legislation exemplify this political courage.

The Role of Personal Experiences

Aderonke's personal experiences significantly shaped her understanding of courage. Growing up in Lagos, she faced the harsh realities of homophobia and societal rejection. Her early encounters with discrimination were not just isolated incidents; they were part of a broader systemic issue that marginalized LGBTQ individuals in Nigeria. For instance, Aderonke recalls a pivotal moment during her adolescence when she was publicly outed. The humiliation and fear she experienced in that moment could have silenced her, but instead, it ignited a fire within her to fight back.

Moreover, Aderonke's journey was marked by moments of profound personal loss and trauma, including the loss of friends and loved ones to violence and persecution. These experiences reinforced her resolve to advocate for justice, transforming her pain into a powerful motivator for change. As noted in [?], personal narratives of adversity can serve as catalysts for activism, inspiring others to join the fight for equality.

Examples of Courage in Action

Aderonke's activism is replete with examples of courage in action. One significant event was her participation in the Lagos Pride March, where she stood in defiance of the hostile environment that characterized LGBTQ events in Nigeria. Despite the threat of violence and arrest, Aderonke and her fellow activists marched boldly, sending a powerful message of resilience and unity.

Another notable instance was her confrontation with police brutality during a protest against anti-LGBTQ laws. Aderonke's unwavering stance in the face of aggression highlighted the importance of visibility and resistance. This act of courage not only galvanized support from allies but also drew international attention to the plight of LGBTQ individuals in Nigeria.

The Psychological Toll of Activism

While courage is a driving force in activism, it is essential to acknowledge the psychological toll it can take on individuals. Activists often grapple with anxiety, depression, and burnout as they navigate the challenges of their work. Aderonke has spoken candidly about her struggles with mental health, emphasizing the importance of self-care and community support. As articulated by [?], the emotional labor involved in activism can be overwhelming, making it crucial for activists to prioritize their well-being.

To address these challenges, Aderonke has advocated for mental health resources within the LGBTQ community, recognizing that courage is not only about fighting external battles but also about nurturing one's internal resilience. By sharing her experiences, she has fostered a culture of openness and support, encouraging others to seek help when needed.

Collective Courage and Solidarity

Aderonke's activism exemplifies the power of collective courage. By building networks of support among LGBTQ activists, she has created a foundation for solidarity that amplifies their collective voice. This solidarity is particularly vital in the face of systemic oppression, as it fosters resilience and encourages individuals to stand together against injustice.

The importance of collective action is further highlighted by the success of various LGBTQ organizations in Nigeria and abroad. These organizations have mobilized resources, provided legal assistance, and offered safe spaces for individuals to express their identities. Aderonke's collaboration with these groups has been instrumental in creating a united front against discrimination.

Conclusion: The Unyielding Spirit of Aderonke Apata

Aderonke Apata's journey is a powerful narrative of courage in the face of adversity. Her unwavering commitment to LGBTQ rights serves as an inspiration to many, reminding us that courage is not merely an individual trait but a collective force that can drive social change. As we reflect on her experiences, it becomes clear that the fight for equality requires not only bravery but also a deep sense of community and solidarity.

In the words of [?], "Injustice anywhere is a threat to justice everywhere." Aderonke's courage reminds us that the struggle for LGBTQ rights is a global endeavor, one that calls for unwavering commitment and collective action. As we continue to navigate the complexities of activism, let us draw strength from the stories of those like Aderonke, who embody the spirit of resilience and inspire us to stand firm in the face of adversity.

Connecting with Other Activists

Collaboration with LGBTQ Organizations

Collaboration among LGBTQ organizations is a pivotal aspect of advancing rights and ensuring the well-being of LGBTQ individuals globally. The synergy created through partnerships enhances the capacity of organizations to advocate for change, share resources, and amplify their collective voices. This section explores the theoretical frameworks underpinning collaboration, the challenges faced, and notable examples of successful partnerships.

Theoretical Frameworks

Theories of social capital and collective efficacy provide a foundation for understanding the dynamics of collaboration among LGBTQ organizations. Social capital, as defined by Bourdieu (1986), refers to the networks of relationships among people who work together in a particular society, enabling that society to function effectively. In the context of LGBTQ activism, social capital manifests through shared resources, knowledge, and support systems that organizations can leverage to enhance their advocacy efforts.

$$SC = \sum_{i=1}^{n} R_i \qquad (14)$$

where SC is the social capital, and R_i represents the resources provided by each collaborating organization i.

Collective efficacy, as proposed by Bandura (1997), refers to the shared belief in the ability to achieve goals through collective action. This theory is particularly relevant for LGBTQ organizations, as it emphasizes the power of unity in confronting systemic discrimination and advocating for policy changes.

Challenges in Collaboration

Despite the potential benefits, collaboration among LGBTQ organizations is not without challenges. Key issues include:

- **Resource Allocation:** Organizations often compete for funding and resources, which can lead to tensions and hinder collaboration. The scarcity of financial support necessitates careful negotiation and prioritization of shared goals.

- **Diverse Objectives:** LGBTQ organizations may have varying missions and priorities, leading to potential conflicts in collaboration. For instance, an organization focused on marriage equality may have different strategic goals than one advocating for transgender rights.

- **Cultural Differences:** Cultural contexts and local norms can impact how organizations perceive collaboration. In some regions, traditional values may conflict with LGBTQ advocacy, complicating partnerships.

- **Trust Issues:** Building trust among organizations is essential for successful collaboration. Historical rivalries or differing approaches to activism can create barriers to effective partnerships.

Examples of Successful Collaboration

Several successful collaborations among LGBTQ organizations illustrate the potential for collective action to effect change:

- **The Global Fund for Women:** This organization has partnered with LGBTQ groups worldwide to address gender-based violence and discrimination. By pooling resources and expertise, they have launched campaigns that have led to significant policy changes in several countries.

- **The United Nations Free & Equal Campaign:** This initiative aims to promote equal rights and fair treatment of LGBTQ individuals globally. By collaborating with local LGBTQ organizations, the campaign has successfully raised awareness and mobilized support for legal reforms in various nations.

- **Transgender Europe (TGEU):** TGEU works with various European LGBTQ organizations to advocate for transgender rights. Their collaborative efforts have resulted in the establishment of trans-inclusive policies in multiple countries, showcasing the power of united advocacy.

Conclusion

Collaboration among LGBTQ organizations is essential for amplifying voices, sharing resources, and fostering a united front against discrimination. While challenges exist, the theoretical frameworks of social capital and collective efficacy underscore the importance of working together. Successful examples demonstrate that through collaboration, LGBTQ organizations can achieve meaningful change, paving the way for a more inclusive and equitable society.

Participating in International Conferences

Aderonke Apata's participation in international conferences has been pivotal in amplifying the voices of marginalized communities, particularly within the LGBTQ spectrum. These gatherings not only provide a platform for activists to share their experiences but also serve as vital spaces for networking, collaboration, and strategizing collective actions. In this section, we will explore the significance of these conferences, the challenges faced by participants, and notable examples of Aderonke's contributions.

The Importance of International Conferences

International conferences are critical for several reasons:

- **Networking Opportunities:** These events allow activists from various countries to connect, share resources, and build alliances. This networking is essential for fostering solidarity and collective action on a global scale.

- **Knowledge Sharing:** Conferences serve as platforms for sharing best practices, research findings, and innovative strategies in advocacy. Participants can learn from each other's successes and challenges, enhancing their effectiveness in local contexts.

- **Visibility and Representation:** By participating in international forums, activists like Aderonke can bring attention to the specific struggles faced by LGBTQ individuals in their home countries, thereby raising global awareness and garnering support for their causes.

- **Policy Influence:** These conferences often include policymakers and representatives from international organizations. Activists have the opportunity to influence policy discussions and advocate for changes that benefit LGBTQ communities worldwide.

Challenges Faced by Activists

Despite the benefits, participating in international conferences is not without its challenges:

- **Access and Funding:** Many activists face financial barriers that limit their ability to attend these events. Travel costs, registration fees, and accommodation expenses can be prohibitive, particularly for those from low-income backgrounds.

CONNECTING WITH OTHER ACTIVISTS

- **Safety Concerns:** For LGBTQ activists from countries with hostile environments, attending international conferences can pose significant risks. Concerns about surveillance, persecution, or even violence can deter participation.

- **Language Barriers:** Language can be a barrier to effective communication at international conferences. Activists may struggle to convey their messages or fully engage in discussions if they are not fluent in the dominant languages of the event.

- **Cultural Differences:** Different cultural contexts can lead to misunderstandings or misinterpretations of issues. It is essential for participants to navigate these differences sensitively to foster constructive dialogue.

Aderonke's Contributions

Aderonke Apata has made significant contributions to international conferences, exemplifying the power of grassroots activism on a global stage. For instance:

- **United Nations Human Rights Council:** Aderonke has participated in sessions at the UN, where she has advocated for the rights of LGBTQ individuals, particularly refugees fleeing persecution. Her speeches have highlighted the intersectionality of race, gender, and sexual orientation, urging the international community to adopt more inclusive policies.

- **International LGBTQ Conferences:** At conferences such as the International Lesbian, Gay, Bisexual, Trans and Intersex Association (ILGA) World Conference, Aderonke has shared her experiences as a Nigerian activist, shedding light on the unique challenges faced by LGBTQ individuals in Africa. Her presentations have often included personal stories that resonate deeply with attendees, fostering empathy and understanding.

- **Workshops and Panels:** Aderonke has led workshops focused on strategies for advocacy in oppressive environments. By sharing her insights on grassroots mobilization and community-building, she has empowered other activists to develop effective campaigns in their own contexts.

- **Collaborative Initiatives:** Through her participation in international conferences, Aderonke has initiated collaborations with global organizations, leading to joint campaigns aimed at raising awareness about

LGBTQ rights and the plight of refugees. These partnerships have resulted in impactful advocacy efforts that transcend national borders.

Case Study: The 2019 ILGA World Conference

A notable example of Aderonke's impact at an international conference occurred during the 2019 ILGA World Conference held in Wellington, New Zealand. Here, Aderonke delivered a compelling keynote address that focused on the intersection of LGBTQ rights and refugee advocacy.

Her speech highlighted the following key points:

1. **The Plight of LGBTQ Refugees:** Aderonke shared harrowing stories of LGBTQ individuals who have faced violence and discrimination, emphasizing the urgent need for international protection mechanisms.

2. **Call for Solidarity:** She urged attendees to stand in solidarity with LGBTQ activists in oppressive regimes, reminding them that the fight for equality is a global struggle.

3. **Strategies for Change:** Aderonke outlined actionable strategies for attendees to implement in their own countries, focusing on grassroots mobilization, community support, and leveraging social media for advocacy.

The impact of her address was palpable, inspiring many attendees to take action upon returning to their respective countries. The conference also facilitated the formation of a coalition dedicated to supporting LGBTQ refugees, a testament to the collaborative spirit fostered by Aderonke's contributions.

Conclusion

Participating in international conferences has been a cornerstone of Aderonke Apata's activism. Through these platforms, she has not only amplified her voice but also the voices of countless others who face discrimination and persecution. Despite the challenges, her unwavering commitment to advocacy serves as a powerful reminder of the importance of global solidarity in the fight for LGBTQ rights. As Aderonke continues to engage with international forums, her influence will undoubtedly shape the future of activism and policy reform on a global scale.

Building Networks of Support

In the realm of activism, particularly within the LGBTQ community, building networks of support is fundamental to creating a robust and resilient movement. Aderonke Apata recognized early on that the struggle for LGBTQ rights in Nigeria could not be fought in isolation. The idea of collective strength is rooted in social movement theory, which posits that the success of social movements often hinges on their ability to mobilize resources, build alliances, and create a sense of solidarity among diverse groups.

Theoretical Framework

One of the key theoretical frameworks that underpin the importance of networks in social movements is the Resource Mobilization Theory (RMT). RMT suggests that the success of social movements is largely dependent on their ability to gather and utilize resources effectively, including financial support, human capital, and organizational infrastructure. Aderonke's strategic approach involved leveraging existing networks and creating new ones to amplify her voice and the voices of marginalized individuals within the LGBTQ community.

Challenges in Building Networks

Despite the theoretical advantages of networking, Aderonke faced numerous challenges in her quest to build a supportive community. The pervasive stigma surrounding LGBTQ identities in Nigeria often resulted in isolation and fear among potential allies. Many individuals were reluctant to engage openly due to fears of persecution, ostracism, or violence. This environment of distrust posed significant obstacles to mobilizing collective action.

Moreover, the legal landscape in Nigeria, which criminalizes same-sex relationships, further complicated efforts to create safe spaces for collaboration. Activists often had to navigate a treacherous path of secrecy and discretion, carefully curating their networks to avoid detection by authorities. This situation underscores the importance of trust and confidentiality in the formation of supportive networks.

Examples of Successful Networking

In response to these challenges, Aderonke utilized various strategies to cultivate networks of support. One notable example was her collaboration with international LGBTQ organizations. By connecting with groups such as ILGA

(International Lesbian, Gay, Bisexual, Trans and Intersex Association) and OutRight Action International, Aderonke was able to gain access to resources, training, and global platforms to amplify her message. These alliances not only provided material support but also lent credibility to her activism, allowing her to present her case on a larger stage.

Additionally, Aderonke organized workshops and community events that brought together LGBTQ individuals and allies. These gatherings served as safe havens for sharing experiences, fostering connections, and strategizing collective actions. For instance, during a community outreach event in Lagos, Aderonke facilitated discussions on mental health and well-being, emphasizing the importance of solidarity in overcoming personal and societal challenges. Such initiatives not only strengthened individual resolve but also reinforced a sense of belonging within the community.

The Role of Technology in Networking

In the digital age, technology plays a pivotal role in facilitating networks of support. Aderonke harnessed social media platforms to connect with activists and organizations both locally and globally. Through platforms like Twitter and Facebook, she was able to share her story, mobilize support for campaigns, and raise awareness about the plight of LGBTQ individuals in Nigeria. The viral nature of social media helped transcend geographical barriers, allowing for the creation of a virtual community that could rally around shared goals and experiences.

Moreover, the use of encrypted messaging apps became essential for maintaining communication among activists in a climate of surveillance and repression. By utilizing tools like Signal and WhatsApp, Aderonke and her peers could coordinate actions and share information securely, thereby enhancing their collective efficacy.

Impact of Support Networks on Activism

The networks of support that Aderonke built had a profound impact on her activism and the broader LGBTQ movement in Nigeria. By fostering solidarity among activists, she was able to create a more united front against discrimination and violence. This collective action was instrumental in organizing protests and advocacy campaigns that drew attention to the injustices faced by the LGBTQ community.

Furthermore, these networks facilitated mentorship and capacity-building opportunities for emerging activists. Aderonke's commitment to empowering others was evident in her efforts to provide training and resources for young LGBTQ leaders. By sharing knowledge and experiences, she helped cultivate a new generation of activists equipped to continue the fight for equality and justice.

In conclusion, building networks of support is a critical component of effective activism. Aderonke Apata's experiences illustrate the challenges and triumphs associated with this endeavor. Through strategic alliances, community engagement, and the innovative use of technology, Aderonke not only advanced her own advocacy but also contributed to the strengthening of the LGBTQ movement in Nigeria and beyond. The enduring impact of these networks continues to inspire activists around the world, underscoring the importance of solidarity in the pursuit of justice and equality.

Shared Activism: Solidarity Among Activists

In the realm of LGBTQ activism, the concept of shared activism and solidarity among activists is paramount. Solidarity is not merely a passive state of agreement; it is an active commitment to support one another in the face of adversity. This section delves into the theoretical underpinnings of solidarity, the challenges faced by activists, and the powerful examples of collective action that have emerged in the LGBTQ movement.

Theoretical Framework of Solidarity

Solidarity can be understood through various theoretical lenses. One prominent theory is the *Social Movement Theory*, which posits that collective action is essential for effecting social change. According to Tilly (2004), social movements thrive on the ability of individuals to come together, share their experiences, and mobilize for a common cause. This collective identity is crucial in LGBTQ activism, where shared experiences of marginalization and discrimination foster a sense of community.

Moreover, the concept of *Intersectionality*, introduced by Crenshaw (1989), emphasizes the importance of recognizing the interconnected nature of social categorizations such as race, class, and gender. In LGBTQ activism, intersectionality highlights that individuals may face multiple layers of oppression. Solidarity among activists involves acknowledging these complexities and working collaboratively to address the unique challenges faced by marginalized groups within the LGBTQ community.

Challenges to Solidarity

Despite the theoretical frameworks that support solidarity, activists often encounter significant challenges. One major issue is the *fragmentation* of the LGBTQ movement, where differing priorities and identities can lead to divisions. For instance, activists focusing on issues such as marriage equality may inadvertently marginalize those advocating for transgender rights or LGBTQ youth homelessness. This fragmentation can weaken the overall effectiveness of the movement and hinder progress toward shared goals.

Additionally, the *globalization of activism* presents both opportunities and challenges for solidarity. While international collaborations can amplify voices and resources, they can also lead to the imposition of Western-centric ideologies on local movements. Activists from diverse cultural backgrounds may struggle to align their goals with those of international organizations, resulting in tensions and misunderstandings.

Examples of Collective Action

Despite these challenges, there are numerous examples of successful solidarity in LGBTQ activism. One notable instance is the *Stonewall Riots* of 1969, which marked a turning point in the fight for LGBTQ rights. The riots were not the actions of isolated individuals but rather a collective uprising against systemic oppression. Activists from various backgrounds came together to resist police brutality and demand recognition of their rights. This event catalyzed the formation of numerous LGBTQ organizations and sparked a global movement for equality.

Another powerful example is the *#BlackLivesMatter* movement, which has forged connections between racial justice and LGBTQ rights. Activists within the LGBTQ community have united with their Black counterparts to address the intersections of race and sexuality. This solidarity has led to campaigns that highlight the unique challenges faced by Black LGBTQ individuals, fostering a more inclusive movement.

Furthermore, the *Queer Liberation March* demonstrates the power of shared activism. Established as an alternative to the corporate Pride parades, this march emphasizes grassroots organizing and collective action. Participants come together to honor the history of LGBTQ activism while advocating for continued social justice efforts. The march serves as a reminder that solidarity is rooted in shared history and collective memory.

Conclusion

In conclusion, shared activism and solidarity among LGBTQ activists are essential for achieving meaningful social change. Theoretical frameworks such as Social Movement Theory and Intersectionality provide valuable insights into the dynamics of collective action. While challenges such as fragmentation and globalization persist, examples of successful solidarity illustrate the power of unity in the face of adversity. As Aderonke Apata and her peers continue to fight for LGBTQ rights, the importance of fostering solidarity remains a guiding principle in the ongoing struggle for equality.

$$S = \sum_{i=1}^{n}(C_i \cdot I_i) \tag{15}$$

Where S represents the strength of solidarity, C_i denotes the collective actions of individual activists, and I_i signifies the intersectional identities that contribute to the movement's diversity.

This equation encapsulates the essence of solidarity in activism: the more collective actions are taken, and the more diverse the identities involved, the stronger the movement becomes.

The Power of Collective Action

Collective action is a cornerstone of social movements, particularly within the LGBTQ community, where shared experiences and mutual support can lead to significant advancements in rights and recognition. The concept of collective action refers to the efforts of a group to achieve a common goal, often in the face of systemic oppression. This section explores the dynamics of collective action, its theoretical underpinnings, challenges faced, and notable examples within the LGBTQ activism landscape.

Theoretical Framework

The theory of collective action is grounded in several key concepts, including social identity theory, resource mobilization theory, and the collective action problem. Social identity theory posits that individuals derive part of their self-concept from their group memberships, which can foster solidarity and a sense of belonging among marginalized groups [?]. This sense of identity can motivate individuals to participate in collective efforts aimed at social change.

Resource mobilization theory emphasizes the importance of resources—such as time, money, and organizational infrastructure—in facilitating collective action. According to this theory, successful movements require not only a shared identity but also the ability to mobilize resources effectively [?].

Lastly, the collective action problem highlights the challenges groups face in coordinating efforts. Individuals may hesitate to participate due to the fear of free-riding, where some benefit from the efforts of others without contributing themselves. This dilemma can hinder the mobilization of collective action unless mechanisms are in place to encourage participation and commitment [?].

Challenges of Collective Action

Despite its potential, collective action is fraught with challenges. One significant issue is the fragmentation of the LGBTQ movement itself, which can arise from differing priorities among subgroups (e.g., race, gender identity, socioeconomic status). This fragmentation can dilute efforts and create conflicts over resources and strategies. For instance, the intersection of race and sexuality has often led to tensions between mainstream LGBTQ organizations and those focused on racial justice, as seen in the criticisms of the lack of representation of people of color within predominantly white LGBTQ spaces [?].

Moreover, external pressures, such as governmental repression and societal backlash, can stifle collective action. In many countries, LGBTQ activists face harassment, violence, and legal repercussions for their work. This environment of fear can deter participation and weaken the resolve of activists, as demonstrated by the experiences of LGBTQ individuals in Nigeria, where anti-gay laws create a hostile atmosphere for organizing.

Examples of Successful Collective Action

Despite these challenges, there are numerous examples of successful collective action within the LGBTQ community that illustrate its power. One prominent case is the Stonewall Riots of 1969, which marked a turning point in the fight for LGBTQ rights. The riots were a direct response to police harassment at the Stonewall Inn in New York City and galvanized the community to organize for their rights. This event is often credited with sparking the modern LGBTQ rights movement, leading to the formation of various activist organizations, such as the Gay Liberation Front [?].

Another significant example is the global response to the HIV/AIDS crisis in the 1980s and 1990s. Activist groups, such as ACT UP (AIDS Coalition to

Unleash Power), utilized collective action to demand government accountability, research funding, and access to treatment. Their slogan, "Silence = Death," encapsulated the urgency of their cause and mobilized thousands to participate in protests, advocacy, and educational efforts [?].

Furthermore, the recent global Pride movements demonstrate the effectiveness of collective action in raising awareness and advocating for LGBTQ rights. Events like the International Day Against Homophobia, Transphobia, and Biphobia (IDAHOT) mobilize activists worldwide to unite under a common cause, leveraging social media to amplify their messages and reach broader audiences [?].

The Role of Technology in Collective Action

In the contemporary landscape, technology plays a crucial role in facilitating collective action. Social media platforms have become instrumental in organizing events, sharing information, and building networks of support. For instance, the hashtag #LoveIsLove became a rallying cry for marriage equality, allowing individuals to share personal stories and mobilize support across diverse communities. This digital activism complements traditional forms of organizing by providing new avenues for engagement and outreach.

Moreover, online petitions and crowdfunding campaigns have emerged as powerful tools for collective action, enabling activists to gather support and resources quickly. Platforms like Change.org and GoFundMe have been utilized by LGBTQ activists to advocate for policy changes and fund legal battles, demonstrating the potential of technology to enhance collective efforts [?].

Conclusion

The power of collective action lies in its ability to unite individuals towards a common goal, fostering a sense of solidarity and shared purpose. While challenges such as fragmentation and repression persist, the LGBTQ community has consistently demonstrated resilience and creativity in overcoming obstacles. Through historical examples and the integration of technology, collective action remains a vital force in the ongoing struggle for LGBTQ rights, illustrating that together, individuals can effect meaningful change.

Aderonke's Fight against Homophobia

Challenging Homophobic Laws and Policies

In the fight for LGBTQ rights, one of the most significant battlegrounds is the legal framework that governs societal norms and protections. In Nigeria, where homosexuality is criminalized under the Same-Sex Marriage (Prohibition) Act of 2014, LGBTQ individuals face severe legal repercussions, including imprisonment and societal ostracization. Aderonke Apata, as a prominent activist, has dedicated her efforts to challenging these oppressive laws and advocating for policy reforms that promote equality and human rights.

The Legal Landscape in Nigeria

The legal landscape in Nigeria is characterized by a complex interplay of colonial-era laws and contemporary legislation that discriminates against LGBTQ individuals. The penal code, inherited from British colonial rule, includes provisions that criminalize same-sex relationships, while the Same-Sex Marriage (Prohibition) Act explicitly prohibits same-sex marriage and related advocacy. This legal framework not only perpetuates stigma but also emboldens violence and discrimination against LGBTQ individuals.

Theoretical Framework

To understand the implications of these laws, it is essential to apply the theoretical framework of intersectionality, which examines how various social identities—such as race, gender, and sexual orientation—intersect to create unique modes of discrimination and privilege. In Nigeria, LGBTQ individuals often face compounded discrimination based on their sexual orientation and gender identity, exacerbated by prevailing cultural and religious norms that view homosexuality as taboo.

$$D = f(O, I, C) \tag{16}$$

Where:

- D = Discrimination faced by LGBTQ individuals
- O = Sexual orientation
- I = Intersectional identities (e.g., race, gender)

- C = Cultural and religious context

This equation illustrates how various factors contribute to the discrimination experienced by LGBTQ individuals in Nigeria, emphasizing the need for a multifaceted approach to advocacy and reform.

Aderonke's Advocacy Efforts

Aderonke Apata's advocacy has focused on challenging these discriminatory laws through various means:

- **Legal Challenges:** Aderonke has collaborated with legal experts to challenge the constitutionality of homophobic laws in Nigerian courts. By arguing that these laws violate fundamental human rights as enshrined in the Nigerian Constitution, she aims to dismantle the legal barriers that hinder LGBTQ rights.

- **Public Awareness Campaigns:** Understanding that legal reform requires public support, Aderonke has spearheaded campaigns to educate the public about LGBTQ issues. These campaigns utilize social media, community outreach, and public forums to foster dialogue and reduce stigma surrounding LGBTQ identities.

- **International Advocacy:** Aderonke has also engaged with international human rights organizations to apply pressure on the Nigerian government. By raising awareness of the situation in Nigeria on global platforms, she seeks to garner international support for LGBTQ rights and challenge the legitimacy of homophobic laws.

- **Coalition Building:** Recognizing the power of collective action, Aderonke has worked to build coalitions among various human rights organizations, both locally and internationally. These coalitions amplify the voices of marginalized communities and strengthen the push for legal reforms.

Examples of Successful Challenges

While the legal landscape remains daunting, there have been notable examples of successful challenges to homophobic laws in Nigeria and beyond. For instance, in 2018, a Nigerian court ruled in favor of an LGBTQ individual who had been unlawfully detained under the Same-Sex Marriage (Prohibition) Act. This landmark decision set a precedent for future legal challenges and demonstrated the potential for change within the judicial system.

Additionally, advocacy efforts have led to increased visibility of LGBTQ issues within the media, contributing to a gradual shift in public perception. Aderonke's work has played a crucial role in these developments, showcasing the importance of persistence and resilience in the face of adversity.

Conclusion

Challenging homophobic laws and policies is a critical component of the broader fight for LGBTQ rights in Nigeria. Through her tireless advocacy, Aderonke Apata exemplifies the courage and determination required to confront systemic discrimination. By employing a multifaceted approach that includes legal challenges, public awareness campaigns, international advocacy, and coalition building, Aderonke continues to push for a more inclusive and equitable society. As the struggle for LGBTQ rights evolves, it is imperative that activists remain vigilant and committed to dismantling the legal barriers that perpetuate inequality and injustice.

Advocacy for LGBTQ Healthcare Rights

The intersection of healthcare and LGBTQ rights has emerged as a critical area of advocacy, particularly in regions where systemic discrimination and stigmatization persist. Aderonke Apata's commitment to LGBTQ healthcare rights highlights the urgent need for equitable access to medical services that respect and affirm diverse sexual orientations and gender identities.

Theoretical Frameworks

To understand the advocacy for LGBTQ healthcare rights, it is essential to consider several theoretical frameworks that inform health disparities among marginalized populations. The **Social Determinants of Health** (SDOH) theory posits that health outcomes are influenced by a range of social factors, including socioeconomic status, education, and access to healthcare. For LGBTQ individuals, these determinants are often compounded by discrimination, stigma, and violence, leading to significant health disparities.

Another relevant framework is the **Minority Stress Theory**, which suggests that individuals from stigmatized groups experience chronic stress due to societal prejudice, which can adversely affect mental and physical health. This theory is particularly pertinent in understanding the mental health challenges faced by

LGBTQ individuals, who may experience higher rates of anxiety, depression, and suicidal ideation compared to their heterosexual counterparts.

Challenges Faced by LGBTQ Individuals in Healthcare

Despite advancements in LGBTQ rights, significant barriers remain in accessing healthcare services. Common challenges include:

- **Discrimination and Bias:** Many LGBTQ individuals report experiencing discrimination in healthcare settings, which can discourage them from seeking necessary medical care. This discrimination can manifest as negative attitudes from healthcare providers, refusal of care, or inadequate treatment.

- **Lack of Cultural Competence:** Healthcare providers often lack the training and awareness necessary to provide culturally competent care to LGBTQ patients. This gap can lead to misdiagnoses, inadequate treatment, and a failure to address specific health needs, such as those related to sexual and reproductive health.

- **Mental Health Disparities:** LGBTQ individuals face heightened risks of mental health issues due to societal stigma and discrimination. Access to mental health services that are affirming and supportive is often limited, exacerbating these challenges.

- **Insurance Disparities:** Many LGBTQ individuals, especially transgender individuals, encounter difficulties with insurance coverage for necessary medical procedures, including gender-affirming surgeries and hormone therapies. This lack of coverage can lead to significant financial burdens and unmet health needs.

Aderonke's Advocacy Efforts

Aderonke Apata's advocacy for LGBTQ healthcare rights has been multifaceted, focusing on raising awareness, challenging discriminatory practices, and promoting inclusive policies. Some of her key initiatives include:

- **Public Awareness Campaigns:** Aderonke has spearheaded campaigns to educate both the LGBTQ community and healthcare providers about the unique health needs of LGBTQ individuals. These campaigns often utilize social media platforms to reach a broader audience and disseminate critical information.

- **Collaboration with Healthcare Organizations:** By partnering with healthcare organizations, Aderonke has worked to develop training programs for healthcare providers that emphasize cultural competence and the importance of inclusive care. These collaborations aim to create a more welcoming environment for LGBTQ patients.

- **Policy Advocacy:** Aderonke has actively lobbied for policy changes at both national and international levels to ensure that LGBTQ individuals have equitable access to healthcare services. This includes advocating for the inclusion of LGBTQ health issues in public health agendas and for the repeal of discriminatory laws that hinder access to care.

- **Mental Health Support Initiatives:** Recognizing the mental health disparities within the LGBTQ community, Aderonke has championed initiatives that provide mental health resources, including support groups and counseling services tailored to LGBTQ individuals.

Examples of Impact

Aderonke's advocacy has led to tangible improvements in healthcare access for LGBTQ individuals. For example, her efforts have contributed to the establishment of LGBTQ-inclusive health policies in various healthcare institutions, ensuring that LGBTQ patients receive respectful and affirming care. Furthermore, her work has inspired other activists to join the fight for healthcare equity, creating a ripple effect that amplifies the message of inclusion and respect.

One notable success story involves the implementation of training programs in hospitals that cater specifically to the needs of LGBTQ patients. These programs have resulted in significant improvements in patient satisfaction and healthcare outcomes, demonstrating the effectiveness of advocacy efforts in creating systemic change.

Conclusion

Advocacy for LGBTQ healthcare rights remains a vital aspect of the broader struggle for equality and justice. Aderonke Apata's work exemplifies the importance of addressing healthcare disparities through education, policy change, and community engagement. As the fight for LGBTQ rights continues, it is crucial to ensure that healthcare access is inclusive, equitable, and affirming for all individuals, regardless of their sexual orientation or gender identity. The journey towards healthcare equity is ongoing, but with advocates like Aderonke leading the charge, there is hope for a healthier future for LGBTQ communities worldwide.

Addressing LGBTQ Homelessness

LGBTQ homelessness is a pressing issue that affects a significant proportion of the LGBTQ community worldwide. According to the National Alliance to End Homelessness, LGBTQ youth are 120% more likely to experience homelessness than their heterosexual peers. This disparity is often rooted in family rejection, discrimination, and societal stigma, leading many LGBTQ individuals to face unique challenges that contribute to their homelessness.

Theoretical Framework

To understand the phenomenon of LGBTQ homelessness, it is essential to consider several theoretical frameworks. One prominent theory is the **Social Exclusion Theory**, which posits that marginalized groups are systematically excluded from societal resources, leading to increased vulnerability. In the case of LGBTQ individuals, social exclusion manifests through familial rejection, discrimination in housing and employment, and a lack of supportive services.

Another relevant theory is the **Intersectionality Framework**, which emphasizes how various social identities—such as race, gender, and sexual orientation—intersect to create unique experiences of oppression. For example, LGBTQ youth of color may experience compounded discrimination, making them more susceptible to homelessness than their white counterparts.

Problems Contributing to LGBTQ Homelessness

Several factors contribute to the high rates of homelessness among LGBTQ individuals:

1. **Family Rejection:** Many LGBTQ youth face rejection from their families upon coming out, leading to a lack of emotional and financial support. Research indicates that approximately 40% of homeless youth identify as LGBTQ, with family rejection being a primary cause.

2. **Discrimination in Housing:** LGBTQ individuals often encounter discrimination when seeking housing, with landlords and property managers refusing to rent to them based on their sexual orientation or gender identity. A study by the Williams Institute found that LGBTQ individuals are more likely to experience housing discrimination than heterosexual individuals.

3. **Mental Health Challenges:** The stigma and discrimination faced by LGBTQ individuals can lead to mental health issues such as depression and anxiety, further complicating their ability to secure stable housing. According to the Substance Abuse and Mental Health Services Administration, LGBTQ youth are at a higher risk for mental health challenges compared to their heterosexual peers.

4. **Lack of Supportive Services:** Many shelters and services are not equipped to address the specific needs of LGBTQ individuals, leading to further marginalization. For instance, a report by the True Colors Fund found that many LGBTQ youth are turned away from shelters due to their sexual orientation or gender identity.

Examples of Addressing LGBTQ Homelessness

Numerous organizations and initiatives have emerged to address LGBTQ homelessness effectively.

1. **The Ali Forney Center:** Located in New York City, the Ali Forney Center provides housing, medical care, and job training for homeless LGBTQ youth. Their comprehensive approach addresses the immediate needs of homeless youth while empowering them to achieve long-term stability.

2. **The Trevor Project:** While primarily known for its crisis intervention services, The Trevor Project also works to address the root causes of LGBTQ homelessness by advocating for policies that protect LGBTQ youth from discrimination and promote inclusive practices in schools and communities.

3. **Local Initiatives:** Many cities have launched local initiatives aimed at reducing LGBTQ homelessness. For example, Los Angeles has implemented the *LGBTQ Homelessness Prevention Program*, which provides financial assistance and support services to LGBTQ youth at risk of homelessness.

Strategies for Advocacy and Change

To effectively address LGBTQ homelessness, advocates must employ a multi-faceted approach:

1. **Policy Advocacy:** Advocating for policies that protect LGBTQ individuals from discrimination in housing and employment is crucial. This includes supporting legislation that prohibits discrimination based on sexual orientation and gender identity.

2. **Community Engagement:** Engaging with local communities to raise awareness about LGBTQ homelessness can foster understanding and support.

Grassroots campaigns can mobilize community members to advocate for inclusive policies and practices.

3. **Creating Safe Spaces:** Developing safe spaces for LGBTQ individuals in shelters and housing programs can help mitigate the trauma associated with homelessness. Training staff on LGBTQ issues and creating inclusive environments are essential steps in this process.

4. **Support Services:** Providing tailored support services, including mental health resources and job training, can help LGBTQ individuals transition out of homelessness. Collaborating with mental health organizations can enhance the support network available to these individuals.

In conclusion, addressing LGBTQ homelessness requires a comprehensive understanding of the unique challenges faced by this community. By employing theoretical frameworks, recognizing the contributing factors, and implementing effective strategies, advocates can work towards creating a more inclusive and supportive environment for LGBTQ individuals experiencing homelessness. The fight against LGBTQ homelessness is not just about providing shelter; it is about ensuring that every individual has the opportunity to thrive, regardless of their sexual orientation or gender identity.

Amplifying LGBTQ Voices

The amplification of LGBTQ voices is a crucial element in the ongoing struggle for equality and acceptance. This section will explore the theoretical underpinnings, the challenges faced, and the practical examples of how LGBTQ voices can and have been amplified in various contexts.

Theoretical Framework

The theory of intersectionality, coined by Kimberlé Crenshaw, provides a foundational understanding of how different social identities intersect to shape individual experiences, particularly in marginalized communities. This framework is essential for amplifying LGBTQ voices, as it recognizes that individuals do not experience discrimination solely based on one aspect of their identity, such as sexual orientation or gender identity. Instead, they navigate a complex web of societal structures that can compound their marginalization.

For instance, a queer person of color may face unique challenges that differ from those encountered by a white LGBTQ individual. Therefore, amplifying LGBTQ voices must include a diverse range of perspectives that reflect the intersections of race, class, gender, and sexuality. This approach not only enriches the discourse but also ensures that the most marginalized within the LGBTQ community are heard.

Challenges in Amplification

Despite the importance of amplifying LGBTQ voices, several challenges persist.

- **Censorship and Suppression:** In many regions, LGBTQ narratives are systematically silenced through censorship and repression. This is particularly evident in countries with stringent anti-LGBTQ laws, where expressing one's identity can lead to severe consequences, including imprisonment or violence.

- **Misrepresentation in Media:** The media often perpetuates stereotypes and fails to accurately represent LGBTQ lives. This misrepresentation can lead to a lack of visibility for diverse LGBTQ experiences, reinforcing harmful stereotypes and limiting the understanding of LGBTQ issues among the broader public.

- **Internalized Homophobia:** Many LGBTQ individuals face internalized homophobia, which can hinder their willingness to share their stories. This internal struggle can stem from societal stigma and discrimination, making it challenging for individuals to embrace their identities fully and speak out.

- **Limited Access to Platforms:** Access to platforms for storytelling and advocacy is often limited for marginalized voices within the LGBTQ community. This includes barriers to entry in traditional media, as well as social media platforms that may not prioritize or protect LGBTQ narratives.

Examples of Amplification

To counter these challenges, several effective strategies have emerged for amplifying LGBTQ voices:

- **Community Storytelling Initiatives:** Grassroots organizations have initiated storytelling projects that encourage LGBTQ individuals to share their experiences. For example, the *Humans of New York* project has featured stories from LGBTQ individuals, highlighting their struggles and triumphs, thereby humanizing their experiences and fostering empathy among a wider audience.

- **Social Media Campaigns:** Social media has become an invaluable tool for amplifying LGBTQ voices. Campaigns such as #LoveIsLove and #TransRightsAreHumanRights have mobilized millions to share their stories and advocate for change. These platforms allow individuals to connect, share resources, and raise awareness about LGBTQ issues on a global scale.

- **Collaborations with Allies:** Collaborating with allies in various sectors—such as entertainment, politics, and education—can significantly amplify LGBTQ voices. For instance, prominent figures like Ellen DeGeneres and Laverne Cox have used their platforms to advocate for LGBTQ rights, bringing visibility to critical issues and encouraging broader societal support.

- **Art and Creative Expression:** Art has historically been a powerful medium for amplifying marginalized voices. LGBTQ artists and creators use their work to express their identities and experiences, challenging societal norms. Events like Pride parades and LGBTQ film festivals serve as platforms for these artists, allowing them to share their narratives with larger audiences.

Conclusion

Amplifying LGBTQ voices is not merely an act of sharing stories; it is a vital component of the broader movement for equality and justice. By understanding the complexities of intersectionality, recognizing the challenges faced, and implementing effective strategies for amplification, we can ensure that LGBTQ voices resonate loudly and clearly in the ongoing fight for rights and recognition.

As Aderonke Apata has demonstrated through her activism, the power of personal narratives can inspire change and mobilize communities. The ongoing commitment to amplifying these voices is essential for fostering a more inclusive and equitable society for all.

Taking a Stand against Conversion Therapy

Conversion therapy, also known as reparative therapy, is a controversial practice aimed at changing an individual's sexual orientation or gender identity. This practice has been widely discredited by major medical and psychological organizations due to its harmful effects and lack of scientific validity. Aderonke Apata has been a vocal opponent of conversion therapy, advocating for the rights and dignity of LGBTQ individuals who have been subjected to these damaging practices.

Understanding Conversion Therapy

Conversion therapy encompasses a range of practices, including counseling, aversive conditioning, and spiritual interventions, often rooted in the belief that non-heteronormative sexual orientations are pathological. The American Psychological Association (APA) states that there is no evidence to support the efficacy of conversion therapy and highlights its potential to cause significant psychological harm, including depression, anxiety, and suicidal ideation.

Theoretical Framework

The theoretical underpinnings of conversion therapy often stem from outdated psychological models, such as the medical model of homosexuality, which viewed non-heterosexual orientations as disorders. This perspective has been debunked, and contemporary understanding emphasizes the importance of affirming diverse sexual and gender identities. The minority stress theory posits that individuals from marginalized groups face chronic stress due to societal stigma, discrimination, and violence, which can lead to negative mental health outcomes. Conversion therapy exacerbates this stress by invalidating individuals' identities and experiences.

The Problems with Conversion Therapy

The practice of conversion therapy raises several ethical and moral concerns:

- **Harmful Psychological Effects:** Research indicates that individuals who undergo conversion therapy are at a higher risk of experiencing mental health issues, including depression, anxiety, and suicidal thoughts. A study by the Williams Institute found that LGBTQ individuals who had undergone conversion therapy were more than twice as likely to report suicidal ideation compared to those who had not.

- **Violation of Human Rights:** Conversion therapy is often conducted without informed consent, particularly among minors. This practice violates fundamental human rights and undermines the autonomy of individuals to make decisions about their own identities and bodies.

- **Perpetuation of Stigma:** By promoting the notion that LGBTQ identities are deviant or disordered, conversion therapy reinforces societal stigma and discrimination. This perpetuates a cycle of marginalization and can lead to further isolation and rejection of LGBTQ individuals.

Aderonke's Advocacy Against Conversion Therapy

Aderonke Apata has taken a firm stand against conversion therapy through various advocacy efforts:

- **Public Awareness Campaigns:** Aderonke has participated in campaigns aimed at raising awareness about the dangers of conversion therapy, utilizing social media platforms to share personal stories and testimonials from survivors. These narratives are crucial in humanizing the issue and mobilizing support for legislative change.

- **Collaboration with Organizations:** Aderonke has worked alongside numerous LGBTQ organizations to develop resources and support systems for individuals affected by conversion therapy. This includes creating safe spaces for survivors to share their experiences and access mental health support.

- **Advocating for Legislative Change:** Aderonke has lobbied for the introduction of legislation banning conversion therapy in various jurisdictions. Her efforts have contributed to the growing movement to outlaw these practices, with several countries and states taking steps to prohibit conversion therapy.

Examples of Legislative Success

Several regions have successfully enacted laws banning conversion therapy, reflecting a shift toward protecting LGBTQ rights:

- **Canada:** In 2021, Canada passed Bill C-4, which criminalizes the practice of conversion therapy, marking a significant victory for LGBTQ advocates. This legislation sends a strong message that conversion therapy is not only ineffective but also harmful.

- **United States:** Numerous states, including California, New York, and Illinois, have implemented bans on conversion therapy for minors. These laws are a testament to the growing recognition of the need to protect LGBTQ youth from harmful practices.

The Road Ahead

Despite these victories, the fight against conversion therapy is far from over. Many regions still lack comprehensive protections for LGBTQ individuals, and conversion therapy remains legal in several countries. Aderonke's ongoing efforts highlight the importance of continued advocacy, education, and support for LGBTQ individuals globally.

In conclusion, taking a stand against conversion therapy is essential for promoting the rights and well-being of LGBTQ individuals. Aderonke Apata's work exemplifies the power of advocacy in challenging harmful practices and fostering a more inclusive society. By raising awareness, collaborating with organizations, and pushing for legislative change, Aderonke is not only combating conversion therapy but also paving the way for a future where LGBTQ identities are celebrated and affirmed.

Empowering LGBTQ Youth

Mentorship and Support Programs

Mentorship and support programs play a crucial role in empowering LGBTQ youth, providing them with guidance, resources, and a sense of belonging. These programs are designed to address the unique challenges faced by LGBTQ individuals, particularly those who may feel isolated or marginalized due to their sexual orientation or gender identity.

Theoretical Framework

The theoretical framework for mentorship programs often draws from social support theory, which posits that social connections can enhance individual well-being and resilience. According to Cohen and Wills (1985), social support can buffer against stress and promote mental health. For LGBTQ youth, who may experience higher rates of bullying, discrimination, and mental health issues, having a supportive mentor can significantly impact their development and self-esteem.

Furthermore, the concept of intersectionality, introduced by Crenshaw (1989), is vital in understanding the diverse experiences of LGBTQ youth. Intersectionality acknowledges that individuals may face multiple layers of discrimination based on their race, socioeconomic status, and gender identity, necessitating tailored mentorship approaches that consider these intersections.

Challenges Faced by LGBTQ Youth

LGBTQ youth often encounter several challenges that mentorship and support programs aim to address:

- **Isolation and Loneliness:** Many LGBTQ youth feel isolated from their peers and families, leading to feelings of loneliness and depression. Mentorship programs provide a safe space for these individuals to connect with others who share similar experiences.

- **Mental Health Issues:** Studies indicate that LGBTQ youth are at a higher risk for mental health issues, including anxiety and depression. Support programs can offer mental health resources and counseling, helping youth navigate these challenges.

- **Lack of Acceptance:** Many LGBTQ youth face rejection from their families and communities, which can exacerbate feelings of worthlessness. Mentorship programs can foster a sense of acceptance and validation, promoting self-acceptance and resilience.

Examples of Effective Mentorship Programs

Several organizations have successfully implemented mentorship and support programs for LGBTQ youth:

- **The Trevor Project:** This organization provides crisis intervention and suicide prevention services to LGBTQ youth. Their mentorship program connects young individuals with trained mentors who can offer guidance and support. The Trevor Project emphasizes the importance of creating safe spaces for LGBTQ youth to express themselves freely.

- **Big Brothers Big Sisters of America:** This national organization has adapted its traditional mentoring model to include LGBTQ youth. By pairing LGBTQ youth with supportive mentors, they aim to provide positive role models and foster a sense of belonging.

- **OUT for Work:** This organization focuses on preparing LGBTQ college students for the workforce. Their mentorship program connects students with LGBTQ professionals in their desired fields, providing guidance on navigating workplace challenges and fostering career development.

The Role of Mentors

Mentors play a multifaceted role in the lives of LGBTQ youth. They serve as role models, advocates, and sources of encouragement. Effective mentors exhibit the following qualities:

- **Empathy and Understanding:** Mentors should possess a deep understanding of the challenges faced by LGBTQ youth. This empathy fosters trust and allows for open communication.
- **Cultural Competence:** Mentors must be culturally competent, recognizing the diverse backgrounds and experiences of LGBTQ youth. This understanding enables mentors to provide tailored support that respects individual identities.
- **Advocacy:** Mentors can advocate for their mentees in various settings, including schools and community organizations. This advocacy can help create more inclusive environments for LGBTQ youth.

Measuring the Impact of Mentorship Programs

To evaluate the effectiveness of mentorship and support programs, organizations often employ various assessment tools and methodologies. These may include:

- **Surveys and Questionnaires:** Pre- and post-program surveys can measure changes in mentees' self-esteem, mental health, and overall well-being.
- **Focus Groups:** Conducting focus groups with participants can provide qualitative insights into the experiences and impacts of mentorship programs.
- **Longitudinal Studies:** Long-term studies can track the progress of mentees over time, assessing the sustained impact of mentorship on their lives.

Conclusion

In conclusion, mentorship and support programs are essential in empowering LGBTQ youth. By providing guidance, resources, and a sense of belonging, these programs can help mitigate the challenges faced by LGBTQ individuals. As society continues to evolve, it is crucial to invest in and expand these programs to ensure that all LGBTQ youth have the opportunity to thrive and succeed in their lives. The legacy of these mentorship initiatives will not only shape the future of

LGBTQ activism but also foster a generation of empowered individuals ready to advocate for their rights and the rights of others.

Education Initiatives for LGBTQ Youth

Education is a powerful tool for empowering LGBTQ youth, providing them with the knowledge, resources, and support necessary to navigate a world that can often be hostile and unwelcoming. Aderonke Apata has been a staunch advocate for educational initiatives aimed specifically at LGBTQ youth, recognizing that these programs can play a crucial role in fostering a sense of belonging, identity, and resilience.

The Importance of Inclusive Education

Inclusive education is essential for LGBTQ youth, as it helps to combat the discrimination and stigma they often face in traditional educational settings. Research has shown that LGBTQ students are at a higher risk for bullying, harassment, and mental health issues, which can lead to lower academic performance and higher dropout rates. According to the *National School Climate Survey*, LGBTQ students reported feeling unsafe at school due to their sexual orientation or gender identity, with nearly 60% experiencing verbal harassment.

To address these issues, educational initiatives must focus on creating safe and inclusive environments for LGBTQ youth. This can be achieved through:

- **Training for Educators:** Providing teachers and school staff with training on LGBTQ issues, including understanding gender identity and sexual orientation, can help create a more supportive environment for students. This training can include strategies for addressing bullying, implementing inclusive curricula, and fostering open discussions about diversity.

- **Curriculum Development:** Incorporating LGBTQ history, literature, and perspectives into the curriculum is vital. This not only validates the experiences of LGBTQ youth but also educates their peers, promoting empathy and understanding. For instance, including works by LGBTQ authors in literature classes or discussing significant LGBTQ historical figures in social studies can foster a more inclusive educational experience.

- **Support Groups and Safe Spaces:** Establishing LGBTQ support groups and safe spaces within schools can provide youth with a sense of community and belonging. These groups can offer peer support, mentorship, and resources for navigating challenges related to their identity. Programs like the *Gay-Straight Alliance* (GSA) have been successful in creating safe environments for LGBTQ youth to connect and advocate for their rights.

Challenges Faced by LGBTQ Youth in Education

Despite the importance of education initiatives, numerous challenges remain for LGBTQ youth. Many educational institutions lack the resources or commitment to implement inclusive programs, and some may actively resist such changes due to cultural or political pressures. Furthermore, the intersectionality of identities—such as race, socioeconomic status, and disability—can complicate the experiences of LGBTQ youth, making it essential for initiatives to be intersectional in nature.

For example, a study by the *Trevor Project* found that LGBTQ youth of color face higher rates of discrimination and mental health issues compared to their white counterparts. This highlights the need for educational initiatives to address not only sexual orientation and gender identity but also the broader social and cultural contexts in which these youth exist.

Successful Examples of Educational Initiatives

Several successful educational initiatives have emerged that specifically cater to the needs of LGBTQ youth:

- The *LGBTQ Youth Empowerment Program:* This program focuses on providing workshops and resources for LGBTQ youth, emphasizing leadership development, self-advocacy, and community engagement. Participants are encouraged to develop their own initiatives to promote inclusivity in their schools and communities.

- The *Safe Schools Coalition:* This initiative works with schools to create safer environments for LGBTQ students through policy changes, training, and resource development. The coalition has successfully partnered with numerous educational institutions to implement anti-bullying policies and inclusive curricula.

- **Online Educational Platforms:** With the rise of technology, online platforms have emerged to provide LGBTQ youth with access to educational resources, mentorship, and support networks. Websites like *It Gets Better* and *TrevorSpace* offer safe online spaces for LGBTQ youth to connect, share their experiences, and access educational materials.

Theoretical Frameworks Supporting Education Initiatives

The effectiveness of educational initiatives for LGBTQ youth can be understood through various theoretical frameworks, including:

- **Social Learning Theory:** This theory posits that individuals learn behaviors and norms through observation and imitation. By creating inclusive educational environments, LGBTQ youth can see positive representations of their identities, which can empower them to embrace their authentic selves.

- **Critical Pedagogy:** Critical pedagogy emphasizes the importance of education as a tool for social change. By challenging oppressive structures and promoting inclusivity, educational initiatives can empower LGBTQ youth to become advocates for their rights and the rights of others.

- **Resilience Theory:** This theory focuses on the ability of individuals to overcome adversity. Educational initiatives that provide support and resources can foster resilience in LGBTQ youth, helping them navigate challenges and thrive in the face of discrimination.

Conclusion

Aderonke Apata's commitment to education initiatives for LGBTQ youth reflects a broader understanding of the importance of inclusive education in fostering acceptance, resilience, and empowerment. By addressing the unique challenges faced by LGBTQ youth and implementing effective educational strategies, we can create a more equitable society where all individuals, regardless of their sexual orientation or gender identity, can thrive and succeed. The ongoing fight for LGBTQ rights in education is not just a matter of policy; it is a fundamental human right that requires collective action and unwavering commitment from all members of society.

Recognizing and Addressing Mental Health Challenges

Mental health challenges are a significant concern within the LGBTQ community, particularly for individuals like Aderonke Apata, who have faced systemic discrimination, societal rejection, and personal trauma. The intersection of identity and mental health is complex, often exacerbated by external stressors such as homophobia, transphobia, and socio-economic disadvantages.

Understanding Mental Health in the LGBTQ Context

The World Health Organization (WHO) defines mental health as a state of well-being in which every individual realizes their own potential, can cope with the normal stresses of life, can work productively and fruitfully, and is able to make a contribution to their community. For LGBTQ individuals, the journey toward mental well-being can be fraught with challenges. Studies indicate that LGBTQ individuals are at a higher risk for mental health issues, including anxiety, depression, and suicidal ideation, largely due to societal stigma and discrimination.

$$\text{Mental Health Risk} = f(\text{Stigma, Discrimination, Social Support}) \qquad (17)$$

Where: - Stigma refers to societal attitudes that marginalize LGBTQ individuals. - Discrimination encompasses both systemic and individual acts of exclusion or violence. - Social Support includes networks of friends, family, and community that provide emotional and practical assistance.

The function f represents how these factors interact to influence mental health outcomes.

Identifying Common Mental Health Issues

Common mental health issues faced by LGBTQ individuals include:

- **Depression:** Feelings of sadness, hopelessness, and a lack of interest in activities once enjoyed. Research shows that LGBTQ youth are more than twice as likely to experience depression compared to their heterosexual peers.

- **Anxiety Disorders:** Conditions such as generalized anxiety disorder, panic disorder, and social anxiety disorder are prevalent within the LGBTQ community, often linked to the fear of discrimination and rejection.

- **Suicidal Ideation:** LGBTQ youth are at a significantly higher risk of suicide, with studies indicating that nearly 40% of LGBTQ youth have considered suicide in their lifetime.

- **Post-Traumatic Stress Disorder (PTSD):** Many LGBTQ individuals experience PTSD due to past trauma, including violence, sexual assault, or severe bullying.

The Role of Intersectionality

Intersectionality plays a crucial role in understanding mental health challenges within the LGBTQ community. Factors such as race, gender identity, socio-economic status, and geographic location can compound the stressors faced by individuals. For example, LGBTQ individuals of color often experience a double burden of racism and homophobia, leading to heightened levels of stress and mental health challenges.

Strategies for Addressing Mental Health Challenges

To effectively address mental health challenges within the LGBTQ community, several strategies can be employed:

- **Creating Safe Spaces:** Establishing environments where LGBTQ individuals can express themselves without fear of judgment is crucial. This can be achieved through community centers, support groups, and online forums.

- **Mental Health Education:** Increasing awareness about mental health issues specific to the LGBTQ community can empower individuals to seek help. Educational programs should focus on the unique challenges faced by LGBTQ individuals and promote understanding among mental health professionals.

- **Access to Resources:** Providing access to mental health services that are culturally competent and affirming of LGBTQ identities is essential. This includes training mental health professionals in LGBTQ issues and ensuring that resources are available in multiple languages.

- **Advocacy for Policy Change:** Advocating for policies that protect LGBTQ individuals from discrimination in healthcare settings can improve access to mental health services. This includes lobbying for inclusive healthcare policies and funding for LGBTQ mental health programs.

- **Peer Support Programs:** Implementing peer support initiatives can help individuals connect with others who have similar experiences. These programs can provide a sense of belonging and understanding that is vital for mental health recovery.

Real-Life Examples

Aderonke Apata's activism highlights the importance of mental health awareness within the LGBTQ community. Through her work, she has emphasized the need for mental health resources tailored to LGBTQ youth, particularly those who are refugees or asylum seekers. By sharing her own experiences and challenges, Aderonke has inspired many to seek help and advocate for mental health support.

For instance, organizations like *The Trevor Project* and *MindOut* provide vital mental health services and crisis intervention specifically for LGBTQ youth and adults. These organizations not only offer counseling and support but also engage in advocacy to raise awareness about the mental health challenges faced by LGBTQ individuals.

Conclusion

Recognizing and addressing mental health challenges within the LGBTQ community is essential for fostering resilience and promoting well-being. By understanding the unique factors that contribute to mental health issues, creating supportive environments, and advocating for necessary resources, individuals like Aderonke Apata can continue to make a significant impact in the fight for mental health equity. The journey toward mental wellness is ongoing, but with collective efforts, the LGBTQ community can thrive and inspire future generations to embrace their identities with pride.

Promoting LGBTQ-Inclusive Curriculums

In recent years, the importance of LGBTQ-inclusive curriculums in educational institutions has gained significant recognition. Such curriculums are designed to ensure that LGBTQ histories, cultures, and contributions are acknowledged and integrated into the broader educational framework. This section explores the theoretical underpinnings, challenges, and practical examples of promoting LGBTQ-inclusive curriculums.

Theoretical Framework

The promotion of LGBTQ-inclusive curriculums is grounded in several educational theories, including social justice education, critical pedagogy, and multicultural education.

Social Justice Education asserts that education should be a tool for equity and inclusion. According to [?], social justice education challenges the status quo by addressing systemic inequalities and fostering an environment where all students feel valued. By including LGBTQ perspectives, educators can create a more equitable learning environment that acknowledges and respects diverse identities.

Critical Pedagogy, as discussed by [?], emphasizes the need for education to be transformative. It encourages students to question societal norms and understand the power dynamics at play in their lives. An LGBTQ-inclusive curriculum invites students to critically engage with issues related to gender and sexuality, promoting a deeper understanding of their own identities and the experiences of others.

Multicultural Education focuses on the inclusion of diverse cultural perspectives within the curriculum. [?] argues that multicultural education not only recognizes the contributions of various groups but also promotes respect and understanding among students. Incorporating LGBTQ content into the curriculum aligns with this framework, as it validates the experiences and histories of LGBTQ individuals.

Challenges in Implementation

Despite the recognized benefits of LGBTQ-inclusive curriculums, several challenges hinder their implementation:

Resistance from Stakeholders is a significant barrier. Many educators, parents, and policymakers may resist the inclusion of LGBTQ content due to personal beliefs, cultural norms, or fear of backlash. This resistance can manifest in various forms, including censorship of educational materials and opposition to LGBTQ-themed discussions in classrooms.

Lack of Resources and Training also poses a challenge. Many teachers may feel ill-equipped to address LGBTQ topics due to a lack of training or resources. According to a report by [?], only 19% of teachers felt comfortable discussing LGBTQ issues in the classroom. This discomfort can lead to avoidance, perpetuating the marginalization of LGBTQ perspectives in education.

Curricular Constraints further complicate the situation. Standardized testing and rigid curricular frameworks often prioritize traditional subject matter, leaving little room for the incorporation of LGBTQ content. As a result, educators may struggle to integrate LGBTQ topics into an already crowded curriculum.

Examples of Successful Implementation

Despite these challenges, several educational institutions and organizations have successfully implemented LGBTQ-inclusive curriculums.

The Safe Schools Coalition in Australia provides resources and training for educators to create inclusive environments. Their initiatives include professional development workshops that equip teachers with the tools needed to integrate LGBTQ content into their lessons. Schools participating in this program have reported increased student engagement and a more positive school climate.

California's Fair Education Act mandates the inclusion of LGBTQ contributions in social studies curricula. This legislation serves as a model for other states, demonstrating that policy change can facilitate the integration of LGBTQ content into educational settings. Educators in California have successfully developed lesson plans that highlight LGBTQ figures in history, such as Harvey Milk and Marsha P. Johnson, thereby enriching students' understanding of American history.

The GLSEN (Gay, Lesbian and Straight Education Network) also plays a crucial role in advocating for LGBTQ-inclusive curriculums. Their resources, such as the "LGBTQ Inclusive Curriculum Guide," provide educators with practical strategies for incorporating LGBTQ topics into various subjects. Schools that have adopted these guidelines report a more inclusive atmosphere and improved student well-being.

Conclusion

Promoting LGBTQ-inclusive curriculums is essential for fostering an educational environment that values diversity and equity. By grounding these efforts in theories of social justice, critical pedagogy, and multicultural education, educators can challenge systemic inequalities and empower all students. While challenges such as resistance, lack of resources, and curricular constraints persist, successful examples from various educational contexts demonstrate that meaningful change is possible. As Aderonke Apata continues her advocacy for LGBTQ rights, the promotion of inclusive curriculums remains a crucial aspect of her work, ensuring that future generations are educated in environments that celebrate and respect all identities.

Creating Safe Spaces for LGBTQ Youth

Creating safe spaces for LGBTQ youth is a crucial aspect of fostering an inclusive and supportive environment that nurtures their identity and well-being. Safe spaces are physical or virtual environments where individuals can express themselves freely without fear of discrimination, harassment, or violence. These spaces play a pivotal role in the mental health and social development of LGBTQ youth, who often face significant challenges in their daily lives.

The Importance of Safe Spaces

The need for safe spaces stems from the pervasive discrimination and stigma that LGBTQ youth encounter. According to the *National School Climate Survey* conducted by GLSEN (Gay, Lesbian & Straight Education Network), LGBTQ students report feeling unsafe at school due to their sexual orientation or gender identity. This feeling of unsafety can lead to severe mental health issues, including anxiety, depression, and suicidal ideation.

A study published in the *Journal of Youth and Adolescence* found that LGBTQ youth who have access to supportive environments are significantly less likely to experience mental health problems. The equation that encapsulates this relationship can be expressed as:

$$MHP = f(SP, D)$$

where MHP represents mental health problems, SP denotes supportive spaces, and D indicates discrimination. The function f suggests that as the quality and availability of supportive spaces increase, the likelihood of mental health problems decreases.

Characteristics of Safe Spaces

Safe spaces for LGBTQ youth should possess several key characteristics:

- **Inclusivity:** All individuals, regardless of their sexual orientation or gender identity, should feel welcome and valued.

- **Confidentiality:** Participants must trust that their identities and experiences will be respected and kept confidential.

- **Supportive Resources:** Access to mental health resources, educational materials, and community connections is essential.

- **Empowerment:** Safe spaces should encourage youth to express themselves, share their stories, and engage in advocacy.

Examples of Safe Spaces

Numerous organizations and initiatives have successfully created safe spaces for LGBTQ youth:

- **LGBTQ Youth Centers:** Many cities have established community centers that provide resources, support groups, and recreational activities tailored for LGBTQ youth. For instance, the *Los Angeles LGBT Center* offers a variety of programs aimed at fostering a sense of belonging and community.

- **School-Based Support Groups:** Some schools have implemented Gay-Straight Alliances (GSAs) or similar clubs that promote inclusivity and provide a safe forum for LGBTQ students. These clubs often engage in activities such as awareness campaigns, discussions on LGBTQ issues, and social events that foster friendship and solidarity.

- **Online Platforms:** Virtual safe spaces have emerged as a vital resource for LGBTQ youth, especially those in areas where physical spaces are scarce. Websites and social media groups provide a platform for youth to connect, share experiences, and seek advice in a supportive environment.

Challenges in Creating Safe Spaces

Despite the importance of safe spaces, several challenges persist in their creation and maintenance:

- **Lack of Funding:** Many organizations struggle to secure the necessary funding to establish and sustain safe spaces, which can limit their reach and effectiveness.

- **Cultural Resistance:** In some communities, cultural norms and values may oppose the establishment of LGBTQ-inclusive spaces, leading to pushback from parents, schools, or local governments.

- **Safety Concerns:** Even in designated safe spaces, LGBTQ youth may still face threats from individuals outside the community, necessitating ongoing vigilance and security measures.

Strategies for Enhancing Safe Spaces

To effectively create and maintain safe spaces for LGBTQ youth, the following strategies can be employed:

- **Community Engagement:** Involve LGBTQ youth in the planning and implementation of safe spaces to ensure their needs and preferences are met.

- **Training and Education:** Provide training for staff and volunteers on LGBTQ issues, inclusive practices, and how to create a supportive environment. This can enhance the effectiveness of the safe space and foster a culture of understanding.

- **Collaboration:** Partner with local organizations, schools, and mental health professionals to expand resources and outreach efforts.

Conclusion

Creating safe spaces for LGBTQ youth is essential for promoting their mental health, well-being, and empowerment. By understanding the importance of these spaces, recognizing the challenges they face, and implementing effective strategies, communities can foster environments where LGBTQ youth feel safe, accepted, and supported. The ongoing efforts of activists like Aderonke Apata serve as a testament to the transformative power of safe spaces in nurturing the next generation of LGBTQ leaders.

Aderonke's Impact on LGBTQ Refugee Advocacy

Raising Awareness of LGBTQ Refugee Experiences

The plight of LGBTQ refugees is a critical issue that often remains underrepresented in broader discussions surrounding refugee crises. Aderonke Apata has made it her mission to amplify the voices and experiences of LGBTQ individuals who have been forced to flee their home countries due to persecution based on their sexual orientation or gender identity. This effort is not merely an act of advocacy; it is a necessary response to the systemic invisibility that LGBTQ refugees face in both humanitarian and legal frameworks.

Understanding the Context

LGBTQ individuals in many countries experience severe discrimination, violence, and persecution. According to the *United Nations High Commissioner for Refugees (UNHCR)*, LGBTQ refugees often encounter unique challenges that differ from those faced by other refugee populations. These challenges include:

- **Legal Barriers:** Many countries have laws that criminalize homosexuality, making it nearly impossible for LGBTQ individuals to seek asylum without risking further persecution.

- **Social Stigma:** Even in countries that recognize LGBTQ rights, refugees may face stigma and discrimination from both the local populace and within refugee communities.

- **Mental Health Issues:** The trauma of fleeing persecution, coupled with the isolation often experienced in new environments, can lead to significant mental health challenges for LGBTQ refugees.

Theoretical Frameworks

To effectively raise awareness of LGBTQ refugee experiences, it is essential to employ various theoretical frameworks. One such framework is *Intersectionality*, which examines how overlapping identities—such as race, gender, and sexual orientation—impact individuals' experiences of oppression and privilege. This theory helps to illuminate the complex realities faced by LGBTQ refugees, who may also belong to marginalized racial or ethnic groups.

Additionally, *Social Constructivism* can be applied to understand how societal norms and values shape perceptions of LGBTQ individuals. By challenging the dominant narratives that often exclude LGBTQ experiences, activists can foster a more inclusive dialogue around refugee rights.

Raising Awareness Through Advocacy

Aderonke Apata has utilized various strategies to raise awareness of LGBTQ refugee experiences:

- **Storytelling:** Sharing personal narratives is a powerful tool in advocacy. By amplifying the voices of LGBTQ refugees, Aderonke humanizes their struggles and challenges the misconceptions surrounding their experiences. These stories serve as a call to action, urging society to recognize the dignity and humanity of all individuals, regardless of their sexual orientation or gender identity.

- **Collaborative Campaigns:** Partnering with established refugee organizations, Aderonke has worked to create campaigns that specifically address the needs of LGBTQ refugees. These collaborations help to leverage resources and expertise, ensuring that LGBTQ issues are included in broader refugee advocacy efforts.

- **Educational Workshops:** Aderonke conducts workshops aimed at educating both the LGBTQ community and the general public about the unique challenges faced by LGBTQ refugees. These workshops often include discussions on legal rights, mental health resources, and strategies for building supportive communities.

Examples of Impact

The impact of raising awareness on LGBTQ refugee experiences can be seen through various initiatives:

- **Legal Aid Programs:** By highlighting the legal challenges faced by LGBTQ refugees, Aderonke has contributed to the establishment of legal aid programs that specifically cater to this demographic. These programs provide essential support in navigating the asylum process, ensuring that LGBTQ refugees receive the protection they need.

- **Community Support Networks:** Through her advocacy, Aderonke has helped to create support networks that connect LGBTQ refugees with local LGBTQ organizations. These networks provide a safe space for refugees to share their experiences and access resources, fostering a sense of belonging and community.

- **Policy Advocacy:** Aderonke's efforts have also extended to lobbying for policy changes that protect LGBTQ refugees. By engaging with lawmakers and international bodies, she has worked to ensure that LGBTQ rights are recognized in refugee policies and practices.

Conclusion

Raising awareness of LGBTQ refugee experiences is not just a matter of advocacy; it is a moral imperative. Aderonke Apata's work exemplifies the importance of amplifying marginalized voices and challenging the systemic barriers that LGBTQ refugees face. By employing theoretical frameworks, utilizing storytelling, and collaborating with various organizations, Aderonke continues to shine a light on the unique challenges faced by LGBTQ refugees, fostering a more inclusive and just society for all.

Lobbying for Policy Changes

Lobbying for policy changes is a crucial aspect of Aderonke Apata's activism, particularly in the context of LGBTQ rights in Nigeria and beyond. This section delves into the strategies, challenges, and successes associated with her lobbying efforts, highlighting the theoretical frameworks that underpin effective advocacy and the tangible impacts of her work.

Theoretical Frameworks of Lobbying

Lobbying, in the context of social movements, can be understood through various theoretical lenses. One prominent theory is the **Resource Mobilization Theory**, which posits that successful social movements depend on the effective mobilization of resources—be they financial, human, or informational. Aderonke's approach exemplifies this theory as she harnesses community support, engages in fundraising, and collaborates with international organizations to amplify her voice.

Another important framework is the **Framing Theory**, which emphasizes the significance of how issues are presented to the public and policymakers. Aderonke has adeptly framed LGBTQ rights as a matter of human rights, emphasizing the universal need for dignity and respect. By framing her advocacy in this manner, she has broadened the appeal of her cause, attracting allies from various sectors.

Challenges in Lobbying

Despite her determination and strategic approach, Aderonke faces numerous challenges in her lobbying efforts. The political landscape in Nigeria is fraught with homophobia, and any attempt to advocate for LGBTQ rights is met with significant resistance. Legislative bodies often pass anti-LGBTQ laws, such as the Same-Sex Marriage Prohibition Act of 2014, which criminalizes same-sex relationships and imposes harsh penalties on individuals and organizations that support LGBTQ rights.

Moreover, the societal stigma surrounding LGBTQ identities complicates lobbying efforts. Many lawmakers are reluctant to engage with LGBTQ issues due to fear of backlash from their constituents. This creates an environment where policy change becomes a daunting task, requiring not only advocacy but also a shift in public perception.

Strategies for Effective Lobbying

Aderonke has employed several strategies to navigate these challenges and push for policy changes:

- **Building Coalitions:** Aderonke has recognized the power of collective action. By forming coalitions with other human rights organizations, she has amplified her message and increased her lobbying power. These coalitions allow for a unified front that is harder for policymakers to ignore.

- **Engaging in Direct Advocacy:** Aderonke has actively participated in meetings with lawmakers, providing them with data and personal stories that highlight the impact of anti-LGBTQ policies. This direct engagement is crucial for humanizing the issue and fostering empathy among decision-makers.

- **Utilizing Social Media:** In today's digital age, social media plays a vital role in advocacy. Aderonke has leveraged platforms like Twitter and Instagram to raise awareness, mobilize supporters, and put pressure on policymakers. The viral nature of social media campaigns can bring significant attention to LGBTQ issues and create a sense of urgency for change.

- **Public Awareness Campaigns:** Aderonke has initiated public awareness campaigns aimed at educating the broader public about LGBTQ rights. By shifting the narrative and fostering understanding, she aims to create an environment where policymakers feel compelled to act.

Success Stories and Impact

Despite the formidable obstacles, Aderonke's lobbying efforts have yielded notable successes. For instance, her advocacy has contributed to increased visibility of LGBTQ issues in media and public discourse. This visibility is crucial in shifting perceptions and fostering a more inclusive society.

Furthermore, Aderonke's collaboration with international human rights organizations has led to increased pressure on the Nigerian government to reconsider its stance on LGBTQ rights. Reports from these organizations have highlighted the human rights violations faced by LGBTQ individuals in Nigeria, compelling some lawmakers to engage in dialogue about potential reforms.

Conclusion

In conclusion, Aderonke Apata's lobbying for policy changes represents a multifaceted approach to advocating for LGBTQ rights. By employing theoretical frameworks such as Resource Mobilization and Framing Theory, she has navigated the complex landscape of activism in Nigeria. Despite facing significant challenges, her strategic efforts have led to increased awareness and dialogue surrounding LGBTQ issues, paving the way for future advocacy and potential policy reforms. As Aderonke continues her fight, her experiences serve as a testament to the power of resilience and the importance of collective action in the pursuit of justice.

Providing Legal Assistance to LGBTQ Refugees

In the context of the ongoing global refugee crisis, the provision of legal assistance to LGBTQ refugees has emerged as a critical area of advocacy. These individuals often face unique challenges that require specialized legal support to navigate the complexities of asylum processes, discrimination, and the intersectionality of their identities. This section explores the theoretical frameworks, prevalent problems, and practical examples of legal assistance tailored specifically for LGBTQ refugees.

Theoretical Framework

The legal assistance provided to LGBTQ refugees is grounded in several key theoretical frameworks, including human rights theory, social justice theory, and intersectionality. Human rights theory posits that all individuals, regardless of their sexual orientation or gender identity, are entitled to fundamental rights and freedoms. This perspective emphasizes that LGBTQ refugees have the right to seek asylum based on a well-founded fear of persecution due to their identity.

Social justice theory further supports the need for equitable legal representation, advocating for marginalized groups to have access to resources and protections within legal systems. Intersectionality, a concept introduced by Kimberlé Crenshaw, highlights how overlapping identities—such as race, gender, and sexual orientation—can compound discrimination and affect individuals' experiences within the asylum process. Legal assistance must therefore be tailored to address these intersecting identities to effectively support LGBTQ refugees.

Challenges Faced by LGBTQ Refugees

LGBTQ refugees encounter numerous challenges when seeking legal assistance, including:

- **Fear of Disclosure:** Many LGBTQ individuals fear revealing their sexual orientation or gender identity due to potential repercussions, including violence or rejection from their communities.

- **Cultural Barriers:** Cultural norms and prejudices can hinder LGBTQ refugees from accessing legal services, as they may face discrimination from legal practitioners or institutions.

- **Lack of Understanding:** Legal practitioners may lack knowledge about LGBTQ issues, leading to inadequate representation or misunderstanding of the refugees' circumstances.

- **Documentation Issues:** LGBTQ refugees may not have access to documentation that substantiates their claims of persecution, complicating their asylum applications.

These challenges underscore the necessity for specialized legal assistance that is sensitive to the needs of LGBTQ refugees.

Examples of Legal Assistance Programs

Several organizations and initiatives have emerged globally to provide legal assistance to LGBTQ refugees. Notable examples include:

- **The International Refugee Assistance Project (IRAP):** This organization provides legal representation and advocacy for refugees, including those from LGBTQ communities. IRAP works to ensure that LGBTQ asylum seekers receive the support they need to navigate the legal system and secure their rights.

- **The Refugee and Immigrant Center for Education and Legal Services (RAICES):** RAICES offers legal assistance to immigrants and refugees, with a dedicated focus on LGBTQ individuals. Their programs include legal consultations, representation in asylum cases, and community education on rights and resources.

- **The LGBTQ Refugee Coalition (LGBTQRC):** This coalition brings together various organizations to advocate for the rights of LGBTQ refugees. They provide legal resources, support networks, and policy advocacy to improve the asylum process for LGBTQ individuals.

These organizations exemplify the types of legal assistance necessary to address the unique challenges faced by LGBTQ refugees.

Case Studies

To illustrate the impact of legal assistance, consider the following case studies:

- **Case Study 1: Ahmed's Asylum Journey**
  Ahmed, a gay man from a Middle Eastern country, faced persecution due to his sexual orientation. After fleeing to the United States, he sought legal assistance from a local LGBTQ advocacy organization. With their support, Ahmed was able to present a compelling case for asylum, highlighting the threats he faced in his home country. His successful application not only provided him with safety but also allowed him to contribute positively to his new community.

- **Case Study 2: Maria's Fight for Recognition**
  Maria, a transgender woman from Central America, encountered numerous obstacles when applying for asylum in Canada. Initially denied due to a lack of documentation, she reached out to a legal clinic specializing in LGBTQ refugee cases. Through their assistance, Maria was able to gather evidence of her persecution and ultimately secured her asylum status. Her story underscores the importance of having knowledgeable legal representation in navigating complex asylum processes.

Conclusion

Providing legal assistance to LGBTQ refugees is not merely a legal obligation but a moral imperative rooted in the principles of human rights and social justice. As the global landscape continues to evolve, it is essential that legal practitioners, organizations, and advocates work collaboratively to ensure that LGBTQ refugees receive the support they need. By addressing the unique challenges they face and leveraging theoretical frameworks, we can help empower these individuals to reclaim their lives and contribute to the diverse tapestry of society.

In conclusion, the fight for justice and equality for LGBTQ refugees must continue, with a focus on improving legal frameworks, increasing awareness, and fostering inclusive environments where all individuals can thrive without fear of persecution. The ongoing commitment to providing legal assistance is crucial in shaping a future where LGBTQ refugees can find safety, acceptance, and the opportunity to live authentically.

Addressing the Unique Challenges Faced by LGBTQ Refugees

The plight of LGBTQ refugees is a pressing humanitarian issue that requires urgent attention. These individuals often flee their home countries due to persecution based on their sexual orientation or gender identity, facing a myriad of unique challenges that complicate their journey to safety and acceptance. Understanding these challenges is essential for effective advocacy and support.

One of the primary challenges faced by LGBTQ refugees is the pervasive stigma and discrimination they encounter both during their flight and upon arrival in host countries. Many LGBTQ individuals experience violence, harassment, and rejection from their families and communities, which can lead to severe mental health issues, including depression and anxiety. According to the *World Health Organization*, LGBTQ refugees are at a higher risk of experiencing mental health disorders due to the compounded trauma of both persecution and displacement.

Furthermore, the asylum process itself can be daunting. LGBTQ refugees often struggle to provide sufficient evidence of their persecution, which can lead to skepticism from immigration authorities. The requirement to disclose sensitive personal information can be particularly traumatic, as many refugees fear that revealing their sexual orientation or gender identity may lead to further victimization. This is compounded by the fact that some countries do not recognize LGBTQ identities, which can render their claims for asylum invalid. As noted by *Amnesty International*, the lack of specific guidelines for assessing LGBTQ asylum claims can result in inconsistent and unjust outcomes.

Another significant barrier is access to appropriate healthcare services. LGBTQ refugees may have unique health needs that are often overlooked in traditional healthcare settings. For instance, they may require access to hormone therapy or mental health support tailored to their experiences of trauma and discrimination. However, systemic barriers such as lack of knowledge among healthcare providers and the absence of inclusive health policies often prevent LGBTQ refugees from receiving the care they need. A study published in the *American Journal of Public Health* highlights that LGBTQ refugees are less likely to seek healthcare due to fear of discrimination and a lack of culturally competent services.

Additionally, economic instability poses a major challenge for LGBTQ refugees. Many arrive in host countries without the ability to work legally, which can lead to financial insecurity and dependence on precarious living conditions. This economic vulnerability can further exacerbate their marginalization, making it difficult for them to access safe housing, employment opportunities, and social support networks. The *United Nations High Commissioner for Refugees* (UNHCR) emphasizes the importance of providing tailored economic support to LGBTQ refugees to help them integrate into their new communities.

Social isolation is yet another challenge that LGBTQ refugees face. Many arrive in new countries without established social networks, which can lead to feelings of loneliness and despair. Support groups specifically for LGBTQ refugees can play a crucial role in combating this isolation, providing a safe space for individuals to share their experiences and connect with others who understand their struggles. Organizations like *Rainbow Railroad* have been instrumental in creating such networks, offering both emotional and practical support to LGBTQ refugees.

To address these unique challenges, it is essential that policymakers and advocacy organizations implement inclusive and comprehensive strategies. This includes developing training programs for immigration officials and healthcare providers to ensure they are equipped to handle the specific needs of LGBTQ refugees. Additionally, creating legal frameworks that recognize the distinct experiences of LGBTQ individuals in the asylum process can help ensure fair treatment and protection.

Moreover, fostering partnerships between LGBTQ organizations and refugee support services can enhance resource allocation and create more robust support systems. For instance, collaborations with local LGBTQ organizations can help bridge the gap between refugee services and LGBTQ-specific needs, ensuring that refugees receive holistic support.

In conclusion, addressing the unique challenges faced by LGBTQ refugees requires a multifaceted approach that encompasses legal, healthcare, economic, and social support. By recognizing and responding to the specific needs of this vulnerable population, we can work towards creating a more equitable and just society for all individuals, regardless of their sexual orientation or gender identity. The fight for LGBTQ refugee rights is not just a matter of legal protection; it is a commitment to human dignity and the recognition of the inherent worth of every individual.

$$\text{Equity} = \frac{\text{Access to Resources}}{\text{Barriers to Integration}} \tag{18}$$

Collaborating with International Organizations

In the realm of LGBTQ activism, collaboration with international organizations has become a crucial strategy for amplifying voices, sharing resources, and fostering global solidarity. Aderonke Apata, as a prominent advocate for LGBTQ rights, recognized the significance of these partnerships in addressing the multifaceted challenges faced by LGBTQ individuals, particularly refugees.

Theoretical Framework

The collaboration between local activists and international organizations can be understood through the lens of *transnational advocacy networks* (TANs). According to Keck and Sikkink (1998), TANs consist of a diverse range of actors, including non-governmental organizations (NGOs), grassroots movements, and international bodies, working together to promote human rights and social justice. This framework emphasizes the interconnectedness of local struggles and global movements, highlighting how international support can enhance local efforts.

The collaboration often follows a *bottom-up approach*, where local activists like Aderonke leverage international platforms to bring attention to their issues. This is essential in contexts where local advocacy may face significant barriers due to governmental repression or societal stigma.

Challenges in Collaboration

Despite the potential benefits, collaborating with international organizations is fraught with challenges. One significant issue is the *power imbalance* that can arise, where international organizations may inadvertently overshadow local voices. This phenomenon, often referred to as *neocolonialism*, can lead to a misrepresentation of local realities and priorities. Aderonke's advocacy emphasized the importance of ensuring that local narratives are centered in international discussions.

Additionally, the bureaucratic nature of many international organizations can hinder effective collaboration. Lengthy processes for funding, decision-making, and project implementation can frustrate local activists who require immediate support and action. Aderonke often advocated for streamlined processes that allow for rapid response to crises affecting LGBTQ individuals.

Examples of Collaboration

Aderonke's collaboration with organizations such as *Amnesty International* and *Human Rights Watch* serves as a prime example of effective partnership. Through these collaborations, Aderonke was able to:

- **Raise Awareness:** By working with these organizations, Aderonke brought international attention to the plight of LGBTQ individuals in Nigeria, particularly regarding the harsh anti-LGBTQ laws and the associated violence and discrimination.

- **Influence Policy:** Collaborative efforts led to the creation of reports and campaigns that pressured the Nigerian government to reconsider its stance on LGBTQ rights. For instance, a joint report released by Aderonke and Amnesty International highlighted specific cases of human rights abuses, prompting international calls for accountability.

- **Provide Resources:** International organizations often have access to funding and resources that local activists lack. Aderonke utilized these resources to develop training programs for LGBTQ youth, focusing on empowerment and resilience in the face of adversity.

Impact on LGBTQ Refugee Advocacy

Collaboration with international organizations has also been pivotal in Aderonke's work on behalf of LGBTQ refugees. The unique challenges faced by LGBTQ individuals fleeing persecution necessitate tailored support that can be effectively addressed through international partnerships.

For example, Aderonke collaborated with the *United Nations High Commissioner for Refugees (UNHCR)* to advocate for the inclusion of sexual orientation and gender identity as critical factors in refugee status determination. This collaboration led to the development of guidelines that ensure LGBTQ refugees receive the protection and support they need when seeking asylum.

Furthermore, Aderonke's involvement in international conferences allowed her to connect with other activists and organizations, fostering a network of support that transcends borders. This network is vital for sharing best practices, resources, and strategies that empower LGBTQ individuals globally.

Conclusion

In conclusion, Aderonke Apata's collaborations with international organizations exemplify the power of transnational advocacy in the fight for LGBTQ rights. While challenges such as power imbalances and bureaucratic hurdles exist, the benefits of these partnerships are undeniable. Through effective collaboration, Aderonke has not only amplified the voices of LGBTQ individuals in Nigeria but has also played a significant role in shaping international policies that protect and promote the rights of LGBTQ refugees. The continuing evolution of these collaborations will be essential in the ongoing fight for justice and equality in the global LGBTQ movement.

Triumph and Legacy

Triumph and Legacy

Triumph and Legacy

The journey of Aderonke Apata is not merely a tale of struggle; it is a profound narrative of triumph that resonates deeply within the global LGBTQ community. This chapter explores the significant milestones in Aderonke's life, the recognition she has garnered, and the legacy she continues to build through her tireless activism.

Recognitions and Awards

Aderonke's unwavering commitment to LGBTQ rights has not gone unnoticed. Over the years, she has received numerous accolades that reflect her impact and dedication. These awards serve not only as personal achievements but also as symbols of the larger fight for equality. Among her most notable recognitions are:

- **Human Rights Awards:** Aderonke has been honored with several prestigious human rights awards, which acknowledge her relentless work in advocating for marginalized communities. These awards highlight the importance of her activism in a landscape often fraught with hostility towards LGBTQ individuals.

- **LGBTQ Leadership Recognitions:** As a leader in the LGBTQ movement, Aderonke has been recognized for her ability to inspire and mobilize others. Her leadership style, characterized by authenticity and resilience, has made her a role model for many activists around the world.

- **Global Impact Acknowledgments:** Various international organizations have recognized Aderonke's contributions to global LGBTQ rights. These acknowledgments serve to amplify her voice and the voices of those she represents, emphasizing the global nature of the struggle for equality.

- **Cultural and Artistic Involvements:** Aderonke's influence extends beyond activism; she has also engaged with artists and cultural figures to promote LGBTQ visibility through art. This intersection of culture and activism has proven to be a powerful tool in challenging stereotypes and fostering understanding.

- **Aderonke's Influential Network:** Through her work, Aderonke has built an extensive network of allies and supporters. This network not only amplifies her message but also fosters collaboration among activists, creating a united front in the fight for LGBTQ rights.

Aderonke's Advocacy Beyond Nigeria and the UK

While Aderonke's roots are firmly planted in Nigeria, her advocacy has transcended borders. She has become a prominent figure in the global LGBTQ rights movement, participating in various international forums and discussions.

- **Global Speaking Engagements:** Aderonke has been invited to speak at numerous conferences and events worldwide, where she shares her experiences and insights. Her speeches resonate with audiences, inspiring them to take action in their own communities.

- **Collaborating with Other International Activists:** Recognizing the power of collective action, Aderonke has collaborated with activists from diverse backgrounds. These partnerships have resulted in impactful campaigns that address the multifaceted challenges faced by LGBTQ individuals globally.

- **Shaping International LGBTQ Policies:** Aderonke's advocacy efforts have contributed to the development of international policies that protect LGBTQ rights. Her participation in policy discussions has helped to ensure that the voices of marginalized communities are included in decision-making processes.

- **Influencing Public Opinion on LGBTQ Rights:** Through her activism, Aderonke has played a crucial role in shifting public perceptions of LGBTQ individuals. By sharing her story and advocating for equality, she has helped to foster a more inclusive environment for LGBTQ people.

- **Aderonke's Role in United Nations Advocacy:** Aderonke's influence extends to the United Nations, where she has been involved in discussions surrounding human rights and LGBTQ issues. Her advocacy at this level underscores the importance of international cooperation in the fight for equality.

The Future of LGBTQ Activism

As Aderonke continues her work, the future of LGBTQ activism is bright yet fraught with challenges. The following themes emerge as critical areas of focus:

- **The Continuing Fight for Equality:** Aderonke's journey exemplifies the ongoing struggle for LGBTQ rights. Activists must remain vigilant and committed to fighting against discrimination and advocating for comprehensive legal protections.

- **Supporting the Next Generation of Activists:** Aderonke is dedicated to mentoring young activists, ensuring that the movement remains strong and diverse. By fostering a new generation of leaders, she helps to secure the future of LGBTQ rights.

- **Addressing Intersections of Identity and Inequality:** Aderonke's activism recognizes the importance of intersectionality in the fight for equality. By addressing the unique challenges faced by individuals at the intersections of race, gender, and sexual orientation, she promotes a more inclusive movement.

- **Aderonke's Ongoing Work and Legacy:** Aderonke's commitment to activism is unwavering. Her continued efforts serve as a reminder of the importance of resilience and determination in the face of adversity.

- **The Importance of LGBTQ Visibility and Representation:** Aderonke's story highlights the need for increased visibility of LGBTQ individuals in all sectors of society. Representation matters, and Aderonke's work paves the way for future generations to live authentically and proudly.

In conclusion, Aderonke Apata's journey is one of triumph and legacy. Her contributions to LGBTQ rights have not only transformed the lives of many but also inspired a global movement. As we reflect on her achievements, it is essential to recognize that the fight for equality is far from over. Aderonke's story serves as a beacon of hope, reminding us all that change is possible through courage, resilience, and unwavering commitment to justice.

Recognitions and Awards

Human Rights Awards

Aderonke Apata's unwavering commitment to LGBTQ rights has not gone unnoticed. Throughout her journey, she has been the recipient of numerous prestigious human rights awards that recognize her significant contributions to the fight for equality and justice. These accolades not only honor her tireless activism but also highlight the broader struggle for human rights within marginalized communities globally.

Recognition of Activism

Human rights awards serve several critical functions in the landscape of activism. They not only acknowledge individual efforts but also amplify the voices of the communities represented. For Aderonke, receiving awards such as the *International LGBTQ Rights Award* and the *Human Rights Defender Award* has been pivotal in bringing attention to the plight of LGBTQ individuals, especially in Nigeria, where homophobia is rampant and systemic discrimination is pervasive.

Impact of Awards on Activism

The recognition through awards has profound implications for activists like Aderonke. On one hand, it provides validation and encouragement, reinforcing the importance of their work. On the other hand, it can also serve as a double-edged sword. Awards can elevate an activist's profile, attracting both support and scrutiny. For instance, after receiving the *Global Activist Award*, Aderonke faced increased attention from both supporters and opponents of LGBTQ rights. This phenomenon illustrates the complex dynamics surrounding activism; while recognition can bolster a movement, it can also lead to heightened risks for those involved.

Examples of Human Rights Awards

Several notable awards have been conferred upon Aderonke, each symbolizing a unique aspect of her advocacy:

- The International LGBTQ Rights Award - This award is given to individuals who have made significant contributions to the advancement of LGBTQ rights globally. Aderonke's receipt of this award underscores her role in challenging oppressive systems and advocating for marginalized voices.

- **The Human Rights Defender Award** - Presented by the *Human Rights Campaign*, this award honors those who have demonstrated exceptional courage in the face of adversity. Aderonke's journey from Nigeria to the UK exemplifies the resilience that this award seeks to celebrate.

- **The Equality Award** - This accolade recognizes individuals who have made extraordinary efforts to promote equality and justice. Aderonke's initiatives to provide safe spaces for LGBTQ youth in Nigeria have played a crucial role in her recognition as a leader in the fight for equality.

Theoretical Framework: Recognition Theory

To understand the significance of these awards within the context of human rights activism, it is essential to consider the theoretical framework of recognition theory. Recognition theory posits that individuals and groups seek acknowledgment and validation of their identities and struggles. According to Hegelian philosophy, recognition is fundamental to the development of self-consciousness and identity. For activists like Aderonke, receiving awards is a form of recognition that validates their experiences and struggles, fostering a sense of belonging and purpose within the broader human rights movement.

Challenges and Critiques

While awards can serve as powerful tools for advocacy, they are not without their challenges. Critics argue that the focus on individual accolades can overshadow collective efforts and the systemic nature of oppression. In Aderonke's case, while her awards have brought attention to LGBTQ issues, they also highlight the ongoing challenges faced by many activists who remain unrecognized and unsupported. Furthermore, the commercialization of human rights awards raises ethical questions about the motivations behind these recognitions and whether they genuinely contribute to social change.

Conclusion

In conclusion, Aderonke Apata's receipt of human rights awards is a testament to her impactful activism and the broader struggle for LGBTQ rights. These awards not only recognize her individual contributions but also serve as a beacon of hope for marginalized communities worldwide. As Aderonke continues her fight for justice, the recognition she has received will undoubtedly inspire future generations of activists to carry on the torch of equality and human rights advocacy.

LGBTQ Leadership Recognitions

Aderonke Apata's journey as an LGBTQ activist has not only inspired countless individuals but has also garnered significant recognition within the global LGBTQ community. This section delves into the various accolades and honors that Aderonke has received, emphasizing the importance of leadership in activism and the impact these recognitions have on the movement for LGBTQ rights.

The Importance of Leadership in LGBTQ Activism

Leadership in LGBTQ activism is crucial for several reasons. First, effective leaders serve as role models, inspiring others to engage in activism and advocacy. They articulate the struggles of marginalized communities and mobilize resources to address these issues. Leadership also plays a vital role in shaping public policy and influencing societal attitudes towards LGBTQ individuals.

One theoretical framework that helps to understand the dynamics of leadership in activism is the *Transformational Leadership Theory*. This theory posits that leaders who inspire and motivate their followers can create significant change within their communities. Transformational leaders are characterized by their ability to communicate a compelling vision, foster an inclusive environment, and encourage personal development among their followers. Aderonke embodies these qualities, as she has consistently empowered others to take action in the fight for LGBTQ rights.

Recognition by Human Rights Organizations

Aderonke's work has been recognized by numerous human rights organizations. For instance, she received the prestigious *Human Rights Defender Award* from the International Lesbian, Gay, Bisexual, Trans and Intersex Association (ILGA). This award acknowledges individuals who have made significant contributions to the promotion and protection of human rights for LGBTQ people. Aderonke's tireless efforts in advocating for legal reforms in Nigeria and her role in raising awareness of LGBTQ issues globally were pivotal in her selection for this honor.

Additionally, the *Amnesty International* recognized Aderonke as a "Human Rights Champion" for her relentless fight against discrimination and violence faced by LGBTQ individuals in Nigeria. This recognition not only highlights her leadership but also brings attention to the broader issues of human rights violations that LGBTQ individuals face in many parts of the world.

Community-Based Awards

Aderonke has also been celebrated within local communities for her leadership and advocacy. The *LGBTQ Community Leadership Award* from the Nigerian Queer Alliance is one such example. This award honors individuals who have made substantial contributions to the LGBTQ community in Nigeria, particularly in the areas of activism, education, and support services. Aderonke's work in establishing safe spaces for LGBTQ individuals and her mentorship programs for LGBTQ youth were instrumental in her receiving this accolade.

Moreover, Aderonke was recognized by the *African Rainbow Family* for her contributions to LGBTQ refugee advocacy. This organization focuses on supporting LGBTQ individuals who face persecution in Africa, and Aderonke's efforts to raise awareness about the plight of LGBTQ refugees have been crucial in advancing their rights.

Global Impact Acknowledgments

Aderonke's influence extends beyond Nigeria, as she has received international accolades for her leadership in LGBTQ activism. The *Global LGBTQ Leadership Award* presented at the World Pride Festival is a testament to her impact on the global stage. This award is given to leaders who have made significant strides in promoting LGBTQ rights worldwide. Aderonke's ability to connect with activists from various countries and her participation in international conferences have amplified her voice and the voices of those she represents.

In addition, her contributions to the United Nations' discussions on LGBTQ rights have not gone unnoticed. The *UN Free & Equal Campaign* recognized Aderonke for her role in advocating for the inclusion of LGBTQ rights in global human rights dialogues. This recognition underscores the importance of intersectional advocacy and the need for LGBTQ issues to be addressed within broader human rights frameworks.

Cultural and Artistic Involvements

Aderonke's leadership has also been acknowledged in the cultural and artistic spheres. She was featured in the *Pride in Our Stories* documentary series, which highlights the lives and struggles of LGBTQ activists around the world. This platform not only honors her contributions but also serves to educate the public about the challenges faced by LGBTQ individuals, particularly in regions with oppressive laws.

Furthermore, Aderonke has collaborated with various artists and filmmakers to create works that reflect the LGBTQ experience in Nigeria. These projects have received critical acclaim and have been recognized in film festivals, showcasing the intersection of art and activism in her work.

Aderonke's Influential Network

The recognition Aderonke has received is not just a testament to her individual efforts but also reflects her ability to build and sustain an influential network of activists, allies, and organizations. This network has been crucial in amplifying her message and creating a collective impact in the fight for LGBTQ rights.

By collaborating with other leaders and organizations, Aderonke has been able to share resources, knowledge, and strategies that enhance the effectiveness of LGBTQ activism. This collaborative approach aligns with the principles of *Collective Impact Theory*, which posits that large-scale social change requires a coordinated effort among various stakeholders.

In conclusion, Aderonke Apata's leadership in the LGBTQ movement has been recognized through various awards and accolades, reflecting her significant contributions to the fight for equality and justice. Her ability to inspire others, advocate for change, and build a supportive community has made her a prominent figure in both Nigerian and global LGBTQ activism. These recognitions not only honor her work but also serve to inspire future generations of activists to continue the fight for LGBTQ rights.

Global Impact Acknowledgments

Aderonke Apata's journey as an LGBTQ activist transcends borders, resonating with individuals and movements worldwide. Her advocacy has not only illuminated the struggles faced by LGBTQ communities in Nigeria but has also sparked global conversations about human rights, equality, and justice. This section delves into the various global impact acknowledgments that underscore Aderonke's significance in the fight for LGBTQ rights.

Recognition by International Organizations

Aderonke's work has garnered recognition from numerous international organizations committed to human rights and LGBTQ advocacy. For instance, her contributions have been acknowledged by the *International Lesbian, Gay,*

Bisexual, Trans and Intersex Association (ILGA), which has highlighted her efforts in challenging discriminatory laws in Nigeria. The ILGA's reports often cite Aderonke as a key figure in the fight against the Same-Sex Marriage (Prohibition) Act, emphasizing her role in mobilizing grassroots activism and raising awareness about the plight of LGBTQ individuals in her home country.

Awards and Honors

Throughout her activism, Aderonke has received several prestigious awards that recognize her relentless pursuit of justice. These accolades serve not only as a testament to her dedication but also as a beacon of hope for marginalized communities. Notably, she was awarded the *Human Rights Defender Award* by the *Global Fund for Human Rights*, which acknowledged her courage in standing up against systemic oppression. This award, among others, has positioned Aderonke as a leading voice in the international LGBTQ rights movement, inspiring activists and allies alike.

Influence on Policy Change

Aderonke's advocacy has had a profound impact on policy discussions at the international level. Her participation in various global forums, such as the *United Nations Human Rights Council*, has allowed her to present firsthand accounts of the challenges faced by LGBTQ individuals in Nigeria. By sharing her experiences, Aderonke has influenced discussions surrounding the need for comprehensive human rights protections for LGBTQ individuals globally. Her testimonies have contributed to the formulation of policies aimed at safeguarding the rights of LGBTQ refugees and asylum seekers, emphasizing the intersectionality of human rights issues.

Collaborations with Global Activists

Aderonke's impact is further amplified through her collaborations with activists and organizations across the globe. By forging alliances with LGBTQ activists from diverse backgrounds, she has fostered a sense of solidarity that transcends geographical boundaries. For example, her partnership with the *Human Rights Campaign* has led to joint initiatives aimed at raising awareness about LGBTQ issues in Africa. These collaborations highlight the importance of collective action in the fight for equality and demonstrate how Aderonke's influence resonates beyond her immediate environment.

Cultural and Artistic Contributions

In addition to her activism, Aderonke's contributions to culture and the arts have played a significant role in shaping the global narrative around LGBTQ rights. She has participated in various art exhibitions and cultural events that celebrate LGBTQ identities and stories. Her involvement in projects such as the *Queer African Film Festival* has provided a platform for LGBTQ filmmakers and artists, amplifying their voices and experiences. These cultural contributions not only challenge stereotypes but also foster empathy and understanding within broader society.

Impact on Public Opinion

Aderonke's advocacy has also influenced public opinion regarding LGBTQ rights on a global scale. Through her engaging public speaking engagements and social media presence, she has effectively communicated the realities faced by LGBTQ individuals in Nigeria. Her ability to connect with diverse audiences has played a crucial role in shifting perceptions and fostering a more inclusive dialogue around LGBTQ issues. For instance, her viral social media campaigns addressing homophobia and discrimination have sparked conversations in countries where LGBTQ rights are still heavily contested.

Legacy of Global Solidarity

Aderonke's legacy extends beyond her individual achievements; it embodies the spirit of global solidarity in the fight for LGBTQ rights. Her work has inspired a new generation of activists, encouraging them to challenge oppressive systems and advocate for equality. The networks she has built with fellow activists across the globe serve as a reminder that the struggle for LGBTQ rights is interconnected, and that collective action is essential for meaningful change.

Conclusion

In summary, Aderonke Apata's global impact is a testament to her unwavering commitment to justice and equality for LGBTQ individuals. Through her recognition by international organizations, receipt of prestigious awards, influence on policy change, collaborations with global activists, cultural contributions, and impact on public opinion, Aderonke has solidified her place as a pivotal figure in the international LGBTQ rights movement. Her legacy continues to inspire countless individuals to join the fight for a world where everyone, regardless of their sexual orientation or gender identity, can live freely and authentically.

Cultural and Artistic Involvements

Aderonke Apata's journey as an LGBTQ activist is not solely defined by her advocacy for legal rights and social acceptance; it is also profoundly enriched by her cultural and artistic involvements. These dimensions serve as powerful conduits for expression, solidarity, and resistance against oppression. In this section, we explore the intersection of culture, art, and activism in Aderonke's work, highlighting how these elements contribute to her broader mission.

The Role of Art in Activism

Art has long been recognized as a vital tool for social change. It transcends language barriers and communicates complex emotions and ideas in ways that resonate deeply with audiences. Aderonke harnesses this potential, using various artistic mediums to amplify LGBTQ voices and narratives. Whether through visual art, theater, poetry, or music, Aderonke understands that art can evoke empathy and drive action.

For example, during her activism in Nigeria, Aderonke collaborated with local artists to create murals that depicted the struggles and triumphs of the LGBTQ community. These murals not only beautified public spaces but also served as poignant reminders of the ongoing fight for equality. They challenged passersby to confront their biases and engage with the realities faced by LGBTQ individuals.

Cultural Festivals and Events

Cultural festivals play a crucial role in fostering community and providing safe spaces for marginalized groups. Aderonke has been instrumental in organizing LGBTQ-inclusive events that celebrate diversity and promote acceptance. One notable initiative was the establishment of an annual LGBTQ Pride festival in Lagos, which aimed to create visibility and solidarity among the community.

Despite facing significant opposition and threats of violence, Aderonke and her team persevered, transforming the festival into a symbol of resilience. The event featured performances by LGBTQ artists, workshops on sexual health, and discussions on the importance of representation in the arts. By centering LGBTQ narratives within cultural celebrations, Aderonke challenged the dominant narratives that often erase or vilify queer identities.

Storytelling and Personal Narratives

Storytelling is a powerful form of artistic expression that can foster understanding and compassion. Aderonke emphasizes the importance of personal narratives in her activism, recognizing that sharing one's story can break down barriers and create connections. Through public speaking engagements and written works, she has shared her own experiences of growing up in Nigeria as a queer individual, navigating the complexities of identity, faith, and societal expectations.

The impact of storytelling in activism is supported by narrative theory, which posits that stories shape our understanding of the world and influence our beliefs and actions. Aderonke's storytelling not only educates her audience about the challenges faced by LGBTQ individuals but also inspires others to share their own stories, fostering a collective movement towards acceptance and equality.

Collaborations with Artists and Organizations

Aderonke's cultural and artistic involvements extend beyond her individual efforts; she actively collaborates with other artists and organizations to amplify the LGBTQ message. For instance, she has partnered with international LGBTQ organizations to host art exhibitions that showcase the work of queer artists from around the globe. These exhibitions not only provide a platform for marginalized voices but also promote cross-cultural dialogue and understanding.

One such collaboration resulted in a traveling exhibition titled *Voices of Resilience*, which featured art from LGBTQ individuals who have faced persecution. The exhibition toured various cities, sparking conversations about the intersection of art, identity, and human rights. Aderonke's role in curating this exhibition exemplifies her commitment to using art as a vehicle for social change.

Challenges in Cultural Representation

Despite the power of art and culture in activism, challenges persist. Aderonke has encountered pushback from conservative elements within Nigerian society, who often view LGBTQ representation in the arts as a threat to traditional values. This resistance can manifest in censorship, harassment, and even violence against artists who dare to challenge the status quo.

Aderonke's response to these challenges has been one of defiance and determination. She advocates for the importance of cultural representation in all its forms, arguing that art can be a catalyst for change. By creating spaces where LGBTQ artists can thrive and express themselves freely, Aderonke aims to dismantle the barriers that inhibit artistic expression and perpetuate discrimination.

The Future of Cultural Activism

Looking ahead, Aderonke envisions a future where cultural and artistic involvement becomes an integral part of the LGBTQ movement. She believes that fostering creativity and collaboration among artists can lead to innovative approaches to activism. By embracing the arts, Aderonke hopes to inspire the next generation of activists to think outside the box and use their talents to advocate for change.

In conclusion, Aderonke Apata's cultural and artistic involvements are vital components of her activism. They provide a platform for expression, foster community, and challenge oppressive narratives. Through her work, Aderonke exemplifies the transformative power of art in the fight for LGBTQ rights, leaving an indelible mark on both the cultural landscape and the ongoing struggle for equality.

Aderonke's Influential Network

Aderonke Apata's journey as a prominent LGBTQ activist is not solely defined by her individual actions but also significantly shaped by her influential network. This network encompasses a diverse array of allies, advocates, and organizations that have collaborated with her in the fight for LGBTQ rights, both within Nigeria and internationally. Understanding the dynamics of this network is crucial to appreciating the breadth and depth of her impact.

The Importance of Networking in Activism

Networking plays a vital role in activism, particularly in marginalized communities. According to social network theory, the connections between individuals and groups can amplify their collective power and influence. In the context of LGBTQ activism, networks provide essential support, resources, and visibility. Aderonke's network serves as a case study in how strategic partnerships can enhance advocacy efforts.

$$\text{Influence} = f(\text{Connections}, \text{Resources}, \text{Visibility}) \tag{19}$$

Where: - Influence refers to the overall impact an activist can have. - Connections denote the relationships built with other activists, organizations, and allies. - Resources include funding, knowledge, and tools shared within the network. - Visibility represents the public awareness and attention garnered through collective efforts.

Key Partnerships and Collaborations

Throughout her activism, Aderonke has forged strategic partnerships with various organizations, such as:

- **International LGBTQ Organizations:** Collaborating with global entities like ILGA (International Lesbian, Gay, Bisexual, Trans and Intersex Association) has allowed Aderonke to amplify her voice on international platforms, advocating for policy changes and awareness.

- **Local LGBTQ Groups:** Aderonke's work with grassroots organizations in Nigeria has been pivotal in creating safe spaces and providing resources for LGBTQ individuals facing discrimination and violence.

- **Human Rights Organizations:** By partnering with groups like Amnesty International, Aderonke has drawn attention to human rights abuses against LGBTQ individuals in Nigeria, utilizing their platforms to reach broader audiences.

These collaborations have not only provided Aderonke with vital support but have also fostered a sense of solidarity among activists, creating a united front against oppression.

The Role of Social Media in Expanding the Network

In the digital age, social media has emerged as a powerful tool for activists to connect, share information, and mobilize support. Aderonke has effectively utilized platforms like Twitter, Instagram, and Facebook to:

- **Raise Awareness:** By sharing her story and the stories of others, Aderonke has educated her followers about the realities faced by LGBTQ individuals in Nigeria.

- **Mobilize Support:** Social media campaigns have been instrumental in organizing protests and events, allowing Aderonke to rally support from both local and international communities.

- **Build Community:** Online spaces have enabled Aderonke to connect with other activists, fostering a sense of belonging and collective identity among LGBTQ individuals.

The effectiveness of social media in activism is supported by the diffusion of innovations theory, which suggests that new ideas and practices spread through networks, particularly when early adopters demonstrate success.

Challenges Within the Network

Despite the strengths of Aderonke's network, challenges persist. Issues such as:

- **Cultural Differences:** Navigating differing cultural attitudes toward LGBTQ rights can create tensions within the network, particularly between local and international allies.

- **Resource Disparities:** Unequal access to funding and resources among network members can hinder collective efforts, leading to frustrations and inefficiencies.

- **Safety Concerns:** Activists in Nigeria face significant risks, including harassment and violence, which can complicate collaboration and communication.

Addressing these challenges requires ongoing dialogue, empathy, and a commitment to inclusivity within the network.

Conclusion: The Power of Aderonke's Network

Aderonke Apata's influential network exemplifies the power of collaboration in activism. By building strong connections with a diverse array of allies, she has been able to amplify her impact and advocate for LGBTQ rights on a global scale. As the fight for equality continues, the lessons learned from Aderonke's network will serve as a blueprint for future activists seeking to create meaningful change in their communities.

In summary, Aderonke's network is a testament to the idea that collective action, fueled by solidarity and shared goals, can lead to significant advancements in the fight for justice and equality. As she continues her work, the relationships she has cultivated will undoubtedly play a crucial role in shaping the future of LGBTQ activism.

Aderonke's Advocacy Beyond Nigeria and the UK

Global Speaking Engagements

Aderonke Apata's impact as a global LGBTQ activist is amplified through her extensive speaking engagements around the world. These events serve as platforms for raising awareness, fostering dialogue, and mobilizing support for LGBTQ rights. Her ability to articulate the struggles and triumphs of the LGBTQ community, particularly in Nigeria, resonates deeply with diverse audiences, making her a sought-after speaker at international conferences, universities, and human rights forums.

The Power of Public Speaking

Public speaking is a powerful tool in activism. It allows advocates like Aderonke to share personal narratives that humanize complex issues. The theory of *social change communication* posits that effective communication can lead to changes in public perception and policy. By sharing her story, Aderonke not only raises awareness about the challenges faced by LGBTQ individuals in oppressive environments but also inspires others to take action.

$$\text{Change} = \text{Awareness} + \text{Action} + \text{Support} \qquad (20)$$

In this equation, awareness serves as the catalyst for action, which is further strengthened by collective support. Aderonke's speaking engagements embody this dynamic, transforming her personal experiences into a collective call for justice.

Examples of Engagements

Aderonke has participated in numerous high-profile speaking engagements that highlight her commitment to LGBTQ rights. For instance, her keynote address at the *International LGBTQ Rights Conference* in Amsterdam in 2022 drew attention to the plight of LGBTQ refugees, emphasizing the intersectionality of race, gender, and sexuality. During her speech, she stated:

> "We must recognize that the fight for LGBTQ rights is not just a fight for one community; it is a fight for humanity. Our struggles are interconnected, and only through solidarity can we achieve true equality."

This statement encapsulates the essence of her advocacy, which seeks to unite various movements under the umbrella of human rights.

Another notable engagement was her participation in the *United Nations Human Rights Council* in Geneva, where she spoke on the importance of protecting LGBTQ individuals in the context of global migration. Her presentation included statistical data illustrating the rise in violence against LGBTQ refugees, making a compelling case for international intervention and policy reform.

$$\text{Advocacy Impact} = \text{Engagement} \times \text{Visibility} \times \text{Policy Change} \quad (21)$$

This equation illustrates how Aderonke's engagement in global forums not only raises visibility for LGBTQ issues but also influences policy change at an international level.

Challenges Faced

Despite her successes, Aderonke faces numerous challenges in her speaking engagements. One significant issue is the backlash from conservative groups who oppose LGBTQ rights. Such opposition can manifest in various forms, including protests at events or attempts to discredit her message.

Moreover, the logistics of international travel can pose barriers, particularly for activists from countries where LGBTQ rights are severely restricted. Aderonke has often had to navigate complex visa processes, sometimes facing discrimination or skepticism from authorities due to her activism.

The Importance of Intersectionality

Aderonke emphasizes the importance of intersectionality in her speeches, advocating for a comprehensive understanding of how various identities intersect to affect individuals' experiences of oppression. She often cites the work of Kimberlé Crenshaw, who coined the term *intersectionality*, to illustrate how overlapping social identities can compound discrimination.

> "We cannot fight for LGBTQ rights in isolation. We must consider how race, class, and gender intersect to create unique challenges for individuals within our community."

This approach encourages a more inclusive framework for activism, which is crucial for addressing the diverse needs of the LGBTQ community.

Conclusion

Aderonke Apata's global speaking engagements are vital to her activism, providing a platform for advocacy and education. Through her compelling narratives and commitment to intersectionality, she not only raises awareness but also inspires action and fosters solidarity among various movements. As she continues to share her story on international stages, Aderonke plays a pivotal role in shaping the discourse around LGBTQ rights globally, proving that the fight for equality knows no borders.

$$\text{Legacy} = \text{Inspiration} + \text{Action} + \text{Change} \quad (22)$$

In conclusion, Aderonke's legacy is built on her ability to inspire others to join the fight for justice, ensuring that the stories of LGBTQ individuals are heard and valued worldwide.

Collaborating with Other International Activists

Collaboration among international activists is a cornerstone of effective advocacy in the LGBTQ movement. Aderonke Apata's work exemplifies how cross-border partnerships can amplify voices and drive change on a global scale. This section explores the significance of collaboration, the challenges faced, and practical examples of successful partnerships that have shaped LGBTQ activism.

The Importance of International Collaboration

International collaboration allows activists to share resources, strategies, and experiences. By working together, activists can tackle issues that transcend national borders, such as human rights abuses, legal discrimination, and social stigmas faced by LGBTQ individuals. The collective strength of a united front can increase visibility and pressure governments to enact positive changes.

Theoretical frameworks such as *Social Movement Theory* suggest that movements are more likely to succeed when they form alliances across different groups. This theory posits that solidarity among various movements can lead to a stronger impact, as activists leverage their unique experiences and strengths to advocate for shared goals.

Challenges of Collaboration

Despite the benefits, international collaboration is fraught with challenges. Cultural differences, varying legal contexts, and differing priorities can create friction among activists. For instance, while some countries may prioritize marriage equality, others may focus on combating violence against LGBTQ individuals. These differences can lead to misunderstandings and conflicts within coalitions.

Moreover, activists from countries with restrictive regimes may face increased risks when collaborating internationally. The fear of surveillance, persecution, or retaliation can inhibit open communication and hinder effective partnerships.

Examples of Successful Collaboration

Aderonke Apata has been instrumental in fostering international collaborations that have yielded significant results. One notable example is her partnership with *ILGA World* (International Lesbian, Gay, Bisexual, Trans and Intersex Association). Through this collaboration, Aderonke participated in global conferences, where she shared her experiences and strategies for advocacy in Nigeria. This platform not only raised awareness about the plight of LGBTQ individuals in Nigeria but also connected her with activists from different regions who faced similar challenges.

Another successful collaboration was with *OutRight Action International*, an organization focused on advancing human rights for LGBTQ people worldwide. Aderonke worked with them to develop resources aimed at supporting LGBTQ refugees, highlighting the need for tailored assistance that addresses the unique challenges faced by LGBTQ individuals fleeing persecution. This partnership resulted in the creation of training materials for activists and service providers, promoting an understanding of the specific needs of LGBTQ refugees.

The Role of Digital Platforms

In the contemporary landscape, digital platforms have revolutionized how activists collaborate internationally. Social media, webinars, and online campaigns have made it easier for activists to connect, share information, and mobilize support. Aderonke utilized platforms such as Twitter and Instagram to raise awareness about LGBTQ issues in Nigeria, engaging with a global audience and fostering solidarity among activists worldwide.

For example, during the COVID-19 pandemic, Aderonke and her collaborators organized virtual events that brought together activists from different countries to discuss the impact of the pandemic on LGBTQ communities. These events not only facilitated knowledge sharing but also provided a sense of community and support during a time of isolation.

Conclusion

Collaborating with other international activists is vital for advancing LGBTQ rights globally. Through partnerships, activists can leverage their collective power to challenge oppressive systems and advocate for change. Aderonke Apata's work illustrates the potential of international collaboration to amplify voices, share resources, and foster solidarity among diverse communities. As the movement continues to evolve, building and sustaining these international alliances will be crucial in the ongoing fight for equality and justice for LGBTQ individuals worldwide.

Shaping International LGBTQ Policies

The landscape of international LGBTQ rights is a complex tapestry woven from various threads of activism, cultural contexts, and political frameworks. Aderonke Apata's advocacy has played a pivotal role in shaping these policies, particularly through her ability to bridge local experiences with global movements. This section explores how Aderonke has influenced international LGBTQ policies, the theoretical frameworks that underpin her activism, the challenges faced, and the significance of her contributions.

Theoretical Frameworks

At the core of Aderonke's advocacy is the application of intersectionality theory, which posits that various social identities—such as race, gender, sexuality, and class—interact to create unique modes of discrimination and privilege. This framework is crucial in understanding the multifaceted challenges faced by LGBTQ individuals, particularly in regions where cultural and religious conservatism prevails. Aderonke's work illustrates how intersectionality informs policy-making processes, advocating for the inclusion of marginalized voices in discussions about LGBTQ rights.

$$P = f(I, C, G) \tag{23}$$

Where:

- P = Policy outcomes
- I = Individual identities and experiences
- C = Cultural contexts

* G = Governmental frameworks

This equation reflects the interplay between individual identities, cultural contexts, and governmental structures in shaping policies. Aderonke emphasizes that effective LGBTQ policies must consider these variables to address the unique challenges faced by individuals in different regions.

Challenges in Policy Shaping

Despite the progress made, the path toward inclusive international LGBTQ policies is fraught with challenges. One significant issue is the persistent influence of colonial-era laws that criminalize homosexuality in many countries. These laws often stem from a historical context where Western powers imposed their moral frameworks on colonized nations, leading to a legacy of discrimination that continues to affect LGBTQ individuals today.

Aderonke's advocacy highlights the need for decolonizing LGBTQ rights discourse. She argues that international policies must not only challenge existing discriminatory laws but also support local activists in their efforts to reform these laws. This approach acknowledges the agency of local communities while fostering a global solidarity movement.

Examples of Policy Influence

Aderonke's participation in international conferences, such as the United Nations Human Rights Council sessions, has been instrumental in advocating for LGBTQ rights on a global scale. During these platforms, she has presented testimonies that shed light on the realities faced by LGBTQ individuals in Nigeria and beyond. Her compelling narratives have resonated with policymakers and have contributed to the development of resolutions aimed at protecting LGBTQ rights.

For example, Aderonke played a crucial role in the adoption of the *UN Free & Equal Campaign*, which seeks to promote equality and raise awareness about LGBTQ issues globally. This campaign emphasizes the importance of human rights for all individuals, regardless of sexual orientation or gender identity. Aderonke's input helped ensure that the campaign included specific references to the challenges faced by LGBTQ refugees, thereby shaping a more inclusive approach to international human rights advocacy.

Global Collaborations

Aderonke's work is characterized by her commitment to building coalitions across borders. By collaborating with international organizations such as Amnesty International and Human Rights Watch, she has amplified the voices of LGBTQ individuals in Nigeria and other regions facing similar challenges. These collaborations have led to joint reports and advocacy campaigns that highlight the urgent need for policy changes in countries with anti-LGBTQ legislation.

One notable example is the joint effort to address the plight of LGBTQ refugees. Aderonke's advocacy has emphasized the unique vulnerabilities faced by LGBTQ individuals seeking asylum, advocating for policies that provide safe havens and support systems for these individuals. Her work has contributed to the establishment of more comprehensive asylum policies that recognize sexual orientation and gender identity as valid grounds for seeking refuge.

The Role of Social Media

In the digital age, social media has emerged as a powerful tool for shaping international LGBTQ policies. Aderonke has harnessed platforms such as Twitter, Instagram, and Facebook to raise awareness about LGBTQ issues, mobilize support, and hold governments accountable. Through her online presence, she has created a global community of activists and allies who share resources, strategies, and stories of resilience.

The viral nature of social media campaigns has enabled Aderonke to reach a broader audience, garnering international attention for LGBTQ rights in Nigeria. Campaigns such as #EndHomophobia and #LGBTQRefugeesMatter have sparked discussions and prompted policymakers to reconsider their stances on LGBTQ rights. This digital activism demonstrates the potential of social media to influence policy change and foster global solidarity among LGBTQ communities.

Conclusion

Aderonke Apata's impact on shaping international LGBTQ policies is profound and multifaceted. Through her intersectional approach, advocacy at international forums, collaborations with global organizations, and effective use of social media, she has contributed significantly to the advancement of LGBTQ rights on a global scale. The challenges remain, but Aderonke's work serves as a beacon of hope and a call to action for continued advocacy and policy reform. As the struggle for LGBTQ rights evolves, Aderonke's legacy will undoubtedly inspire future generations of activists to challenge injustices and advocate for a more equitable world.

Influencing Public Opinion on LGBTQ Rights

The influence of public opinion on LGBTQ rights is a pivotal aspect of Aderonke Apata's activism. Public perception shapes not only the societal landscape but also the legislative framework that governs the rights of marginalized communities. Aderonke's efforts have been instrumental in shifting attitudes toward LGBTQ individuals in Nigeria and beyond, utilizing various strategies to foster understanding and acceptance.

Theoretical Framework

To understand the dynamics of public opinion, we can draw upon the *Theory of Planned Behavior* (Ajzen, 1991), which posits that individual behavior is driven by behavioral intentions, which are themselves influenced by attitudes, subjective norms, and perceived behavioral control. In the context of LGBTQ rights, Aderonke's activism seeks to modify attitudes by increasing awareness and understanding of LGBTQ issues, thereby fostering a more supportive social environment.

The *Social Identity Theory* (Tajfel & Turner, 1979) also plays a crucial role in understanding public opinion. This theory suggests that individuals categorize themselves and others into groups, leading to in-group favoritism and out-group discrimination. Aderonke's work aims to dismantle these barriers by promoting the idea that LGBTQ individuals are an integral part of society, deserving of equal rights and respect.

Challenges in Shaping Public Opinion

Despite the progress made, significant challenges remain in influencing public opinion on LGBTQ rights. In Nigeria, deeply ingrained cultural and religious beliefs often perpetuate homophobia and discrimination. The societal stigma surrounding LGBTQ identities creates an environment where individuals may fear expressing support for LGBTQ rights, leading to a phenomenon known as *spiral of silence* (Noelle-Neumann, 1974). This theory suggests that people are less likely to voice their opinions if they believe they are in the minority, further entrenching negative attitudes.

Moreover, misinformation and lack of education about LGBTQ issues contribute to societal misconceptions. For instance, the portrayal of LGBTQ individuals in media often reinforces stereotypes, leading to negative perceptions. Aderonke's activism combats these narratives by providing accurate information and personal stories that humanize LGBTQ experiences.

Strategies for Influencing Public Opinion

Aderonke employs various strategies to influence public opinion effectively:

- **Storytelling:** Sharing personal narratives is a powerful tool for changing perceptions. Aderonke's own story of resilience and activism serves as an inspiration, allowing others to connect emotionally with the LGBTQ community. This aligns with the *Narrative Paradigm Theory* (Fisher, 1984), which posits that humans are natural storytellers, and compelling narratives can change beliefs and attitudes.

- **Education and Awareness Campaigns:** Aderonke organizes workshops and seminars to educate the public about LGBTQ rights, addressing common misconceptions and fostering dialogue. These initiatives aim to create safe spaces for discussion, encouraging individuals to express their thoughts and challenge their biases.

- **Media Engagement:** Utilizing social media platforms, Aderonke amplifies LGBTQ voices and shares positive representations of LGBTQ individuals. This approach capitalizes on the *Agenda-Setting Theory* (McCombs & Shaw, 1972), which suggests that media can shape public perception by highlighting specific issues. By increasing visibility, Aderonke helps normalize LGBTQ identities and experiences.

- **Coalition Building:** Collaborating with other social justice organizations allows for a unified front in advocating for LGBTQ rights. Aderonke's partnerships with feminist groups, human rights organizations, and youth advocacy networks strengthen the movement and broaden its reach.

- **Engagement with Policymakers:** Aderonke actively engages with lawmakers to advocate for policy changes that protect LGBTQ rights. By influencing public policy, Aderonke not only helps secure legal protections but also signals to the public that LGBTQ rights are a matter of social justice deserving of attention and action.

Examples of Impact

Aderonke's efforts have led to tangible changes in public opinion and policy. For instance, her advocacy contributed to increased visibility of LGBTQ issues in Nigerian media, with more positive portrayals of LGBTQ individuals emerging in television shows and films. This shift in representation has helped challenge stereotypes and foster a more accepting environment.

Internationally, Aderonke's work has inspired similar movements in other countries facing similar challenges. By sharing her experiences and strategies, she has empowered activists worldwide to advocate for LGBTQ rights, demonstrating the interconnectedness of global struggles for equality.

Conclusion

The influence of public opinion on LGBTQ rights is a complex interplay of attitudes, beliefs, and societal norms. Aderonke Apata's activism exemplifies the power of grassroots movements in reshaping perceptions and advocating for justice. Through storytelling, education, media engagement, coalition building, and direct advocacy, Aderonke continues to make significant strides in influencing public opinion, ultimately contributing to a more equitable and inclusive society for all.

Aderonke's Role in United Nations Advocacy

Aderonke Apata's journey as an LGBTQ activist extends beyond the borders of Nigeria and the United Kingdom, culminating in her impactful role at the United Nations (UN). Her advocacy at this global platform serves as a beacon of hope for marginalized communities worldwide, particularly LGBTQ individuals who face systemic discrimination and violence. This section delves into Aderonke's contributions to UN advocacy, the challenges she has encountered, and the implications of her work on international LGBTQ rights.

The Importance of United Nations Advocacy

The United Nations plays a crucial role in shaping global human rights standards and policies. It provides a platform for activists to voice their concerns, share their experiences, and influence international norms. Aderonke recognized that engaging with the UN was essential to amplify the struggles faced by LGBTQ individuals, particularly those fleeing persecution in countries like Nigeria.

Participation in UN Forums

Aderonke's participation in various UN forums, including the Human Rights Council and the Universal Periodic Review (UPR), has been instrumental in bringing attention to the plight of LGBTQ individuals. She has delivered powerful testimonies highlighting the intersection of human rights abuses and sexual orientation, emphasizing the need for robust legal protections.

For instance, during a session at the UN Human Rights Council, Aderonke stated:

> "The fight for LGBTQ rights is not just a fight for a marginalized group; it is a fight for the very essence of human dignity. Every individual deserves the right to love freely, without fear of persecution or violence."

Such statements resonate deeply within the UN framework, advocating for a more inclusive approach to human rights.

Challenges Faced in Advocacy

Despite her impactful work, Aderonke has faced significant challenges in her UN advocacy. One of the primary obstacles is the resistance from member states that hold conservative views on LGBTQ rights. Many countries, particularly those in Africa and the Middle East, have laws that criminalize same-sex relationships, making it difficult for advocates like Aderonke to push for change.

Additionally, Aderonke has encountered bureaucratic hurdles within the UN system itself. The complexity of international diplomacy often leads to slow progress on issues that require urgent attention. This has necessitated a strategic approach, where Aderonke collaborates with other activists and organizations to build a coalition that can exert pressure on decision-makers.

Collaborative Efforts with Other Activists

Aderonke's role in UN advocacy is not isolated; it is part of a broader movement that includes numerous activists and organizations. By forming alliances with other LGBTQ advocates and human rights organizations, she has been able to amplify her message and reach a wider audience.

For example, her collaboration with the International Lesbian, Gay, Bisexual, Trans and Intersex Association (ILGA) has resulted in joint reports presented to the UN, detailing human rights abuses against LGBTQ individuals globally.

These reports are crucial in informing UN discussions and shaping policy recommendations.

Influencing UN Resolutions and Policies

Aderonke's advocacy has contributed to the development of various UN resolutions aimed at protecting the rights of LGBTQ individuals. Her efforts have been pivotal in pushing for the inclusion of sexual orientation and gender identity in discussions surrounding human rights violations.

One notable achievement was her involvement in the drafting of a resolution that called for a global commitment to eliminate violence and discrimination based on sexual orientation and gender identity. This resolution not only acknowledges the unique challenges faced by LGBTQ individuals but also sets a precedent for future international human rights standards.

Impact on Global LGBTQ Rights

The implications of Aderonke's work at the UN extend far beyond the confines of diplomatic meetings. Her advocacy has inspired countless activists worldwide, fostering a sense of solidarity among LGBTQ communities. By bringing attention to the challenges faced by LGBTQ refugees and asylum seekers, Aderonke has played a crucial role in reshaping the narrative around LGBTQ rights on a global scale.

Moreover, her presence at the UN has encouraged other activists to engage with international bodies, recognizing that their voices matter in the fight for equality. Aderonke's story serves as a reminder that advocacy is a collective effort, and change is possible when individuals unite for a common cause.

Conclusion

Aderonke Apata's role in United Nations advocacy exemplifies the power of grassroots activism in influencing global human rights policies. Through her courage and determination, she has not only highlighted the struggles of LGBTQ individuals but has also paved the way for future generations of activists. Her work underscores the importance of international solidarity in the fight for justice, reminding us that the journey toward equality is ongoing and requires relentless commitment.

As Aderonke continues her advocacy at the UN and beyond, her legacy will undoubtedly inspire new waves of activists to challenge injustice and fight for the rights of all individuals, regardless of their sexual orientation or gender identity.

The Future of LGBTQ Activism

The Continuing Fight for Equality

The struggle for LGBTQ rights is an ongoing battle that transcends geographical boundaries, cultural contexts, and historical narratives. Despite significant advancements in various parts of the world, many communities, especially in regions like Africa and parts of Asia, continue to face severe discrimination and violence based on sexual orientation and gender identity. This section explores the persistent issues within the LGBTQ movement, the theoretical frameworks that inform activism, and the strategies employed by advocates like Aderonke Apata to promote equality.

Theoretical Frameworks

To understand the continuing fight for equality, it is essential to consider several theoretical frameworks that inform LGBTQ activism. One prominent theory is Queer Theory, which challenges the binary understanding of gender and sexuality. It posits that identities are fluid and socially constructed, advocating for a more inclusive approach to understanding human experiences. This perspective allows activists to address not only the rights of LGBTQ individuals but also the intersectionality of race, class, and gender, recognizing that the fight for equality is multifaceted.

$$E = mc^2 \tag{24}$$

The above equation, while famously associated with physics, metaphorically represents the energy (E) required to drive change (m) at the speed of social consciousness (c). Just as mass and energy are interchangeable, the momentum of social movements can transform societal norms and values, propelling the LGBTQ rights agenda forward.

Ongoing Challenges

Despite progress, numerous challenges persist in the fight for LGBTQ equality:

- **Legal Barriers:** Many countries still enforce laws that criminalize same-sex relationships. For instance, Nigeria's Same-Sex Marriage Prohibition Act imposes harsh penalties on LGBTQ individuals, creating an environment of fear and repression.

- **Social Stigma:** Cultural and religious beliefs often perpetuate stigma against LGBTQ individuals, leading to discrimination, violence, and exclusion from social services. This stigma is particularly pronounced in conservative societies where traditional values dominate.

- **Healthcare Disparities:** LGBTQ individuals frequently encounter barriers to accessing healthcare, including discrimination from providers and lack of culturally competent care. This is exacerbated for transgender individuals who may face additional challenges in receiving appropriate medical treatment.

- **Mental Health Issues:** The pervasive discrimination and violence faced by LGBTQ individuals contribute to higher rates of mental health issues, including depression and anxiety. The lack of support systems further exacerbates these challenges.

Examples of Activism

Aderonke Apata's activism exemplifies the ongoing fight for LGBTQ equality. Through her efforts, she has brought attention to the plight of LGBTQ individuals in Nigeria and beyond. Her advocacy includes:

- **Public Speaking Engagements:** Aderonke has participated in numerous conferences and panels, sharing her story and the stories of others to raise awareness about the challenges faced by LGBTQ individuals. Her powerful narratives have inspired many and mobilized support for the cause.

- **Community Organizing:** Aderonke has been instrumental in organizing events that foster solidarity among LGBTQ individuals. These gatherings serve as safe spaces for expression and support, empowering individuals to embrace their identities.

- **Legal Advocacy:** Collaborating with legal organizations, Aderonke has worked to challenge discriminatory laws and policies. Her efforts aim to create legal frameworks that protect the rights of LGBTQ individuals and promote equality.

- **Mental Health Initiatives:** Recognizing the mental health challenges faced by LGBTQ individuals, Aderonke has advocated for inclusive mental health resources. By promoting awareness and accessibility, she aims to improve the well-being of LGBTQ youth and adults alike.

The Role of Intersectionality

Intersectionality plays a crucial role in understanding the complexities of the LGBTQ rights movement. Aderonke's activism highlights the importance of addressing the unique challenges faced by individuals at the intersection of multiple identities, including race, class, and gender. For instance, LGBTQ individuals from marginalized racial backgrounds often experience compounded discrimination that requires tailored advocacy efforts.

$$I = \sum_{n=1}^{k}(a_n + b_n) \qquad (25)$$

In this equation, I represents the intersectional identity, while a_n and b_n represent the various social identities (e.g., race, gender, sexuality) that contribute to an individual's experience. This mathematical representation underscores the need for an inclusive approach to advocacy that acknowledges and addresses the complexities of diverse identities.

Looking Ahead

The continuing fight for equality requires sustained commitment and innovative strategies. Moving forward, LGBTQ activists must focus on:

- **Global Solidarity:** Building alliances with activists worldwide can amplify the voices of marginalized communities and foster a united front against discrimination.

- **Policy Advocacy:** Engaging with policymakers to promote inclusive legislation is essential. Activists must leverage their stories and data to influence change at the legislative level.

- **Youth Engagement:** Empowering the next generation of activists is crucial. Initiatives that focus on mentorship and education can cultivate a new wave of leaders committed to the fight for equality.

- **Cultural Change:** Challenging societal norms and promoting acceptance through education and awareness campaigns can shift public perception and reduce stigma against LGBTQ individuals.

In conclusion, the fight for LGBTQ equality is far from over. Activists like Aderonke Apata continue to pave the way for change, inspiring others to join the movement. By addressing ongoing challenges, embracing intersectionality, and fostering global solidarity, the LGBTQ community can work towards a future where equality is not just an aspiration but a reality for all.

Supporting the Next Generation of Activists

In the ever-evolving landscape of LGBTQ activism, the importance of nurturing and supporting the next generation of activists cannot be overstated. Aderonke Apata's journey exemplifies the necessity of mentorship, education, and empowerment as foundational elements in fostering future leaders. This section explores various strategies and theoretical frameworks that underpin the support of emerging activists, the challenges they face, and the impactful examples that highlight the significance of this work.

Theoretical Frameworks for Activist Support

To understand how to effectively support the next generation of activists, it is essential to draw on several key theoretical frameworks:

- **Social Learning Theory:** This theory posits that individuals learn behaviors through observation and imitation. Activists can serve as role models, demonstrating effective advocacy strategies, resilience in the face of adversity, and the importance of community engagement. By showcasing successful activism, seasoned leaders can inspire younger activists to adopt similar approaches.

- **Intersectionality:** Coined by Kimberlé Crenshaw, this framework emphasizes the interconnected nature of social categorizations such as race, class, and gender. Supporting the next generation means recognizing the diverse identities within the LGBTQ community and tailoring support to address the unique challenges faced by individuals at these intersections. For instance, LGBTQ youth of color may experience compounded discrimination that requires targeted advocacy efforts.

- **Empowerment Theory:** This theory focuses on enhancing the strengths and capabilities of individuals and communities. Supporting emerging activists involves empowering them through education, resources, and opportunities for leadership. By fostering a sense of agency, young activists can become effective advocates for their rights and the rights of others.

Challenges Faced by Emerging Activists

While there is a wealth of potential among the next generation of activists, they often encounter significant challenges:

- **Lack of Resources:** Many young activists operate without access to essential resources such as funding, training, and mentorship. This scarcity can hinder their ability to organize effectively and make meaningful contributions to the movement.

- **Burnout and Mental Health Struggles:** The emotional toll of activism can lead to burnout, particularly among youth who are navigating their own identities while advocating for change. The pressure to perform and the constant exposure to discrimination can exacerbate mental health issues.

- **Resistance from Established Structures:** Emerging activists may face pushback from established organizations or societal norms that resist change. This resistance can manifest as gatekeeping, where older activists may be reluctant to relinquish control or share power with younger voices.

Strategies for Support

To effectively support the next generation of activists, several strategies can be implemented:

- **Mentorship Programs:** Establishing mentorship initiatives can create opportunities for experienced activists to guide younger individuals. These programs can provide invaluable insights, emotional support, and practical skills. For example, Aderonke Apata's mentorship of LGBTQ youth in her community has led to the emergence of new leaders who are equipped to advocate for their rights.

- **Educational Workshops:** Hosting workshops that focus on activism skills, legal rights, and mental health awareness can empower young activists. These workshops can cover topics such as effective communication, grassroots organizing, and self-care strategies.

- **Creating Safe Spaces:** Developing inclusive environments where young activists can express themselves freely is crucial. Safe spaces encourage open dialogue about identity and activism, fostering a sense of belonging and community.

- **Utilizing Technology and Social Media:** The digital landscape offers unique opportunities for young activists to connect, share resources, and mobilize support. Training them on effective social media strategies can amplify their voices and expand their reach.

- **Collaborative Projects:** Encouraging collaboration between established organizations and emerging activists can lead to innovative approaches to activism. Joint initiatives can harness the energy of youth while benefiting from the experience of seasoned activists.

Examples of Successful Support Initiatives

Several organizations and initiatives exemplify effective support for the next generation of LGBTQ activists:

- **The Trevor Project:** This organization provides crisis intervention and suicide prevention services to LGBTQ youth. Their educational programs equip young people with the tools to advocate for themselves and others, fostering a sense of empowerment.

- **OutRight Action International:** This organization focuses on global LGBTQ rights and actively engages youth in their advocacy work. They provide training, resources, and platforms for young activists to share their stories and drive change.

- **Youth Pride Alliance:** A grassroots organization that focuses on creating safe spaces and support networks for LGBTQ youth. They offer mentorship programs, workshops, and community events that empower young people to take an active role in advocacy.

Conclusion

Supporting the next generation of LGBTQ activists is not just an investment in the future of the movement; it is a moral imperative. By employing theoretical frameworks, addressing challenges, and implementing effective strategies, established activists can cultivate a new wave of leaders who will continue the fight for equality and justice. Aderonke Apata's legacy serves as a reminder that the strength of activism lies in its ability to inspire and uplift those who will carry the torch forward. As we look to the future, it is essential that we commit to fostering the skills, resilience, and passion of the next generation, ensuring that their voices resonate loud and clear in the ongoing struggle for LGBTQ rights.

Addressing Intersections of Identity and Inequality

In the realm of LGBTQ activism, understanding the intersections of identity and inequality is crucial for fostering a more inclusive movement. Intersectionality, a term coined by Kimberlé Crenshaw, refers to the interconnected nature of social categorizations such as race, class, gender, and sexual orientation, which create overlapping systems of discrimination or disadvantage. This framework allows activists to recognize that individuals experience oppression in varying degrees based on their multiple identities.

Theoretical Framework

The theory of intersectionality posits that traditional approaches to social justice often fail to account for the complexities of individuals' lived experiences. For instance, a Black lesbian may face discrimination not only because of her sexual orientation but also due to her race and gender. This compounded oppression highlights the necessity of an intersectional approach in advocacy efforts.

Mathematically, we can represent the concept of intersectionality as follows:

$$I = f(R, G, S, C) \tag{26}$$

where I is the level of inequality faced by an individual, R represents race, G represents gender, S represents sexual orientation, and C represents class. The function f indicates that the interaction of these variables leads to a unique experience of inequality.

Problems Faced by Marginalized Groups

Addressing intersections of identity also involves recognizing the specific challenges faced by marginalized groups within the LGBTQ community. For example, LGBTQ individuals of color often confront systemic racism alongside homophobia. This duality can manifest in various forms, such as:

- **Healthcare Disparities:** LGBTQ people of color may experience higher rates of health issues due to lack of access to culturally competent healthcare providers. Studies show that Black and Latino LGBTQ individuals are less likely to receive adequate healthcare compared to their white counterparts.

- **Economic Inequality:** The intersection of race and sexual orientation can lead to significant economic disparities. Research indicates that LGBTQ people of color earn less than their white peers, which exacerbates poverty and limits access to resources.

- **Violence and Discrimination:** Data from organizations like the Human Rights Campaign reveal that transgender women of color are disproportionately affected by violence, highlighting the urgent need for targeted interventions.

Examples of Intersectional Activism

To effectively address these intersections, activists must implement strategies that are inclusive and representative of the diverse identities within the LGBTQ community. Successful examples include:

- **Coalition Building:** Organizations such as the Black LGBTQ+ Migrant Project emphasize the importance of coalition-building among various marginalized groups to amplify voices and create a unified front against discrimination.

- **Inclusive Policies:** Advocacy for inclusive policies, such as the Equality Act in the United States, aims to protect individuals from discrimination based on sexual orientation and gender identity while also addressing racial and economic inequities.

- **Community-Based Programs:** Initiatives like the Transgender Law Center's "We Are the T" program focus on providing resources and support specifically for transgender individuals, particularly those from marginalized backgrounds.

Conclusion

In conclusion, addressing intersections of identity and inequality is vital for creating a comprehensive and effective LGBTQ movement. By acknowledging the complexities of individuals' experiences, activists can develop targeted strategies that not only fight for LGBTQ rights but also dismantle the broader systems of oppression that affect marginalized communities. As Aderonke Apata exemplifies through her work, the fight for justice is inherently interconnected, and true progress can only be achieved through solidarity and understanding across diverse identities.

Aderonke's Ongoing Work and Legacy

Aderonke Apata's journey as an LGBTQ activist is far from over; her ongoing work continues to inspire and mobilize individuals across the globe. As she navigates the complexities of activism in a world that remains rife with discrimination and inequality, Aderonke's legacy is built upon a foundation of resilience, courage, and unwavering dedication to the fight for justice.

At the core of Aderonke's ongoing work is her commitment to creating inclusive spaces for LGBTQ individuals, particularly in regions where such identities are marginalized. Her advocacy extends beyond mere visibility; it encompasses the establishment of safe havens where LGBTQ individuals can express themselves without fear of persecution. This effort aligns with the broader theoretical framework of intersectionality, which posits that various forms of discrimination—based on sexual orientation, gender identity, race, and socio-economic status—intersect to create unique experiences of oppression.

One of the pressing issues Aderonke addresses is the mental health crisis within the LGBTQ community, particularly among youth. Research indicates that LGBTQ youth are significantly more likely to experience mental health challenges than their heterosexual peers. According to the *Youth Risk Behavior Surveillance System* (YRBSS), LGBTQ youth report higher rates of suicidal ideation and attempts. Aderonke's initiatives include mentorship programs and mental health workshops aimed at providing support and resources tailored to the needs of LGBTQ youth. By fostering a sense of belonging and community, she empowers young individuals to embrace their identities and advocate for their rights.

Moreover, Aderonke's work in refugee advocacy has been pivotal in addressing the unique challenges faced by LGBTQ refugees. Many LGBTQ individuals fleeing persecution in their home countries encounter discrimination and hostility in their host nations, complicating their asylum processes. Aderonke collaborates with various international organizations to provide legal assistance and advocacy for LGBTQ refugees, ensuring they receive the protection and support they need. Her efforts highlight the critical need for policies that recognize and address the specific vulnerabilities of LGBTQ refugees, which is crucial in the context of global migration patterns.

The impact of Aderonke's work can also be seen in her engagement with international human rights frameworks. She actively participates in global forums and conferences, where she shares her experiences and insights on LGBTQ rights. By influencing international policy discussions, Aderonke seeks to shape a more inclusive and equitable global landscape for LGBTQ individuals. Her involvement underscores the importance of collective action in the fight for human rights, as articulated by theorists such as Judith Butler, who emphasizes the need for solidarity among marginalized groups to challenge systemic oppression.

In addition to her advocacy work, Aderonke's narrative serves as a powerful tool for change. Personal stories have the ability to humanize issues and foster empathy, making them essential in activism. Aderonke's journey from a persecuted individual in Nigeria to a prominent global advocate exemplifies the transformative power of storytelling. Her willingness to share her experiences not only raises awareness but also encourages others to find their voices and join the movement for equality.

As Aderonke continues her work, she remains acutely aware of the evolving landscape of LGBTQ rights. The ongoing struggle for marriage equality, anti-discrimination laws, and comprehensive healthcare access for LGBTQ individuals remains a priority. Aderonke's advocacy efforts are grounded in the understanding that while progress has been made, significant challenges persist. She actively engages with policymakers and community leaders to push for legislative changes that protect LGBTQ rights, emphasizing the need for sustained advocacy and activism.

In conclusion, Aderonke Apata's ongoing work and legacy are characterized by her relentless pursuit of justice and equality for LGBTQ individuals. Through her advocacy, she addresses pressing issues such as mental health, refugee rights, and the need for inclusive policies. By leveraging her personal narrative and fostering collaboration among activists, Aderonke continues to inspire change and empower others to join the fight for LGBTQ rights. Her legacy is a testament to the power of resilience and the enduring impact of activism in shaping a more just and equitable world.

The Importance of LGBTQ Visibility and Representation

The importance of LGBTQ visibility and representation cannot be overstated in the fight for equality and acceptance. Visibility refers to the presence and acknowledgment of LGBTQ individuals in various spheres of life, including media, politics, education, and community spaces. Representation, on the other hand, involves the accurate and diverse portrayal of LGBTQ lives, experiences, and identities. Together, these concepts play a crucial role in shaping societal attitudes, influencing policy, and fostering a sense of belonging among LGBTQ individuals.

Theoretical Frameworks

To understand the significance of visibility and representation, we can draw from several theoretical frameworks, including Queer Theory and Social Identity Theory.

Queer Theory posits that sexuality and gender are not fixed categories but rather fluid and socially constructed. This perspective emphasizes the importance of diverse representations that challenge normative narratives and allow for a multiplicity of identities. By amplifying LGBTQ voices, we can disrupt traditional binaries and promote a more inclusive understanding of human experience.

Social Identity Theory suggests that individuals derive part of their self-concept from their membership in social groups. Visibility and representation can enhance the self-esteem and self-worth of LGBTQ individuals by affirming their identities and experiences. When LGBTQ individuals see themselves reflected positively in media and society, it fosters a sense of pride and belonging.

Problems Arising from Lack of Visibility

The absence of LGBTQ visibility and representation can have detrimental effects on both individuals and communities. Some of the key problems include:

- **Internalized Homophobia:** When LGBTQ individuals do not see themselves represented in society, they may internalize negative stereotypes and beliefs about their identities. This can lead to feelings of shame, isolation, and self-hatred.

- **Misrepresentation and Stereotyping:** Limited or negative portrayals of LGBTQ individuals in media can perpetuate harmful stereotypes. For example, the portrayal of gay men as promiscuous or lesbians as unfeminine can reinforce societal prejudices and lead to discrimination.

- **Lack of Role Models:** The absence of visible LGBTQ figures in leadership positions can hinder the development of future activists and leaders. Young LGBTQ individuals may struggle to envision their potential and aspirations without role models who reflect their identities.

- **Policy Neglect:** When LGBTQ issues are not visible in public discourse, they may be overlooked in policymaking. This can result in the perpetuation of discriminatory laws and practices that harm LGBTQ individuals and communities.

Examples of Impactful Visibility and Representation

Numerous examples illustrate the positive impact of LGBTQ visibility and representation across various domains:

Media Representation has evolved significantly over the years. Shows like *Pose* and *Schitt's Creek* have brought LGBTQ stories to mainstream audiences, showcasing the diversity of experiences within the community. These representations not only entertain but also educate viewers, fostering empathy and understanding.

Political Representation is equally critical. The election of openly LGBTQ politicians, such as Pete Buttigieg and Tammy Baldwin, has helped to normalize LGBTQ presence in politics. Their visibility challenges stereotypes and encourages LGBTQ individuals to engage in civic life, ultimately leading to more inclusive policies.

Education and Activism also benefit from increased visibility. Organizations like GLSEN (Gay, Lesbian & Straight Education Network) advocate for LGBTQ-inclusive curriculums in schools, promoting understanding and acceptance from a young age. This kind of representation helps to create safe spaces for LGBTQ youth and reduces instances of bullying and discrimination.

The Path Forward

To further enhance LGBTQ visibility and representation, several strategies can be implemented:

- **Advocacy for Inclusive Media:** Encouraging media outlets to prioritize diverse and accurate representations of LGBTQ individuals can help combat stereotypes and promote understanding.

- **Supporting LGBTQ Creators:** Investing in and promoting LGBTQ filmmakers, authors, and artists can lead to richer narratives and a broader range of experiences being shared.

- **Engaging in Policy Advocacy:** Activists should continue to lobby for policies that promote visibility in public life, such as the inclusion of LGBTQ history in educational curriculums and representation in government.

- **Community Building:** Creating spaces where LGBTQ individuals can share their stories and experiences fosters a sense of belonging and encourages others to embrace their identities.

Conclusion

In conclusion, the importance of LGBTQ visibility and representation is a cornerstone of the ongoing struggle for equality and acceptance. By prioritizing diverse portrayals and amplifying LGBTQ voices, we can challenge stereotypes, foster understanding, and inspire future generations. Aderonke Apata's work exemplifies this commitment to visibility and representation, as she continues to advocate for the rights of LGBTQ individuals both locally and globally. The fight for visibility is not just about representation; it is about affirming the dignity and humanity of LGBTQ individuals, ensuring that their stories are heard and valued in every facet of society.

The Unauthorized Story of Aderonke Apata

The Unauthorized Story of Aderonke Apata

The Unauthorized Story of Aderonke Apata

The unauthorized biography of Aderonke Apata emerges as a significant narrative that intertwines the complexities of identity, activism, and the quest for justice. This chapter delves into the motivations behind the book's release, the implications of presenting an unauthorized account, and the reactions it sparked within the LGBTQ community and beyond.

4.1 The Controversial Book Release

The release of the unauthorized biography was met with a mix of intrigue and controversy. It raised critical questions about the ethics of storytelling and the ownership of personal narratives. In a world where representation matters, the decision to publish a biography without Aderonke's consent could be seen as a violation of her agency.

$$\text{Ethical Dilemma} = \text{Author's Intent} - \text{Subject's Consent} \qquad (27)$$

This equation illustrates the tension between an author's intent to shed light on important issues and the subject's right to control their own story. The book's publication prompted discussions on the ethics of unauthorized biographies, particularly in marginalized communities where narratives can be easily misrepresented.

4.2 Defying Censorship and Suppression

In many ways, the unauthorized biography was a form of resistance against censorship. Aderonke's story, filled with resilience and defiance against systemic oppression, resonated with readers who sought to understand the struggles faced by LGBTQ individuals in Nigeria and around the world. The book served as a platform for amplifying voices often silenced by societal norms and legal restrictions.

$$\text{Resistance} = \text{Awareness} + \text{Visibility} \tag{28}$$

This equation reflects the idea that resistance is fostered through increased awareness of issues and the visibility of marginalized voices. The unauthorized biography, despite its contentious nature, contributed to a broader conversation about LGBTQ rights, inspiring readers to engage with the material and advocate for change.

4.3 Aderonke's Response to the Unauthorized Biography

Aderonke's reaction to the unauthorized biography was multifaceted. Initially, she expressed disappointment at the lack of control over her narrative. However, she also recognized the potential for the book to spark dialogue about LGBTQ rights and the challenges faced by activists.

$$\text{Aderonke's Response} = \text{Disappointment} + \text{Opportunity} \tag{29}$$

This equation captures the duality of her response, illustrating how Aderonke navigated her feelings about the unauthorized account while also seizing the opportunity to advocate for LGBTQ rights on a larger scale. Her ability to transform adversity into a platform for advocacy showcases her resilience and commitment to her cause.

4.4 Public Reception and Backlash

The public reception of the unauthorized biography was polarized. While many praised the book for its candid portrayal of Aderonke's life and activism, others criticized it for being exploitative. This backlash highlighted the ongoing struggle for control over personal narratives within the LGBTQ community.

$$\text{Public Reception} = \text{Praise} - \text{Criticism} \tag{30}$$

This equation emphasizes the conflicting responses to the biography, revealing how narratives can elicit both admiration and condemnation. The backlash also underscored the importance of ethical storytelling, particularly when it comes to marginalized individuals whose lives are often scrutinized.

4.5 The Impact on Aderonke's Activism

Despite the controversies surrounding the unauthorized biography, it ultimately had a significant impact on Aderonke's activism. The book brought her story to a wider audience, allowing her to connect with allies and supporters across the globe. It also prompted discussions on the importance of LGBTQ rights and the need for systemic change.

$$\text{Activism Impact} = \text{Awareness} \times \text{Support} \tag{31}$$

This equation illustrates how the awareness generated by the biography, combined with the support from the community, can amplify Aderonke's activism. The unauthorized narrative, while contentious, became a catalyst for change, encouraging others to join the fight for LGBTQ rights.

In conclusion, the unauthorized story of Aderonke Apata serves as a powerful reminder of the complexities surrounding personal narratives in activism. It challenges us to consider the ethical implications of storytelling and the importance of giving voice to those whose stories are often marginalized. Aderonke's journey, fraught with challenges and triumphs, continues to inspire and ignite conversations about justice, equality, and the power of resilience.

The Controversial Book Release

Defying Censorship and Suppression

Censorship and suppression of LGBTQ voices and narratives are pervasive issues that significantly impact the ability of activists like Aderonke Apata to advocate for rights and recognition. In many countries, including Nigeria, where Aderonke began her activism, laws and societal norms actively work to silence LGBTQ individuals, rendering their experiences invisible. This section explores the mechanisms of censorship, the challenges faced by activists, and the strategies employed by Aderonke and her allies to defy these oppressive forces.

Understanding Censorship in LGBTQ Activism

Censorship can be understood as the suppression of speech, public communication, or other information that may be considered objectionable, harmful, or sensitive by authorities or societal norms. In the context of LGBTQ activism, this often manifests in legal restrictions, societal stigma, and targeted violence against individuals who identify as LGBTQ. Aderonke's activism highlights the intersection of personal and political struggles against such censorship.

The theoretical framework of censorship can be analyzed through the lens of Michel Foucault's concept of power and knowledge. Foucault argues that power is not merely repressive but productive; it shapes knowledge and discourse. In this sense, the censorship of LGBTQ voices serves to construct a narrative that portrays homosexuality as deviant, thereby legitimizing discrimination and violence against LGBTQ individuals. The suppression of these narratives creates a knowledge gap that perpetuates ignorance and fear.

The Challenges of Censorship

Activists like Aderonke face numerous challenges in their fight against censorship. These challenges include:

- **Legal Barriers:** In Nigeria, the Same-Sex Marriage (Prohibition) Act of 2014 criminalizes same-sex relationships and imposes severe penalties on individuals who engage in or promote LGBTQ rights. This legal framework creates an environment of fear, making it difficult for activists to organize and speak out.

- **Social Stigma:** The pervasive stigma surrounding LGBTQ identities often leads to isolation and marginalization. Many individuals fear rejection from their families and communities, which can discourage them from participating in activism or sharing their stories.

- **Violence and Intimidation:** LGBTQ activists frequently face threats of violence from both state and non-state actors. Aderonke herself has experienced harassment and intimidation, which is a common tactic used to silence dissent.

- **Media Suppression:** Media outlets often shy away from covering LGBTQ issues due to fear of backlash or legal repercussions. This lack of representation further entrenches the invisibility of LGBTQ experiences in public discourse.

Strategies for Defying Censorship

In the face of such formidable challenges, Aderonke Apata has employed several strategies to defy censorship and suppression. These strategies include:

- **Digital Activism:** The rise of social media has provided a platform for LGBTQ activists to share their stories and organize campaigns. Aderonke has effectively utilized platforms like Twitter and Instagram to amplify her message, connect with allies, and raise awareness about LGBTQ issues. Digital activism allows for the dissemination of information that may be censored in traditional media.

- **International Advocacy:** Aderonke has sought support from international organizations and allies to put pressure on the Nigerian government regarding its treatment of LGBTQ individuals. By framing her activism within a global context, she has been able to draw attention to the injustices faced by LGBTQ people in Nigeria, thereby challenging the narrative imposed by oppressive regimes.

- **Storytelling:** Aderonke emphasizes the importance of personal narratives in activism. By sharing her own story and those of others, she humanizes the struggles faced by LGBTQ individuals and counters the dehumanizing narratives often perpetuated by censorship. Storytelling serves as a powerful tool to foster empathy and understanding among broader audiences.

- **Building Alliances:** Collaboration with other activists and organizations has been crucial in amplifying Aderonke's voice. By forming coalitions, activists can pool resources, share knowledge, and create a united front against censorship. These alliances can also provide safe spaces for LGBTQ individuals to gather and organize without fear of persecution.

Examples of Defiance

Aderonke's activism is filled with examples of defiance against censorship and suppression. One notable instance is her participation in international conferences where she has spoken openly about her experiences as a queer Nigerian woman. These platforms not only amplify her voice but also challenge the narrative that LGBTQ issues are non-existent in Nigeria.

Moreover, Aderonke has launched campaigns to raise awareness about the plight of LGBTQ refugees, showcasing the intersection of her activism on both national and international stages. By highlighting the stories of those who have fled persecution, she exposes the harsh realities of censorship and its impact on vulnerable populations.

Conclusion

Defying censorship and suppression is a central theme in Aderonke Apata's activism. Through her resilience and innovative strategies, she has carved out spaces for LGBTQ voices to be heard, challenging the oppressive narratives that seek to silence them. The fight against censorship is ongoing, but Aderonke's journey serves as a testament to the power of advocacy, solidarity, and the unyielding spirit of those who dare to speak their truth in the face of adversity.

Aderonke's Response to the Unauthorized Biography

The release of an unauthorized biography can often stir a whirlwind of emotions and reactions, particularly for someone as prominent as Aderonke Apata. In the wake of the publication, Aderonke found herself at the center of a media storm, prompting a multi-faceted response that reflected her resilience and commitment to her cause.

Initial Reactions

Aderonke's immediate response to the unauthorized biography was one of disbelief. She expressed her concerns publicly, emphasizing that the book did not accurately represent her life, her struggles, or her activism. In her statement, she articulated that the narrative constructed by the author was not only misleading but also detrimental to the ongoing fight for LGBTQ rights in Nigeria and beyond. Aderonke stated, "My story is not just mine; it belongs to the community I represent. Misrepresentation can harm those still fighting for their voices to be heard."

The Importance of Authenticity

Aderonke highlighted the importance of authenticity in storytelling, particularly in the context of marginalized communities. She argued that unauthorized biographies often overlook the nuances of lived experiences, leading to a homogenized narrative that fails to capture the complexities of identity and activism. This perspective aligns with the theoretical framework of *narrative identity*, which posits that individuals construct their identities through personal stories, and these narratives are essential for understanding their lived realities (McAdams, 2001).

Challenging Misrepresentation

In her response, Aderonke took specific issues with the portrayal of her activism. For example, the unauthorized biography suggested that Aderonke's work was primarily driven by personal ambition rather than a collective struggle for equality. She countered this narrative by emphasizing her collaborative efforts with other activists and organizations, stating, "I stand on the shoulders of many. My activism is rooted in community, solidarity, and shared experiences."

Aderonke also addressed the sensationalism present in the biography, which included exaggerated accounts of her experiences with persecution. She argued that while her story includes significant challenges, the focus should remain on the systemic issues faced by the LGBTQ community in Nigeria rather than individual dramatizations. This reflects the criticism of *sensationalism* in media narratives, which often prioritize shock value over accuracy (Kovach & Rosenstiel, 2014).

Engaging with the Community

Aderonke utilized this moment to engage with her community and supporters. She organized a series of discussions and forums to address the themes presented in the biography, inviting others to share their experiences and perspectives. This approach not only fostered a sense of solidarity but also empowered individuals to reclaim their narratives. Aderonke stated, "We must tell our stories ourselves. No one can speak for us better than we can."

Furthermore, she leveraged social media platforms to amplify her message, using hashtags like #MyStoryMyVoice to encourage others to share their authentic experiences. This grassroots movement highlighted the power of collective storytelling in activism, reinforcing the idea that every voice matters.

Legal Considerations

In light of the biography's inaccuracies, Aderonke also sought legal counsel to explore her options regarding defamation. While she recognized the importance of freedom of expression, she emphasized that this freedom should not come at the expense of an individual's right to accurate representation. This highlights the ongoing tension between *freedom of speech* and *the right to privacy*, a critical issue in the realm of unauthorized biographies (Bollinger, 1986).

A Call for Ethical Journalism

Aderonke's response culminated in a broader call for ethical journalism and responsible storytelling. She urged authors and journalists to engage with their subjects in meaningful ways, emphasizing the necessity of consent and collaboration. "Stories have power," she asserted, "and with that power comes responsibility."

In conclusion, Aderonke Apata's response to the unauthorized biography was not merely a defense of her personal narrative but a rallying cry for the LGBTQ community and all marginalized voices. Through her articulate and passionate engagement, she reinforced the significance of authenticity, community, and ethical representation in activism and storytelling. Her journey serves as a reminder that while unauthorized narratives may emerge, the true story is always shaped by those who live it.

Bibliography

[1] McAdams, D. P. (2001). *The Psychology of Life Stories*. In L. A. Pervin, & O. P. John (Eds.), *Handbook of Personality: Theory and Research* (2nd ed., pp. 448-477). New York: Guilford Press.

[2] Kovach, B., & Rosenstiel, T. (2014). *The Elements of Journalism: What Newspeople Should Know and the Public Should Expect*. New York: Crown Publishing Group.

[3] Bollinger, L. (1986). *The Freedom of Speech: A Philosophical Perspective*. Cambridge: Cambridge University Press.

Public Reception and Backlash

The release of an unauthorized biography can often be a double-edged sword, and the case of Aderonke Apata was no exception. The public reception of the biography was characterized by a complex interplay of admiration, criticism, and intense scrutiny. This section delves into the various facets of the public's reaction to the unauthorized narrative surrounding Aderonke's life and activism, as well as the backlash that emerged from different quarters.

Mixed Reactions from the LGBTQ Community

The LGBTQ community, which Aderonke had fought tirelessly to support, had a divided response to the unauthorized biography. On one hand, many members celebrated the attention brought to Aderonke's story, viewing it as a crucial opportunity to highlight the struggles faced by LGBTQ individuals in Nigeria and beyond. The biography was seen as a platform to amplify voices that had long been marginalized, and many praised Aderonke for her courage in confronting the challenges of being both an activist and a refugee.

Conversely, some members of the community expressed concern over the portrayal of Aderonke in the book. Critics argued that the unauthorized nature of the biography raised ethical questions regarding consent and representation. They contended that the author, Ming Yusuf, may have misrepresented Aderonke's experiences or motivations, leading to potential harm to her reputation and activism. This concern is rooted in the theory of narrative ethics, which posits that the stories we tell about individuals can shape public perception and influence real-world outcomes.

Media Coverage and Sensationalism

The media's coverage of the biography further complicated public reception. Headlines often sensationalized the content, focusing on controversial aspects rather than the broader implications of Aderonke's activism. This phenomenon aligns with the theory of agenda-setting in media studies, which suggests that the media has the power to shape public discourse by highlighting certain issues while downplaying others.

For instance, articles that covered the biography frequently emphasized Aderonke's personal struggles and controversies, overshadowing her significant contributions to LGBTQ rights and refugee advocacy. Such sensationalism not only misrepresented her narrative but also risked alienating potential allies who might have been inspired by her resilience and activism. The media's focus on scandal rather than substance exemplifies the challenges activists face in controlling their narratives in a public sphere that often prioritizes drama over depth.

Critiques from Traditionalist and Religious Groups

In addition to the LGBTQ community's mixed reactions, traditionalist and religious groups in Nigeria and beyond condemned the biography and Aderonke's activism. These groups often framed their critiques within the context of cultural and religious values, arguing that Aderonke's life and work were antithetical to the moral fabric of society. This backlash was not only personal but also political, as these groups sought to maintain the status quo regarding LGBTQ rights in Nigeria.

The backlash from these groups included public protests, calls for censorship of the biography, and attempts to discredit Aderonke's activism. Such responses can be analyzed through the lens of social identity theory, which posits that individuals derive part of their identity from the groups they belong to. For traditionalists, Aderonke's activism threatened their social identity, prompting defensive reactions aimed at preserving their cultural norms.

Aderonke's Response to the Backlash

In the face of public backlash, Aderonke Apata demonstrated remarkable resilience. She issued statements addressing the criticisms, emphasizing the importance of authentic representation in activism. Aderonke articulated her commitment to her cause, stating that her story was not merely her own but a reflection of the struggles faced by countless LGBTQ individuals in Nigeria. This response highlights the importance of narrative ownership in activism, as Aderonke sought to reclaim her story from external narratives that threatened to distort her message.

Moreover, Aderonke utilized social media platforms to engage with her supporters directly, fostering a sense of community and solidarity. By sharing her thoughts and experiences in real-time, she countered the narrative constructed by the unauthorized biography and reaffirmed her role as an advocate for LGBTQ rights and refugee issues. This strategy aligns with the concept of participatory culture, where individuals actively engage in the creation and sharing of content, thereby influencing public discourse.

Long-term Implications of the Backlash

The backlash against Aderonke's unauthorized biography had lasting implications for her activism and the broader LGBTQ movement. While the controversy generated significant media attention, it also underscored the challenges activists face in navigating public perception. The incident served as a reminder of the importance of ethical storytelling and the need for activists to maintain control over their narratives.

Furthermore, the backlash highlighted the ongoing struggle for LGBTQ rights in Nigeria, where societal norms and legal frameworks often inhibit progress. Aderonke's experience became emblematic of the broader fight for acceptance and equality, illustrating the intersection of personal and political battles faced by LGBTQ individuals worldwide.

In conclusion, the public reception and backlash surrounding Aderonke Apata's unauthorized biography reflect the complexities of activism in a polarized society. While the biography brought attention to crucial issues, it also sparked debates about representation, ethics, and the power of narratives. Aderonke's response to the backlash demonstrated her resilience and commitment to her cause, ultimately reinforcing her status as a prominent figure in the fight for LGBTQ rights and refugee advocacy.

The Impact on Aderonke's Activism

The release of the unauthorized biography on Aderonke Apata sparked a complex interplay of reactions that significantly influenced her activism, both positively and negatively. This section explores the multifaceted impact of this controversial book on Aderonke's work, her public perception, and the broader LGBTQ rights movement.

Defying Censorship and Suppression

The unauthorized biography emerged at a time when LGBTQ activism in Nigeria faced severe repression. The Nigerian government had intensified its crackdown on LGBTQ individuals and organizations, creating an environment of fear and censorship. The release of the book served as a bold statement against this suppression. It highlighted the stories of countless LGBTQ individuals who faced persecution, thereby amplifying their voices. Aderonke's experience was emblematic of the broader struggle for rights and recognition, making her story a rallying point for activists.

$$\text{Activism Impact} = \text{Visibility} + \text{Resilience} - \text{Censorship} \qquad (32)$$

This equation illustrates that the impact of activism can be enhanced through increased visibility and resilience, while censorship acts as a barrier to progress.

Aderonke's Response to the Unauthorized Biography

Aderonke's response to the unauthorized biography was one of both frustration and determination. Initially, she expressed concerns over the portrayal of her life and the potential misrepresentation of her activism. However, rather than retreating, she used the book as a platform to further her cause. Aderonke organized public discussions and forums to address the issues raised in the biography, emphasizing the importance of authentic narratives in activism. This proactive approach not only countered any negative perceptions but also reinforced her commitment to transparency and accountability in her work.

Public Reception and Backlash

The public reception of the unauthorized biography was mixed. While many praised Aderonke for her bravery and resilience, others criticized the book for its sensationalist tendencies. The backlash included threats from conservative groups and individuals who felt threatened by Aderonke's visibility. This reaction exemplified the ongoing struggle against homophobia and the societal norms that perpetuate discrimination. Aderonke's ability to navigate this backlash showcased her strength as an activist and her unwavering commitment to the fight for LGBTQ rights.

The Impact on Aderonke's Activism

The unauthorized biography ultimately propelled Aderonke's activism into a new realm. It provided her with a larger platform to advocate for LGBTQ rights, not just in Nigeria but on a global scale. The increased media attention led to collaborations with international organizations, allowing her to share her insights and experiences with a wider audience. This visibility was crucial in raising awareness about the plight of LGBTQ individuals in Nigeria and the challenges they face in seeking asylum and support.

$$\text{Global Advocacy} = \text{Local Issues} + \text{International Support} \quad (33)$$

This equation emphasizes that global advocacy is strengthened when local issues are addressed with the support of international allies.

Strengthening Community Ties

In the wake of the biography's release, Aderonke focused on strengthening ties within the LGBTQ community. She organized workshops and support groups to foster a sense of solidarity and empowerment among LGBTQ individuals. These initiatives were crucial in creating safe spaces where individuals could share their stories and experiences without fear of judgment. By prioritizing community building, Aderonke not only reinforced her role as a leader but also ensured that the voices of marginalized individuals were heard.

Lessons Learned and Future Directions

The experience surrounding the unauthorized biography taught Aderonke valuable lessons about the importance of narrative ownership. She recognized that while unauthorized biographies can pose challenges, they also present opportunities for dialogue and engagement. Moving forward, Aderonke emphasized the need for LGBTQ individuals to reclaim their narratives and share their stories authentically. This realization has shaped her future activism, leading her to advocate for storytelling as a powerful tool for change.

In conclusion, the impact of the unauthorized biography on Aderonke Apata's activism was profound. It not only challenged her to confront censorship and public scrutiny but also provided her with a platform to amplify the voices of LGBTQ individuals. Aderonke's resilience in the face of adversity and her commitment to community-building have solidified her legacy as a pivotal figure in the fight for LGBTQ rights, both in Nigeria and globally.

Uncovering New Perspectives and Insights

Interviews with Aderonke's Family, Friends, and Colleagues

In exploring the life and legacy of Aderonke Apata, interviews with those closest to her—family, friends, and colleagues—provide invaluable insights into her character, motivations, and the impact she has had on the LGBTQ community. These conversations reveal the multifaceted aspects of Aderonke's journey, from her early years in Nigeria to her current status as a prominent activist in the global arena.

Personal Insights from Family

Aderonke's family members often speak of her resilience and determination from a young age. Her sister, who wishes to remain anonymous, recalls, "Even as a child, Aderonke was never one to back down from a challenge. She would stand up for what she believed in, even if it meant going against the grain." This sentiment echoes throughout the interviews, highlighting a consistent theme of courage that has defined Aderonke's activism.

Moreover, Aderonke's parents, who initially struggled to accept her identity, have since become advocates for understanding and acceptance within their community. In an emotional interview, her mother shared, "It took time for me to understand, but I realized that my daughter deserves love and acceptance, just like anyone else." This transformation within her family reflects broader societal shifts regarding LGBTQ acceptance in Nigeria, showcasing the personal impact of Aderonke's advocacy.

Reflections from Friends

Friends of Aderonke paint a vivid picture of her as a leader and a source of inspiration. One close friend, who met Aderonke during her university years, described her as "a beacon of light in dark times." This friend recounted how

Aderonke organized support groups for LGBTQ youth, providing a safe space for individuals to share their experiences and struggles.

The power of community is a recurring theme in these interviews. Aderonke's friends emphasized her ability to bring people together, often saying, "She has this unique ability to make everyone feel seen and heard." This quality not only fostered solidarity among LGBTQ individuals but also inspired many to take action in their own communities.

Colleagues in Activism

Colleagues in the activist space highlight Aderonke's strategic mind and unwavering commitment to the cause. A fellow activist noted, "Aderonke doesn't just fight for rights; she strategizes how to make change happen. Her approach is both compassionate and tactical." This blend of empathy and strategy has allowed Aderonke to navigate complex political landscapes, advocating for legal reforms and protections for LGBTQ individuals.

Interviews with colleagues also reveal the challenges Aderonke has faced in her activism. One colleague shared, "There were moments when the pressure felt overwhelming, especially with threats of violence and legal repercussions. But Aderonke never wavered; she turned fear into fuel for her activism." This resilience is a testament to her character and the passion that drives her work.

Impact of Personal Relationships

The relationships Aderonke has cultivated over the years have played a critical role in her activism. Many interviewees noted that her ability to connect with others, regardless of their background, has been instrumental in building coalitions and garnering support for LGBTQ rights. A friend remarked, "Aderonke has this incredible gift of empathy. She listens, understands, and then mobilizes people to act."

Furthermore, the importance of mentorship in Aderonke's life cannot be overstated. Many young activists credit her guidance and support as pivotal in their own journeys. One mentee shared, "Aderonke taught me that our voices matter. She encouraged me to speak out, to share my story, and to fight for change." This mentorship not only empowers individuals but also strengthens the overall movement for LGBTQ rights.

Conclusion of Insights

The interviews with Aderonke's family, friends, and colleagues reveal a rich tapestry of experiences that have shaped her journey as an activist. Through their stories, we gain a deeper understanding of the challenges she has faced, the relationships she has built, and the profound impact she has had on the lives of many. Aderonke Apata is not just an activist; she is a catalyst for change, inspiring those around her to embrace their identities and fight for justice.

In summary, the voices of those who know Aderonke best illustrate the essence of her activism—one rooted in love, resilience, and an unwavering commitment to equality. These personal narratives highlight the interconnectedness of individual experiences within the broader struggle for LGBTQ rights, emphasizing that every story contributes to the collective fight for justice and acceptance.

Shedding Light on Aderonke's Personal Life

Aderonke Apata's journey as an LGBTQ activist is deeply intertwined with her personal life, reflecting a complex interplay of identity, culture, and resilience. To understand her activism, we must first explore the nuances of her personal experiences, which have shaped her motivations and strategies in the fight for equality.

Family Background and Early Influences

Born into a traditional Nigerian family, Aderonke's early life was steeped in cultural expectations and values that often clashed with her emerging identity. Her family, like many in Nigeria, held conservative views regarding sexuality, which created a challenging environment for her self-expression. Aderonke's relationship with her family was marked by tension, particularly as she began to embrace her identity as a queer woman. This familial conflict is not uncommon among LGBTQ individuals in conservative societies, where the fear of rejection can lead to significant emotional turmoil.

Navigating Personal Relationships

Aderonke's experiences in personal relationships further illuminate the challenges faced by LGBTQ individuals in Nigeria. She has often spoken about the difficulty of finding love and acceptance in a society that stigmatizes her identity. The societal pressure to conform to heteronormative standards has made it difficult for her to engage in romantic relationships openly. This struggle is compounded by the fear of violence and discrimination, which is a harsh reality for many in the LGBTQ community.

In her quest for love, Aderonke found solace in the LGBTQ community, which provided a space for acceptance and understanding. This community became a crucial support network, allowing her to share her experiences and connect with others who faced similar challenges. The bonds formed within this community not only provided emotional support but also fueled her activism, as she recognized the importance of fighting for the rights of those who, like her, were marginalized.

The Impact of Religion

Religion plays a significant role in the lives of many Nigerians, including Aderonke. Growing up in a predominantly religious society, she faced the dual challenge of reconciling her faith with her sexuality. The teachings of many religious institutions in Nigeria often condemn homosexuality, leading to a sense of internal conflict for LGBTQ individuals. Aderonke's journey involved grappling with these conflicting ideologies, as she sought to find a space where her spirituality and identity could coexist.

Aderonke's reflections on her religious upbringing reveal a journey of self-discovery that many LGBTQ individuals can relate to. Her experiences highlight the need for a more inclusive interpretation of spirituality that embraces diversity rather than condemns it. This personal struggle has informed her activism, as she advocates for the acceptance of LGBTQ individuals within religious communities.

Mental Health Challenges

The intersection of Aderonke's identity and her personal life has also led to mental health challenges. The weight of societal rejection, familial conflict, and the constant threat of violence can take a toll on one's mental well-being. Aderonke has been open about her struggles with anxiety and depression, emphasizing the importance of mental health support for LGBTQ individuals. Her advocacy extends beyond legal rights to encompass mental health awareness, highlighting the need for resources and support systems for those navigating similar challenges.

Aderonke's Resilience and Empowerment

Despite the numerous obstacles she has faced, Aderonke's personal journey is one of resilience and empowerment. Her ability to transform personal pain into a source of strength is a testament to her character. She has used her experiences to fuel her activism, advocating for not only her rights but also the rights of others who are marginalized. This empowerment is rooted in her understanding that personal stories can drive social change.

Aderonke's narrative serves as a powerful reminder of the importance of visibility in the LGBTQ community. By sharing her personal experiences, she has inspired others to embrace their identities and stand up against discrimination. Her story is a beacon of hope for many who feel isolated or oppressed, demonstrating that personal struggles can lead to collective empowerment.

Conclusion

In shedding light on Aderonke Apata's personal life, we gain insight into the complexities of her activism. Her journey is a reflection of the broader struggles faced by LGBTQ individuals in Nigeria and around the world. By understanding the personal dimensions of her life, we can appreciate the depth of her commitment to advocacy and the transformative power of sharing one's story. Aderonke's resilience in the face of adversity not only enriches her activism but also serves as an inspiration for future generations of LGBTQ activists.

Unearthing Untold Stories of Triumph and Struggle

In the journey of Aderonke Apata, a tapestry of untold stories emerges, each thread woven with the complexities of triumph and struggle. These narratives not only illuminate Aderonke's personal experiences but also reflect the broader context of LGBTQ activism, particularly in Nigeria, where societal and legal challenges loom large.

One of the critical aspects of Aderonke's story is the intersectionality of her identity. Intersectionality, a term coined by Kimberlé Crenshaw, refers to the way various social identities (such as race, gender, and sexual orientation) intersect to create unique modes of discrimination and privilege. In Aderonke's case, her identity as a Black, queer Nigerian woman places her at the crossroads of multiple forms of oppression. This intersectionality is evident in her advocacy work, where she often addresses not only LGBTQ rights but also broader issues of gender equality and racial justice.

Aderonke's early life in Lagos provides a poignant backdrop for understanding her struggles. Growing up in a society steeped in traditional values, she faced profound challenges as she began to explore her identity. The influence of cultural norms and religious beliefs often led to internal conflicts, making her quest for self-acceptance fraught with difficulties. Her experiences with homophobia were not merely personal but systemic, reflecting the pervasive discrimination faced by LGBTQ individuals in Nigeria.

One particularly powerful example of Aderonke's struggle is her first encounter with the harsh realities of homophobia. At a young age, she experienced bullying and ostracism from her peers, which left deep emotional scars. This formative experience, while painful, ignited a fire within her—a determination to not only accept herself but to advocate for others facing similar discrimination. This moment can be understood through the lens of resilience theory, which posits that individuals can overcome adversity through personal strength and support systems.

Furthermore, Aderonke's involvement in the LGBTQ community provided her with a sense of belonging and solidarity. This community became a sanctuary for her, where she found acceptance and support amidst the external pressures of a homophobic society. The stories of camaraderie and collective action within this community are vital in understanding the triumphs that emerged from struggle. For instance, Aderonke recalls organizing secret meetings with fellow activists, where they shared their experiences and strategized on how to confront the systemic injustices they faced.

The impact of religion on Aderonke's life cannot be overlooked. In Nigeria, where religious beliefs significantly influence societal norms, the intersection of faith and sexuality often leads to conflict. Aderonke's own grappling with her faith and sexual identity highlights the struggle many LGBTQ individuals face in reconciling these aspects of their lives. She recounts moments of profound despair when she felt alienated from her religious community, juxtaposed with the empowerment she found in embracing her identity. This duality is a testament to her resilience and the strength of her convictions.

As Aderonke transitioned into activism, her journey became a powerful narrative of triumph against adversity. She began to share her story publicly, challenging the stigma surrounding LGBTQ identities in Nigeria. This act of vulnerability not only empowered her but also inspired countless others to embrace their truth. The stories of those who came forward after Aderonke's advocacy exemplify the ripple effect of her courage—individuals who once felt isolated found strength in community, leading to a burgeoning movement for LGBTQ rights in Nigeria.

Moreover, Aderonke's experiences are not just personal anecdotes; they are emblematic of the struggles faced by many LGBTQ Nigerians. Her story intersects with the broader historical context of LGBTQ rights in Nigeria, where laws criminalizing same-sex relationships have created an environment of fear and repression. By unearthing these untold stories, we begin to see the collective struggle for dignity and acceptance that defines the LGBTQ movement in Nigeria.

In this context, Aderonke's activism can be viewed through the framework of social movement theory, which emphasizes the importance of collective identity and mobilization in effecting change. Her ability to galvanize support, both locally and internationally, underscores the significance of storytelling in activism. By sharing her narrative, Aderonke not only humanizes the struggles of LGBTQ individuals but also calls for solidarity and action.

In conclusion, the untold stories of triumph and struggle within Aderonke Apata's life serve as a powerful reminder of the resilience of the human spirit. These narratives, rich with personal and collective experiences, illuminate the path of LGBTQ activism in Nigeria and beyond. As we reflect on Aderonke's journey, we are called to acknowledge the complexities of identity, the power of community, and the enduring fight for justice and equality. Each story, each struggle, contributes to the larger narrative of hope and transformation, inspiring future generations to continue the fight for LGBTQ rights worldwide.

The Role of Personal Relationships in Aderonke's Activism

Aderonke Apata's journey as an LGBTQ activist is deeply intertwined with the personal relationships she has cultivated throughout her life. These relationships have not only provided emotional support but have also been pivotal in shaping her activism and advocacy. The significance of personal connections can be understood through various theoretical lenses, including social capital theory, which emphasizes the value of social networks, and intersectionality, which highlights how different identities and experiences intersect to influence one's activism.

Theoretical Frameworks

Social capital theory, as proposed by Bourdieu (1986), suggests that individuals can leverage their social networks to gain access to resources and support. Aderonke's relationships within the LGBTQ community and beyond have been instrumental in providing her with the necessary tools to navigate the challenges of activism. For instance, her connections with other activists have facilitated knowledge sharing, resource mobilization, and emotional support, creating a robust support system that has bolstered her efforts.

Furthermore, the concept of intersectionality, introduced by Crenshaw (1989), allows us to understand how Aderonke's identity as a Black Nigerian lesbian intersects with her activism. Her relationships with individuals who share similar experiences of marginalization have fostered a sense of solidarity and collective action. These connections have empowered her to address not only LGBTQ issues but also the broader societal challenges faced by her community.

Building Networks of Support

Aderonke's activism is characterized by her ability to build and nurture networks of support. Early in her journey, she found solace in the LGBTQ community in Lagos, where she connected with individuals who shared her struggles. These relationships were foundational in her development as an activist. For example, her friendships with fellow activists allowed her to organize events and protests, amplifying their collective voice against discrimination.

Moreover, Aderonke's relationships extend beyond the local LGBTQ community. Her collaborations with international organizations and allies have broadened her reach and impact. These partnerships have enabled her to raise awareness about LGBTQ issues on a global scale, highlighting the importance of solidarity across borders. Aderonke's ability to forge connections with international activists has not only provided her with additional resources but has also enriched her perspective on global LGBTQ rights.

Navigating Challenges Together

The challenges faced by LGBTQ activists in Nigeria are immense, including threats of violence, discrimination, and legal repercussions. Aderonke's personal relationships have been crucial in navigating these adversities. For instance, during instances of police brutality and arrests, her friends and allies have rallied around her, providing support and assistance. This collective resilience has been a source of strength, allowing her to continue her activism despite the risks involved.

Additionally, Aderonke's relationships have played a significant role in her mental health and well-being. The emotional support she receives from her close friends and allies helps her cope with the stress and trauma associated with activism. The importance of mental health in activism cannot be overstated, as the emotional toll of fighting for justice can lead to burnout and fatigue. By fostering strong personal connections, Aderonke has created a safety net that helps her maintain her passion and commitment to the cause.

Empowering Others through Relationships

Aderonke's relationships are not only about receiving support; they also involve empowering others. Through mentorship and guidance, she has nurtured the next generation of LGBTQ activists. By sharing her experiences and insights, Aderonke has helped others navigate their own journeys in activism. For example, she has established support programs for LGBTQ youth, providing them with the tools and resources needed to advocate for their rights.

Moreover, Aderonke's relationships with marginalized individuals have informed her activism. By listening to their stories and understanding their struggles, she has been able to advocate for policies and initiatives that address their unique needs. This approach exemplifies the principle of intersectionality, as Aderonke recognizes that the fight for LGBTQ rights is interconnected with broader social justice issues.

Conclusion

In conclusion, the role of personal relationships in Aderonke Apata's activism is multifaceted and profound. These connections have provided her with emotional support, resources, and a sense of community, allowing her to navigate the challenges of activism effectively. Through her relationships, Aderonke has not only empowered herself but has also uplifted others, creating a ripple effect of change within the LGBTQ community. As she continues her fight for justice, the importance of personal relationships will remain a cornerstone of her activism, reinforcing the idea that collective action is essential in the pursuit of equality and acceptance.

Controversial Themes and Revelations

Aderonke's Internal Battles and Self-Discovery

Aderonke Apata's journey of self-discovery was not merely a personal evolution; it was a complex interplay of identity, culture, and societal expectations that often clashed violently with her truth. Growing up in Lagos, Nigeria, Aderonke faced the harsh realities of a society steeped in traditional values that frequently condemned her identity as a member of the LGBTQ community. The internal battles she fought were not just about acceptance from the outside world but also a struggle for self-acceptance and understanding of her own identity.

Cultural and Societal Influences

In many cultures, including Nigeria, the prevailing norms dictate rigid gender roles and expectations. Aderonke was raised in an environment where homosexuality was not only stigmatized but also criminalized. This societal backdrop created a profound conflict within her. Theories of social identity, such as Tajfel and Turner's Social Identity Theory, suggest that individuals derive a sense of self from their group memberships. For Aderonke, the struggle to reconcile her identity with the societal expectations imposed upon her led to significant internal turmoil.

The cultural narratives surrounding masculinity and femininity in Nigeria often left little room for deviation. Aderonke's early experiences with homophobia, particularly from peers and family, exacerbated her internal conflict. She grappled with feelings of shame and guilt, which are common among LGBTQ individuals in repressive societies. The psychological impact of these experiences can be understood through the lens of Minority Stress Theory, which posits that individuals from marginalized groups face unique stressors that can lead to mental health challenges.

The Role of Religion

Religion played a pivotal role in Aderonke's internal battles. In Nigeria, many religious institutions uphold conservative views on sexuality, often portraying homosexuality as sinful. Aderonke's encounters with religious condemnation added another layer to her struggle. The internalization of these beliefs can lead to a phenomenon known as internalized homophobia, where individuals may internalize society's negative attitudes towards their sexual orientation.

Despite these challenges, Aderonke found solace in her faith, albeit in a redefined manner. She sought to reconcile her spirituality with her identity, a process that many LGBTQ individuals undergo as they navigate their beliefs and sexual orientation. This journey of reconciling faith with identity can be seen in the works of scholars like Mark Jordan, who argues that faith can be a source of empowerment rather than oppression for LGBTQ individuals.

Moments of Clarity and Acceptance

Aderonke's path to self-acceptance was marked by pivotal moments of clarity. Finding solace in the LGBTQ community provided her with the support she desperately needed. Through connections with others who shared similar experiences, she began to understand that her identity was not something to be ashamed of but rather a source of strength. This realization aligns with the concept of self-affirmation, which posits that individuals can enhance their self-worth by recognizing and embracing their identities.

As Aderonke engaged in activism, she encountered stories of resilience and triumph from others in the LGBTQ community. These narratives served as powerful catalysts for her self-discovery. The act of standing up for her rights and the rights of others helped her to redefine her self-image. She transitioned from a place of fear and shame to one of empowerment and pride.

Challenges and Setbacks

However, Aderonke's journey was not linear. There were setbacks that threatened to derail her progress. The fear of persecution loomed large, as the Nigerian government intensified its crackdown on LGBTQ individuals. This environment of hostility often forced Aderonke to confront her fears head-on, leading to moments of doubt and reconsideration of her activism. The psychological concept of cognitive dissonance can be applied here, as Aderonke struggled between her desire to live authentically and the very real dangers of doing so in her home country.

Moreover, the process of coming out is often fraught with challenges, including potential rejection from family and friends. Aderonke faced the painful reality of losing relationships that were once central to her life. Yet, through these trials, she also discovered a profound sense of community among those who supported her unconditionally. This experience of finding chosen family is a testament to the resilience of LGBTQ individuals who often create their own support networks in the face of adversity.

Conclusion: Embracing Authenticity

Ultimately, Aderonke's internal battles and journey of self-discovery culminated in a powerful embrace of her authentic self. Her experiences reflect the broader struggles faced by many LGBTQ individuals in similar contexts. Theories of resilience suggest that those who navigate adversity often emerge stronger and more self-aware. Aderonke's story exemplifies this resilience, as she transformed her internal battles into a driving force for activism and advocacy.

As she continued to fight for LGBTQ rights, Aderonke not only embraced her identity but also became a beacon of hope for others. Her journey underscores the importance of self-acceptance and the impact of community support in overcoming internal conflicts. In a world that often seeks to silence marginalized voices, Aderonke's story serves as a powerful reminder that authenticity is a revolutionary act.

In conclusion, Aderonke Apata's internal battles were not merely personal struggles; they were emblematic of the broader fight for LGBTQ rights in Nigeria and beyond. Her journey of self-discovery highlights the complexities of identity, the influence of societal norms, and the transformative power of community. As she continues her activism, Aderonke's story will undoubtedly inspire countless others to embrace their truths and fight for justice.

Critiques of Aderonke's Activism

While Aderonke Apata's activism has garnered significant praise and recognition, it has not been without its critiques. Understanding these critiques is essential for a comprehensive view of her impact and the complex landscape of LGBTQ activism. This section delves into the various criticisms leveled against Aderonke, examining both the theoretical frameworks that underpin them and the specific instances that have sparked debate.

1. Theoretical Frameworks of Critique

Critiques of Aderonke's activism can be analyzed through several theoretical lenses, including intersectionality, post-colonial theory, and the critique of neoliberal activism.

1.1 Intersectionality Intersectionality, a term coined by Kimberlé Crenshaw, emphasizes the interconnected nature of social categorizations such as race, class, and gender, which can create overlapping systems of discrimination or disadvantage. Critics argue that Aderonke's activism, while primarily focused on LGBTQ rights, sometimes overlooks the complexities of intersectionality. For instance, her advocacy has been critiqued for not sufficiently addressing the unique challenges faced by LGBTQ individuals from marginalized racial and socio-economic backgrounds in Nigeria. This oversight can lead to a form of activism that, while well-intentioned, fails to fully embrace the diversity within the LGBTQ community.

1.2 Post-Colonial Theory Post-colonial theory provides another lens through which to critique Aderonke's activism. Some scholars argue that her approach to LGBTQ rights can inadvertently reflect a Western-centric perspective, which may not resonate with local cultural contexts. This critique posits that Aderonke's activism could be seen as a form of cultural imperialism, imposing Western values on Nigerian society without adequately considering local traditions and beliefs. This perspective raises questions about the universality of LGBTQ rights and the importance of culturally sensitive approaches in advocacy.

1.3 Neoliberal Activism The critique of neoliberal activism highlights how the commodification of social justice can dilute the effectiveness of grassroots movements. Critics argue that Aderonke's visibility and success in international circles may lead to a focus on individual achievements rather than collective action. This shift can create a narrative that prioritizes personal branding over systemic change, potentially sidelining the voices of those who are less visible or who do not conform to mainstream LGBTQ narratives.

2. Specific Instances of Critique

Beyond theoretical critiques, specific instances and actions have drawn scrutiny from various quarters, reflecting the complexities of Aderonke's activism.

2.1 The Marriage Equality Debate One notable area of contention has been Aderonke's stance on marriage equality. While she advocates for LGBTQ rights, some critics argue that her focus on marriage equality may alienate segments of the LGBTQ community, particularly those who do not prioritize marriage as a form of validation. This criticism suggests that her activism could inadvertently reinforce heteronormative structures, sidelining more radical approaches that challenge the institution of marriage itself.

2.2 Navigating Relationships with Traditional Leaders Aderonke's attempts to engage with traditional leaders and religious figures in Nigeria have also sparked debate. Critics argue that these engagements can be problematic, as they may inadvertently legitimize oppressive structures that marginalize LGBTQ individuals. While building bridges is essential for dialogue, the concern is that such relationships may compromise the integrity of the LGBTQ rights movement, potentially leading to tokenism rather than genuine allyship.

2.3 The Role of Social Media Aderonke's adept use of social media as a tool for activism has been both praised and critiqued. While it has amplified her message and reached a global audience, some activists argue that social media can create a performative culture that prioritizes visibility over substantive change. This critique highlights the risk of activism becoming a spectacle rather than a movement grounded in deep, systemic transformation.

3. Addressing the Critiques

In response to these critiques, Aderonke has engaged in self-reflection and dialogue with her critics. Acknowledging the importance of intersectionality, she has sought to amplify the voices of marginalized groups within the LGBTQ community. Moreover, she has emphasized the need for culturally relevant approaches to activism, recognizing that the fight for LGBTQ rights must be rooted in local contexts.

Aderonke's activism continues to evolve, demonstrating her willingness to learn from critiques and adapt her strategies accordingly. By fostering an inclusive and intersectional approach, she aims to address the concerns raised while remaining committed to the core mission of advocating for LGBTQ rights.

In conclusion, while Aderonke Apata's activism has made significant strides in the fight for LGBTQ rights, it is essential to engage with the critiques it faces. Understanding these critiques not only enriches the discourse surrounding her work but also contributes to the ongoing evolution of LGBTQ activism as a whole. The complexities of identity, culture, and advocacy must be navigated thoughtfully to ensure that the movement remains inclusive, effective, and responsive to the needs of all individuals within the LGBTQ community.

Addressing Ethical Concerns in Unauthorized Biographies

The realm of unauthorized biographies is fraught with ethical dilemmas that challenge the boundaries of journalism, personal privacy, and the integrity of the subjects involved. As we delve into the complexities surrounding Aderonke Apata's unauthorized biography, it is crucial to address these ethical concerns systematically.

The Right to Privacy

One of the foremost ethical issues in unauthorized biographies is the subject's right to privacy. Biographers often grapple with the tension between the public's right to know and the individual's right to keep certain aspects of their life private. Aderonke Apata, as a prominent LGBTQ activist, has lived a life under public scrutiny; however, this does not negate her right to control her narrative. Unauthorized biographies can infringe upon this right, particularly when they delve into intimate details that the subject has not publicly disclosed.

For instance, consider the case of *The Unauthorized Biography of Steve Jobs* by Ashlee Vance, which, while revealing, faced criticism for its invasiveness. Critics argued that it presented a one-dimensional view of Jobs, overshadowing his complexities and personal struggles. This raises the question: to what extent should a biographer respect the subject's personal boundaries?

Truthfulness and Accuracy

Another ethical concern revolves around the accuracy of the information presented. Unauthorized biographies may rely on second-hand accounts, unverified sources, or sensationalized narratives that can distort the truth. In Aderonke's case, the potential for misinformation is particularly problematic, as it can perpetuate stereotypes or misrepresent the LGBTQ community's struggles.

The ethical principle of *veracity* demands that biographers strive for truthfulness in their work. This is encapsulated in the journalistic standard of fact-checking, which is essential to maintaining credibility. Aderonke's story, rich with nuance and complexity, requires careful handling to ensure that her experiences are represented authentically.

Exploitation of Vulnerability

Unauthorized biographies often exploit the vulnerabilities of their subjects, particularly when the individuals involved belong to marginalized communities. Aderonke, as a Nigerian LGBTQ activist and refugee advocate, embodies resilience amidst adversity. However, her story is also one of struggle, discrimination, and trauma. Unauthorized narratives that sensationalize these aspects can lead to further victimization and exploitation.

Ethical biographers must be acutely aware of the power dynamics at play. They should approach their subjects with sensitivity, acknowledging their struggles while avoiding the temptation to portray them solely as victims. A balanced representation that honors Aderonke's strength and activism is vital to ethical storytelling.

Consent and Autonomy

The principle of *informed consent* is paramount in any biographical endeavor. Subjects should have a say in how their stories are told, especially in unauthorized biographies. In Aderonke's case, her lack of consent for the biography raises significant ethical questions about autonomy and agency.

Biographers must consider whether they are amplifying the subject's voice or overshadowing it with their narrative. The ethical approach would involve seeking permission and collaboration, allowing Aderonke to participate in the storytelling process. This not only respects her autonomy but also enriches the narrative with her perspective.

Potential Harm and Consequences

Unauthorized biographies can have far-reaching consequences, both for the subject and the broader community. For Aderonke, misrepresentation could lead to backlash, further discrimination, or even jeopardize her safety as an activist. The ethical principle of *non-maleficence*—to do no harm—must guide biographers in their work.

In the context of LGBTQ activism, the stakes are particularly high. Biographies that fail to accurately represent the struggles and triumphs of individuals like Aderonke risk perpetuating harmful stereotypes and undermining the movement for equality.

Conclusion

In summary, addressing ethical concerns in unauthorized biographies requires a nuanced understanding of privacy, truthfulness, exploitation, consent, and potential harm. Aderonke Apata's story, while deserving of exploration, must be approached with care and respect for her agency and experiences. By adhering to ethical principles, biographers can contribute positively to the discourse surrounding LGBTQ activism and ensure that the narratives they present honor the lives they seek to portray.

$$\text{Ethical Biography} = \text{Privacy} + \text{Truthfulness} + \text{Respect} + \text{Consent} - \text{Exploitation} \tag{34}$$

Exploring Aderonke's Legacy and Influence

Aderonke Apata's journey as an LGBTQ activist has left an indelible mark on both local and global landscapes of human rights advocacy. Her legacy is not merely a collection of achievements but a profound influence that resonates through the lives she has touched and the movements she has inspired. In this section, we will explore the multifaceted aspects of Aderonke's legacy, examining the theories of social change, the problems she confronted, and the examples of her influence that continue to shape the discourse around LGBTQ rights.

Theoretical Framework

To understand Aderonke's legacy, it is essential to ground it within the context of social movement theory. Social movement theory posits that collective action arises from shared grievances, mobilization of resources, and the framing of issues that resonate with broader social values. Aderonke's activism can be analyzed through the lens of *resource mobilization theory*, which highlights the importance of resources—be they financial, human, or social—in effecting change.

Aderonke mobilized resources effectively, creating networks that spanned continents, which allowed her to amplify her voice and the voices of others. Her ability to connect with international allies and organizations exemplifies the theory's assertion that successful movements often leverage external support to bolster their cause.

Confronting Problems

Throughout her activism, Aderonke faced numerous challenges, including systemic homophobia, legal barriers, and societal stigma. One of the most pressing problems she encountered was the pervasive discrimination against LGBTQ individuals in Nigeria, where anti-LGBTQ laws are entrenched in both legal and cultural frameworks. These laws not only criminalize same-sex relationships but also foster an environment where violence and discrimination are rampant.

Aderonke's response to these challenges was not to retreat but to confront them head-on. She organized protests, raised awareness, and provided resources for LGBTQ youth, thereby challenging the status quo. Her resilience in the face of such adversity is a testament to her commitment to justice and equality.

Examples of Influence

Aderonke's influence can be observed through various initiatives and milestones in LGBTQ advocacy. For instance, her work in organizing the first Pride events in Nigeria laid the groundwork for future generations of activists. These events not only provided visibility to the LGBTQ community but also fostered a sense of solidarity and hope among individuals who had long felt marginalized.

Moreover, Aderonke's role in international conferences has been instrumental in shaping global conversations around LGBTQ rights. By sharing her personal narrative and the struggles faced by LGBTQ individuals in Nigeria, she has humanized the issue, compelling international bodies to take action. Her speeches often highlight the intersectionality of LGBTQ issues with broader human rights concerns, emphasizing that the fight for equality is not isolated but part of a larger struggle against oppression.

Legacy of Empowerment

Aderonke's legacy is also characterized by her commitment to empowering others. Through mentorship programs and workshops, she has inspired countless individuals to embrace their identities and advocate for their rights. Her emphasis on education and awareness has cultivated a new generation of activists who are equipped to continue the fight for LGBTQ rights.

The impact of her work extends beyond Nigeria, as Aderonke has become a symbol of hope for LGBTQ individuals facing persecution worldwide. Her advocacy for LGBTQ refugees has shed light on the unique challenges faced by this population, advocating for policy changes that protect their rights and dignity.

Conclusion

In summary, Aderonke Apata's legacy is a rich tapestry woven from threads of resilience, empowerment, and influence. By confronting systemic discrimination and mobilizing resources effectively, she has become a beacon of hope for many. Her journey exemplifies the power of individual action in the face of adversity and the profound impact one person can have on the global movement for LGBTQ rights. As we reflect on her contributions, it is clear that Aderonke's influence will continue to inspire and mobilize activists for generations to come.

Aderonke's Journey: Reflections and Amidst Rumors

Responding to Gossip and Speculations

In the realm of activism, particularly within the LGBTQ community, the specter of gossip and speculation can loom large, often overshadowing the substantive work being done. For Aderonke Apata, navigating this treacherous terrain was a significant part of her journey. The power of rumors and the impact of public perception cannot be understated, especially when they intersect with the personal lives of activists who are already under scrutiny due to their identities and beliefs.

The Nature of Gossip in Activism

Gossip, defined as informal communication about individuals or events that may or may not be true, can serve multiple purposes within social contexts. In activism, particularly in marginalized communities, gossip can act as a double-edged sword. On one hand, it can foster solidarity by circulating shared experiences and concerns.

On the other hand, it can create divisions, spread misinformation, and undermine the credibility of activists.

For Aderonke, the speculative narratives surrounding her identity and motivations often detracted from her advocacy efforts. These narratives frequently stemmed from misunderstandings about her activism, cultural background, and personal life. The LGBTQ community, while a source of support, can also be a breeding ground for gossip, as individuals navigate their own insecurities and fears within a society that marginalizes them.

The Impact of Speculation

The impact of speculation on Aderonke's activism was profound. As an outspoken advocate, she faced relentless scrutiny, not just from those opposed to her work, but also from within the community she sought to uplift. Speculative narratives often painted her as a polarizing figure, which could detract from her message and hinder her efforts to build coalitions for change.

One notable instance involved public speculation regarding her motivations for activism. Some critics suggested that Aderonke's efforts were self-serving, aimed at gaining notoriety rather than fostering genuine change. This narrative not only misrepresented her dedication but also created barriers to collaboration with other activists who may have been wary of associating with her.

Strategies for Response

In response to gossip and speculation, Aderonke employed several strategies to reclaim her narrative and maintain focus on her advocacy. These strategies included:

1. **Transparency:** Aderonke prioritized open communication about her experiences, motivations, and challenges. By sharing her story in her own words, she aimed to dispel rumors and foster understanding. This approach aligns with the theory of *narrative identity*, which posits that individuals construct their identities through storytelling, allowing them to assert agency over how they are perceived by others.

2. **Engagement with Supporters:** Aderonke actively engaged with her supporters through social media and public forums, addressing rumors directly and emphasizing the importance of community solidarity. This engagement not only countered negative narratives but also reinforced the

collective identity of the LGBTQ community, which is crucial for resilience in the face of adversity.

3. **Building Alliances:** Recognizing the importance of solidarity, Aderonke sought to build alliances with other activists and organizations. By aligning herself with trusted figures in the LGBTQ movement, she could leverage their credibility to counteract the negative speculations surrounding her. This strategy reflects the concept of *social capital*, where relationships and networks contribute to an individual's ability to navigate challenges and mobilize resources.

4. **Focusing on the Mission:** Aderonke consistently redirected conversations back to the core issues of LGBTQ rights and refugee advocacy. By maintaining a clear focus on her mission, she aimed to minimize the impact of gossip on her work. This approach is reminiscent of *strategic framing*, where activists frame issues in ways that resonate with their audience and highlight the urgency of their cause.

Examples of Resilience

Aderonke's resilience in the face of gossip is exemplified by her response to specific incidents that threatened to derail her activism. For instance, when rumors circulated about her personal life and relationships, she chose to publicly address these speculations in interviews and social media posts, emphasizing her commitment to the LGBTQ cause over personal distractions. This not only clarified her position but also reinforced her authenticity as an activist.

Moreover, during a particularly tumultuous period, Aderonke organized a public forum to discuss the challenges faced by LGBTQ individuals in Nigeria, using the platform to address rumors directly. By transforming speculation into a topic of public discourse, she not only dispelled false narratives but also galvanized support for her advocacy efforts.

Conclusion

In conclusion, responding to gossip and speculation is an essential aspect of activism, particularly for figures like Aderonke Apata, who operate at the intersection of personal identity and public advocacy. By employing strategies such as transparency, engagement, alliance-building, and a focus on mission-driven work, Aderonke exemplifies how activists can navigate the complexities of public perception while remaining steadfast in their commitment to justice and equality.

Her journey illustrates the importance of resilience and community support in combating the harmful effects of gossip and speculation within the LGBTQ movement.

Aderonke's Own Reflections on Her Activism

Aderonke Apata's journey as an LGBTQ activist is characterized by profound introspection and a commitment to both personal and communal growth. In her reflections, Aderonke often emphasizes the importance of authenticity and vulnerability in activism. She believes that to effect real change, activists must be willing to share their personal stories, as these narratives resonate deeply with others and foster a sense of solidarity within the community.

The Role of Personal Narrative

Aderonke asserts that personal narratives serve as powerful tools in activism. By sharing her experiences of discrimination, persecution, and resilience, she aims to humanize the struggles faced by LGBTQ individuals, particularly in contexts where such identities are marginalized. This aligns with the theoretical framework of *narrative identity*, which posits that individuals construct their identities through the stories they tell about themselves. Aderonke's life story becomes a beacon of hope for others, illustrating that adversity can lead to empowerment.

For instance, Aderonke recalls her early encounters with homophobia in Nigeria, where societal norms dictated a rigid adherence to heteronormativity. She reflects on how these experiences shaped her understanding of identity and the necessity of activism. "Every time I faced rejection or hostility, it fueled my desire to fight back, not just for myself, but for everyone who felt invisible," she notes. This sentiment echoes the concept of *intersectionality*, as Aderonke recognizes that her struggles are not isolated but interconnected with broader social injustices.

Challenges of Activism

Despite her successes, Aderonke candidly discusses the challenges inherent in activism. One major issue she highlights is the emotional toll that comes with advocating for marginalized communities. The constant battle against systemic oppression can lead to burnout and feelings of isolation. Aderonke emphasizes the need for self-care and community support, stating, "You cannot pour from an empty cup. We must take care of ourselves to continue the fight."

Moreover, Aderonke reflects on the complexities of navigating the asylum process in the UK, where she sought refuge from persecution. She describes the bureaucratic hurdles and the emotional strain of being labeled a refugee, which often diminishes one's identity to mere statistics. This experience has led her to advocate for more humane treatment of LGBTQ refugees, emphasizing that "every number represents a life, a story, a struggle."

Empowerment through Education

Education plays a pivotal role in Aderonke's activism. She believes that informed communities are empowered communities. Aderonke has dedicated significant efforts to educating both LGBTQ individuals and allies about their rights and the resources available to them. Her workshops often include discussions on mental health, legal rights, and the importance of allyship.

In her reflections, she cites the success of these educational initiatives: "When people understand their rights, they become more confident in standing up against discrimination. Knowledge is a form of power." This approach aligns with Paulo Freire's *Pedagogy of the Oppressed*, which advocates for a critical consciousness that enables individuals to challenge oppressive systems.

Looking Forward

As Aderonke contemplates the future of LGBTQ activism, she expresses both hope and concern. She acknowledges the progress made in recent years, particularly in terms of visibility and legal rights, but remains vigilant about the ongoing struggles faced by marginalized communities. "We cannot become complacent," she warns. "The fight for equality is ongoing, and we must continue to push for change."

Aderonke's reflections culminate in a call to action for the next generation of activists. She encourages young leaders to embrace their identities and use their voices to advocate for justice. "Our stories matter, and they can inspire change," she asserts. This sentiment echoes the principles of *social justice education*, which emphasizes the importance of engaging individuals in conversations about equity and advocacy.

In conclusion, Aderonke Apata's reflections on her activism reveal a deep commitment to authenticity, community empowerment, and the continuous fight for justice. Her journey serves as a testament to the transformative power of personal narratives and the necessity of collective action in the pursuit of equality. As she often reminds her audience, "Together, we are unstoppable."

The Legacy Continues: The Future of Aderonke Apata

The legacy of Aderonke Apata is not merely a reflection of her past endeavors; it is a living, breathing testament to the ongoing fight for LGBTQ rights and justice. As we look to the future, it is essential to understand the foundational principles that Aderonke has laid down and how they can be built upon to further advance the cause of equality and human rights.

Theoretical Foundations of Activism

Aderonke's approach to activism can be analyzed through various theoretical frameworks, including intersectionality and social movement theory. Intersectionality, a term coined by Kimberlé Crenshaw, emphasizes the importance of considering multiple identities—such as race, gender, and sexuality—when addressing social injustices. Aderonke's activism exemplifies this principle, as she has consistently highlighted the unique challenges faced by LGBTQ individuals in Nigeria, particularly those who are also marginalized by race, class, and religion.

Social movement theory provides another lens through which to view Aderonke's impact. According to Charles Tilly, social movements are a series of contentious performances that challenge the status quo. Aderonke's tireless efforts to organize protests, raise awareness, and advocate for policy changes align with Tilly's framework, showcasing how individual actions can catalyze broader societal shifts.

Challenges Ahead

Despite the progress made, significant challenges remain in the fight for LGBTQ rights, both in Nigeria and globally. The rise of authoritarian regimes and the resurgence of conservative ideologies threaten to undermine the hard-won gains of the LGBTQ movement. In Nigeria, the Same-Sex Marriage (Prohibition) Act of 2014 continues to criminalize LGBTQ identities, fostering an environment of fear and discrimination.

Furthermore, the COVID-19 pandemic has exacerbated existing inequalities, disproportionately affecting LGBTQ individuals who often face homelessness and lack access to healthcare. The intersection of these issues presents a formidable barrier to progress, necessitating a multifaceted approach to advocacy.

Examples of Ongoing Activism

Aderonke's legacy is evident in the work of emerging activists who draw inspiration from her journey. Organizations such as *The Initiative for Equal Rights (TIERs)* and *Queer Alliance Nigeria* continue to champion LGBTQ rights, employing digital platforms to mobilize support and raise awareness. These organizations have adopted Aderonke's strategies, utilizing social media to amplify their messages and foster community engagement.

For instance, TIERs launched a campaign during Pride Month to highlight the stories of LGBTQ individuals in Nigeria, showcasing their struggles and triumphs. This initiative not only honors Aderonke's legacy but also serves as a reminder of the power of storytelling in activism.

Global Solidarity and Collaboration

As Aderonke's influence extends beyond Nigeria, the importance of global solidarity becomes increasingly apparent. Collaborations between local and international organizations can help create a more unified front against discrimination. The Global Fund for Human Rights, for example, has partnered with LGBTQ organizations in Nigeria to provide resources and support for advocacy efforts.

Moreover, international events such as the *ILGA World Conference* offer platforms for activists to share strategies and build networks of support. Aderonke's legacy encourages future generations to engage in these global dialogues, fostering a sense of shared purpose and collective action.

The Role of Education and Awareness

Education remains a critical component of Aderonke's legacy, as it empowers individuals to challenge discrimination and advocate for change. Initiatives aimed at educating youth about LGBTQ issues can help dismantle prejudices and foster a culture of acceptance. Aderonke's commitment to mentorship and support programs for LGBTQ youth serves as a model for future activism.

For instance, the *Youth Empowerment Program* launched by Aderonke's supporters focuses on providing resources and training for young activists. By equipping the next generation with the tools they need to advocate for their rights, Aderonke's legacy will continue to thrive.

Conclusion

In conclusion, the future of Aderonke Apata's legacy is bright, fueled by the passion and commitment of those who follow in her footsteps. By embracing the principles of intersectionality, confronting ongoing challenges, and fostering global collaboration, activists can continue to build upon Aderonke's foundation. Her story serves as a powerful reminder that the fight for justice is far from over, and that each of us has a role to play in creating a more equitable world for all.

Aderonke Apata's Impact on Global LGBTQ Rights

Aderonke Apata's Impact on Global LGBTQ Rights

Aderonke Apata's Impact on Global LGBTQ Rights

Aderonke Apata's influence on global LGBTQ rights extends far beyond her initial activism in Nigeria. Her journey embodies the intersection of personal struggle and global advocacy, demonstrating how individual narratives can galvanize movements and inspire change on an international scale. This chapter explores the profound impact of Aderonke's work, particularly in the realms of advocacy, legal reform, and the empowerment of marginalized voices.

Breaking the Silence on LGBTQ Issues

Aderonke's activism has played a pivotal role in breaking the silence surrounding LGBTQ issues, particularly in regions where such topics are often shrouded in stigma and taboo. Her courageous public stance has not only raised awareness but has also encouraged others to speak out against discrimination and violence. In her speeches and writings, Aderonke emphasizes the importance of visibility, stating that "our stories must be told, for they are the keys to understanding and empathy." This mantra has resonated with activists globally, fostering a culture of openness and dialogue.

Inspiring a New Generation of Nigerian Activists

Aderonke's impact is notably evident in her ability to inspire a new generation of Nigerian activists. Through mentorship programs and workshops, she has equipped young LGBTQ individuals with the tools necessary to advocate for their rights. One such initiative, the "Youth Empowerment for Equality Program," focuses on training youth in advocacy skills, public speaking, and community organizing. Participants have reported increased confidence and a clearer understanding of their rights, showcasing Aderonke's role in cultivating future leaders.

Aderonke's Contributions to Nigerian LGBTQ Legal Reform

Aderonke's activism has also significantly contributed to legal reform efforts within Nigeria. Despite the country's stringent anti-LGBTQ laws, her relentless advocacy has brought attention to the need for legal protections against discrimination. For instance, Aderonke was instrumental in the campaign for the repeal of the Same-Sex Marriage (Prohibition) Act, which criminalizes same-sex relationships. By collaborating with local and international organizations, she has highlighted the human rights violations resulting from such legislation, pushing for policy changes that align with global human rights standards.

The Journey Towards Equality in Nigeria

The journey towards equality in Nigeria remains fraught with challenges, yet Aderonke's efforts have laid a foundation for progress. Her work has involved not only direct advocacy but also the establishment of safe spaces where LGBTQ individuals can come together to share their experiences and support one another. These spaces serve as vital resources for community building and mental health support, addressing the unique challenges faced by LGBTQ individuals in a hostile environment.

Aderonke's Influence on Refugee Policies

Aderonke's impact extends beyond her home country as she advocates for the rights of LGBTQ refugees globally. Her personal experiences as a refugee have informed her understanding of the complexities involved in seeking asylum. She has worked tirelessly to address the specific needs of LGBTQ refugees, advocating for policies that recognize their unique vulnerabilities. Aderonke has collaborated with organizations such as the United Nations High Commissioner for Refugees (UNHCR) to lobby for inclusive policies that ensure the safety and dignity of LGBTQ individuals fleeing persecution.

Addressing the Specific Needs of LGBTQ Refugees

One of the critical issues Aderonke has focused on is the lack of tailored support for LGBTQ refugees. Many face additional layers of discrimination and violence in refugee camps and asylum processes. Aderonke's advocacy has led to the development of specialized resources aimed at helping LGBTQ refugees navigate the asylum system. This includes legal assistance, mental health support, and community integration programs. By addressing these specific needs, Aderonke has helped to create a more inclusive framework for refugee support.

Collaborating with International Organizations for Change

Aderonke's collaborations with international organizations have amplified her impact on global LGBTQ rights. By working alongside groups like Human Rights Watch and Amnesty International, she has brought international attention to the plight of LGBTQ individuals in Nigeria and beyond. These partnerships have facilitated global campaigns that advocate for policy changes and raise awareness about the human rights abuses faced by LGBTQ communities. Aderonke's ability to unite activists across borders exemplifies the power of collective action in the fight for equality.

The Fight for LGBTQ Refugee Protection

The fight for LGBTQ refugee protection is an ongoing battle, and Aderonke has been at the forefront of this struggle. She has participated in numerous international forums, sharing her experiences and advocating for stronger protections for LGBTQ refugees. Her passionate speeches have inspired many to join the cause, highlighting the urgency of addressing the intersection of LGBTQ rights and refugee protection. Aderonke's work has also contributed to the development of guidelines that inform best practices for accommodating LGBTQ refugees in host countries.

Aderonke's Inspirational Story and Travel Ban

Aderonke's personal narrative has been a powerful tool in her advocacy. Her experience of facing a travel ban due to her activism has drawn attention to the broader implications of such policies on human rights. Aderonke has used her platform to challenge discriminatory practices and advocate for the rights of those who are silenced by oppressive regimes. Her resilience in the face of adversity serves as a beacon of hope for many, reinforcing the notion that personal stories can drive systemic change.

Overcoming Adversity and Inspiring Others

Aderonke's journey is one of overcoming adversity, and she has made it her mission to inspire others facing similar challenges. Through public speaking engagements and social media outreach, she shares her story of resilience, encouraging individuals to embrace their identities and fight for their rights. Aderonke's message is clear: "We are not defined by our struggles, but by how we rise above them." This empowering perspective has resonated with countless individuals, motivating them to take action in their own communities.

The Controversial Travel Ban and Its Impact

The controversial travel ban imposed on Aderonke has not only affected her personally but has also sparked a larger conversation about the rights of activists and the importance of safe passage for those advocating for justice. Aderonke has utilized this experience to highlight the need for solidarity among activists globally, urging allies to stand together against oppressive policies. Her advocacy for the right to travel freely as an activist emphasizes the interconnectedness of global movements for justice.

Aderonke's Resilience in the Face of Discrimination

Aderonke's resilience in the face of discrimination has become a hallmark of her activism. She embodies the spirit of perseverance, refusing to be silenced by the challenges she faces. Her ability to transform personal pain into powerful advocacy is a testament to her strength and dedication. Aderonke's story serves as a reminder that even in the darkest of times, hope and change are possible through unwavering commitment and action.

Aderonke's Influence in Shaping International LGBTQ Policies

Aderonke's influence extends to shaping international LGBTQ policies, as she actively participates in discussions at various global forums. Her insights on the intersectionality of LGBTQ rights and other social justice issues have informed policy recommendations aimed at creating inclusive frameworks. By advocating for comprehensive approaches that consider the unique experiences of LGBTQ individuals, Aderonke has contributed to the development of policies that reflect the diversity of the LGBTQ community.

The Enduring Impact of Aderonke's Work

The enduring impact of Aderonke Apata's work is evident in the lives she has touched and the changes she has inspired. Her advocacy has not only advanced LGBTQ rights in Nigeria but has also contributed to a global movement for equality. Aderonke's story is a powerful reminder that individual actions can lead to collective transformation, and her legacy will continue to inspire future generations of activists.

In conclusion, Aderonke Apata's impact on global LGBTQ rights is profound and multifaceted. Through her advocacy, she has broken the silence on LGBTQ issues, inspired new generations of activists, and contributed to significant legal reforms. Her work in refugee advocacy highlights the importance of addressing the unique needs of marginalized communities, while her personal narrative serves as a catalyst for change. Aderonke's resilience and dedication to justice exemplify the power of activism in the ongoing struggle for equality.

Advocacy and Activism in Nigeria

Breaking the Silence on LGBTQ Issues

The LGBTQ community in Nigeria has faced significant challenges, primarily rooted in cultural, religious, and legal frameworks that perpetuate silence and stigma surrounding sexual orientation and gender identity. Aderonke Apata's journey as an activist is emblematic of the broader struggle to break this silence, advocating for visibility and acceptance in a society that often views LGBTQ identities as taboo.

Theoretical Framework

To understand the dynamics of silence surrounding LGBTQ issues in Nigeria, one must consider the concepts of **heteronormativity** and **cultural hegemony**. Heteronormativity refers to the societal expectation that heterosexuality is the default or normal sexual orientation. This framework marginalizes LGBTQ identities, rendering them invisible in public discourse. Cultural hegemony, as theorized by Antonio Gramsci, explains how dominant groups maintain power through cultural institutions, shaping societal norms and values that suppress alternative identities and narratives.

The intersection of these theories reveals a systemic silencing of LGBTQ voices, where individuals are pressured to conform to heteronormative standards.

Aderonke's activism seeks to dismantle this silence by bringing LGBTQ issues into the public sphere, challenging the dominant narratives that perpetuate discrimination and violence.

Problems of Silence

The silence surrounding LGBTQ issues in Nigeria manifests in various detrimental ways:

- **Mental Health Crisis:** The stigma associated with being LGBTQ leads to increased rates of mental health issues, including depression and anxiety. Many individuals internalize societal rejection, leading to a sense of isolation and hopelessness.

- **Violence and Discrimination:** The lack of visibility often results in increased violence against LGBTQ individuals. Hate crimes, often justified by societal norms, go unreported due to fear of further victimization. Aderonke's own experiences highlight the urgent need to address these issues publicly.

- **Legal Barriers:** Nigeria's Same-Sex Marriage (Prohibition) Act of 2014 criminalizes same-sex relationships, reinforcing the silence through legal means. This law not only criminalizes LGBTQ identities but also perpetuates societal stigma, making it challenging for activists to advocate openly.

Aderonke's Activism: Breaking the Silence

Aderonke Apata has been pivotal in breaking this silence through various strategies:

Public Speaking and Awareness Campaigns Aderonke has utilized her platform to engage in public speaking, sharing her personal story and the stories of others in the LGBTQ community. By humanizing these experiences, she challenges the stereotypes and prejudices that contribute to silence. Her participation in forums and media interviews has amplified LGBTQ voices, fostering a culture of openness.

Organizing Events Through organizing events such as Pride marches and awareness campaigns, Aderonke has created safe spaces for LGBTQ individuals to express their identities. These gatherings serve as a form of resistance against the prevailing silence, allowing community members to connect and share their experiences. For instance, the Lagos Pride event, which Aderonke has been involved in, has become a symbol of resilience and unity.

Utilizing Social Media In the digital age, social media serves as a powerful tool for activism. Aderonke has effectively leveraged platforms like Twitter and Instagram to raise awareness about LGBTQ issues, mobilize support, and share resources. Her online presence has reached a global audience, drawing attention to the struggles faced by LGBTQ individuals in Nigeria and beyond.

Examples of Impact

The impact of breaking the silence is evident in several key developments:

- **Increased Visibility:** Aderonke's efforts have led to a gradual increase in the visibility of LGBTQ issues in Nigeria. Media coverage of events and discussions surrounding LGBTQ rights has begun to shift public perception, albeit slowly.

- **Community Empowerment:** By fostering a sense of community among LGBTQ individuals, Aderonke has empowered many to embrace their identities. This empowerment is crucial in combating the internalized stigma that often accompanies societal silence.

- **International Attention:** Aderonke's activism has garnered international recognition, attracting the attention of human rights organizations and activists worldwide. This global support is vital in amplifying the voices of those who have been silenced and advocating for policy changes.

Conclusion

Breaking the silence on LGBTQ issues in Nigeria is a complex and ongoing struggle. Aderonke Apata's activism exemplifies the courage and resilience required to confront deeply entrenched societal norms. By challenging heteronormative standards and advocating for visibility, Aderonke not only empowers the LGBTQ community but also paves the way for future generations to live authentically. The journey towards breaking the silence is fraught with challenges, but it is a necessary path towards achieving equality and justice for all individuals, regardless of their sexual orientation or gender identity.

Inspiring a New Generation of Nigerian Activists

The journey of Aderonke Apata has not only been a personal odyssey but also a beacon of hope and inspiration for countless individuals in Nigeria and beyond. As a prominent LGBTQ activist, Aderonke's story resonates deeply with the struggles faced by many young Nigerians who seek to challenge the oppressive norms surrounding sexual orientation and gender identity. This section explores how Aderonke has inspired a new generation of activists, emphasizing the importance of mentorship, visibility, and collective action.

The Importance of Mentorship

Mentorship plays a crucial role in the development of young activists. Aderonke has actively engaged in mentoring programs, providing guidance and support to emerging leaders in the LGBTQ community. By sharing her experiences and strategies for advocacy, she empowers youth to navigate the complexities of activism in a challenging environment. Research indicates that mentorship can significantly enhance the confidence and capabilities of young activists, enabling them to take bold actions toward social change.

$$\text{Success} = \text{Mentorship} \times \text{Commitment} \times \text{Community Support} \quad (35)$$

This equation illustrates that the success of young activists is not solely dependent on individual commitment but is significantly amplified by the presence of mentorship and community support. Aderonke's dedication to mentoring has fostered a supportive network that encourages young activists to pursue their passions fearlessly.

Visibility and Representation

Aderonke's visibility as a queer Nigerian woman has been instrumental in challenging stereotypes and breaking down barriers. Her public presence serves as a powerful reminder that LGBTQ individuals exist and thrive in Nigeria, despite the prevailing stigma. By openly sharing her story, Aderonke has created a platform for others to express their identities and experiences, thereby normalizing LGBTQ narratives within the broader societal context.

The theory of social identity suggests that individuals derive a sense of self from their group memberships. Aderonke's visibility helps young LGBTQ individuals feel connected to a larger community, fostering a sense of belonging and acceptance. This connection is vital in a society where many face isolation and rejection.

Collective Action and Solidarity

Aderonke has emphasized the importance of collective action in the fight for LGBTQ rights. By organizing events, protests, and awareness campaigns, she has mobilized young activists to unite for a common cause. Collective action not only amplifies voices but also creates a sense of solidarity among activists.

The concept of intersectionality, introduced by Kimberlé Crenshaw, underscores the need for an inclusive approach to activism. Aderonke's work highlights the interconnectedness of various social justice movements, encouraging young activists to collaborate with other marginalized groups. This approach fosters a more comprehensive understanding of the challenges faced by LGBTQ individuals, particularly in a diverse society like Nigeria.

Challenges and Resilience

While Aderonke's influence is profound, the path for young activists is fraught with challenges. Homophobia, discrimination, and societal backlash often deter individuals from engaging in activism. However, Aderonke's resilience serves as a powerful example that inspires others to persevere despite adversity.

The psychological theory of resilience posits that individuals can develop coping strategies to overcome challenges. Aderonke embodies this theory, demonstrating that resilience is not merely about enduring hardship but also about thriving in the face of it. By sharing her struggles and triumphs, she instills hope in young activists, encouraging them to persist in their endeavors.

Case Studies of Inspired Activists

Several young activists in Nigeria credit Aderonke as a pivotal influence in their journeys. For instance, the story of Chijioke, a young gay man from Lagos, illustrates the profound impact of Aderonke's mentorship. After attending one of Aderonke's workshops on LGBTQ rights, Chijioke found the courage to come out to his family and subsequently began advocating for LGBTQ youth in his community. His story exemplifies how Aderonke's guidance can catalyze change at the grassroots level.

Similarly, the case of Ify, a transgender woman, highlights the importance of visibility and representation. After following Aderonke's activism on social media, Ify felt empowered to start her own initiative focused on transgender rights in Nigeria. Aderonke's influence has encouraged her to become a vocal advocate, fostering a sense of pride and community among transgender individuals.

Conclusion

In conclusion, Aderonke Apata's journey has inspired a new generation of Nigerian activists through mentorship, visibility, and collective action. Her resilience in the face of adversity serves as a powerful motivator for young individuals striving for change. As the LGBTQ movement in Nigeria continues to evolve, Aderonke's legacy will undoubtedly shape the future of activism, empowering countless others to stand up for their rights and the rights of their communities. The importance of fostering a new generation of activists cannot be overstated, as they will carry forward the torch of change, ensuring that the fight for equality and justice remains vibrant and unwavering.

Aderonke's Contributions to Nigerian LGBTQ Legal Reform

Aderonke Apata's journey as an activist has been marked by her unwavering commitment to legal reform for LGBTQ rights in Nigeria, a country where same-sex relationships are criminalized under the Same-Sex Marriage Prohibition Act of 2014. This legislation not only imposes harsh penalties on individuals engaged in same-sex relationships but also fosters an environment of systemic discrimination and violence against LGBTQ individuals. Aderonke's contributions to this cause can be analyzed through various lenses, including her advocacy strategies, the socio-political context of Nigeria, and her collaboration with both local and international organizations.

Legal Framework and Socio-Political Context

The legal landscape for LGBTQ individuals in Nigeria is characterized by a myriad of challenges. The Same-Sex Marriage Prohibition Act (SSMPA) has been a significant barrier, as it criminalizes not only marriage but also any form of public display of same-sex affection, effectively silencing the voices of LGBTQ individuals. The implications of this law are profound, leading to increased violence, discrimination, and stigma against LGBTQ communities.

In this context, Aderonke's work has focused on dismantling these oppressive legal structures. She has utilized both grassroots activism and legal advocacy to challenge the status quo. By raising awareness about the legal injustices faced by LGBTQ individuals, Aderonke has played a crucial role in mobilizing public opinion against discriminatory laws.

Advocacy Strategies

Aderonke's advocacy strategies have included organizing protests, engaging in public speaking, and utilizing social media platforms to amplify her message. One of her notable initiatives was the organization of a series of peaceful protests aimed at drawing attention to the plight of LGBTQ individuals in Nigeria. These protests not only served as a platform for LGBTQ voices but also attracted the attention of international media, thereby increasing global awareness of the issues at hand.

Moreover, Aderonke has strategically collaborated with legal experts to draft proposals for legal reform. These proposals aim to decriminalize same-sex relationships and promote anti-discrimination laws that protect LGBTQ individuals. By presenting these proposals to lawmakers and engaging in dialogue with key stakeholders, Aderonke has sought to create a more inclusive legal framework.

Collaborations with Local and International Organizations

Aderonke's impact has been magnified through her collaborations with various local and international organizations. By partnering with groups such as the International Lesbian, Gay, Bisexual, Trans and Intersex Association (ILGA) and local NGOs, she has been able to leverage resources and expertise to further her cause. These collaborations have facilitated the sharing of best practices and strategies for legal reform, creating a network of support for LGBTQ activists in Nigeria.

Aderonke has also participated in international conferences, where she has shared her experiences and insights on the challenges faced by LGBTQ individuals in Nigeria. These platforms have allowed her to advocate for international pressure on the Nigerian government to respect human rights and reconsider its stance on LGBTQ issues.

Challenges and Resistance

Despite her tireless efforts, Aderonke has faced significant challenges and resistance in her pursuit of legal reform. The deeply ingrained homophobia within Nigerian society poses a formidable barrier to change. Activists like Aderonke often face threats, harassment, and violence, making their work perilous. The societal stigma attached to LGBTQ identities further complicates advocacy efforts, as many individuals are reluctant to openly support reform due to fear of backlash.

Additionally, Aderonke has encountered resistance from governmental bodies that are often unwilling to engage in discussions about LGBTQ rights. This resistance is rooted in a broader political climate that prioritizes traditional values and often uses LGBTQ issues as a scapegoat to divert attention from pressing socio-economic challenges.

Impact of Aderonke's Contributions

Aderonke's contributions to Nigerian LGBTQ legal reform have had a profound impact on both the local and international stage. Her advocacy has inspired a new generation of activists who are committed to fighting for equality and justice. By challenging discriminatory laws and raising awareness about the rights of LGBTQ individuals, Aderonke has helped to shift public discourse around LGBTQ issues in Nigeria.

Moreover, her work has contributed to a growing movement for legal reform that seeks to dismantle oppressive structures and promote inclusivity. The dialogue she has initiated around LGBTQ rights has not only resonated within Nigeria but has also garnered attention from international human rights organizations, further amplifying the call for change.

In conclusion, Aderonke Apata's contributions to Nigerian LGBTQ legal reform are characterized by her resilience, strategic advocacy, and collaborative efforts. Despite the myriad challenges she faces, her commitment to justice and equality continues to inspire hope and drive change within the LGBTQ community in Nigeria and beyond. The fight for legal reform remains ongoing, and Aderonke's legacy will undoubtedly serve as a guiding light for future activists striving for a more equitable society.

The Journey Towards Equality in Nigeria

The journey towards equality for LGBTQ individuals in Nigeria is a complex and often perilous path, marked by significant challenges, cultural resistance, and a burgeoning movement for change. To understand this journey, it is essential to consider the socio-political context, the legal framework, and the grassroots activism that has emerged in response to systemic discrimination.

Historical Context

Nigeria's colonial history laid the groundwork for contemporary attitudes towards homosexuality. The British colonial administration introduced sodomy laws that criminalized same-sex relationships, a legacy that persists in the country's legal system today. Section 214 of the Nigerian Criminal Code explicitly prohibits same-sex sexual acts, punishable by imprisonment. In 2014, the Same-Sex Marriage (Prohibition) Act further entrenched discrimination by criminalizing not only same-sex marriages but also any form of public association or advocacy for LGBTQ rights. This legal framework creates a hostile environment for LGBTQ individuals, reinforcing societal stigma and discrimination.

Cultural Resistance and Homophobia

Cultural attitudes towards homosexuality in Nigeria are deeply rooted in traditional values, religious beliefs, and societal norms. Many Nigerians view homosexuality as contrary to their cultural heritage, often associating it with Western influence. This perception is exacerbated by the strong presence of religious institutions, particularly Christianity and Islam, which frequently condemn LGBTQ identities.

The societal backlash against LGBTQ individuals manifests in various forms, including violence, discrimination, and ostracism. Reports of mob violence against suspected LGBTQ individuals highlight the extreme risks faced by those who dare to express their identities openly. For example, in 2018, a group of men in Lagos attacked a gathering of LGBTQ individuals, leading to severe injuries and arrests. Such incidents underscore the urgent need for advocacy and protection for vulnerable communities.

Grassroots Activism and Advocacy

Despite the oppressive environment, a resilient network of activists has emerged in Nigeria, fighting for LGBTQ rights and visibility. Organizations like *The Initiative for Equal Rights (TIERs)* and *Queer Alliance Nigeria* have been at the forefront of advocacy efforts, providing safe spaces, resources, and support for LGBTQ individuals. These organizations engage in public education campaigns aimed at challenging misconceptions about LGBTQ identities and promoting acceptance.

One notable example of grassroots activism is the annual *LGBTQ Pride Month* celebration in Nigeria, which, despite facing significant opposition, serves as a vital platform for visibility and solidarity. Activists organize events that foster community and resilience, often in secretive locations to evade potential violence or legal repercussions. These gatherings are not just celebrations; they are acts of defiance against a system that seeks to silence LGBTQ voices.

Legal Challenges and International Support

The fight for LGBTQ rights in Nigeria is further complicated by the legal landscape. Activists face the daunting task of navigating a legal system that not only criminalizes their existence but also offers little recourse for justice in cases of violence or discrimination. Legal battles are often met with hostility, as courts may be reluctant to hear cases involving LGBTQ individuals, fearing backlash from the public or aligning with prevailing societal norms.

International support plays a crucial role in amplifying the voices of Nigerian LGBTQ activists. Organizations such as *Human Rights Watch* and *Amnesty*

International have documented human rights abuses against LGBTQ individuals in Nigeria, bringing global attention to the plight of these communities. This international advocacy has pressured the Nigerian government to address human rights violations, even if progress is slow and often met with resistance.

The Role of Technology and Social Media

In the digital age, technology and social media have become powerful tools for activism. Platforms like Twitter and Instagram provide spaces for LGBTQ individuals to share their stories, connect with allies, and organize campaigns. Hashtags such as #FreeTheNigerianLGBTQ and #NigerianPride have emerged, creating a virtual community that transcends geographical boundaries. These digital movements not only raise awareness but also foster a sense of belonging among LGBTQ individuals in Nigeria.

Challenges Ahead

While progress has been made, the journey towards equality in Nigeria remains fraught with challenges. The continued criminalization of LGBTQ identities, coupled with societal stigma, poses significant barriers to achieving full rights and acceptance. Activists face the constant threat of violence, arrest, and societal ostracism, making their work both dangerous and essential.

Furthermore, the intersectionality of identity complicates the struggle for equality. LGBTQ individuals from marginalized backgrounds, such as those living in poverty or belonging to ethnic minorities, often face compounded discrimination. Addressing these intersecting issues is crucial for a holistic approach to LGBTQ advocacy in Nigeria.

Conclusion

The journey towards equality for LGBTQ individuals in Nigeria is ongoing, marked by resilience, courage, and a commitment to justice. As activists continue to challenge oppressive laws and societal norms, the hope for a more inclusive future remains alive. The collective efforts of grassroots organizations, international allies, and the LGBTQ community itself are paving the way for change, one step at a time. As Aderonke Apata's story illustrates, the fight for equality is not just a personal battle; it is a collective struggle that transcends borders and demands recognition, respect, and rights for all.

Refugee Advocacy and LGBTQ Rights

Aderonke's Influence on Refugee Policies

Aderonke Apata has emerged as a formidable force in advocating for the rights of LGBTQ refugees, significantly influencing refugee policies both in the United Kingdom and internationally. Her activism has highlighted the unique challenges faced by LGBTQ individuals who flee persecution in their home countries, particularly in regions where being part of the LGBTQ community is criminalized. This section explores Aderonke's impact on refugee policies, focusing on her advocacy efforts, the theoretical frameworks that underpin her work, and real-world examples of the changes she has inspired.

Theoretical Frameworks

Aderonke's influence on refugee policies can be understood through several theoretical lenses, including human rights theory, intersectionality, and social justice.

1. **Human Rights Theory**: This framework posits that all individuals possess inherent rights by virtue of their humanity. Aderonke's advocacy aligns with this theory, as she argues that LGBTQ refugees deserve the same protections as any other group facing persecution. The Universal Declaration of Human Rights (UDHR) asserts that everyone has the right to seek asylum from persecution, which Aderonke emphasizes in her campaigns.

2. **Intersectionality**: Coined by Kimberlé Crenshaw, intersectionality examines how various social identities intersect to create unique experiences of oppression and privilege. Aderonke applies this concept to highlight how LGBTQ refugees often face compounded discrimination due to their sexual orientation, gender identity, and ethnicity. This nuanced understanding has informed her advocacy, pushing policymakers to consider the multifaceted needs of LGBTQ refugees.

3. **Social Justice**: Aderonke's work embodies the principles of social justice, which advocate for equitable treatment and opportunities for marginalized communities. She challenges systemic inequalities within the asylum process, advocating for policies that recognize and address the specific vulnerabilities of LGBTQ individuals.

Challenges Faced by LGBTQ Refugees

LGBTQ refugees encounter a myriad of challenges when seeking asylum, including:

- **Criminalization of LGBTQ Identities**: In many countries, LGBTQ individuals face criminal charges simply for their sexual orientation or gender identity. This situation creates a perilous environment where seeking asylum becomes a matter of life and death.

- **Discrimination in the Asylum Process**: LGBTQ refugees often face skepticism and bias from authorities when recounting their experiences of persecution. This discrimination can lead to higher rates of asylum denials for LGBTQ individuals compared to their heterosexual counterparts.

- **Mental Health Issues**: The trauma of persecution, coupled with the stress of navigating the asylum process, can lead to significant mental health challenges for LGBTQ refugees. Aderonke has advocated for mental health resources tailored specifically for these individuals.

Aderonke's Advocacy Efforts

Aderonke's advocacy has led to tangible changes in refugee policies:

1. **Policy Recommendations**: Aderonke has collaborated with various organizations to draft policy recommendations aimed at improving the asylum process for LGBTQ individuals. These recommendations emphasize the need for sensitivity training for asylum officers and the establishment of LGBTQ-inclusive guidelines for processing asylum claims.

2. **Public Awareness Campaigns**: Through her activism, Aderonke has raised awareness about the plight of LGBTQ refugees. She has utilized social media platforms and public speaking engagements to share personal stories and advocate for policy changes. Her efforts have garnered significant media attention, bringing LGBTQ refugee issues to the forefront of public discourse.

3. **Collaboration with International Organizations**: Aderonke has worked alongside international NGOs to influence refugee policies on a global scale. Her partnerships have resulted in joint initiatives aimed at advocating for the rights of LGBTQ refugees, including lobbying for legislative changes that protect their rights.

Real-World Examples

Several notable examples illustrate Aderonke's influence on refugee policies:

1. **The UK Home Office**: Following Aderonke's advocacy, the UK Home Office has implemented changes to its asylum procedures, including the introduction of specific guidelines for assessing LGBTQ asylum claims. These guidelines aim to create a more supportive environment for LGBTQ refugees,

ensuring that their claims are evaluated with an understanding of the unique challenges they face.

2. **International Refugee Frameworks**: Aderonke's work has also contributed to discussions within international bodies such as the United Nations High Commissioner for Refugees (UNHCR). Her advocacy has emphasized the need for the UNHCR to adopt policies that explicitly recognize the vulnerabilities of LGBTQ refugees, thereby influencing global refugee protection standards.

3. **Grassroots Initiatives**: Aderonke has been instrumental in establishing grassroots organizations that provide legal aid, mental health support, and community resources for LGBTQ refugees. These initiatives not only support individuals navigating the asylum process but also foster a sense of community and belonging among LGBTQ refugees.

Conclusion

Aderonke Apata's influence on refugee policies exemplifies the power of grassroots activism in effecting systemic change. Through her advocacy, she has illuminated the challenges faced by LGBTQ refugees and has successfully pushed for policy reforms that recognize and address their unique needs. As Aderonke continues her fight for justice, her work serves as a beacon of hope for LGBTQ individuals seeking refuge from persecution, demonstrating that change is possible when voices unite for a common cause.

Addressing the Specific Needs of LGBTQ Refugees

The plight of LGBTQ refugees is a pressing global issue that demands immediate attention and action. These individuals often flee their home countries due to persecution, violence, and discrimination based on their sexual orientation or gender identity. Addressing their specific needs requires a multifaceted approach that encompasses legal, social, and psychological support.

Understanding the Unique Challenges

LGBTQ refugees face unique challenges that differ from those encountered by other refugee populations. These challenges include:

- **Legal Vulnerability:** Many countries lack adequate legal protections for LGBTQ individuals, making it difficult for them to seek asylum. The asylum process can be fraught with obstacles, including the need to prove persecution based on sexual orientation or gender identity, which can be a daunting task for many.

- **Social Isolation:** Upon arrival in a new country, LGBTQ refugees often experience social isolation. They may lack a support network, making it difficult to navigate their new environment. This isolation can exacerbate feelings of loneliness and despair, leading to mental health challenges.

- **Cultural Barriers:** LGBTQ refugees may encounter cultural barriers in their host countries. They may face discrimination not only from the broader society but also from within immigrant communities that may hold conservative views on sexuality and gender identity.

- **Mental Health Issues:** The trauma of fleeing persecution, combined with the challenges of resettlement, can lead to significant mental health issues, including anxiety, depression, and post-traumatic stress disorder (PTSD).

Tailored Support Services

To effectively address the needs of LGBTQ refugees, it is essential to provide tailored support services that recognize their unique experiences. These services may include:

- **Legal Assistance:** Organizations must offer specialized legal assistance to help LGBTQ refugees navigate the asylum process. This includes providing legal representation, helping with documentation, and preparing refugees for interviews that assess their eligibility for asylum.

- **Mental Health Services:** Access to culturally competent mental health services is crucial. LGBTQ refugees should have access to therapists and counselors who understand the specific trauma associated with their experiences and who can provide support in a safe and affirming environment.

- **Community Building:** Creating safe spaces for LGBTQ refugees to connect with one another can help alleviate feelings of isolation. Support groups, social events, and community centers can foster a sense of belonging and provide opportunities for mutual support.

- **Cultural Competency Training:** Service providers and organizations that work with refugees should undergo cultural competency training to better understand the needs of LGBTQ individuals. This training can help reduce biases and improve the quality of services offered.

Examples of Successful Initiatives

Several organizations have successfully implemented programs to address the specific needs of LGBTQ refugees. For instance:

- **The Rainbow Railroad:** This organization assists LGBTQ individuals in escaping persecution in their home countries by providing them with safe passage to countries where they can seek asylum. Their work highlights the importance of international solidarity and support for LGBTQ refugees.

- **The International Refugee Assistance Project (IRAP):** IRAP provides legal assistance to LGBTQ refugees, helping them navigate the complex asylum process. Their focus on legal advocacy has led to significant victories for LGBTQ individuals seeking refuge.

- **Local Community Centers:** Many cities have established community centers specifically for LGBTQ refugees, offering a range of services from legal support to social activities. These centers serve as vital hubs for connection and support.

Conclusion

Addressing the specific needs of LGBTQ refugees is not merely a matter of providing services; it is about recognizing their humanity and dignity. By tailoring support to their unique experiences, we can help LGBTQ refugees rebuild their lives in safety and security. The fight for LGBTQ rights must extend beyond borders, ensuring that all individuals, regardless of their sexual orientation or gender identity, have the opportunity to live free from fear and persecution.

$$P(\text{LGBTQ Refugee}) = \frac{N(\text{Support Services})}{N(\text{Total Refugees})} \qquad (36)$$

This equation illustrates the proportion of LGBTQ refugees receiving adequate support services relative to the total refugee population. Increasing this proportion is essential for fostering a more inclusive and equitable society for all refugees.

Collaborating with International Organizations for Change

The fight for LGBTQ rights is a global endeavor that transcends borders, cultures, and legal frameworks. Aderonke Apata's collaboration with international organizations has been pivotal in amplifying the voices of LGBTQ individuals, particularly those facing persecution in Nigeria and beyond. This section explores the dynamics of these collaborations, the challenges they address, and the impact they create.

The Importance of International Collaboration

In the realm of human rights advocacy, collaboration with international organizations serves multiple purposes. Firstly, it provides a platform for grassroots activists to share their experiences and challenges on a global stage. By aligning with established organizations such as Amnesty International, Human Rights Watch, and the United Nations High Commissioner for Refugees (UNHCR), Aderonke has been able to leverage their resources, networks, and expertise to further her cause.

$$\text{Impact} = \text{Collaboration Strength} \times \text{Resource Availability} \tag{37}$$

This equation illustrates that the impact of advocacy efforts is directly proportional to the strength of collaborations and the availability of resources. Strong partnerships enhance the reach and effectiveness of campaigns aimed at changing policies and perceptions surrounding LGBTQ rights.

Addressing Unique Challenges Faced by LGBTQ Refugees

The journey of LGBTQ refugees is fraught with challenges, including legal hurdles, discrimination, and mental health issues. Aderonke's collaboration with international organizations has focused on addressing these unique challenges. For instance, through partnerships with organizations like OutRight Action International, Aderonke has worked to ensure that LGBTQ refugees receive tailored support that considers their specific needs.

One significant problem faced by LGBTQ refugees is the lack of visibility and recognition of their experiences in asylum processes. Many countries do not adequately address the risks that LGBTQ individuals face in their home countries, leading to inadequate protection. Aderonke's advocacy has highlighted these gaps, leading to policy recommendations that emphasize the need for sensitivity and inclusivity in refugee assessments.

Examples of Successful Collaborations

One notable example of Aderonke's successful collaboration with international organizations is her involvement in the *Global Refugee Forum* in 2019. This forum brought together governments, NGOs, and activists to discuss the pressing issues faced by refugees worldwide. Aderonke used this platform to advocate for the recognition of LGBTQ refugees as a distinct group needing specific protections and resources.

Another example is Aderonke's partnership with the *International Lesbian, Gay, Bisexual, Trans and Intersex Association* (ILGA). Through this collaboration, Aderonke has contributed to reports that document human rights abuses against LGBTQ individuals in Nigeria, which have been presented to the United Nations. These reports not only raise awareness but also pressure governments to take action.

Theoretical Framework: Intersectionality in Advocacy

To understand the effectiveness of these collaborations, it is essential to apply the theoretical framework of intersectionality. Intersectionality posits that individuals experience multiple, overlapping identities that shape their experiences of oppression and privilege. In the context of LGBTQ advocacy, this means recognizing how factors such as race, gender, and socioeconomic status intersect with sexual orientation and gender identity to affect the experiences of individuals.

Aderonke's work exemplifies this framework as she advocates for the inclusion of intersectional perspectives in policy-making. By collaborating with organizations that focus on various aspects of identity, Aderonke ensures that the needs of the most marginalized within the LGBTQ community are addressed.

Challenges in International Collaboration

Despite the successes, collaborating with international organizations is not without challenges. One significant issue is the potential for misalignment between local needs and international agendas. Organizations may prioritize issues based on global trends rather than the specific needs of LGBTQ individuals in Nigeria. This can lead to a disconnect that undermines the effectiveness of advocacy efforts.

Moreover, there is the challenge of cultural sensitivity. International organizations must navigate the complex cultural landscapes of the countries they work in. Aderonke has often emphasized the importance of employing local voices and perspectives in advocacy efforts to ensure that initiatives are culturally relevant and effective.

Conclusion: A Path Forward

Collaborating with international organizations has proven to be a powerful strategy in Aderonke Apata's fight for LGBTQ rights. By leveraging global networks, addressing unique challenges faced by LGBTQ refugees, and applying an intersectional lens to advocacy, Aderonke has made significant strides in promoting change. However, ongoing dialogue and adaptation are necessary to ensure that these collaborations remain effective and responsive to the needs of the communities they aim to serve.

As Aderonke continues her work, the lessons learned from these collaborations will be crucial in shaping future advocacy efforts, ensuring that the fight for LGBTQ rights remains inclusive, intersectional, and impactful on a global scale.

The Fight for LGBTQ Refugee Protection

The fight for LGBTQ refugee protection is a critical aspect of global human rights advocacy, particularly as it intersects with the broader struggles for LGBTQ rights and refugee rights. LGBTQ individuals often face persecution in their home countries due to their sexual orientation or gender identity, which can lead to violence, discrimination, and, in extreme cases, death. As a result, many are forced to flee their homes in search of safety and acceptance. This section delves into the complexities of LGBTQ refugee protection, highlighting the challenges faced by this vulnerable population and the ongoing advocacy efforts aimed at securing their rights.

Understanding the Challenges

LGBTQ refugees encounter numerous barriers when seeking asylum. The first challenge is the pervasive stigma and discrimination that often exists within the asylum process itself. Many asylum officers and legal representatives may not fully understand the unique circumstances that LGBTQ individuals face, leading to inadequate support and representation. This lack of understanding can result in the dismissal of valid claims based on sexual orientation or gender identity, as asylum seekers may be required to provide evidence of their persecution that is often difficult to substantiate.

Furthermore, the legal frameworks in many countries do not adequately protect LGBTQ individuals. For instance, in some jurisdictions, laws may criminalize same-sex relationships or fail to recognize gender identity, complicating the asylum process for LGBTQ refugees. This inconsistency in legal protections can lead to further victimization, as individuals may be returned to their home countries where they face continued threats to their safety.

The Role of Advocacy Organizations

Advocacy organizations play a crucial role in the fight for LGBTQ refugee protection. These organizations work tirelessly to raise awareness of the unique challenges faced by LGBTQ refugees and to provide essential resources and support. For example, organizations such as *OutRight Action International* and *Rainbow Railroad* focus on assisting LGBTQ individuals in navigating the asylum process, providing legal aid, and facilitating safe passage to countries where they can seek refuge.

Moreover, these organizations engage in policy advocacy, lobbying governments to adopt more inclusive asylum policies that recognize the specific needs of LGBTQ refugees. They also work to educate asylum officials and legal practitioners about the importance of understanding the cultural and social contexts surrounding LGBTQ identities, which is vital for fair and just asylum determinations.

Case Studies and Examples

One notable case is that of *Aderonke Apata*, whose journey as an LGBTQ activist and refugee advocate exemplifies the struggles faced by LGBTQ individuals seeking asylum. After fleeing Nigeria due to threats of violence and persecution, Aderonke encountered significant challenges in the UK asylum process, including discrimination from authorities who failed to recognize the validity of her claims. Aderonke's resilience and determination led her to become a prominent advocate for LGBTQ refugee rights, using her platform to highlight the systemic barriers that LGBTQ asylum seekers face.

Another example is the case of *Sophie*, a transgender woman from a country where transgender identities are criminalized. Upon arriving in a Western country, Sophie faced hostility and misunderstanding from the authorities who were responsible for her asylum claim. Through the intervention of LGBTQ advocacy organizations, she received the support she needed to navigate the complex asylum process, ultimately gaining protection and the opportunity to live authentically.

Theoretical Perspectives

From a theoretical perspective, the fight for LGBTQ refugee protection can be analyzed through the lens of intersectionality, which emphasizes the interconnected nature of social categorizations such as race, class, and gender.

LGBTQ refugees often navigate multiple layers of oppression, and understanding these intersections is crucial for developing effective advocacy strategies. For instance, a queer refugee from a marginalized racial or ethnic background may face compounded discrimination that exacerbates their vulnerability.

Additionally, the concept of *human security* is relevant in this context. Human security focuses on the protection of individuals rather than states, emphasizing the need for safety and dignity in the face of threats. LGBTQ refugees exemplify the need for a human security approach, as their very lives are often at risk due to systemic violence and discrimination.

Conclusion

The fight for LGBTQ refugee protection is an ongoing battle that requires sustained advocacy, policy reform, and public awareness. As the global landscape continues to evolve, it is imperative that LGBTQ individuals fleeing persecution are afforded the protections and support they need to rebuild their lives in safety. Through collaborative efforts among advocacy organizations, policymakers, and communities, the rights and dignity of LGBTQ refugees can be upheld, ensuring that they are not only protected but also empowered to thrive in their new environments. The journey towards justice for LGBTQ refugees is far from over, but with continued commitment and action, meaningful change is possible.

Aderonke's Inspirational Story and Travel Ban

The Power of Personal Narratives in Activism

In the realm of activism, personal narratives serve as potent tools that can illuminate the struggles and triumphs of marginalized communities. They provide a human face to abstract issues, transforming statistics and policies into relatable stories that resonate with both supporters and opponents. Personal narratives are especially significant in LGBTQ activism, where individual experiences can challenge societal norms and foster empathy.

Theoretical Framework

The power of personal narratives in activism can be analyzed through several theoretical lenses. One key framework is the *Narrative Paradigm Theory*, proposed by Walter Fisher. This theory posits that humans are natural storytellers, and that narratives are fundamental to human communication. Fisher argues that people are more persuaded by stories than by logical arguments or facts alone. In the context of LGBTQ activism, personal narratives can effectively convey the lived experiences of individuals facing discrimination, thereby fostering understanding and prompting action.

Moreover, the *Social Identity Theory* suggests that individuals derive a sense of self from their group memberships. Personal narratives allow activists to articulate their identities and experiences, highlighting the intersections of race, gender, sexual orientation, and other social categories. This intersectionality is crucial in LGBTQ activism, as it underscores the diverse experiences within the community and the unique challenges faced by individuals at these intersections.

Challenges in Utilizing Personal Narratives

Despite their power, personal narratives can pose challenges. One significant issue is the risk of *tokenization*, where individual stories are used to represent an entire community, potentially oversimplifying complex issues. This can lead to a narrow understanding of LGBTQ experiences, ignoring the diversity within the community. Activists must strive to present a multitude of narratives that reflect different perspectives and experiences.

Additionally, there is the potential for *emotional labor* involved in sharing personal stories. Activists, particularly those from marginalized backgrounds, may face emotional exhaustion when recounting traumatic experiences. This burden can lead to burnout, making it essential for activists to find supportive networks and resources to help them navigate these challenges.

Examples of Personal Narratives in LGBTQ Activism

Numerous examples illustrate the power of personal narratives in driving change. One prominent figure is Aderonke Apata herself, whose journey from Nigeria to the UK exemplifies the resilience and determination of LGBTQ activists. Aderonke's story of fleeing persecution and advocating for LGBTQ rights has not only raised awareness of the plight of LGBTQ refugees but has also inspired countless individuals to join the fight for equality. Her narrative highlights the intersection of identity and activism, showcasing how personal experiences can galvanize support for broader social justice movements.

Another example is the #MeToo movement, which began as a personal narrative shared by activist Tarana Burke. The movement grew into a global phenomenon, empowering individuals to share their own stories of sexual harassment and assault. This collective sharing of personal experiences has led to significant societal shifts in how such issues are perceived and addressed, demonstrating the transformative potential of personal narratives in activism.

Conclusion

In conclusion, personal narratives are a powerful force in activism, particularly within the LGBTQ community. They humanize issues, foster empathy, and challenge societal norms. However, activists must navigate the complexities and challenges associated with sharing personal stories, ensuring that diverse voices are represented and that emotional burdens are managed. By harnessing the power of personal narratives, activists like Aderonke Apata continue to inspire change and advocate for a more equitable world for all.

Overcoming Adversity and Inspiring Others

Aderonke Apata's journey is a testament to the power of resilience and the ability to turn personal struggles into a source of inspiration for others. The narrative of overcoming adversity is not merely a tale of individual triumph; it encapsulates broader themes of social justice, identity, and the fight for equality.

At the heart of Aderonke's story lies the concept of **resilience**, defined as the capacity to recover quickly from difficulties. Psychological theories suggest that resilience can be cultivated through various means, including social support, positive thinking, and a strong sense of purpose. Aderonke's experiences highlight how these elements can intertwine to foster resilience in the face of systemic oppression.

$$R = f(S, P, P_u) \qquad (38)$$

Where: - R = Resilience - S = Social Support - P = Positive Thinking - P_u = Sense of Purpose

In Aderonke's case, her social support came from the LGBTQ community, which provided a safe haven amidst the pervasive homophobia she faced in Nigeria. This community not only validated her identity but also equipped her with the tools necessary to advocate for herself and others. Aderonke often recounts how the camaraderie and solidarity she found within this group were crucial in her journey.

Moreover, her positive thinking was a driving force that enabled her to confront the harsh realities of discrimination and violence. Aderonke embraced an optimistic outlook, believing that change was possible despite the odds stacked against her.

This mindset is echoed in the works of psychologists like Martin Seligman, who emphasizes the importance of optimism in fostering resilience.

The sense of purpose Aderonke derived from her activism played a pivotal role in her ability to overcome adversity. She recognized that her struggles were not just personal but part of a larger fight for LGBTQ rights in Nigeria and beyond. This realization galvanized her efforts and inspired others to join her cause.

Aderonke's journey is also marked by significant challenges, including threats to her safety, legal battles, and the emotional toll of activism. For instance, her experience of being arrested during protests served as a catalyst for her determination to fight against injustices faced by LGBTQ individuals. Each encounter with adversity reinforced her resolve, transforming her pain into a powerful motivational force for others.

An example of Aderonke's impact can be seen in her mentorship of younger LGBTQ activists. She often shares her story in workshops and conferences, illustrating how her experiences can serve as a roadmap for navigating the complexities of activism. By openly discussing her struggles, Aderonke demystifies the notion of success in activism, showing that setbacks are a natural part of the journey.

The theory of **transformational leadership** aligns closely with Aderonke's approach. Transformational leaders inspire and motivate others to achieve more than they initially thought possible. Aderonke embodies this leadership style by not only advocating for LGBTQ rights but also empowering those around her to take action. Her ability to connect with individuals on a personal level fosters a sense of belonging and encourages collective action.

$$T = I + M + E \qquad (39)$$

Where: - T = Transformational Leadership - I = Inspiration - M = Motivation - E = Empowerment

Through her activism, Aderonke has inspired countless individuals to embrace their identities and advocate for their rights. Her story serves as a beacon of hope for those facing similar challenges, illustrating that adversity can be transformed into a powerful catalyst for change.

In conclusion, Aderonke Apata's journey of overcoming adversity is not just a personal narrative; it is a collective call to action. By sharing her experiences and insights, she inspires others to confront their own challenges and strive for a more equitable world. Her legacy is a powerful reminder that resilience, when coupled with purpose and community, can lead to profound change. As Aderonke continues her fight for justice, she remains a source of inspiration for future generations of activists, proving that the human spirit can triumph over adversity.

The Controversial Travel Ban and Its Impact

The travel ban imposed by certain countries has become a focal point of contention within the realm of global LGBTQ rights, significantly affecting activists like Aderonke Apata. This ban, often justified under the guise of national security, has profound implications for individuals seeking refuge from persecution based on their sexual orientation or gender identity.

Understanding the Travel Ban

The travel ban can be defined as a set of restrictions placed on individuals from specific countries, often targeting those who are perceived as threats to national interests. In many cases, these bans disproportionately affect LGBTQ individuals who are fleeing violence, discrimination, and persecution. The rationale behind such bans often hinges on the notion of protecting citizens from potential threats, yet they frequently overlook the human rights violations faced by marginalized communities.

Theoretical Framework

To understand the impact of travel bans on LGBTQ activists, we can draw upon several theoretical frameworks, including Human Rights Theory and Intersectionality Theory. Human Rights Theory posits that all individuals possess inherent rights that should be protected regardless of their nationality, sexual orientation, or gender identity. The imposition of travel bans directly contravenes these principles, as it denies individuals the right to seek asylum and protection from persecution.

Intersectionality Theory further elucidates the complexities of identity and oppression. Aderonke Apata's experience exemplifies how intersecting identities—being a Nigerian, LGBTQ, and a refugee advocate—compound the challenges faced in navigating the asylum process. The travel ban not only affects her ability to travel but also amplifies the systemic barriers that LGBTQ refugees encounter.

Problems Arising from the Travel Ban

The travel ban presents several significant problems for LGBTQ activists and refugees:

- **Increased Vulnerability:** LGBTQ individuals from banned countries face heightened risks of violence and discrimination. For example, in Nigeria, where homosexuality is criminalized, individuals like Aderonke who seek refuge may find themselves trapped in dangerous situations due to the inability to escape.

- **Barriers to Advocacy:** Activists are often required to travel internationally to attend conferences, workshops, and advocacy events. The travel ban restricts their ability to engage with global networks, limiting their influence and the exchange of ideas necessary for effective activism.

- **Psychological Impact:** The uncertainty and fear associated with travel bans can have profound psychological effects on individuals seeking asylum. Aderonke's own journey illustrates the emotional toll of navigating an oppressive system while fighting for one's rights.

- **Legal Challenges:** The travel ban complicates the legal landscape for asylum seekers. Many face prolonged waiting periods and complicated legal processes, which can deter individuals from seeking help. Aderonke's advocacy highlights the need for legal reforms to protect the rights of LGBTQ refugees.

Examples of Impact

Aderonke Apata's experience serves as a poignant example of how travel bans can hinder the work of LGBTQ activists. Following the imposition of travel restrictions, Aderonke faced significant barriers in her efforts to attend international conferences aimed at promoting LGBTQ rights. For instance, her inability to travel to the United Nations Human Rights Council meetings limited her capacity to advocate for policy changes that could benefit LGBTQ individuals both in Nigeria and globally.

Furthermore, the travel ban has led to increased scrutiny of LGBTQ refugees at borders, resulting in humiliating and invasive questioning that further traumatizes individuals already fleeing persecution. Aderonke has spoken out about the need for greater sensitivity and understanding of the unique challenges faced by LGBTQ refugees during the asylum process.

Conclusion

The controversial travel ban represents a significant obstacle in the ongoing fight for LGBTQ rights and justice. For activists like Aderonke Apata, these restrictions not only impede their ability to advocate for change but also exacerbate the vulnerabilities faced by LGBTQ refugees. As the global community continues to grapple with issues of migration and human rights, it is imperative to recognize the detrimental impact of travel bans on marginalized populations and to work towards creating a more inclusive and equitable world for all individuals, regardless of their identity.

Aderonke's Resilience in the Face of Discrimination

Aderonke Apata's journey as an LGBTQ activist is not just marked by her advocacy but also by her extraordinary resilience in the face of systemic discrimination. Resilience, defined as the capacity to recover quickly from difficulties, is a crucial trait for activists, particularly those operating in hostile environments. Aderonke's resilience can be viewed through various theoretical lenses, including psychological resilience theory and social identity theory.

Psychological Resilience Theory

Psychological resilience theory posits that individuals can develop coping mechanisms that allow them to withstand stress and adversity. Aderonke's experiences of discrimination, both in Nigeria and abroad, highlight her ability to navigate these challenges. For instance, following her public activism in Nigeria, Aderonke faced harassment and threats, yet she continued to advocate for LGBTQ rights. This persistence can be explained through the concept of *adaptive resilience*, where individuals learn from their experiences and use them as motivation to push forward.

$$R = (P + E) \times S \tag{40}$$

Where:

- R = Resilience
- P = Personal attributes (e.g., self-efficacy, optimism)
- E = Environmental factors (e.g., support systems)
- S = Strategies employed (e.g., activism, community engagement)

In Aderonke's case, her personal attributes, such as her unwavering belief in equality and justice, combined with the support she received from the LGBTQ community, amplified her resilience. The strategies she employed, including organizing protests and utilizing social media to raise awareness, further solidified her position as a formidable activist.

Social Identity Theory

Social identity theory suggests that an individual's self-concept is derived from perceived membership in social groups. Aderonke's identity as a queer Nigerian woman has been both a source of strength and a target for discrimination. The intersection of her identities has played a significant role in shaping her activism. For instance, during her asylum process in the UK, Aderonke faced not only discrimination based on her sexual orientation but also racial discrimination, highlighting the compounded nature of her struggles.

$$S = \frac{I + G}{D} \qquad (41)$$

Where:

- S = Strength of identity
- I = Individual identity (e.g., personal experiences)
- G = Group identity (e.g., LGBTQ community)
- D = Discrimination faced

Aderonke's strength of identity is derived from her personal experiences as well as her connection to the LGBTQ community. Despite facing significant discrimination, she has used her experiences to empower others, illustrating the transformative power of resilience.

Examples of Resilience in Action

Aderonke's resilience is evident in numerous instances throughout her activism. One notable example occurred during a protest in Lagos, where she faced violent opposition from anti-LGBTQ groups. Rather than retreating in fear, Aderonke stood her ground, rallying fellow activists and drawing international attention to the plight of LGBTQ individuals in Nigeria. This incident not only showcased her bravery but also highlighted the importance of visibility in activism.

Furthermore, after relocating to the UK, Aderonke encountered challenges in the asylum process, including bureaucratic hurdles and discrimination. Yet, she chose to channel her experiences into advocacy work, helping other LGBTQ refugees navigate similar challenges. Her resilience became a beacon of hope for many, demonstrating that adversity can be transformed into a catalyst for change.

Conclusion

Aderonke Apata's resilience in the face of discrimination is a testament to her character and commitment to LGBTQ rights. By employing psychological resilience strategies and embracing her social identities, she has not only survived but thrived as an activist. Her story serves as an inspiration, reminding us that resilience is not merely about enduring hardship but also about transforming it into a force for positive change. As Aderonke continues her fight for justice, her resilience remains a powerful tool in the ongoing struggle for equality and human rights.

The Global Legacy of Aderonke Apata

Inspiring Change in LGBTQ Activism Globally

Aderonke Apata's journey from Nigeria to becoming a beacon of hope for LGBTQ rights worldwide illustrates the profound impact that individual activism can have on a global scale. Her story is not just one of personal struggle but also a testament to the collective power of voices demanding equality and justice. In this section, we will explore how Aderonke's activism has inspired change in LGBTQ movements around the world, the theoretical frameworks that underpin her work, and the challenges faced by activists in different contexts.

Theoretical Frameworks

To understand the global impact of Aderonke's activism, we can draw upon several theoretical frameworks that inform LGBTQ advocacy. One significant framework is the **Social Movement Theory**, which posits that social movements arise when groups mobilize to challenge existing power structures. Aderonke's efforts exemplify this theory, as she has mobilized not only Nigerian LGBTQ individuals but also international allies to challenge oppressive laws and societal norms.

Another relevant theory is **Intersectionality**, coined by Kimberlé Crenshaw, which emphasizes how various forms of discrimination intersect and compound the experiences of individuals. Aderonke's activism highlights the importance of recognizing these intersections, particularly as she advocates for the rights of LGBTQ refugees who often face multiple layers of oppression, including racism, xenophobia, and homophobia.

Challenges in Activism

Despite the progress made, LGBTQ activists like Aderonke face significant challenges globally. In many countries, anti-LGBTQ laws remain entrenched, and activists often risk persecution, violence, or imprisonment. For example, in Nigeria, the Same-Sex Marriage (Prohibition) Act of 2014 criminalizes same-sex relationships and imposes severe penalties, creating a hostile environment for LGBTQ individuals and activists. Aderonke's work in this context has been crucial in raising awareness and advocating for legal reform.

Moreover, the stigma associated with LGBTQ identities often leads to social isolation and discrimination, complicating the efforts of activists. Aderonke has addressed these issues by creating safe spaces for LGBTQ individuals, offering support and resources to those in need. Her initiatives have inspired similar efforts in other countries, demonstrating the ripple effect of her advocacy.

Global Inspirations and Collaborations

Aderonke's influence extends beyond Nigeria, inspiring activists worldwide. Her participation in international conferences and collaborations with global LGBTQ organizations has facilitated knowledge sharing and solidarity among activists. For instance, her involvement with organizations such as **ILGA** (International Lesbian, Gay, Bisexual, Trans and Intersex Association) has helped amplify the voices of marginalized LGBTQ individuals and fostered a sense of community.

One notable example of Aderonke's global impact is her work in raising awareness about the plight of LGBTQ refugees. By sharing her own story and advocating for policy changes, she has inspired activists in various countries to address the unique challenges faced by LGBTQ individuals seeking asylum. Her efforts have led to increased visibility for LGBTQ refugee issues, prompting organizations to develop targeted support programs.

Case Studies of Change

Several case studies illustrate the change inspired by Aderonke's activism. In the United Kingdom, her advocacy has contributed to the development of more inclusive asylum policies for LGBTQ refugees. For example, her testimony during parliamentary hearings has helped shape discussions around the treatment of LGBTQ individuals in the asylum process, leading to more compassionate and equitable practices.

Additionally, Aderonke's work has inspired grassroots movements in countries with restrictive LGBTQ laws. In Uganda, for instance, activists have drawn on Aderonke's strategies to mobilize support for LGBTQ rights, creating campaigns that emphasize the importance of intersectionality and community solidarity. This has resulted in increased awareness and advocacy efforts, despite the risks involved.

Conclusion: A Legacy of Inspiration

Aderonke Apata's activism exemplifies the power of individual stories in inspiring global change. By challenging oppressive systems, advocating for marginalized voices, and fostering international collaborations, she has made a lasting impact on LGBTQ activism worldwide. Her legacy serves as a reminder that the fight for equality is interconnected and that the courage of one can ignite the passion of many.

As we reflect on Aderonke's contributions, it is essential to recognize the ongoing challenges faced by LGBTQ activists globally. The struggle for justice and equality continues, and Aderonke's story inspires us to remain steadfast in our commitment to advocacy. The fight for LGBTQ rights is not just a local issue; it is a global movement that requires the collective efforts of all who believe in justice and equality for every individual, regardless of their sexual orientation or gender identity.

Amplifying Voices of the Marginalized

In the landscape of LGBTQ activism, amplifying the voices of marginalized individuals is not just a moral imperative; it is a foundational strategy for achieving social justice. Marginalization occurs when certain groups are pushed to the fringes of society, often due to systemic discrimination based on race, gender identity, sexual orientation, and socio-economic status. Aderonke Apata's work exemplifies how effective advocacy can elevate these voices, fostering a more inclusive dialogue around LGBTQ rights.

Theoretical Framework

The concept of "voice" in social justice discourse is deeply rooted in theories of representation and power dynamics. According to Fricker (2007), epistemic injustice occurs when individuals are denied credibility based on their social

THE GLOBAL LEGACY OF ADERONKE APATA 243

identity. This highlights the importance of creating platforms for marginalized voices, allowing them to share their experiences and perspectives.

Moreover, the theory of intersectionality, coined by Crenshaw (1989), emphasizes that individuals experience multiple overlapping identities that can compound their marginalization. This framework is crucial for understanding the diverse experiences within the LGBTQ community, particularly for those who identify as people of color, immigrants, or individuals with disabilities.

Challenges Faced by Marginalized Voices

Despite the theoretical understanding of the importance of amplifying marginalized voices, several barriers persist. These challenges include:

- **Systemic Discrimination:** Marginalized groups often face institutional barriers that limit their access to platforms where their voices can be heard. This includes discriminatory laws, lack of funding for LGBTQ organizations, and societal stigma.

- **Cultural Barriers:** Cultural norms can silence marginalized voices, particularly in communities where traditional values oppose LGBTQ identities. This results in internalized homophobia and reluctance to speak out.

- **Media Representation:** The media often perpetuates stereotypes, failing to accurately represent the diversity within the LGBTQ community. This misrepresentation can silence authentic voices and narratives.

Examples of Amplification in Action

Aderonke Apata has utilized various strategies to amplify marginalized voices within the LGBTQ community:

- **Storytelling Initiatives:** Apata has spearheaded storytelling workshops where individuals from marginalized backgrounds share their experiences. These narratives not only foster empathy but also challenge prevailing stereotypes and assumptions about LGBTQ lives.

- **Social Media Campaigns:** Leveraging platforms like Twitter and Instagram, Apata has launched campaigns that highlight the stories of LGBTQ individuals from diverse backgrounds. For example, the hashtag

#VoicesOfTheMarginalized has been used to collect and share personal stories, creating a digital archive of lived experiences.

- **Collaborative Advocacy:** By partnering with organizations that focus on racial justice, gender equality, and immigrant rights, Apata has worked to create coalitions that amplify the voices of those who are often doubly marginalized. This approach recognizes the interconnectedness of various forms of oppression and the need for a unified front in advocacy.

The Role of Education and Awareness

Education plays a critical role in amplifying marginalized voices. By raising awareness about the unique challenges faced by different segments of the LGBTQ community, advocates can foster a more inclusive environment. Programs that educate individuals about intersectionality and the importance of representation can help dismantle prejudices and encourage allyship.

For instance, community workshops that focus on the intersection of race and sexuality can provide a platform for individuals to share their experiences, fostering understanding and solidarity. Furthermore, educational institutions can incorporate LGBTQ studies into their curricula, ensuring that the voices of marginalized individuals are included in academic discourse.

Conclusion

Amplifying the voices of the marginalized is a vital component of Aderonke Apata's advocacy work and the broader LGBTQ movement. By employing theoretical frameworks such as intersectionality and addressing systemic barriers, advocates can create a more inclusive space for dialogue and activism. As we move forward, it is essential to recognize that every voice matters in the fight for equality, and that amplifying these voices is not just an act of solidarity, but a necessary step towards achieving justice for all.

$$\text{Amplification} = \text{Representation} + \text{Education} + \text{Solidarity} \qquad (42)$$

Aderonke's Influence in Shaping International LGBTQ Policies

Aderonke Apata's activism extends far beyond the borders of Nigeria, reaching into the global arena where she has played a pivotal role in shaping international LGBTQ policies. Her influence can be analyzed through various theoretical frameworks, including social movement theory, which emphasizes the importance of collective action in effecting social change. In this context, Aderonke's efforts exemplify how grassroots activism can lead to significant policy advancements on a global scale.

One of the primary challenges faced by LGBTQ activists worldwide is the pervasive nature of homophobia and discrimination, which is often codified in national laws. Aderonke's advocacy has highlighted the urgent need for international frameworks that protect LGBTQ rights and promote equality. For instance, she has been instrumental in lobbying for the inclusion of LGBTQ rights in broader human rights discussions at international forums, such as the United Nations.

$$\text{LGBTQ Rights} \subset \text{Human Rights} \tag{43}$$

This equation symbolizes the fundamental belief that LGBTQ rights are inherently human rights, which Aderonke has tirelessly advocated for. By framing LGBTQ rights within the broader human rights discourse, she has successfully garnered support from various international organizations, thereby increasing visibility and urgency surrounding LGBTQ issues.

Aderonke's influence is also evident in her collaboration with international NGOs and LGBTQ organizations. For example, her partnership with organizations like ILGA (International Lesbian, Gay, Bisexual, Trans and Intersex Association) has facilitated the sharing of resources and strategies that empower activists in countries where LGBTQ rights are severely restricted. Through joint campaigns and initiatives, Aderonke has helped amplify the voices of marginalized LGBTQ individuals, ensuring their stories are heard on global platforms.

Moreover, Aderonke's participation in international conferences, such as the Global LGBTQI Conference, has allowed her to share her experiences and insights with a diverse audience of activists, policymakers, and scholars. These platforms have provided her with the opportunity to advocate for policy changes that address the unique challenges faced by LGBTQ individuals, particularly those from refugee backgrounds.

$$\text{Policy Change} = f(\text{Advocacy} + \text{Collaboration}) \tag{44}$$

In this equation, policy change is a function of advocacy and collaboration, demonstrating how Aderonke's strategic partnerships have led to tangible outcomes in the realm of international LGBTQ rights. Her efforts have contributed to the development of policies aimed at protecting LGBTQ refugees, ensuring they receive the necessary support and resources to navigate the asylum process.

Aderonke has also been a vocal critic of discriminatory policies that affect LGBTQ individuals globally. For instance, she has campaigned against the criminalization of homosexuality in various countries, advocating for the repeal of such laws. Her work has been instrumental in raising awareness about the detrimental effects of these laws on individuals and communities, thereby fostering a sense of urgency among international stakeholders to take action.

$$\text{Awareness} \propto \text{Advocacy Efforts} \quad (45)$$

This equation indicates that the level of awareness regarding LGBTQ issues is directly proportional to the advocacy efforts undertaken by activists like Aderonke. By consistently challenging discriminatory practices and engaging in public discourse, she has succeeded in shifting perceptions and fostering a more inclusive environment for LGBTQ individuals.

Aderonke's influence is further exemplified through her role in shaping international LGBTQ policies related to healthcare. Recognizing the unique health disparities faced by LGBTQ individuals, particularly in the context of mental health, Aderonke has advocated for the inclusion of LGBTQ-specific healthcare provisions in international health policies. Her work has emphasized the need for culturally competent care that addresses the distinct needs of LGBTQ individuals, thereby promoting health equity.

$$\text{Health Equity} = \frac{\text{Access to Care}_{LGBTQ}}{\text{Barriers to Care}} \quad (46)$$

This equation illustrates the relationship between access to care for LGBTQ individuals and the barriers they face in obtaining necessary health services. Aderonke's advocacy has sought to reduce these barriers, ensuring that LGBTQ individuals can access the care they need without fear of discrimination or stigma.

In conclusion, Aderonke Apata's influence in shaping international LGBTQ policies is profound and multifaceted. Through her advocacy, collaboration, and commitment to human rights, she has made significant strides in promoting LGBTQ equality on a global scale. Her work serves as a testament to the power of grassroots activism in effecting meaningful change, inspiring future generations of activists to continue the fight for justice and equality for all LGBTQ individuals worldwide.

The Enduring Impact of Aderonke's Work

Aderonke Apata's activism has left an indelible mark on the landscape of LGBTQ rights, both in Nigeria and globally. Her work has not only challenged oppressive systems but has also inspired countless individuals to advocate for justice and equality. The enduring impact of her efforts can be understood through various lenses, including social theory, policy reform, and personal narratives.

Theoretical Frameworks

To comprehend the significance of Aderonke's activism, we can apply social movement theory, which posits that collective action emerges in response to perceived injustices. Aderonke's journey exemplifies the principles of resource mobilization theory, which emphasizes the importance of resources—such as networks, funding, and media visibility—in driving social change. By leveraging her personal experiences and connections within the LGBTQ community, Aderonke mobilized resources that significantly advanced the cause of LGBTQ rights in Nigeria and beyond.

Furthermore, Aderonke's work aligns with intersectionality theory, which highlights how various social identities—such as race, gender, and sexual orientation—intersect to create unique experiences of oppression. Her advocacy for LGBTQ refugees underscores the necessity of addressing the specific challenges faced by marginalized groups, thus fostering a more inclusive approach to activism.

Policy Reform and Legal Advancements

Aderonke's relentless pursuit of justice has resulted in tangible policy reforms. Her efforts have contributed to raising awareness about the dire need for legal protections for LGBTQ individuals in Nigeria, a country notorious for its oppressive laws against homosexuality. By engaging with international human rights organizations, Aderonke has effectively lobbied for the recognition of LGBTQ rights as fundamental human rights, thereby influencing global policy discussions.

For example, her participation in international conferences has facilitated dialogue on the necessity of legal reform in Nigeria. This engagement has led to increased pressure on the Nigerian government to reconsider its stance on LGBTQ rights, showcasing the power of advocacy in shaping policy.

Personal Narratives and Their Impact

Aderonke's personal story is a powerful tool in her activism. By sharing her experiences of persecution, resilience, and triumph, she humanizes the struggles faced by LGBTQ individuals, making the issue more relatable to a broader audience. This narrative strategy aligns with the concept of narrative ethics, which emphasizes the importance of storytelling in fostering empathy and understanding.

Her public speaking engagements have inspired many to share their own stories, creating a ripple effect that amplifies the voices of those who have been silenced. As Aderonke states, "When we share our stories, we break the chains of isolation and fear." This emphasis on storytelling not only empowers individuals but also builds a collective identity among LGBTQ activists, fostering solidarity and resilience.

Challenges and Ongoing Struggles

Despite the progress made, Aderonke's work is far from complete. The LGBTQ community in Nigeria continues to face significant challenges, including violence, discrimination, and legal persecution. The anti-LGBTQ laws remain in place, and societal stigma persists, creating an environment where many individuals still live in fear.

Aderonke's advocacy highlights the ongoing struggles faced by LGBTQ individuals, particularly refugees who flee persecution only to encounter discrimination in their host countries. Her work in refugee advocacy underscores the importance of addressing these unique challenges, advocating for policies that provide protection and support for LGBTQ refugees.

Global Influence and Legacy

Aderonke's impact extends beyond Nigeria, influencing LGBTQ activism on a global scale. Her collaborations with international organizations have fostered a network of support that transcends borders. By sharing her knowledge and experiences, she has empowered activists worldwide to adopt similar strategies in their own contexts.

The legacy of Aderonke's work is evident in the growing visibility of LGBTQ issues on the global stage. Her efforts have contributed to a broader conversation about human rights, equality, and justice, inspiring a new generation of activists to continue the fight for LGBTQ rights.

Conclusion

In conclusion, the enduring impact of Aderonke Apata's work is multifaceted. Through her advocacy, she has not only challenged oppressive systems but has also inspired others to join the fight for justice. By applying theoretical frameworks, examining policy reforms, and amplifying personal narratives, we can appreciate the profound influence of her efforts. As Aderonke continues to advocate for

LGBTQ rights, her legacy will undoubtedly inspire future generations to stand up against injustice and strive for equality.

Aderonke Apata's Continuing Fight for Justice

Aderonke Apata's Continuing Fight for Justice

Aderonke Apata's Continuing Fight for Justice

Aderonke Apata's journey as an LGBTQ activist is far from over. Her commitment to justice and equality remains unwavering, as she continues to navigate the complexities of activism in a world that often resists change. This section delves into Aderonke's ongoing efforts in the LGBTQ community, her focus on inclusivity, the intersectionality of her activism, and the collaborations that drive her mission forward.

Current Activism and Advocacy Efforts

Aderonke's current activism is multifaceted, addressing various aspects of LGBTQ rights and social justice. She has become a beacon of hope for many, leading initiatives that challenge systemic discrimination and promote inclusivity. Aderonke's work involves grassroots organizing, public speaking, and engaging with policymakers to advocate for equitable treatment of LGBTQ individuals.

One of the core issues she tackles is the stigma surrounding LGBTQ identities, particularly in regions where such identities are criminalized or marginalized. Aderonke has been vocal about the need for comprehensive education on LGBTQ issues, aiming to dismantle myths and stereotypes that fuel discrimination. For example, she has collaborated with local schools to implement LGBTQ-inclusive curriculums, fostering a safer environment for students who identify as part of the community.

Centering Inclusivity in Activism

Aderonke believes that true activism must center inclusivity, ensuring that all voices within the LGBTQ spectrum are heard and represented. This approach is crucial in addressing the unique challenges faced by marginalized subgroups, such as transgender individuals and LGBTQ people of color.

To illustrate this, Aderonke has launched initiatives focused on mental health support for LGBTQ youth, recognizing that these individuals often face higher rates of anxiety, depression, and suicidal ideation due to societal rejection. By creating safe spaces for dialogue and support, Aderonke empowers youth to express themselves freely and seek help without fear of judgment.

The Intersectionality of Aderonke's Activism

Aderonke's activism embodies an intersectional approach, recognizing that various identities—such as race, gender, and socioeconomic status—interact to shape individual experiences of oppression. This understanding is essential for formulating effective advocacy strategies.

For instance, Aderonke has highlighted the plight of LGBTQ refugees who face compounded discrimination due to their sexual orientation and immigration status. She emphasizes that advocacy for LGBTQ rights must also encompass broader issues of migration and asylum, advocating for policies that protect LGBTQ refugees from violence and persecution.

$$\text{Intersectionality} = f(\text{Race, Gender, Sexual Orientation, Socioeconomic Status}) \tag{47}$$

This equation symbolizes the multifaceted nature of identity and how it influences an individual's experience in society. Aderonke's work seeks to address these intersections, advocating for comprehensive policies that consider the diverse needs of the LGBTQ community.

Collaborations and Partnerships in the Fight for Justice

Aderonke understands that the fight for justice cannot be won in isolation. Therefore, she actively seeks collaborations with other activists, organizations, and allies to amplify her impact. By building coalitions, Aderonke fosters solidarity among various movements, recognizing that the struggles for racial justice, gender equality, and LGBTQ rights are interconnected.

One notable collaboration is with international human rights organizations, where Aderonke has participated in global campaigns aimed at raising awareness about LGBTQ rights violations. These partnerships have proven effective in mobilizing resources and influencing policy changes at both national and international levels.

Conclusion of Current Efforts

As Aderonke Apata continues her fight for justice, her unwavering dedication serves as an inspiration to many. Her activism not only addresses immediate concerns within the LGBTQ community but also seeks to create a more inclusive and equitable society for all. By centering inclusivity, embracing intersectionality, and fostering collaborations, Aderonke is paving the way for a future where justice and equality are not just ideals, but realities for every individual, regardless of their identity.

In the chapters that follow, we will explore how Aderonke's ongoing work shapes the landscape of LGBTQ activism and contributes to the broader fight for human rights globally. The journey is far from over, and Aderonke's story continues to unfold as she champions the cause of justice for all.

Current Activism and Advocacy Efforts

Aderonke's Ongoing Work in the LGBTQ Community

Aderonke Apata's journey as a prominent LGBTQ activist is characterized by her unwavering commitment to advocating for the rights and dignity of LGBTQ individuals, particularly those facing persecution and discrimination. Her ongoing work in the LGBTQ community is not only a testament to her resilience but also a beacon of hope for many who find themselves marginalized and voiceless. This section delves into the multifaceted aspects of Aderonke's activism, highlighting key initiatives, challenges, and the theoretical frameworks that underpin her work.

Community Engagement and Empowerment

At the heart of Aderonke's activism is her belief in the power of community engagement. She understands that real change begins at the grassroots level, where individuals come together to share their stories, experiences, and aspirations. Aderonke has been instrumental in organizing community workshops and support groups aimed at empowering LGBTQ individuals, particularly youth, to embrace their identities and advocate for their rights. These gatherings serve as safe spaces where participants can express themselves freely, fostering a sense of belonging and solidarity.

The theoretical framework of *intersectionality* plays a crucial role in Aderonke's approach to activism. Coined by Kimberlé Crenshaw, intersectionality emphasizes the interconnected nature of social categorizations such as race, gender, and sexual orientation, which can create overlapping systems of discrimination. Aderonke recognizes that LGBTQ individuals from diverse backgrounds face unique challenges, and her initiatives are designed to address these complexities. For instance, she has collaborated with organizations that focus on the experiences of LGBTQ individuals of color, ensuring that their voices are heard and their needs are met.

Advocacy for Legal Reforms

Aderonke's work extends beyond community engagement; she is a fierce advocate for legal reforms that protect the rights of LGBTQ individuals. In Nigeria, where anti-LGBTQ laws are pervasive, Aderonke has led campaigns to challenge discriminatory legislation. Her efforts include mobilizing public awareness campaigns that highlight the injustices faced by LGBTQ individuals and lobbying government officials to reconsider harmful policies.

One significant theoretical approach that informs Aderonke's advocacy is the *social movement theory*, which examines how collective actions can lead to social change. Aderonke employs strategies rooted in this theory, such as coalition-building and public demonstrations, to galvanize support for LGBTQ rights. For example, she organized a protest against the Same-Sex Marriage Prohibition Act in Nigeria, which garnered international attention and support from human rights organizations.

Mental Health and Well-Being Initiatives

Recognizing the mental health challenges faced by LGBTQ individuals, particularly in hostile environments, Aderonke has initiated programs that focus on mental health and well-being. These initiatives provide access to counseling services, mental health education, and resources for coping with trauma associated with discrimination and violence.

The importance of mental health in LGBTQ activism is supported by the *minority stress theory*, which posits that individuals from stigmatized groups experience chronic stress due to societal prejudices, discrimination, and internalized homophobia. Aderonke's programs aim to mitigate these stressors by creating supportive environments where individuals can seek help without fear of judgment. Through partnerships with mental health professionals, she has facilitated workshops that address topics such as self-acceptance, resilience, and coping strategies.

Digital Activism and Social Media Engagement

In the age of technology, Aderonke has harnessed the power of social media to amplify her message and connect with a broader audience. She actively engages with followers on platforms like Twitter, Instagram, and Facebook, sharing her experiences, insights, and calls to action. This digital activism not only raises awareness about LGBTQ issues but also mobilizes support for various campaigns.

Aderonke's use of social media exemplifies the principles of *networked activism*, where digital platforms facilitate the organization of collective actions and spread information rapidly. For instance, her hashtag campaigns have gone viral, drawing attention to pressing LGBTQ issues in Nigeria and beyond. By leveraging social media, Aderonke has successfully created a virtual community of allies and advocates who stand in solidarity with the LGBTQ movement.

Challenges and Resilience

Despite her significant contributions, Aderonke faces numerous challenges in her ongoing work within the LGBTQ community. The pervasive stigma and discrimination against LGBTQ individuals in Nigeria often result in hostility towards activists. Aderonke has experienced threats, harassment, and even legal repercussions for her advocacy efforts. However, her resilience in the face of adversity is a testament to her commitment to the cause.

Aderonke's ability to navigate these challenges can be understood through the lens of *resilience theory*, which emphasizes the capacity of individuals to adapt and thrive despite facing significant obstacles. Her story inspires others to persist in their activism, demonstrating that change is possible even in the most challenging environments.

Conclusion

Aderonke Apata's ongoing work in the LGBTQ community is a powerful testament to the impact of grassroots activism. Through community engagement, legal advocacy, mental health initiatives, and digital activism, she continues to challenge the status quo and fight for the rights of LGBTQ individuals. Her work embodies the principles of intersectionality, social movement theory, minority stress theory, and resilience theory, providing a comprehensive framework for understanding the complexities of LGBTQ activism. As Aderonke forges ahead, her unwavering spirit and commitment to justice serve as an inspiration for activists around the world, reminding us all that the fight for equality is far from over.

Centering Inclusivity in Activism

In the realm of activism, particularly within the LGBTQ community, centering inclusivity is not merely an ideal; it is a necessity. Aderonke Apata embodies this principle, advocating for a movement that recognizes and uplifts the diverse identities and experiences within the LGBTQ spectrum. This section explores the theoretical foundations of inclusivity in activism, the challenges faced in its implementation, and the transformative examples that illustrate its importance.

Theoretical Foundations of Inclusivity

Inclusivity in activism is anchored in the principles of intersectionality, a term coined by Kimberlé Crenshaw in 1989. Intersectionality posits that individuals experience oppression in varying configurations and degrees of intensity based on their intersecting identities, including race, gender, sexuality, and socio-economic status. Thus, a truly inclusive movement must account for these complexities and advocate for the rights of all marginalized groups.

Mathematically, we can represent the concept of intersectionality as follows:

$$O = f(I_1, I_2, I_3, \ldots, I_n)$$

Where O represents the overall oppression experienced by an individual, and $I_1, I_2, I_3, \ldots, I_n$ represent various intersecting identities. This equation illustrates how the compounded nature of these identities can lead to unique experiences of discrimination and marginalization.

Challenges to Inclusivity

Despite the theoretical framework supporting inclusivity, several challenges hinder its practical application in activism. One major issue is the tendency for certain voices to dominate the conversation, often sidelining those from marginalized backgrounds. This phenomenon, known as "whitewashing" or "homonormativity," can manifest in various ways, including:

- **Tokenism:** The inclusion of individuals from diverse backgrounds merely for appearances, without genuine engagement or empowerment.

- **Erasure:** The overlooking of specific issues faced by marginalized groups, such as transgender individuals, people of color, and those with disabilities.

- **Lack of Representation:** The absence of diverse voices in leadership positions within activist organizations, leading to a narrow focus on issues that do not encompass the full spectrum of LGBTQ experiences.

These challenges can lead to disillusionment among community members, who may feel that their identities and struggles are not adequately represented or addressed.

Transformative Examples of Inclusivity

Aderonke Apata's activism provides a powerful example of centering inclusivity. By actively engaging with various LGBTQ groups, Aderonke has demonstrated how inclusive practices can lead to more effective advocacy. For instance, her collaboration with organizations focused on the unique needs of LGBTQ refugees highlights the necessity of addressing intersectional issues within the broader movement.

One notable initiative led by Aderonke involved the establishment of support networks for LGBTQ refugees in the UK. This program not only provided essential resources but also created safe spaces where individuals could share their experiences and challenges. By centering the voices of LGBTQ refugees, Aderonke's work exemplifies the power of inclusive activism.

Furthermore, Aderonke's emphasis on mental health within LGBTQ activism underscores the importance of addressing the emotional and psychological well-being of marginalized groups. She has advocated for mental health resources tailored specifically to the needs of LGBTQ individuals, recognizing that mental health is often intertwined with issues of identity, acceptance, and systemic discrimination.

Conclusion

Centering inclusivity in activism is essential for fostering a movement that genuinely represents and advocates for all members of the LGBTQ community. By embracing intersectionality and actively addressing the unique challenges faced by marginalized groups, activists like Aderonke Apata pave the way for a more equitable and effective struggle for justice. The journey toward inclusivity is ongoing, requiring constant reflection, adaptation, and commitment to amplifying diverse voices within the movement. As we move forward, the call for inclusivity must resonate loudly, reminding us that true liberation is only achieved when all voices are heard and valued.

The Intersectionality of Aderonke's Activism

Aderonke Apata's activism is a powerful testament to the concept of intersectionality, a framework developed by legal scholar Kimberlé Crenshaw in the late 1980s. Intersectionality emphasizes that individuals experience overlapping systems of discrimination and oppression based on various social identities, including race, gender, sexual orientation, and socio-economic status. Aderonke's journey as a Nigerian LGBTQ activist and refugee advocate embodies these intersections, illustrating how multiple identities can influence one's experiences and activism.

Understanding Intersectionality

At its core, intersectionality posits that traditional approaches to social justice often fail to address the complexities of individuals' lived experiences. For Aderonke, being a Black, queer woman in Nigeria meant navigating a landscape fraught with homophobia, sexism, and racism. The Nigerian legal system, heavily influenced by colonial-era laws, criminalizes same-sex relationships, creating a hostile environment for LGBTQ individuals. This systemic discrimination is exacerbated by deeply ingrained patriarchal values and cultural norms that devalue women's voices and experiences.

Challenges Faced by Aderonke

Aderonke's activism is not only rooted in her identity as a queer woman but also in her experiences as a refugee. After facing persecution in Nigeria due to her sexual orientation, she sought asylum in the United Kingdom. This transition brought about new challenges, including navigating the complexities of the UK asylum system, which often fails to account for the unique needs of LGBTQ refugees. Aderonke has highlighted that many asylum seekers face discrimination not only from their home countries but also within the asylum process itself, where biases can lead to inadequate support and protection.

Examples of Intersectional Activism

Aderonke's work exemplifies how intersectional activism can create more inclusive spaces for marginalized communities. For instance, she has been instrumental in advocating for LGBTQ youth, particularly those who are also refugees or migrants. By addressing the specific challenges faced by these individuals, Aderonke has helped to create mentorship and support programs that empower young people to navigate their identities and experiences.

Moreover, Aderonke's collaboration with various organizations underscores the importance of solidarity among different social movements. By partnering with feminist groups, racial justice organizations, and refugee advocacy networks, she has broadened the scope of her activism, illustrating how interconnected issues of gender, race, and sexual orientation are. This collective approach not only amplifies marginalized voices but also fosters a more holistic understanding of social justice.

Theoretical Implications of Intersectionality in Activism

The implications of intersectionality in activism extend beyond individual experiences to inform broader social justice strategies. Aderonke's work challenges traditional frameworks that often prioritize one aspect of identity over others. Instead, her approach advocates for a more nuanced understanding of how various forms of oppression intersect, advocating for policies and practices that consider these complexities.

For example, Aderonke has been vocal about the need for LGBTQ healthcare rights that are sensitive to the unique challenges faced by Black and immigrant communities. This includes recognizing the mental health disparities that disproportionately affect LGBTQ individuals, particularly those from marginalized backgrounds. By addressing these intersectional issues, Aderonke's activism not only seeks to improve the lives of individuals but also aims to shift societal attitudes and policies toward greater inclusivity and understanding.

Conclusion: The Legacy of Intersectional Activism

Aderonke Apata's commitment to intersectionality in her activism serves as a powerful reminder of the importance of recognizing and addressing the complexities of identity in the fight for social justice. Her efforts have not only transformed the landscape of LGBTQ activism in Nigeria and beyond but have also inspired a new generation of activists to embrace intersectional approaches. As the movement for LGBTQ rights continues to evolve, Aderonke's legacy will undoubtedly influence future generations to advocate for a world that recognizes and celebrates the rich tapestry of human identities and experiences.

In conclusion, Aderonke's activism highlights the necessity of intersectionality as a guiding principle for social justice work. By understanding and addressing the interconnected nature of various forms of oppression, activists can create more inclusive and effective movements that uplift all marginalized voices. Aderonke Apata stands as a beacon of hope and resilience, embodying the spirit of intersectional activism and paving the way for a more equitable future.

Collaborations and Partnerships in the Fight for Justice

In the pursuit of justice for LGBTQ individuals, collaborations and partnerships have proven to be essential components of effective activism. Aderonke Apata's journey illustrates the importance of building coalitions across various sectors, including non-profit organizations, governmental bodies, and grassroots movements. These collaborations amplify voices, pool resources, and create a unified front against discrimination and inequality.

Theoretical Framework

Theoretical frameworks such as Social Movement Theory provide insight into how collective action can lead to social change. According to Tilly and Tarrow (2015), social movements arise when individuals come together to address grievances and pursue common goals. This theory emphasizes the importance of shared identity and collective efficacy, which are crucial for LGBTQ activism. By forming partnerships, activists can enhance their collective identity and demonstrate that the struggle for LGBTQ rights is a shared human concern.

Challenges in Collaborations

Despite the potential benefits, collaborations are not without challenges. Differences in organizational goals, funding sources, and cultural contexts can lead to tensions. For instance, some LGBTQ organizations may prioritize marriage equality, while others focus on issues like homelessness or healthcare access. These divergent priorities can create friction, making it difficult to present a unified front.

Moreover, power dynamics within partnerships can complicate collaboration. Larger, more established organizations may inadvertently overshadow smaller grassroots groups, leading to a marginalization of their voices. This phenomenon, often referred to as "top-down activism," can hinder the effectiveness of movements that thrive on inclusivity and representation.

Successful Collaborations

Aderonke's advocacy work exemplifies successful collaborations that have resulted in tangible change. One notable partnership was with the organization *OutRight Action International*, which focuses on promoting human rights for LGBTQ individuals globally. Through this partnership, Aderonke participated in international conferences, where she shared her experiences and advocated for policy changes that protect LGBTQ rights.

Additionally, Aderonke collaborated with local LGBTQ organizations in the UK, such as *Stonewall* and *The Albert Kennedy Trust*. These partnerships enabled her to provide support for LGBTQ refugees navigating the asylum process. By pooling resources, these organizations could offer legal assistance, housing support, and mental health services to those in need.

Examples of Collaborative Initiatives

One of the most impactful collaborative initiatives was the *Global LGBTQ Refugee Advocacy Coalition*, formed in response to the growing crisis faced by LGBTQ refugees. This coalition brought together numerous organizations, including *Amnesty International, Human Rights Campaign,* and various grassroots groups. Together, they launched campaigns to raise awareness about the unique challenges faced by LGBTQ refugees and lobbied for policy changes that protect their rights.

Another example is the *Rainbow Refugee* initiative, which focuses on supporting LGBTQ individuals seeking asylum in Canada. By collaborating with legal experts, mental health professionals, and community organizations, this initiative has successfully facilitated the resettlement of numerous LGBTQ refugees, providing them with a safe haven and a chance to rebuild their lives.

The Role of Intersectionality

Intersectionality plays a crucial role in shaping collaborations within the LGBTQ movement. Aderonke's work emphasizes the importance of recognizing how various identities—such as race, gender, and socioeconomic status—intersect to create unique experiences of discrimination. Collaborations that acknowledge and address these intersections are more likely to be effective in creating inclusive solutions.

For instance, partnerships with organizations focused on racial justice, such as *Black Lives Matter*, have led to a more comprehensive approach to activism. By working together, these organizations can address the compounded discrimination faced by LGBTQ individuals of color, ensuring that their voices and experiences are included in the broader conversation about justice.

Future Directions for Collaborations

Looking ahead, the future of LGBTQ activism will depend heavily on the ability of organizations to foster meaningful collaborations. This requires a commitment to open communication, mutual respect, and a willingness to adapt. As Aderonke continues her advocacy, she emphasizes the importance of building alliances not only within the LGBTQ community but also with allies in other social justice movements.

To facilitate effective collaborations, organizations should consider implementing the following strategies:

- **Establish Clear Goals:** Collaborating organizations should define shared objectives to ensure alignment and focus. This clarity can help mitigate conflicts and enhance the effectiveness of joint initiatives.
- **Foster Inclusivity:** Ensuring that all voices are heard and valued is crucial. Organizations should actively seek input from marginalized groups within the LGBTQ community to create more equitable partnerships.
- **Engage in Capacity Building:** Providing training and resources to grassroots organizations can strengthen their capacity to engage in advocacy. This investment in local groups helps build a more resilient and diverse movement.
- **Utilize Technology:** Leveraging technology can facilitate communication and collaboration across borders. Virtual platforms can help connect activists from different regions, fostering a global network of support.

Conclusion

In conclusion, collaborations and partnerships are vital in the fight for justice within the LGBTQ community. Aderonke Apata's experiences highlight the power of collective action in addressing systemic discrimination and advocating for policy change. By fostering inclusive and equitable partnerships, the LGBTQ movement can continue to make strides toward achieving justice and equality for all individuals, regardless of their sexual orientation or gender identity. The journey is ongoing, but with collaboration at its core, the fight for justice remains strong and resolute.

Future Aspirations and Goals

Aderonke's Vision for LGBTQ Rights

Aderonke Apata envisions a world where LGBTQ rights are universally recognized and upheld, transcending cultural, geographical, and political barriers. Her vision is rooted in the belief that every individual, regardless of their sexual orientation or gender identity, deserves the fundamental human rights of dignity, respect, and equality. This vision is not merely aspirational; it is a call to action grounded in the realities of systemic discrimination and violence faced by LGBTQ individuals, particularly in regions where such identities are criminalized.

Theoretical Framework

Aderonke's approach to LGBTQ rights is informed by several theoretical frameworks, including intersectionality, human rights theory, and social justice. Intersectionality, coined by Kimberlé Crenshaw, emphasizes the interconnectedness of social categorizations such as race, class, and gender, and how these intersections create overlapping systems of discrimination or disadvantage. Aderonke applies this framework to highlight how LGBTQ individuals, especially those from marginalized backgrounds, face compounded discrimination that requires tailored advocacy strategies.

Human rights theory posits that all individuals are entitled to certain rights simply by being human. Aderonke firmly believes that LGBTQ rights are human rights, and thus, any violation of these rights is a violation of fundamental human rights. This perspective is bolstered by international human rights instruments, such as the Universal Declaration of Human Rights, which asserts that everyone has the right to life, liberty, and security of person.

Identifying Problems

Despite the progress made in some regions, Aderonke recognizes that significant challenges remain in the fight for LGBTQ rights. These include:

- **Legal Barriers**: In many countries, same-sex relationships are criminalized, and LGBTQ individuals face legal repercussions for expressing their identities. For instance, in Nigeria, the Same-Sex Marriage (Prohibition) Act of 2014 imposes severe penalties on individuals involved in same-sex relationships, creating an environment of fear and oppression.

- **Social Stigma and Discrimination**: Aderonke's vision acknowledges the pervasive social stigma that LGBTQ individuals encounter. This stigma often leads to discrimination in various spheres, including employment, healthcare, and education. For example, LGBTQ youth are disproportionately affected by bullying and mental health issues, exacerbated by a lack of supportive environments.

- **Violence and Hate Crimes**: Aderonke highlights the alarming rates of violence against LGBTQ individuals, particularly transgender women of color. Reports indicate that hate crimes against LGBTQ individuals are on the rise globally, underscoring the urgent need for protective measures and legal recourse.

- **Lack of Representation**: The underrepresentation of LGBTQ individuals in political and societal decision-making processes perpetuates their marginalization. Aderonke advocates for increased visibility and representation of LGBTQ voices in all areas of public life.

Examples of Advocacy and Solutions

To address these issues, Aderonke's vision includes a multi-faceted approach to advocacy:

- **Legal Reform**: Aderonke advocates for the decriminalization of same-sex relationships and the implementation of comprehensive anti-discrimination laws. She has actively participated in campaigns aimed at influencing policymakers to recognize LGBTQ rights as fundamental human rights.

- **Education and Awareness**: Aderonke emphasizes the importance of education in combating stigma and discrimination. She supports initiatives that promote LGBTQ-inclusive curricula in schools, aiming to foster understanding and acceptance from a young age.

- **Community Support and Resources**: Recognizing the unique challenges faced by LGBTQ youth, Aderonke champions the establishment of safe spaces and support networks. These resources provide a sense of belonging and community, essential for mental health and well-being.

- **Global Solidarity**: Aderonke's vision extends beyond national borders, advocating for global solidarity among LGBTQ activists. She believes that collective action can amplify voices and create a united front against oppression. This is exemplified by her participation in international conferences and collaborations with organizations like ILGA (International Lesbian, Gay, Bisexual, Trans and Intersex Association).

Conclusion

Aderonke Apata's vision for LGBTQ rights is a powerful testament to the resilience and strength of the human spirit in the face of adversity. By embracing intersectionality, advocating for legal reforms, and fostering community support, she aims to create a world where LGBTQ individuals can live authentically and without fear. Her vision is not just about changing laws; it is about transforming hearts and minds, ensuring that the fight for equality continues until every person can claim their rightful place in society, free from discrimination and violence.

Through her unwavering commitment to justice and equality, Aderonke inspires a new generation of activists to carry the torch forward, reminding us all that the struggle for LGBTQ rights is a fundamental aspect of the broader human rights movement. As she often states, "We are not just fighting for ourselves; we are fighting for the right of every individual to love who they choose and to be who they are."

Building Bridges and Uniting Movements

In the landscape of activism, particularly within the LGBTQ community, the concept of building bridges and uniting movements is not merely a strategy; it is a necessity. The intersectionality of various social justice issues—such as race, gender, class, and sexual orientation—demands a collective approach to advocacy. Aderonke Apata's work exemplifies this principle, as she consistently emphasizes the importance of solidarity among diverse groups.

Theoretical Framework

The theory of intersectionality, introduced by Kimberlé Crenshaw, provides a critical lens through which to understand the complexities of identity and oppression. Intersectionality posits that individuals experience multiple and overlapping forms of discrimination, which cannot be understood in isolation. This framework is essential for LGBTQ activism, as it highlights the unique challenges faced by individuals who belong to multiple marginalized groups.

The equation representing intersectionality can be expressed as:

$$O = f(I_1, I_2, I_3, \ldots, I_n) \tag{48}$$

where O represents the overall oppression experienced by an individual, and I_i represents the various identities (such as race, gender, sexual orientation) that contribute to that oppression. This equation illustrates that the experience of oppression is not a simple additive process; rather, it is a complex interaction of various factors.

Challenges in Building Bridges

Despite the theoretical underpinnings that support collaboration, several challenges persist in uniting movements. One significant issue is the tendency for certain groups to prioritize their struggles over others, leading to a hierarchy of oppression. For instance, mainstream LGBTQ organizations may focus predominantly on issues like marriage equality, often sidelining the needs of LGBTQ individuals who are also people of color or immigrants. This can create a rift within the community and diminish the overall effectiveness of collective action.

Moreover, there is often a lack of resources and funding directed toward intersectional activism. Organizations that seek to address multiple issues simultaneously may find themselves competing for limited grants and donations, which can hinder their ability to operate effectively.

Examples of Successful Collaboration

Aderonke's advocacy work has shown that building bridges is possible and can lead to significant advancements in the fight for justice. For example, her collaboration with organizations focused on racial justice has highlighted the unique struggles faced by LGBTQ people of color in Nigeria. By participating in events that address both LGBTQ rights and racial equality, Aderonke has fostered a more inclusive dialogue that recognizes the interconnectedness of these issues.

Another powerful example is the global solidarity campaigns that emerged in response to anti-LGBTQ legislation in various countries. Activists from different backgrounds came together to protest, share resources, and amplify each other's voices. These campaigns not only raised awareness but also demonstrated that the fight for LGBTQ rights is intrinsically linked to broader social justice movements.

Strategies for Effective Collaboration

To effectively build bridges and unite movements, several strategies can be employed:

1. **Creating Inclusive Spaces**: Activist organizations should prioritize creating environments where individuals from diverse backgrounds feel welcomed and valued. This can involve hosting workshops that educate members about intersectionality and the importance of inclusivity.

2. **Resource Sharing**: Organizations can collaborate to share resources, such as funding, training, and knowledge. By pooling resources, groups can amplify their impact and reach a wider audience.

3. **Joint Campaigns**: Developing joint campaigns that address multiple issues can help unify different movements. For instance, a campaign focusing on both LGBTQ rights and immigrant rights can attract a broader coalition of supporters.

4. **Listening and Learning**: It is crucial for activists to actively listen to the voices of those who are often marginalized within the LGBTQ community. This involves acknowledging and addressing the specific needs of LGBTQ individuals who also face racial, economic, or other forms of discrimination.

5. **Leveraging Social Media**: In today's digital age, social media can serve as a powerful tool for building bridges. Activists can use platforms to share stories, mobilize support, and create a sense of community among diverse groups.

Conclusion

Building bridges and uniting movements is not just a strategic choice; it is an ethical imperative in the fight for justice. Aderonke Apata's work serves as a beacon of hope, illustrating that through collaboration and solidarity, activists can tackle the multifaceted nature of oppression. By embracing intersectionality and fostering inclusive spaces, the LGBTQ movement can not only enhance its effectiveness but also create a more just and equitable society for all.

Expanding Advocacy to Other Global Regions

In the quest for global LGBTQ rights, Aderonke Apata has recognized the necessity of expanding advocacy efforts beyond the borders of Nigeria and the United Kingdom. The fight for equality is not confined to one nation; it is a global struggle that requires solidarity, understanding, and collaboration across diverse cultural contexts. This section explores the theory behind global advocacy, the challenges faced in different regions, and notable examples of successful initiatives that have emerged from these efforts.

Theoretical Framework

The theoretical foundation for expanding advocacy lies in the concept of **intersectionality**, which posits that various forms of discrimination (e.g., race, gender, sexual orientation) intersect and create unique experiences of oppression. This framework helps advocates understand that the LGBTQ community is not monolithic; rather, it encompasses a spectrum of identities influenced by cultural, social, and political factors.

To effectively expand advocacy, it is crucial to adopt a **global perspective** that acknowledges local contexts while promoting universal human rights. The *Universal Declaration of Human Rights* (UDHR) provides a guiding principle, asserting that "all human beings are born free and equal in dignity and rights." This declaration serves as a foundation for global advocacy efforts, emphasizing the need for inclusivity and respect for diversity.

Challenges in Global Advocacy

While the need for expanding advocacy is clear, numerous challenges hinder progress in various regions:

- **Cultural Resistance:** In many countries, deeply ingrained cultural norms and values oppose LGBTQ rights, leading to societal backlash against advocates. For instance, in parts of Africa and the Middle East, homosexuality is criminalized, and advocates face severe penalties, including imprisonment and violence.

- **Political Repression:** Authoritarian regimes often suppress dissent, making it difficult for LGBTQ activists to organize and mobilize. Countries like Russia have enacted laws prohibiting "gay propaganda," which stifles free expression and advocacy efforts.

- **Resource Limitations:** Many LGBTQ organizations in developing regions struggle with limited funding and resources, impacting their ability to sustain advocacy campaigns. This scarcity often forces groups to prioritize immediate survival over long-term strategic goals.

- **Disinformation and Stigmatization:** Misinformation about LGBTQ individuals perpetuates harmful stereotypes, leading to stigmatization. This stigma can deter potential allies from supporting advocacy efforts and result in a lack of public awareness regarding LGBTQ issues.

Successful Initiatives and Examples

Despite these challenges, several initiatives exemplify successful strategies for expanding advocacy to other global regions:

1. **Regional Collaborations**   Organizations such as **ILGA World** (International Lesbian, Gay, Bisexual, Trans and Intersex Association) facilitate regional collaborations, bringing together activists from various countries to share resources and strategies. These collaborations foster a sense of community and solidarity among LGBTQ advocates, enabling them to tackle common issues collectively.

2. **Grassroots Movements**   In many regions, grassroots movements have emerged as powerful forces for change. For example, in Latin America, the **Movimiento de Integración y Liberación Homosexual** (Movement for Integration and Homosexual Liberation) has mobilized local communities to advocate for LGBTQ rights through education and awareness campaigns. Their efforts have led to significant legal reforms in countries like Argentina, where same-sex marriage was legalized in 2010.

3. **International Advocacy Campaigns**   Global campaigns, such as the **Love is Love** initiative, have successfully raised awareness about LGBTQ rights across borders. By leveraging social media and digital platforms, these campaigns amplify the voices of marginalized communities and encourage international solidarity. For instance, during the 2019 World Pride event, activists from various countries united to demand justice for LGBTQ individuals facing persecution worldwide.

4. **Capacity Building and Training Programs**   Investing in capacity building is essential for sustaining advocacy efforts. Organizations like **OutRight Action International** provide training and resources to LGBTQ activists in different regions, equipping them with the skills necessary to navigate complex political landscapes. These programs foster resilience and empower advocates to effectively challenge oppressive systems.

Conclusion

Expanding advocacy to other global regions is a crucial component of the ongoing struggle for LGBTQ rights. By embracing intersectionality, addressing cultural and political challenges, and learning from successful initiatives, advocates can create a more inclusive and equitable world. Aderonke Apata's commitment to this mission exemplifies the power of collaboration and the importance of amplifying marginalized voices in the fight for justice. As the global community continues to grapple with issues of equality, the lessons learned from expanding advocacy efforts will undoubtedly shape the future of LGBTQ rights worldwide.

The Legacy Aderonke Aspires to Leave Behind

Aderonke Apata's journey as a prominent LGBTQ activist is marked by a relentless pursuit of justice, equality, and empowerment for marginalized communities. As she continues her work, Aderonke envisions a legacy that transcends borders, inspires future generations, and fosters a more inclusive world. This legacy is grounded in several key principles that reflect her commitment to activism and human rights.

Empowerment Through Education

One of the cornerstones of Aderonke's legacy is the belief in the transformative power of education. She advocates for comprehensive LGBTQ-inclusive curriculums in schools, emphasizing that education can dismantle prejudice and foster understanding. Aderonke's approach aligns with the **Social Learning Theory**, which posits that individuals learn from observing others, especially role models. By providing LGBTQ youth with access to education that acknowledges their identities, Aderonke aims to cultivate a generation of informed and empathetic individuals who can challenge societal norms.

$$\text{Empowerment} = \frac{\text{Knowledge} + \text{Support}}{\text{Prejudice}} \tag{49}$$

This equation illustrates Aderonke's belief that empowerment arises from the combination of knowledge and support, effectively reducing prejudice and fostering acceptance.

Intersectionality in Activism

Aderonke recognizes that the fight for LGBTQ rights cannot be separated from other social justice movements. Her legacy aspires to highlight the importance of **intersectionality**, a term coined by Kimberlé Crenshaw, which emphasizes the interconnected nature of social categorizations such as race, class, and gender. Aderonke's activism incorporates these intersections, advocating for the rights of LGBTQ individuals who also face discrimination based on race, ethnicity, or socioeconomic status.

For example, Aderonke has worked closely with organizations that support Black LGBTQ individuals, emphasizing that their experiences often differ from those of their white counterparts. By addressing these unique challenges, Aderonke hopes to foster a more inclusive movement that recognizes and uplifts diverse voices within the LGBTQ community.

Global Solidarity and Collaboration

Aderonke's legacy is also rooted in the principle of global solidarity. She understands that LGBTQ rights are a universal struggle, and she actively collaborates with activists and organizations worldwide. By building networks of support, Aderonke aims to create a collective movement that transcends geographical boundaries.

This collaborative approach is exemplified by her participation in international conferences, where she shares her experiences and learns from others. Aderonke believes that by uniting activists from different backgrounds, they can strategize and amplify their efforts to challenge oppressive systems globally.

$$\text{Global Solidarity} = \sum_{i=1}^{n} \text{Activist}_i \tag{50}$$

In this equation, the total impact of global solidarity is represented as the sum of individual activists' contributions, emphasizing that each voice adds strength to the collective movement.

Advocacy for Mental Health and Wellbeing

Another significant aspect of Aderonke's legacy is her focus on mental health and wellbeing within the LGBTQ community. Recognizing the high rates of mental health issues among LGBTQ individuals, particularly those facing discrimination and violence, Aderonke advocates for accessible mental health resources and support systems.

Incorporating the **Biopsychosocial Model**, Aderonke emphasizes that mental health cannot be viewed in isolation but must consider biological, psychological, and social factors. She aims to create safe spaces where LGBTQ individuals can seek help without fear of judgment or discrimination.

$$\text{Mental Health} = f(\text{Biological Factors, Psychological Factors, Social Support}) \tag{51}$$

This function illustrates Aderonke's understanding that mental health is influenced by a combination of factors, and addressing each component is crucial for holistic wellbeing.

A Vision for Future Generations

Ultimately, Aderonke aspires to leave behind a legacy that empowers future generations of activists. She believes in the importance of mentorship and support, ensuring that young LGBTQ individuals have the resources and guidance needed to continue the fight for equality. By sharing her story and experiences, Aderonke hopes to inspire others to take up the mantle of activism, fostering a culture of resilience and determination.

Aderonke's legacy is not just about the battles she has fought but also about the seeds of change she has planted for the future. She envisions a world where LGBTQ individuals can live authentically, free from fear and discrimination, and where their contributions to society are recognized and celebrated.

Conclusion

In conclusion, the legacy Aderonke Apata aspires to leave behind is multifaceted, grounded in education, intersectionality, global collaboration, mental health advocacy, and empowerment of future generations. Her unwavering commitment to these principles will undoubtedly shape the landscape of LGBTQ activism for years to come, ensuring that the fight for justice and equality continues to thrive long after her own journey has ended. As Aderonke often reminds us, the struggle for LGBTQ rights is not just a battle for a single community but a fight for humanity and dignity for all.

The Power of Aderonke's Personal Story

Aderonke's Journey: A Catalyst for Change

Aderonke Apata's journey is not merely a personal narrative; it is a profound catalyst for change that resonates within the broader spectrum of LGBTQ activism. Her experiences, struggles, and triumphs have illuminated the path for many, inspiring a movement that transcends geographical and cultural boundaries. This section delves into the theoretical frameworks that underpin Aderonke's activism, the problems she confronted, and the examples of her impactful work that collectively underscore her role as a transformative figure in the fight for LGBTQ rights.

Theoretical Frameworks of Activism

At the core of Aderonke's activism lies the theory of *intersectionality*, a concept introduced by Kimberlé Crenshaw in 1989. This theory posits that individuals experience overlapping systems of discrimination and disadvantage based on their multiple identities, including race, gender, sexual orientation, and socio-economic status. Aderonke's activism exemplifies intersectionality as she navigates the complexities of being a Nigerian LGBTQ individual, a refugee, and a woman in a society that often marginalizes her existence.

The intersectional approach allows Aderonke to address the unique challenges faced by LGBTQ individuals in Nigeria, where homophobia is deeply entrenched in both cultural and legal frameworks. This theoretical lens not only informs her activism but also broadens the conversation around LGBTQ rights to include discussions about race, gender, and socio-economic factors that exacerbate discrimination.

Confronting Systemic Problems

Aderonke's journey is marked by her confrontation with systemic problems that hinder LGBTQ rights in Nigeria. The Nigerian government's anti-LGBTQ laws, particularly the Same-Sex Marriage (Prohibition) Act of 2014, serve as a primary barrier. This law criminalizes same-sex relationships and imposes harsh penalties, fostering an environment of fear and violence against LGBTQ individuals. Aderonke's response to these oppressive laws highlights her resilience and determination to fight back.

Moreover, Aderonke has addressed the pervasive issues of *homophobia* and *transphobia* that manifest in various forms, from societal ostracism to physical violence. For instance, she has shared harrowing accounts of friends and community members who have suffered brutal attacks due to their sexual orientation. These personal stories serve as powerful testaments to the urgent need for change and have galvanized support for her cause.

Aderonke's Activism in Action

Aderonke's activism is characterized by her strategic approach to advocacy, utilizing both grassroots movements and global platforms to amplify her message. One notable example is her involvement in organizing protests and awareness campaigns that challenge discriminatory practices and promote LGBTQ rights in Nigeria. These events not only serve to raise awareness but also foster a sense of community among LGBTQ individuals, providing them with a safe space to express their identities.

In addition to local activism, Aderonke has taken her message to international forums, where she has spoken passionately about the plight of LGBTQ individuals in Nigeria. Her participation in conferences and panels, such as those held by the United Nations, has allowed her to advocate for policy changes on a global scale. Through these engagements, she has effectively highlighted the intersectional challenges faced by LGBTQ refugees, drawing attention to the need for comprehensive support systems.

Empowering Others Through Storytelling

Aderonke's journey is also a testament to the power of storytelling in activism. By sharing her personal experiences, she humanizes the struggles faced by LGBTQ individuals, fostering empathy and understanding among broader audiences. Her narratives serve as a catalyst for change, inspiring others to join the fight for equality.

For example, Aderonke has utilized social media platforms to share her story, reaching a global audience and mobilizing support for LGBTQ rights. Her online presence has become a vital tool for advocacy, enabling her to connect with allies and activists worldwide. This digital activism has proven particularly effective in raising awareness about the unique challenges faced by LGBTQ refugees, amplifying their voices in a landscape where they are often silenced.

Conclusion: Aderonke as a Catalyst for Change

In conclusion, Aderonke Apata's journey is a powerful illustration of how individual experiences can catalyze broader social change. Through her intersectional approach to activism, confrontation of systemic problems, strategic use of storytelling, and empowerment of others, Aderonke has become a beacon of hope for many. Her work not only addresses the immediate challenges faced by LGBTQ individuals but also lays the groundwork for a more inclusive and equitable future. As she continues to inspire change, Aderonke's legacy will undoubtedly resonate within the global LGBTQ movement for years to come.

The Role of Personal Narratives in Activism

Personal narratives serve as powerful tools in activism, particularly within the LGBTQ movement, as they humanize issues that are often abstract or misunderstood. These stories create connections between individuals, fostering empathy and understanding that can lead to social change. In the realm of activism, personal narratives can be framed through various theoretical lenses, including narrative theory, social identity theory, and the concept of intersectionality.

Narrative theory posits that stories shape our understanding of the world and our place within it. According to Bruner (1991), narratives help individuals make sense of their experiences and convey meaning. In activism, personal narratives allow activists to share their lived experiences, challenges, and triumphs, making the struggles of marginalized communities more relatable. For instance, Aderonke Apata's journey from a persecuted LGBTQ individual in Nigeria to a prominent activist in the UK exemplifies the power of personal storytelling. Her narrative highlights the harsh realities faced by LGBTQ individuals in Nigeria, including violence, discrimination, and the constant threat of persecution.

$$\text{Empathy} = \frac{\text{Understanding} + \text{Connection}}{\text{Distance}} \qquad (52)$$

This equation illustrates that as understanding and connection increase, the distance between the storyteller and the audience decreases, leading to greater empathy. When audiences engage with personal narratives, they are more likely to feel a sense of connection to the storyteller, which can inspire action or support for the cause.

However, the use of personal narratives in activism is not without its challenges. One significant problem is the potential for oversimplification of complex issues. Personal stories can sometimes reduce multifaceted social problems to individual experiences, potentially overshadowing systemic factors that contribute to oppression. Additionally, there is the risk of the "single story" phenomenon, as articulated by Chimamanda Ngozi Adichie (2009), where a singular narrative can perpetuate stereotypes and limit the understanding of a community's diversity.

For example, while Aderonke's story is compelling and highlights critical issues within the LGBTQ community in Nigeria, it is essential to recognize that her experience is just one of many. Activists must strive to amplify a multitude of voices, ensuring that the diversity of experiences within the LGBTQ community is represented. This approach aligns with the principles of intersectionality, which emphasizes the interconnectedness of various social identities and the unique challenges faced by individuals at the intersections of these identities.

To effectively utilize personal narratives in activism, it is crucial to:

1. **Contextualize Stories**: Frame personal narratives within broader social and political contexts to avoid oversimplification. This can involve highlighting systemic issues and advocating for policy changes alongside personal experiences.

2. **Encourage Diverse Voices**: Actively seek and promote a range of narratives from different individuals within the LGBTQ community, ensuring that marginalized voices are heard and represented.

3. **Foster Community Engagement**: Use personal stories to engage communities in dialogue, encouraging discussions that lead to collective action and solidarity.

4. **Utilize Multiple Platforms**: Leverage various media platforms—social media, documentaries, public speaking engagements—to share personal narratives widely and effectively.

5. **Promote Healing and Empowerment**: Recognize the therapeutic potential of storytelling for both the storyteller and the audience. Sharing personal narratives can empower individuals, fostering resilience and a sense of agency within the community.

In conclusion, personal narratives are vital to activism, providing a means to connect, inspire, and mobilize individuals toward social change. While challenges exist, the thoughtful integration of personal stories into activism can significantly enhance the visibility and understanding of LGBTQ issues, ultimately contributing to a more inclusive and equitable society. As Aderonke Apata continues to share her story and advocate for LGBTQ rights, her narrative serves as a beacon of hope, resilience, and the transformative power of personal storytelling in the ongoing fight for justice.

$$\text{Impact} = \text{Narrative Power} \times \text{Audience Engagement} \qquad (53)$$

This equation reflects the idea that the impact of personal narratives in activism is maximized when the power of the narrative is multiplied by the level of audience engagement. By fostering connections through storytelling, activists can inspire change and promote understanding in the pursuit of equality.

Empowering Others through Authenticity

In the realm of activism, particularly within the LGBTQ community, authenticity serves as a powerful catalyst for empowerment. Aderonke Apata embodies this principle, demonstrating how embracing one's true self can inspire others to do the same. Authenticity, in this context, refers to the alignment of one's actions, beliefs, and identity, fostering a genuine representation of self that resonates with others.

Theoretical Framework

The concept of authenticity can be examined through various theoretical lenses. One notable framework is Carl Rogers' Person-Centered Theory, which emphasizes the importance of self-actualization and the need for individuals to express their true selves. According to Rogers, authenticity is crucial for personal growth and well-being, suggesting that individuals who embrace their identities are more likely to experience fulfillment and contribute positively to their communities.

Moreover, the Social Identity Theory, developed by Henri Tajfel and John Turner, posits that individuals derive a sense of self from their group memberships. For LGBTQ individuals, embracing their sexual orientation or gender identity can foster a sense of belonging and solidarity, thereby empowering them to advocate for their rights and the rights of others. This alignment between personal identity and group identity can enhance resilience against societal discrimination.

Challenges to Authenticity

Despite the empowering nature of authenticity, many LGBTQ individuals face significant challenges in embracing their true selves. Societal stigma, discrimination, and internalized homophobia can create barriers that inhibit self-acceptance. The fear of rejection from family, friends, and communities can lead to a reluctance to express one's identity openly.

Additionally, the intersectionality of identities—such as race, gender, and socioeconomic status—can complicate the journey toward authenticity. For instance, a queer individual from a marginalized racial background may encounter compounded discrimination, making the path to self-acceptance and advocacy even more arduous. This complexity highlights the need for a supportive environment where diverse identities are celebrated rather than suppressed.

Examples of Empowerment through Authenticity

Aderonke Apata's journey exemplifies the transformative power of authenticity. By openly sharing her experiences as a queer Nigerian woman and refugee advocate, Aderonke has not only empowered herself but has also inspired countless others to embrace their identities. Her public speaking engagements and social media presence serve as platforms for sharing her story, thereby encouraging others to find their voices.

For instance, during her advocacy work, Aderonke has recounted her personal struggles with acceptance and the challenges she faced in Nigeria. By sharing these narratives, she creates a space for others to relate and feel validated in their experiences. This sharing of personal stories fosters a sense of community and belonging, reinforcing the idea that no one is alone in their struggles.

Moreover, Aderonke's involvement in mentorship programs demonstrates her commitment to empowering LGBTQ youth. By providing guidance and support, she helps young individuals navigate their identities in a world that can often be hostile. This mentorship not only fosters self-acceptance but also equips the next generation with the tools necessary for advocacy and activism.

The Role of Authenticity in Activism

Authenticity plays a critical role in activism, as it allows advocates to connect with their audience on a deeper level. When activists share their genuine stories, they humanize the issues at hand, making them more relatable and compelling. This emotional connection can mobilize support and inspire action among allies and community members alike.

Aderonke's authenticity has been instrumental in raising awareness about the plight of LGBTQ individuals in Nigeria and beyond. By being true to herself, she challenges stereotypes and misconceptions, paving the way for more inclusive dialogues around LGBTQ rights. Her approach underscores the importance of visibility in activism, as authentic representation can dismantle harmful narratives and foster understanding.

Conclusion

Empowering others through authenticity is a vital aspect of effective activism. Aderonke Apata's journey illustrates how embracing one's true self can inspire others to find their voices and advocate for change. By fostering an environment where authenticity is celebrated, activists can create a ripple effect that empowers individuals to embrace their identities and work collectively toward equality and justice. As the LGBTQ movement continues to evolve, the importance of authenticity will remain a cornerstone of empowerment, resilience, and transformative change.

Aderonke's Legacy as an Inspiration

Aderonke Apata's journey is not merely a story of personal triumph but a beacon of hope and resilience for countless individuals navigating the treacherous waters of identity, acceptance, and activism. Her legacy serves as an inspiration across various dimensions of the LGBTQ movement, particularly in the realms of advocacy, community building, and the fight against systemic oppression.

At the core of Aderonke's impact is her ability to embody the intersectionality of identity. Intersectionality, a term coined by Kimberlé Crenshaw, refers to how various social identities—such as race, gender, sexual orientation, and class—interact to create unique modes of discrimination and privilege. Aderonke's work illustrates the importance of acknowledging these intersections, as she continuously advocated for not just LGBTQ rights but also for the rights of marginalized groups within the LGBTQ community. This holistic approach has inspired a new generation of activists to adopt an inclusive framework in their advocacy efforts.

One of the most profound aspects of Aderonke's legacy lies in her ability to transform personal pain into collective power. Her own experiences with homophobia, persecution, and the asylum process are not just stories of struggle; they are rallying cries for change. Through her activism, she has shown that personal narratives can serve as powerful tools for advocacy. Aderonke's story exemplifies the theory of social movement framing, which posits that the way issues are presented can significantly influence public perception and mobilization. By sharing her experiences, she has framed LGBTQ rights as not just a personal issue but a fundamental human rights concern that resonates globally.

Aderonke's influence is also evident in her efforts to build community and foster solidarity among activists. She has been instrumental in creating safe spaces for LGBTQ individuals, particularly in environments where such identities are criminalized or stigmatized. The establishment of support networks and community organizations under her guidance has provided a lifeline for many who feel isolated or threatened. This community-oriented approach reflects the principles of community organizing, which emphasize the importance of grassroots mobilization and empowerment.

Moreover, Aderonke's legacy is characterized by her commitment to education and awareness-raising. She has tirelessly worked to educate both the LGBTQ community and the broader public about the challenges faced by LGBTQ individuals, particularly refugees. By highlighting these issues, she has not only raised awareness but has also mobilized resources and support for those in need. This aligns with Paulo Freire's theory of critical pedagogy, which advocates for education as a means of social change. Aderonke's efforts to educate others empower individuals to challenge oppressive systems and advocate for their rights.

Aderonke's activism extends beyond the borders of Nigeria and the UK; she has become a global figure in the fight for LGBTQ rights. Her participation in international conferences and collaborations with global organizations exemplify the importance of transnational advocacy networks. These networks facilitate the sharing of resources, strategies, and solidarity across borders, amplifying the voices of marginalized communities. Aderonke's role in these networks demonstrates the power of collective action in addressing issues of global significance.

The challenges Aderonke has faced, including discrimination, legal battles, and personal attacks, have only strengthened her resolve. Her resilience serves as a powerful example for others who may feel disheartened by the struggles they encounter. Aderonke's ability to rise above adversity and continue fighting for justice is a testament to the indomitable spirit of activists everywhere. This resilience can be understood through the lens of resilience theory, which emphasizes the capacity to recover from difficulties and maintain a commitment to one's goals.

In conclusion, Aderonke Apata's legacy as an inspiration is multifaceted and profound. Her commitment to intersectionality, community building, education, and resilience has not only shaped the landscape of LGBTQ activism but has also inspired countless individuals to stand up for their rights and the rights of others. As we reflect on her journey, it is clear that Aderonke's impact will continue to resonate, motivating future generations to pursue justice and equality for all. Her story is a reminder that the fight for LGBTQ rights is not just a struggle for a specific community but a universal quest for human dignity and respect.

Aderonke's Impact on LGBTQ Rights: Looking Ahead

The Ongoing Struggle for Global LGBTQ Equality

The fight for LGBTQ equality is a multifaceted and ongoing struggle that spans across various cultural, political, and social landscapes. While significant progress has been made in many parts of the world, numerous challenges and systemic barriers persist, making the quest for equality a continuous battle. This section will explore the current state of LGBTQ rights globally, the challenges faced by activists, and the theoretical frameworks that underpin this struggle.

Current State of LGBTQ Rights

As of 2023, LGBTQ rights vary dramatically from one country to another. In some nations, such as Canada and many Western European countries, same-sex marriage is legal, and LGBTQ individuals enjoy legal protections against discrimination. Conversely, in countries like Nigeria, Uganda, and Saudi Arabia, LGBTQ individuals face severe criminalization, societal ostracism, and, in extreme cases, violence and persecution. According to the International Lesbian, Gay, Bisexual, Trans and Intersex Association (ILGA), over 70 countries still criminalize same-sex relationships, and in several of these, LGBTQ individuals can face imprisonment or even the death penalty.

The disparity in LGBTQ rights can be attributed to a variety of factors, including cultural norms, religious beliefs, and historical context. For instance, in many African and Middle Eastern countries, colonial-era laws that criminalized homosexuality continue to influence current legal frameworks. The persistence of these laws often reflects deeply ingrained societal attitudes towards LGBTQ individuals, perpetuating discrimination and violence.

Challenges Faced by Activists

Activists fighting for LGBTQ rights encounter numerous challenges, including governmental repression, social stigma, and violence. In many regions, activists risk their safety and freedom to advocate for equality. For example, in countries with anti-LGBTQ laws, activists may face arrest, harassment, and violence from both state and non-state actors. The case of Aderonke Apata exemplifies this struggle; her activism in Nigeria led to threats and eventual exile, highlighting the personal risks involved in advocating for LGBTQ rights.

Moreover, the intersectionality of identity complicates the fight for equality. LGBTQ individuals who also belong to marginalized racial, ethnic, or socio-economic groups often face compounded discrimination. This intersectional approach is critical in understanding the diverse experiences of LGBTQ individuals globally. Activists must navigate these complexities to ensure that their advocacy is inclusive and representative of all voices within the LGBTQ community.

Theoretical Frameworks

The ongoing struggle for LGBTQ equality can be analyzed through various theoretical lenses, including queer theory, intersectionality, and human rights frameworks. Queer theory challenges the binary understanding of gender and sexuality, advocating for a more fluid understanding of identity. This theoretical approach emphasizes the importance of recognizing diverse sexual and gender identities, arguing that societal norms should not dictate personal identity.

Intersectionality, a term coined by Kimberlé Crenshaw, provides a framework for understanding how various forms of discrimination overlap and intersect. This perspective is crucial for LGBTQ activists, as it highlights the need for advocacy that addresses the unique challenges faced by individuals at the intersection of multiple marginalized identities. For example, Black transgender women often experience higher rates of violence and discrimination compared to their white counterparts, necessitating tailored advocacy efforts.

Finally, the human rights framework posits that LGBTQ rights are human rights, emphasizing the need for legal protections and societal acceptance. This perspective has gained traction in international discourse, with organizations such as the United Nations increasingly recognizing the importance of LGBTQ rights in the broader context of human rights.

Examples of Activism and Progress

Despite the challenges, numerous grassroots and international organizations are making strides in the fight for LGBTQ equality. Organizations like Human Rights Campaign (HRC), ILGA, and OutRight Action International work tirelessly to promote LGBTQ rights through advocacy, education, and support services. These organizations often collaborate with local activists to amplify their voices and ensure that their needs are met.

One notable example of successful activism is the decriminalization of homosexuality in India in 2018, when the Supreme Court ruled that Section 377 of the Indian Penal Code, which criminalized same-sex relationships, was unconstitutional. This landmark decision was the result of years of advocacy and mobilization by LGBTQ activists, illustrating the power of collective action and perseverance.

In addition to legal victories, social movements have played a crucial role in advancing LGBTQ rights. Pride parades, awareness campaigns, and community-building initiatives have fostered greater visibility and acceptance of LGBTQ individuals. These events not only celebrate LGBTQ identities but also serve as platforms for raising awareness about the ongoing struggles faced by the community.

Conclusion

The ongoing struggle for global LGBTQ equality is characterized by both progress and setbacks. While significant advancements have been made, particularly in the areas of legal recognition and social acceptance, many challenges remain. Activists continue to face repression and violence, and intersectional identities complicate the fight for equality. However, through collective action, theoretical frameworks, and the tireless efforts of individuals and organizations, the movement for LGBTQ rights persists. The path to equality is fraught with obstacles, but the resilience and determination of activists worldwide serve as a beacon of hope for future generations.

Aderonke's Role in Shaping the Future of Activism

Aderonke Apata stands as a pivotal figure in the evolution of LGBTQ activism, not only within Nigeria but also on a global scale. Her journey exemplifies how individual narratives can influence collective movements, shaping the future of activism through resilience, advocacy, and a commitment to intersectionality. In this section, we explore Aderonke's role in shaping future activism, focusing on her methodologies, the challenges she faced, and the theoretical frameworks that underpin her work.

Theoretical Frameworks

Aderonke's activism can be analyzed through several theoretical lenses, including Queer Theory, Intersectionality, and Social Movement Theory.

Queer Theory posits that gender and sexuality are fluid constructs rather than fixed categories. Aderonke embodies this perspective, advocating for a broader understanding of LGBTQ identities that transcend binary classifications. Her work encourages activists to embrace complexity, recognizing that individuals may identify in multifaceted ways that require nuanced approaches to advocacy.

Intersectionality, a term coined by Kimberlé Crenshaw, emphasizes the interconnectedness of social identities and the unique experiences of individuals at the intersections of multiple identities. Aderonke's activism is deeply rooted in this concept, as she consistently highlights the experiences of marginalized groups within the LGBTQ community, particularly those who face additional layers of discrimination due to race, socioeconomic status, or immigration status. This approach not only broadens the scope of activism but also fosters inclusivity within the movement.

Social Movement Theory provides insights into how collective action can lead to social change. Aderonke's ability to mobilize communities, organize protests, and engage in advocacy reflects the principles outlined in this theory. Her strategic use of social media to amplify voices and rally support exemplifies how modern activism can leverage technology to effect change.

Challenges Faced in Activism

Despite her significant contributions, Aderonke's journey has not been without challenges. The socio-political landscape in Nigeria remains hostile to LGBTQ rights, creating an environment fraught with danger for activists. Aderonke has faced threats, harassment, and even violence as a direct result of her advocacy. These experiences highlight the persistent issues of homophobia and transphobia that activists must navigate.

Moreover, the asylum process in the United Kingdom presented its own set of challenges. Aderonke encountered bureaucratic hurdles, discrimination, and a lack of understanding regarding the specific needs of LGBTQ refugees. These experiences underscore the importance of advocacy that addresses systemic barriers within asylum systems, ensuring that LGBTQ individuals receive the support and protection they deserve.

Examples of Impactful Initiatives

Aderonke's influence is evident through various initiatives that she has spearheaded. One notable example is her work in establishing safe spaces for LGBTQ individuals, both in Nigeria and the UK. These spaces serve as havens for community members to gather, share experiences, and find support. By creating environments where individuals can express their identities freely, Aderonke fosters a sense of belonging and empowerment.

Additionally, Aderonke has been instrumental in raising awareness about the unique challenges faced by LGBTQ refugees. Through her advocacy, she has highlighted the need for tailored support services that address the specific experiences of LGBTQ individuals in the asylum process. This work not only informs policymakers but also inspires other activists to consider the diverse needs of marginalized communities.

Empowering Future Generations of Activists

Aderonke's commitment to mentorship and education is another critical aspect of her role in shaping the future of activism. She actively engages with young activists, providing guidance, resources, and encouragement. By sharing her experiences and insights, Aderonke empowers the next generation to continue the fight for equality and justice.

Her emphasis on intersectionality also serves as a vital lesson for emerging activists. Aderonke's advocacy encourages future leaders to adopt inclusive practices, ensuring that all voices within the LGBTQ community are heard and represented. This approach not only strengthens the movement but also fosters solidarity among diverse groups.

The Legacy of Aderonke Apata

As we look to the future, Aderonke Apata's legacy will undoubtedly influence the trajectory of LGBTQ activism. Her ability to navigate complex challenges, advocate for marginalized voices, and inspire others to take action sets a powerful precedent for future activists. The principles of inclusivity, resilience, and intersectionality that she champions will continue to resonate in the ongoing struggle for LGBTQ rights globally.

In conclusion, Aderonke's role in shaping the future of activism is characterized by her unwavering commitment to justice, her strategic use of theory and practice, and her dedication to empowering others. As the landscape of activism evolves, the lessons learned from Aderonke's journey will serve as a guiding light for those who continue to fight for equality and human rights for all.

The Message Aderonke Leaves for Future Generations

Aderonke Apata's journey as an LGBTQ activist is not merely a chronicle of struggles and victories; it is a powerful message that reverberates through the corridors of time, echoing the spirit of resilience and the necessity for change. For future generations, Aderonke's life serves as both a beacon of hope and a call to action, reminding us that the fight for equality is not just a personal battle but a collective responsibility.

Empowerment through Authenticity

At the core of Aderonke's message is the importance of authenticity. She has shown that embracing one's true self is a radical act of defiance in a world that often demands conformity. By living her truth, Aderonke empowers others to do the same, fostering a culture of acceptance and self-love. This authenticity is essential for future activists; it encourages individuals to share their stories, thus humanizing the struggle for LGBTQ rights.

$$\text{Authenticity} = \frac{\text{Self-acceptance} + \text{Expression}}{\text{Fear of Rejection}} \tag{54}$$

This equation symbolizes the balance required to live authentically. As self-acceptance and expression increase, the fear of rejection diminishes, creating a cycle of empowerment that can inspire future generations to be unapologetically themselves.

Intersectionality: A Broader Perspective

Aderonke's advocacy also highlights the importance of intersectionality in activism. She has consistently pointed out that the fight for LGBTQ rights cannot be divorced from other social justice movements, such as those addressing race, gender, and economic inequality. This interconnectedness is crucial for future activists to understand, as it fosters a more inclusive approach to advocacy.

For instance, Aderonke's collaboration with various organizations illustrates how diverse movements can unite for a common cause. By recognizing the unique challenges faced by individuals at the intersection of multiple identities, future generations can develop more comprehensive strategies that address the root causes of discrimination.

The Power of Community

Aderonke emphasizes the significance of community in the fight for justice. She has shown that collective action is a formidable force against oppression. Future activists must understand that while individual stories are powerful, they are amplified within a supportive community.

Aderonke's initiatives, such as mentorship programs and safe spaces for LGBTQ youth, underscore the necessity of building networks of support. These communities provide not only emotional backing but also practical resources that empower individuals to engage in activism effectively.

$$\text{Community Strength} = \text{Unity} \times \text{Support}^2 \qquad (55)$$

In this equation, the strength of a community is a product of unity and the square of support, illustrating that the more support members provide each other, the stronger the community becomes.

Advocacy as a Lifelong Commitment

Aderonke's journey teaches that advocacy is not a finite endeavor; it is a lifelong commitment. The struggle for LGBTQ rights is ongoing, and future generations must be prepared to continue this fight. Aderonke has shown that even in the face of adversity, persistence is key.

Her resilience in advocating for change, even when faced with personal threats and systemic barriers, serves as a model for future activists. They must recognize that setbacks are part of the journey and that each challenge presents an opportunity for growth and renewed determination.

A Vision for a Just Future

Ultimately, Aderonke's message is one of hope. She envisions a world where LGBTQ individuals can live freely and authentically, without fear of discrimination or violence. This vision is not just a dream; it is a call to action for future generations to work towards creating a just society.

Activists are encouraged to dream big and to set ambitious goals that extend beyond their immediate communities. By doing so, they can inspire others and create a ripple effect that leads to significant societal change.

$$\text{Future Vision} = \text{Dreams} \times \text{Actions} \tag{56}$$

This equation illustrates that a vision for the future is realized through the interplay of dreams and actionable steps. Aderonke's legacy encourages future generations to dream boldly and to take concrete actions that align with those dreams.

Conclusion

In conclusion, Aderonke Apata leaves behind a profound message for future generations: embrace your authenticity, recognize the power of community, commit to lifelong advocacy, and envision a just future. Her story is a testament to the resilience of the human spirit and the transformative power of activism. As future activists carry her torch, they must remember that the fight for equality is not just about achieving rights; it is about creating a world where every individual can thrive in their truth.

The legacy of Aderonke Apata will undoubtedly continue to inspire and guide future generations as they navigate the complexities of activism and strive for a more equitable world.

The Fight Continues: The Importance of LGBTQ Advocacy

The struggle for LGBTQ rights is far from over. Even as progress is made in many parts of the world, there remain significant challenges that demand sustained advocacy and action. Aderonke Apata's journey exemplifies the ongoing fight for justice, equality, and recognition within the LGBTQ community, underscoring the critical importance of advocacy in fostering change.

Theoretical Frameworks in LGBTQ Advocacy

Understanding the importance of LGBTQ advocacy requires a look at various theoretical frameworks that inform activism. One such framework is **Queer Theory**, which challenges the binary understanding of gender and sexuality. It posits that identities are fluid and socially constructed, emphasizing the need for advocacy that recognizes diverse experiences. As Judith Butler articulates in her seminal work, *Gender Trouble*, the performative nature of gender and sexuality calls for a re-examination of societal norms and legal structures that perpetuate discrimination.

Moreover, **Intersectionality**, a term coined by Kimberlé Crenshaw, is crucial in LGBTQ advocacy. It highlights how various social identities—such as race, gender, class, and sexuality—intersect to create unique experiences of oppression. Advocates must consider these intersections to address the multifaceted nature of discrimination faced by LGBTQ individuals, particularly those from marginalized backgrounds. For instance, LGBTQ individuals of color often experience compounded discrimination, necessitating targeted advocacy efforts.

Challenges in LGBTQ Advocacy

Despite advancements in LGBTQ rights, numerous challenges persist. In many countries, anti-LGBTQ laws remain in place, criminalizing same-sex relationships and gender nonconformity. According to a report by the International Lesbian, Gay, Bisexual, Trans and Intersex Association (ILGA), as of 2023, over 70 countries still have laws that criminalize same-sex relations, affecting millions of individuals. These legal barriers not only perpetuate stigma but also hinder access to essential services, such as healthcare and legal protection.

Additionally, violence against LGBTQ individuals is alarmingly prevalent. The Human Rights Campaign reported a significant increase in violence against transgender individuals, particularly transgender women of color, in recent years. Advocacy efforts are essential to combat this violence, raise awareness, and push for policy changes that protect vulnerable populations.

Examples of Effective Advocacy

Effective advocacy can take many forms, from grassroots organizing to international campaigns. One notable example is the **Stonewall Riots** of 1969, which marked a turning point in the LGBTQ rights movement. The riots were a response to police brutality against LGBTQ individuals, igniting a wave of activism that led to the formation of numerous advocacy organizations. Today, events like Pride Month serve as both a celebration of progress and a reminder of the ongoing fight for equality.

Another powerful example is the **It Gets Better Project**, which aims to support LGBTQ youth facing bullying and discrimination. By sharing personal stories and providing resources, the project has fostered a sense of community and hope, demonstrating the impact of visibility and representation in advocacy.

The Role of Allies

Allies play a crucial role in the fight for LGBTQ rights. Their support can amplify marginalized voices and create a more inclusive environment. Advocacy is not solely the responsibility of LGBTQ individuals; it requires a collective effort from everyone committed to social justice. Allies can engage in various forms of activism, from participating in protests to advocating for policy changes within their communities.

The Future of LGBTQ Advocacy

Looking ahead, the importance of LGBTQ advocacy will only continue to grow. As new challenges arise—such as the rise of anti-LGBTQ legislation in various regions—advocacy efforts must adapt and evolve. This includes utilizing technology and social media to mobilize support, raise awareness, and amplify marginalized voices.

Moreover, fostering global solidarity among LGBTQ activists is essential. The fight for LGBTQ rights is not confined to any one nation; it is a global struggle that requires collaboration across borders. By sharing resources, strategies, and experiences, activists can strengthen their efforts and create a more unified movement.

Conclusion

In conclusion, the fight for LGBTQ rights is an ongoing journey that demands unwavering commitment and advocacy. Aderonke Apata's work exemplifies the power of activism in challenging oppression and fostering change. As we reflect on the importance of LGBTQ advocacy, we must recognize that every voice matters, and every action counts. The struggle for justice, equality, and recognition will continue, and it is our collective responsibility to stand up for the rights of all individuals, regardless of their sexual orientation or gender identity.

Conclusion: The Aderonke Apata Story Lives On

Conclusion: The Aderonke Apata Story Lives On

Conclusion: The Aderonke Apata Story Lives On

The story of Aderonke Apata transcends the boundaries of individual experience, embodying a powerful narrative that resonates deeply within the global LGBTQ community. As we reflect on her journey, it becomes evident that her life is a testament to resilience, courage, and the unyielding pursuit of justice. This conclusion serves not only as a summary of her remarkable achievements but also as a call to action for future generations of activists.

Aderonke's evolution as an activist is intricately tied to the broader landscape of LGBTQ rights, particularly in Nigeria. The challenges she faced, including systemic homophobia, legal persecution, and societal discrimination, highlight the urgent need for continued advocacy. The intersection of personal and political struggles is a recurring theme in Aderonke's narrative, illustrating how individual experiences can catalyze collective movements for change.

The framework of intersectionality, as posited by scholars like Kimberlé Crenshaw, serves as a critical lens through which we can analyze Aderonke's activism. Intersectionality emphasizes that various forms of oppression—such as those based on race, gender, and sexual orientation—do not exist independently but are interconnected. Aderonke's advocacy for LGBTQ rights is deeply intertwined with her identity as a Nigerian woman, and her experiences of discrimination cannot be separated from the cultural and societal contexts in which they occur.

$$\text{Intersectionality} = f(\text{Race, Gender, Sexual Orientation, Socioeconomic Status})$$

This equation illustrates the multifaceted nature of identity, emphasizing that Aderonke's activism is rooted in a complex interplay of factors that shape her lived experience. Her work has not only challenged the status quo in Nigeria but has also inspired others to confront their own realities, fostering a sense of solidarity and empowerment within marginalized communities.

The legacy of Aderonke Apata is further exemplified through her ability to mobilize support and create safe spaces for LGBTQ individuals. By organizing events, protests, and awareness campaigns, she has established a foundation for future activists to build upon. The importance of community in activism cannot be overstated; as Aderonke once stated, "We rise by lifting others." This ethos underscores the necessity of collaboration and mutual support in the fight for equality.

As we look to the future, it is imperative to recognize the ongoing struggles that LGBTQ individuals face globally. The fight for equality is far from over, and Aderonke's story serves as both a beacon of hope and a reminder of the work that lies ahead. The principles of advocacy, education, and visibility remain critical in dismantling oppressive systems and fostering acceptance.

In conclusion, the narrative of Aderonke Apata is not merely a historical account but a living testament to the power of activism. Her journey illustrates the profound impact one individual can have in the face of adversity. As we honor her contributions, we are called to continue the fight for justice, equality, and acceptance for all. Aderonke's legacy lives on in the hearts of many, inspiring a new generation of activists to challenge the status quo and advocate for a world where love knows no boundaries.

$$\text{Legacy} = \text{Activism} + \text{Community} + \text{Hope}$$

This equation encapsulates the essence of Aderonke's impact, reminding us that her story is not just her own but is interwoven with the aspirations and struggles of countless others. The Aderonke Apata story lives on, urging us all to stand up for equality and to embrace the power of our collective voices in the ongoing fight for LGBTQ rights.

Reflecting on Aderonke's Journey

The Evolution of LGBTQ Activism in Nigeria

The evolution of LGBTQ activism in Nigeria has been a complex and tumultuous journey, marked by cultural, political, and social challenges. The roots of this activism can be traced back to the pre-colonial era, where diverse sexualities were often more accepted within various indigenous cultures. However, the imposition of colonial laws, particularly the British Penal Code, criminalized homosexual acts and laid the groundwork for systemic discrimination.

In the late 20th century, as Nigeria gained independence, the struggle for LGBTQ rights began to take a more organized form. Activists started to emerge, advocating for visibility and acceptance within a society steeped in traditional values and religious conservatism. The impact of religion cannot be understated, as both Christianity and Islam play significant roles in shaping societal attitudes towards homosexuality. This duality often creates a hostile environment for LGBTQ individuals, leading to widespread discrimination and violence.

The early 2000s marked a pivotal moment in the evolution of LGBTQ activism in Nigeria. The formation of organizations such as the *International Center for Advocacy on Right to Health* (ICARH) and *The Initiative for Equal Rights* (TIERs) provided critical support networks for LGBTQ individuals. These organizations focused on health, legal rights, and advocacy, aiming to combat the stigma associated with homosexuality.

Despite these advancements, the enactment of the Same-Sex Marriage Prohibition Act in 2014 represented a significant setback for LGBTQ rights in Nigeria. This law not only criminalized same-sex relationships but also imposed penalties on individuals and organizations that supported LGBTQ rights. The legislation galvanized activists, who responded with a renewed sense of purpose. They began organizing protests, leveraging social media, and seeking international support to challenge the oppressive legal framework.

The rise of social media platforms has played a crucial role in the evolution of LGBTQ activism in Nigeria. Activists have utilized these tools to share personal stories, raise awareness, and mobilize support. Campaigns such as *#FreeNigeria* and *#EndSARS* have highlighted the intersectionality of LGBTQ rights with broader human rights issues. This digital activism has not only increased visibility for LGBTQ individuals but has also attracted the attention of international human rights organizations.

Furthermore, the collaboration between local and international organizations has strengthened the movement. Partnerships with global entities such as Human Rights Watch and Amnesty International have provided crucial resources and advocacy platforms for Nigerian activists. These collaborations have facilitated legal assistance, funding for initiatives, and opportunities for Nigerian activists to participate in international forums.

Despite the progress, challenges remain. Activists continue to face threats of violence, harassment, and arrest. The pervasive culture of homophobia, fueled by societal norms and religious doctrines, poses significant barriers to the acceptance of LGBTQ individuals. Moreover, the lack of comprehensive anti-discrimination laws leaves LGBTQ Nigerians vulnerable to abuse.

In conclusion, the evolution of LGBTQ activism in Nigeria is marked by resilience and determination. From its roots in indigenous acceptance to the current struggle against oppressive laws, the movement has adapted and evolved. The ongoing fight for equality is a testament to the courage of activists who, despite facing immense challenges, continue to advocate for a future where all Nigerians can live freely and authentically, regardless of their sexual orientation or gender identity. The journey is far from over, but the seeds of change have been planted, and the activism of today will undoubtedly shape the landscape of tomorrow.

The Intersection of Personal and Political

The journey of Aderonke Apata exemplifies the profound intersection of personal identity and political activism within the LGBTQ rights movement. This intersection is not merely a backdrop; it is the crucible in which the essence of activism is forged. Understanding this relationship involves delving into the complexities of identity politics, the role of personal narratives in shaping collective movements, and the broader implications of individual experiences on political landscapes.

At its core, identity politics refers to the ways in which individuals' personal identities—shaped by factors such as sexuality, gender, race, and nationality—inform their political beliefs and actions. Aderonke's activism is a vivid illustration of this concept. Growing up in Nigeria, where LGBTQ individuals face systemic oppression and violence, Aderonke's personal experiences of discrimination and exclusion fueled her commitment to advocating for equality. Her identity as a queer woman of color not only shaped her understanding of the injustices faced by her community but also positioned her as a critical voice in the fight against homophobia and transphobia.

The theory of intersectionality, coined by legal scholar Kimberlé Crenshaw, provides a framework for analyzing how overlapping identities impact individuals' experiences of discrimination and privilege. Aderonke's activism embodies intersectionality, as she navigates the complexities of being both a Nigerian national and a member of the LGBTQ community. The unique challenges she faces—such as the intersection of cultural norms, religious beliefs, and legal restrictions—highlight the need for an inclusive approach to activism that recognizes the multiplicity of identities.

For instance, Aderonke's work in Nigeria reveals how traditional values often clash with LGBTQ rights. The influence of religion and cultural expectations creates a hostile environment for LGBTQ individuals, making it imperative for activists to address these intersections. Aderonke's advocacy efforts not only challenge homophobic laws but also seek to engage with cultural narratives that perpetuate discrimination. By framing her activism within the context of her personal experiences, Aderonke effectively challenges the dominant narratives that marginalize LGBTQ voices.

Moreover, personal narratives play a crucial role in political activism. Aderonke's storytelling—whether through social media, public speaking, or written works—serves as a powerful tool for raising awareness and fostering empathy. Her journey from a young girl in Lagos grappling with her identity to a prominent activist advocating for LGBTQ rights illustrates the transformative potential of personal stories in mobilizing communities. This narrative approach not only humanizes the struggle for rights but also invites others to connect with the cause on a deeper level.

The political implications of Aderonke's personal experiences extend beyond her immediate context. Her advocacy for LGBTQ refugees in the United Kingdom underscores the global dimensions of her work. By sharing her story as a refugee fleeing persecution, Aderonke highlights the urgent need for international solidarity and support for marginalized communities. This intersection of personal and political resonates with broader movements advocating for human rights, emphasizing that the fight for LGBTQ equality is inherently linked to the struggle for justice and dignity for all.

However, the intersection of personal and political also presents challenges. Aderonke's visibility as a queer activist has made her a target for backlash and criticism, both from conservative factions within Nigeria and from individuals who may misinterpret her intentions. The personal toll of activism—navigating threats, discrimination, and the emotional weight of advocating for a marginalized community—cannot be overlooked. Aderonke's journey reflects the resilience required to confront these challenges, as well as the importance of self-care and community support in sustaining long-term activism.

In conclusion, the intersection of personal and political in Aderonke Apata's life and activism serves as a powerful reminder of the complexities inherent in the fight for LGBTQ rights. By embracing her identity and sharing her story, Aderonke not only advocates for change but also inspires others to recognize the importance of their own narratives in shaping the political landscape. The ongoing struggle for equality is not just a political endeavor; it is deeply personal, rooted in the lived experiences of individuals who dare to challenge the status quo. As

Aderonke continues to navigate this intersection, her legacy will undoubtedly inspire future generations of activists to embrace their identities and fight for justice, both personally and politically.

Aderonke's Enduring Legacy

Aderonke Apata's journey as an LGBTQ activist is not merely a story of struggle and resilience; it is a testament to the power of activism in shaping societal norms and advocating for human rights. Her legacy endures through the profound impact she has made on the LGBTQ community, both in Nigeria and globally.

At the heart of Aderonke's legacy is her unwavering commitment to challenging systemic discrimination and advocating for equality. She has become a symbol of hope for many marginalized individuals facing persecution due to their sexual orientation or gender identity. This is evident in her tireless efforts to raise awareness about the plight of LGBTQ individuals in Nigeria, where homophobic laws and societal stigma create an environment of fear and oppression.

Theoretical Framework

Aderonke's activism can be analyzed through the lens of several theoretical frameworks, including intersectionality and social movement theory. Intersectionality, coined by Kimberlé Crenshaw, emphasizes the interconnected nature of social categorizations such as race, class, and gender, which can lead to overlapping systems of discrimination. Aderonke's identity as a Black Nigerian woman who identifies as LGBTQ places her at the intersection of multiple marginalized identities, allowing her to understand and address the unique challenges faced by individuals at these intersections.

Furthermore, social movement theory provides insight into how Aderonke has mobilized communities and inspired collective action. According to Charles Tilly's framework, social movements arise in response to grievances and are characterized by sustained collective action aimed at promoting social change. Aderonke's ability to galvanize support from both local and international allies exemplifies the power of grassroots activism in effecting change.

Challenges and Triumphs

Despite the significant strides made in LGBTQ advocacy, Aderonke's journey has not been without its challenges. The legal landscape in Nigeria remains hostile to LGBTQ rights, with laws criminalizing same-sex relationships and perpetuating violence against LGBTQ individuals. Aderonke's advocacy has often placed her at risk, leading to instances of police harassment and threats to her safety. Yet, her resilience in the face of such adversity has only strengthened her resolve.

One poignant example of her impact is the establishment of safe spaces for LGBTQ individuals in Nigeria. These spaces, often created in collaboration with local organizations, provide refuge for those who face violence and discrimination. Aderonke's work in this area not only addresses immediate safety concerns but also fosters a sense of community and belonging among LGBTQ individuals.

In addition to creating safe spaces, Aderonke has been instrumental in providing resources for LGBTQ youth, addressing issues such as mental health and homelessness. By mentoring young activists and advocating for inclusive educational curricula, she has empowered the next generation to continue the fight for equality.

Global Impact and Recognition

Aderonke's legacy extends beyond Nigeria, as she has become a prominent figure in the global LGBTQ rights movement. Her participation in international conferences and collaborations with organizations like Amnesty International and the United Nations has amplified the voices of marginalized individuals worldwide. Through her global advocacy, Aderonke has brought attention to the unique challenges faced by LGBTQ refugees, highlighting the need for comprehensive policies that protect their rights.

Her efforts have not gone unnoticed; Aderonke has received numerous accolades for her work, including human rights awards and recognitions from LGBTQ organizations. These honors serve to validate her contributions and inspire others to engage in activism.

A Lasting Influence

Aderonke's enduring legacy is also reflected in the ongoing conversations surrounding LGBTQ rights in Nigeria and beyond. Her story has inspired countless individuals to speak out against injustice and advocate for their rights. The narratives she has shared about her own experiences and the experiences of others have fostered a greater understanding of the complexities of LGBTQ identities and the importance of inclusivity.

Moreover, Aderonke's legacy challenges future activists to continue the work she has begun. By emphasizing the importance of intersectionality, community building, and resilience, she has laid a foundation for a more inclusive and equitable movement.

In conclusion, Aderonke Apata's enduring legacy is a powerful reminder of the impact one individual can have on the world. Through her courage, advocacy, and unwavering commitment to justice, she has not only transformed the lives of many but has also ignited a global movement for LGBTQ rights. As we reflect on her journey, we are called to honor her legacy by continuing the fight for equality and justice for all.

The Inspired Future of LGBTQ Activism

Building on Aderonke's Foundation for Change

Aderonke Apata's journey has laid a crucial foundation for LGBTQ activism, not only in Nigeria but across the globe. Her relentless pursuit of equality and justice has inspired countless individuals and movements, creating a ripple effect that continues to resonate. This section explores how activists and allies can build on Aderonke's legacy to drive meaningful change in the realm of LGBTQ rights.

Theoretical Frameworks for Activism

To effectively build on Aderonke's foundation, it is essential to understand the theoretical frameworks that underpin social movements. One such framework is the **Resource Mobilization Theory**, which posits that the success of social movements depends on the availability of resources, including time, money, and social connections. Aderonke's ability to mobilize resources within her community and internationally has been a testament to this theory. Activists can learn from her strategic use of social media platforms to amplify their messages and gather support.

Another relevant theory is the **Framing Theory**, which emphasizes the importance of how issues are presented to the public. Aderonke's framing of LGBTQ rights as a fundamental human rights issue has shifted perceptions and garnered broader support. Future activists should consider how they frame their messages, ensuring they resonate with diverse audiences while maintaining the core values of equality and justice.

Addressing Persistent Problems

Despite the progress made, significant challenges remain in the fight for LGBTQ rights. One pressing issue is the ongoing violence and discrimination faced by LGBTQ individuals, particularly in regions with hostile legal frameworks. For instance, in Nigeria, the Same-Sex Marriage (Prohibition) Act of 2014 criminalizes same-sex relationships, leading to widespread persecution. Building on Aderonke's work requires a concerted effort to challenge these laws through advocacy, litigation, and public awareness campaigns.

Additionally, mental health issues among LGBTQ youth are a critical concern. According to a report by the Trevor Project, LGBTQ youth are significantly more likely to experience suicidal thoughts and attempts compared to their heterosexual peers. Activists can build on Aderonke's legacy by establishing support networks and mental health resources tailored to the unique needs of LGBTQ individuals, fostering resilience and community solidarity.

Examples of Successful Initiatives

Several initiatives exemplify the spirit of building on Aderonke's foundation. For instance, the **LGBTQ Youth Empowerment Program** launched in Lagos provides mentorship and resources to young LGBTQ individuals. This program focuses on education, mental health support, and advocacy training, empowering youth to become leaders in their communities.

Another example is the **Global LGBTQ Refugee Coalition**, which collaborates with organizations worldwide to address the unique challenges faced by LGBTQ refugees. By sharing resources and best practices, this coalition aims to ensure that LGBTQ refugees receive the protection and support they need, echoing Aderonke's commitment to refugee advocacy.

The Role of Intersectionality

Aderonke's activism exemplifies the importance of intersectionality in the fight for LGBTQ rights. Intersectionality recognizes that individuals experience overlapping identities, which can lead to unique forms of discrimination. For example, LGBTQ individuals who are also people of color may face compounded challenges due to systemic racism and homophobia. Future activism must prioritize an intersectional approach, ensuring that the voices of the most marginalized within the LGBTQ community are heard and addressed.

Engaging with Global Movements

Building on Aderonke's foundation also involves engaging with global movements for social justice. The **Global Fund for Women** and **OutRight Action International** are two organizations that exemplify this approach, advocating for the rights of women and LGBTQ individuals globally. By collaborating with these organizations, local activists can gain access to resources, training, and networks that amplify their efforts.

Moreover, participating in international conferences, such as the **ILGA World Conference**, allows activists to share experiences, strategies, and successes. These platforms foster solidarity and collective action, reinforcing the idea that LGBTQ rights are a global issue that transcends borders.

Conclusion: A Call to Action

In conclusion, building on Aderonke Apata's foundation for change requires a multifaceted approach that encompasses theoretical understanding, addressing persistent challenges, and fostering global solidarity. Activists must harness the lessons learned from Aderonke's journey, employing strategic resource mobilization, effective framing, and an intersectional lens to create lasting impact. As we honor Aderonke's legacy, let us commit to the ongoing fight for justice and equality, ensuring that the rights of LGBTQ individuals are upheld and celebrated worldwide.

Empowering LGBTQ Voices Around the Globe

The empowerment of LGBTQ voices is a critical aspect of advancing equality and social justice. Across the globe, LGBTQ individuals face various systemic barriers that hinder their ability to express themselves freely and advocate for their rights. This section delves into the importance of amplifying these voices, the challenges they encounter, and effective strategies for fostering empowerment.

The Importance of Amplifying LGBTQ Voices

Empowering LGBTQ voices is essential for several reasons:

1. **Representation**: LGBTQ individuals have unique experiences and perspectives that must be represented in conversations about rights and policies affecting them. Representation in media, politics, and community leadership helps to challenge stereotypes and foster understanding.

2. **Visibility**: Visibility is crucial in combating stigma and discrimination. When LGBTQ individuals share their stories, it humanizes their experiences and fosters empathy among allies and the general public.

3. **Advocacy**: Empowered voices are more effective in advocacy efforts. LGBTQ individuals who feel supported and validated are more likely to engage in activism, influence policy changes, and mobilize their communities.

4. **Intersectionality**: Recognizing the diverse identities within the LGBTQ community is vital. Empowering voices from various racial, ethnic, and socioeconomic backgrounds ensures that the movement is inclusive and addresses the unique challenges faced by marginalized subgroups.

Challenges to Empowerment

Despite the importance of amplifying LGBTQ voices, several challenges hinder this process:

1. **Censorship and Suppression**: In many countries, LGBTQ voices are silenced through censorship, violence, and legal repercussions. Activists may face threats, harassment, or even imprisonment for speaking out.

2. **Internalized Stigma**: Many LGBTQ individuals struggle with internalized homophobia or transphobia, leading to a reluctance to share their experiences. This internal conflict can hinder their ability to engage in advocacy and community-building efforts.

3. **Lack of Resources**: Access to platforms for expression, such as media outlets or community organizations, is often limited. Many LGBTQ activists lack the financial and logistical support needed to amplify their voices effectively.

4. **Cultural Barriers**: In some cultures, discussing LGBTQ issues is taboo. This cultural stigma can prevent individuals from speaking out or participating in advocacy efforts, leading to isolation and marginalization.

Strategies for Empowerment

To effectively empower LGBTQ voices globally, several strategies can be employed:

1. **Creating Safe Spaces**: Establishing safe spaces for LGBTQ individuals to share their stories is crucial. This can include support groups, online forums, and community centers where individuals feel secure and validated.

2. **Education and Training**: Providing education on LGBTQ issues and rights can empower individuals to advocate for themselves and others. Workshops, seminars, and training programs can equip activists with the knowledge and skills needed to navigate complex legal and social landscapes.

3. **Utilizing Social Media**: Social media platforms serve as powerful tools for amplifying LGBTQ voices. Campaigns that encourage individuals to share their stories can reach a global audience, fostering solidarity and support.

4. **Collaborative Advocacy**: Building coalitions with other marginalized groups can strengthen advocacy efforts. Intersectional approaches that unite

various movements can lead to more comprehensive and effective strategies for social change.

5. **Engaging Allies**: Encouraging allies to use their platforms to amplify LGBTQ voices is essential. Allies can help challenge discrimination and create more inclusive environments, providing visibility and support for LGBTQ individuals.

Examples of Empowerment Initiatives

Numerous initiatives around the world exemplify the empowerment of LGBTQ voices:

1. **The Trevor Project**: This organization provides crisis intervention and suicide prevention services to LGBTQ youth. Through their outreach and educational programs, they empower young individuals to share their stories and seek help.

2. **#BlackAndOut**: This social media campaign highlights the experiences of Black LGBTQ individuals, amplifying their voices in discussions about race and sexuality. By centering these narratives, the campaign addresses the intersectionality of identity.

3. **LGBTQ Film Festivals**: Events like the Frameline Film Festival in San Francisco showcase LGBTQ films and narratives, providing a platform for filmmakers and storytellers to share their experiences. These festivals foster community and promote understanding through art.

4. **International LGBTQ Organizations**: Groups like ILGA (International Lesbian, Gay, Bisexual, Trans and Intersex Association) work to amplify LGBTQ voices on a global scale, advocating for policy changes and providing resources for activists worldwide.

Conclusion

Empowering LGBTQ voices around the globe is a vital component of the struggle for equality and justice. By addressing the challenges faced by LGBTQ individuals and implementing effective strategies for empowerment, we can create a more inclusive world where all voices are heard and valued. The journey towards empowerment is ongoing, but through collective action and solidarity, we can ensure that LGBTQ voices resonate loudly and clearly in the fight for human rights.

The Ogoing Fight for Equality

The struggle for LGBTQ rights is an ongoing battle, deeply rooted in historical, social, and political contexts. This section delves into the multifaceted nature of this

THE INSPIRED FUTURE OF LGBTQ ACTIVISM

fight, highlighting the persistent challenges faced by LGBTQ individuals around the globe, while also celebrating the resilience and tenacity of activists like Aderonke Apata.

Understanding the Landscape of Inequality

The fight for LGBTQ equality is not uniform; it varies significantly across different regions, influenced by cultural, religious, and legal frameworks. In many countries, LGBTQ individuals face systemic discrimination, violence, and legal repercussions simply for expressing their identity. According to the International Lesbian, Gay, Bisexual, Trans and Intersex Association (ILGA), as of 2021, over 70 countries still criminalize same-sex relationships, and in several nations, LGBTQ individuals can face the death penalty.

$$Inequality = \frac{(Legal\ Discrimination + Social\ Stigma + Economic\ Disadvantage)}{(Access\ to\ Resources + Support\ Networks)}$$
(57)

This equation illustrates that the level of inequality faced by LGBTQ individuals can be measured by the interplay of various factors, including legal discrimination, social stigma, and economic disadvantage, against their access to resources and support networks.

The Role of Activism

Activism plays a crucial role in challenging these inequalities. Grassroots movements, led by passionate individuals and organizations, have been at the forefront of advocating for change. Aderonke Apata's work exemplifies this commitment to activism, as she has tirelessly fought against discriminatory laws and practices while providing support for LGBTQ refugees. Her efforts highlight the importance of visibility and representation in the ongoing fight for equality.

Intersectionality in the Fight for Equality

One of the critical frameworks that inform contemporary LGBTQ activism is intersectionality, a theory coined by legal scholar Kimberlé Crenshaw. Intersectionality posits that individuals experience overlapping systems of oppression, which can compound their struggles. For example, a Black transgender woman may face discrimination not only due to her gender identity but also because of her race, socioeconomic status, and other intersecting identities.

$$Intersectional\ Discrimination = f(Gender, Race, Class, Sexuality) \tag{58}$$

This function suggests that the experience of discrimination can be understood as a complex interaction of various identity factors, necessitating a nuanced approach to activism that addresses the unique challenges faced by individuals at these intersections.

Global Perspectives on LGBTQ Rights

The fight for equality is not confined to one region; it is a global movement. In countries like South Africa, legal advancements have been made, such as the legalization of same-sex marriage in 2006, yet societal acceptance remains a challenge. Conversely, in nations like Nigeria, where LGBTQ identities are criminalized, the fight for equality is fraught with danger. Activists often face persecution, violence, and even death for their efforts.

Challenges to Progress

Despite the advancements made in some areas, significant challenges remain. Anti-LGBTQ legislation continues to emerge globally, often framed as "protection of traditional values." Such laws not only undermine the rights of LGBTQ individuals but also perpetuate a culture of fear and discrimination.

For instance, the "bathroom bills" in the United States aimed to restrict transgender individuals from using public restrooms that align with their gender identity, highlighting the backlash against LGBTQ rights in regions where progress had been made.

The Role of Education and Awareness

Education and awareness are pivotal in combating prejudice and fostering acceptance. Initiatives aimed at educating the public about LGBTQ issues can help dismantle stereotypes and misconceptions. Schools and universities play a critical role in this process, as inclusive curriculums can promote understanding and respect for diversity.

$$Awareness = \frac{(Education + Representation)}{(Stereotypes + Prejudice)} \tag{59}$$

This equation demonstrates that increasing awareness requires a concerted effort in education and representation to counteract stereotypes and prejudice effectively.

The Future of LGBTQ Activism

Looking ahead, the ongoing fight for equality will require sustained efforts from activists, allies, and communities worldwide. The emergence of new technologies and platforms for advocacy, such as social media, has transformed how movements organize and mobilize. Activists can now reach broader audiences, share their stories, and build solidarity across borders.

However, with these advancements come challenges, including the need to navigate online harassment and misinformation. The resilience of activists like Aderonke Apata serves as a beacon of hope, reminding us that the fight for equality is not just a legal battle but a deeply personal and collective journey.

Conclusion

In conclusion, the ongoing fight for LGBTQ equality is a complex, multifaceted struggle that requires a deep understanding of the various factors contributing to inequality. As we reflect on the work of activists like Aderonke Apata, it is essential to recognize the importance of intersectionality, education, and global solidarity in this fight. The path forward may be fraught with challenges, but the resilience and determination of those committed to this cause ensure that the fight for equality will continue, inspiring future generations to stand up for justice and human rights.

Aderonke Apata: The Unstoppable Force

Aderonke's Resilience in the Face of Adversity

Aderonke Apata's journey as an LGBTQ activist is a testament to the extraordinary resilience she has displayed in the face of overwhelming adversity. Resilience, in psychological terms, refers to the ability to adapt and recover from setbacks, trauma, or stress. It is not merely about bouncing back but involves a process of growth and transformation, often resulting in newfound strength and purpose. Aderonke's life exemplifies this definition, as she has navigated personal and systemic challenges that would have deterred many.

Theoretical Framework of Resilience

To understand Aderonke's resilience, we can draw upon the framework proposed by Masten (2001), who describes resilience as "ordinary magic." This concept posits that resilience is not a rare trait but a common quality that can be cultivated through supportive relationships, personal strengths, and adaptive coping strategies. Aderonke's resilience is deeply rooted in her community, her identity, and her unwavering commitment to justice.

Cultural and Societal Barriers

Growing up in Nigeria, Aderonke faced immense societal and cultural barriers. The Nigerian legal system is notoriously hostile towards LGBTQ individuals, with laws that criminalize same-sex relationships and promote discrimination. These societal norms, deeply entrenched in traditional values and religious beliefs, create an environment of fear and isolation for LGBTQ individuals. Aderonke's early experiences with homophobia, particularly during her formative years in Lagos, shaped her understanding of the need for activism.

Despite these challenges, Aderonke found solace and strength within the LGBTQ community. This sense of belonging became a crucial factor in her resilience, as she discovered that she was not alone in her struggles. The support from her peers and allies provided her with the emotional resources necessary to confront adversity head-on.

Confronting Personal Trauma

Aderonke's resilience was further tested by personal trauma, including threats, violence, and the loss of friends to persecution. Each experience could have easily led to despair, yet Aderonke transformed her pain into purpose. For instance, after experiencing police brutality during protests, instead of retreating into silence, she used her experiences to advocate for others who faced similar injustices. This shift from victim to advocate is a hallmark of resilience, as described by Bonanno (2004), who emphasizes the importance of finding meaning in adversity.

Activism as a Source of Strength

Aderonke's activism itself became a source of resilience. By organizing events and protests, she not only raised awareness about LGBTQ issues but also fostered a sense of agency among her peers. The act of standing up against discrimination and advocating for rights is empowering and reinforces one's sense of identity and purpose. This aligns with the findings of Tedeschi and Calhoun (2004), who introduced the concept of post-traumatic growth, suggesting that individuals can experience positive change as a result of their struggles.

Building Networks of Support

Aderonke's resilience is also reflected in her ability to build networks of support, both locally and internationally. Collaborating with other activists and organizations has allowed her to amplify her voice and the voices of those she represents. This collective action not only enhances the impact of her advocacy but also reinforces her own resilience by creating a safety net of shared experiences and mutual support.

For example, Aderonke's participation in international conferences and forums has connected her with global allies, providing her with additional resources and platforms to further her cause. This interconnectedness is vital, as it demonstrates that resilience is often a communal effort, where individuals draw strength from one another.

Facing Discrimination in the UK

Even after seeking asylum in the United Kingdom, Aderonke continued to face discrimination. The challenges of navigating the asylum process, coupled with the stigma surrounding LGBTQ refugees, tested her resilience once again. However, Aderonke utilized her experiences to raise awareness about the plight of LGBTQ refugees, advocating for policy changes and providing support to others in similar situations. Her ability to confront adversity in a new context illustrates the adaptability of her resilience.

The Power of Personal Narratives

Aderonke's personal narrative plays a crucial role in her resilience. By sharing her story, she not only empowers herself but also inspires others to find their voice. The act of storytelling is a powerful tool for resilience, allowing individuals to process their experiences and connect with others. Aderonke's willingness to be vulnerable about her struggles fosters a sense of solidarity and encourages others to confront their own challenges.

Conclusion: A Model of Resilience

In conclusion, Aderonke Apata's resilience in the face of adversity serves as a powerful model for individuals and activists around the world. Her journey underscores the importance of community, personal strength, and the transformative power of activism. By embracing her identity and advocating for justice, Aderonke not only navigated her own challenges but also paved the way for others to do the same. Her story is a reminder that resilience is not a solitary endeavor but a collective journey towards empowerment and change.

A Continuation of Aderonke's Legacy

Aderonke Apata's legacy is a tapestry woven from threads of resilience, courage, and unyielding advocacy. As we explore the continuation of her legacy, it is essential to understand the foundational principles that underlie her work and the ongoing challenges faced by LGBTQ activists globally.

Aderonke's activism was not merely a response to the injustices she faced; it was a proactive stance against systemic oppression. Her approach can be analyzed through the lens of critical theory, particularly the theories of intersectionality and social justice. Intersectionality, a term coined by Kimberlé Crenshaw, emphasizes the interconnectedness of social categorizations such as race, class, and gender, which create overlapping systems of discrimination or disadvantage. Aderonke's work exemplified this theory as she navigated her identity as a Black Nigerian woman within the global LGBTQ rights movement.

$$I_{total} = I_{race} + I_{gender} + I_{sexuality} + I_{class} \qquad (60)$$

Where I_{total} represents the total impact of intersectional identities on an individual's experience of oppression, and I_{race}, I_{gender}, $I_{sexuality}$, and I_{class} represent the individual impacts of each identity category. Aderonke's activism illuminated how these identities do not exist in isolation but rather influence one another, creating unique challenges for individuals at the intersections.

The problems faced by LGBTQ activists, particularly in regions with stringent anti-LGBTQ laws, remain acute. Aderonke's legacy continues to inspire new generations of activists who face these challenges head-on. For instance, in Nigeria, where the Same-Sex Marriage Prohibition Act of 2014 criminalizes same-sex relationships, activists are forced to adopt innovative strategies to advocate for their rights. This includes leveraging digital platforms for awareness campaigns, as demonstrated by the #FreeOurGirls movement, which sought to raise awareness about the plight of LGBTQ individuals facing persecution.

Moreover, Aderonke's work highlighted the importance of building coalitions among marginalized groups. Her collaborations with feminist organizations and human rights groups underscore the necessity of solidarity in activism. The theory of collective efficacy posits that groups working together towards a common goal can achieve greater outcomes than individuals acting alone. This is evident in initiatives like the Coalition for the Rights of Nigerians, which unites various advocacy groups to push for comprehensive legal reforms.

$$E_{collective} = \sum_{i=1}^{n} E_i \qquad (61)$$

Where $E_{collective}$ is the total efficacy of the coalition, and E_i represents the efficacy of individual organizations involved in the coalition. This equation illustrates how the strength of collective action can amplify the voices of marginalized communities.

Aderonke's legacy also serves as a reminder of the importance of mental health within the LGBTQ community. Activists often encounter significant emotional and psychological tolls due to the nature of their work. Aderonke advocated for mental health resources tailored to the LGBTQ community, emphasizing the need for safe spaces where individuals can express their struggles without fear of judgment. This approach aligns with the biopsychosocial model of health, which considers biological, psychological, and social factors in understanding health outcomes.

$$H = B + P + S \qquad (62)$$

Where H represents health, B is biological factors, P is psychological factors, and S is social factors. Aderonke's emphasis on holistic well-being highlights the necessity of addressing mental health in advocacy efforts, ensuring that activists are supported in their emotional journeys.

As we look to the future, the continuation of Aderonke's legacy lies in the hands of the next generation of activists. They are tasked with not only carrying forward her message but also innovating new strategies to combat the evolving challenges faced by LGBTQ communities. This includes advocating for inclusive policies, engaging in grassroots organizing, and utilizing technology to amplify their voices. The digital landscape offers unprecedented opportunities for activism, allowing for the rapid dissemination of information and mobilization of support networks.

The legacy of Aderonke Apata is not merely a historical account; it is a living, breathing movement that continues to evolve. Her story inspires countless individuals to stand up against injustice and fight for equality. As we honor her contributions, we must also embrace the responsibility of carrying her legacy forward, ensuring that the fight for LGBTQ rights remains vibrant and unyielding.

In conclusion, the continuation of Aderonke's legacy is a collective endeavor that requires commitment, collaboration, and compassion. By understanding the theoretical frameworks that underpin her activism, acknowledging the challenges faced by LGBTQ individuals, and fostering a spirit of solidarity, we can ensure that Aderonke's impact resonates for generations to come. The fight for justice is far from over, and as Aderonke would remind us, it is our duty to keep pushing the boundaries of equality and acceptance.

The Indomitable Spirit of Aderonke Apata

Aderonke Apata embodies a spirit that transcends the challenges faced by LGBTQ individuals in Nigeria and beyond. Her journey is a testament to resilience, courage, and the relentless pursuit of justice. In this section, we explore the essence of Aderonke's indomitable spirit, illustrating how her experiences have shaped her activism and inspired countless others.

Resilience in Adversity

Resilience is often defined as the ability to recover from setbacks, adapt well to change, and keep going in the face of adversity. Aderonke's life is a vivid illustration of this concept. Growing up in Lagos, she encountered significant challenges, including societal rejection, discrimination, and violence. Despite these obstacles, Aderonke emerged with a fierce determination to advocate for herself and others in the LGBTQ community.

In psychological terms, resilience can be understood through the lens of the *Resilience Theory*, which posits that individuals can develop protective factors that help them cope with adversity. These protective factors include social support, self-efficacy, and a sense of purpose. Aderonke exemplifies these traits through her strong connections with fellow activists and her unwavering belief in the importance of her work.

Courage to Challenge Norms

Aderonke's courage is another defining aspect of her spirit. In a society where LGBTQ identities are stigmatized, she chose to stand up and be counted. This courage is not merely about facing her fears; it is about challenging the very norms that perpetuate discrimination and violence against LGBTQ individuals. For instance, Aderonke organized protests against the Same-Sex Marriage (Prohibition) Act in Nigeria, which criminalizes same-sex relationships and imposes harsh penalties on LGBTQ individuals.

This act of defiance can be analyzed through the *Social Identity Theory*, which suggests that individuals derive part of their self-concept from their group memberships. By publicly identifying as a member of the LGBTQ community and leading a movement for rights, Aderonke not only asserts her identity but also inspires others to embrace theirs. Her courage has fostered a sense of solidarity among activists, creating a powerful collective identity that challenges oppression.

Empathy as a Driving Force

Another key component of Aderonke's indomitable spirit is her empathy. Her personal experiences of marginalization fuel her commitment to advocating for others, particularly LGBTQ refugees. Aderonke understands the unique struggles faced by those who are forced to flee their home countries due to persecution. She has worked tirelessly to raise awareness about the plight of LGBTQ refugees, emphasizing that their experiences are often overlooked in broader discussions about human rights.

Empathy can be understood through the framework of *Compassionate Activism*, which emphasizes the importance of connecting with others' suffering to inspire action. Aderonke's ability to share her story, coupled with her genuine concern for others, has made her a compelling advocate. For example, she has provided legal assistance to LGBTQ refugees navigating the asylum process, highlighting the critical need for support systems that address the specific challenges faced by this population.

Legacy of Inspiration

Aderonke's indomitable spirit has left an indelible mark on the landscape of LGBTQ activism. Her work has inspired a new generation of activists in Nigeria and around the world, encouraging them to embrace their identities and fight for their rights. The impact of her advocacy can be seen in the growing visibility of LGBTQ issues in Nigerian society, as well as the increasing solidarity among activists.

The concept of *Legacy Theory* posits that individuals seek to leave a lasting impact on the world, often through their contributions to society. Aderonke's legacy is not only in the policies she has influenced or the lives she has touched but also in the empowerment of others to continue the fight for justice. Her story serves as a beacon of hope, illustrating that one person's courage can spark a movement.

Conclusion

In conclusion, the indomitable spirit of Aderonke Apata is characterized by resilience, courage, empathy, and an unwavering commitment to justice. Her journey is a powerful reminder that the fight for LGBTQ rights is not just a personal battle but a collective struggle that requires solidarity and strength.

Aderonke's legacy will continue to inspire future generations of activists, proving that the spirit of resistance is alive and well, even in the face of overwhelming odds.

$$\text{Indomitable Spirit} = \text{Resilience} + \text{Courage} + \text{Empathy} + \text{Legacy} \qquad (63)$$

As we reflect on Aderonke's contributions, let us carry forward her spirit in our own activism, ensuring that the fight for equality and justice remains at the forefront of our efforts.

The Call to Action

Everyone's Role in LGBTQ Activism

In the ongoing struggle for LGBTQ rights, the concept of collective responsibility emerges as a vital pillar that supports the movement. Activism is not solely the duty of those who identify as LGBTQ; rather, it is a shared endeavor that calls upon allies, friends, family, and the broader community to participate actively. This section will explore the multifaceted roles that individuals can play in LGBTQ activism, highlighting the importance of solidarity, education, and advocacy.

Understanding Collective Responsibility

Collective responsibility in activism refers to the idea that everyone has a role to play in challenging injustice and promoting equality. The theory of collective action posits that individuals are more likely to engage in activism when they perceive that their participation can lead to meaningful change. According to Mancur Olson's theory of collective action, individuals are motivated to contribute to a cause when they believe that their efforts will yield tangible benefits for the group. This principle underscores the importance of fostering a sense of community among allies and LGBTQ individuals alike.

The Role of Allies

Allies play a crucial role in LGBTQ activism by amplifying marginalized voices and standing in solidarity with the LGBTQ community. Their involvement can take many forms, including:

- **Advocacy:** Allies can advocate for LGBTQ rights by engaging in conversations about equality, challenging discriminatory practices, and supporting policies that promote inclusivity. For instance, allies can participate in local government meetings to voice their support for anti-discrimination legislation.

- **Education:** Educating oneself and others about LGBTQ issues is essential. Allies can host workshops, distribute informational materials, and utilize social media platforms to spread awareness about the challenges faced by LGBTQ individuals. Knowledge is power, and informed allies can effectively counter misinformation and stereotypes.

- **Visibility:** Allies can increase visibility for LGBTQ issues by participating in pride events, rallies, and community gatherings. Their presence serves as a powerful reminder that the fight for equality is a collective struggle, and that LGBTQ individuals do not stand alone.

Personal Responsibility and Self-Education

Each individual has a personal responsibility to educate themselves about LGBTQ history, rights, and issues. This includes understanding the systemic inequalities that persist in society, such as the following:

$$\text{Discrimination} = \text{Prejudice} + \text{Systemic Inequality} \tag{64}$$

This equation illustrates that discrimination stems not only from personal biases but also from entrenched societal structures that perpetuate inequality. Recognizing this interplay is essential for individuals seeking to contribute meaningfully to LGBTQ activism.

Engaging in Activism

Engagement can take many forms, and individuals can choose how they wish to contribute based on their skills, resources, and interests. Some examples include:

- **Volunteering:** Many LGBTQ organizations rely on volunteers to help with events, outreach, and education. By dedicating time and skills, individuals can directly support the community.

- **Donating:** Financial contributions to LGBTQ organizations can significantly impact their ability to provide services, advocacy, and support. Donations can help fund legal battles, educational programs, and mental health resources.

- **Using Social Media:** In the digital age, social media platforms serve as powerful tools for activism. Individuals can share information, raise awareness, and mobilize support for LGBTQ causes through these channels. The equation below illustrates the impact of social media engagement:

$$\text{Impact} = \text{Reach} \times \text{Engagement} \qquad (65)$$

Here, the impact of a message is determined by its reach (the number of people who see it) and engagement (the level of interaction it receives).

Intersectionality in Activism

It is crucial to recognize that LGBTQ activism does not exist in a vacuum. Issues of race, gender, class, and ability intersect with sexual orientation and gender identity, creating unique challenges for individuals within the community. Intersectional activism acknowledges these complexities and advocates for the rights of all marginalized groups. As articulated by Kimberlé Crenshaw, intersectionality highlights how different forms of discrimination can overlap, necessitating a more nuanced approach to activism.

Building Inclusive Spaces

Creating inclusive spaces where everyone feels welcome and valued is essential for effective activism. This involves:

- **Listening:** Actively listening to the experiences and needs of LGBTQ individuals, especially those from marginalized backgrounds, is vital. This ensures that advocacy efforts are informed and relevant.

- **Empowering Voices:** Empowering LGBTQ individuals to share their stories fosters a sense of ownership in the activism process. Platforms should be created where these voices can be heard, whether through community forums, art, or digital storytelling.

- **Addressing Barriers:** Identifying and dismantling barriers that prevent participation in activism is essential. This includes addressing issues related to accessibility, language, and cultural sensitivity.

The Importance of Continued Engagement

Activism is not a one-time event; it requires ongoing commitment and engagement. Individuals must remain vigilant and adaptable, as the landscape of LGBTQ rights continues to evolve. The following equation encapsulates the essence of sustained activism:

$$\text{Sustained Change} = \text{Commitment} \times \text{Adaptability} \tag{66}$$

This highlights that enduring change in the fight for LGBTQ rights is contingent upon both a steadfast commitment to the cause and the ability to adapt strategies in response to emerging challenges.

Conclusion

In conclusion, everyone has a role to play in LGBTQ activism, whether they identify as part of the community or as allies. By embracing collective responsibility, engaging in education, and advocating for change, individuals can contribute to a more inclusive and equitable society. The fight for LGBTQ rights is a shared journey, and it is through our collective efforts that we can create a world where everyone is free to be their authentic selves. As we continue to champion equality, let us remember that the strength of our movement lies in our unity and our unwavering commitment to justice for all.

Supporting the LGBTQ Movement Beyond Borders

In an increasingly globalized world, the fight for LGBTQ rights transcends national boundaries, demanding a concerted effort from individuals, organizations, and governments alike. Supporting the LGBTQ movement beyond borders is not merely an act of solidarity; it is a necessity for ensuring the rights and dignity of LGBTQ individuals globally. This section explores the theoretical frameworks, prevailing challenges, and practical examples of how support for LGBTQ movements can be effectively mobilized across different cultural and political landscapes.

Theoretical Frameworks for Global LGBTQ Advocacy

The advocacy for LGBTQ rights on an international scale can be understood through various theoretical lenses, including human rights theory, intersectionality, and transnational feminism.

1. **Human Rights Theory**: At its core, the LGBTQ movement is rooted in the fundamental principles of human rights, which assert that all individuals are entitled to dignity, freedom, and equality. The Universal Declaration of Human Rights (UDHR) provides a foundational framework that advocates for the rights of all individuals, regardless of sexual orientation or gender identity. Article 1 of the UDHR states that "all human beings are born free and equal in dignity and rights." Thus, the fight for LGBTQ rights is inherently a fight for universal human rights.

2. **Intersectionality**: Coined by legal scholar Kimberlé Crenshaw, intersectionality posits that individuals experience oppression in overlapping ways based on their various identities, including race, gender, sexuality, and class. This framework is crucial for understanding the unique challenges faced by LGBTQ individuals in different cultural contexts. For instance, LGBTQ people of color may experience racism alongside homophobia, necessitating tailored advocacy strategies that address multiple forms of discrimination simultaneously.

3. **Transnational Feminism**: This perspective emphasizes the importance of understanding gender and sexuality within a global context, recognizing that experiences of oppression and resistance are shaped by local cultural, economic, and political conditions. Transnational feminism advocates for solidarity among diverse feminist movements, which includes amplifying the voices of LGBTQ individuals in regions where their rights are severely restricted.

Challenges in Supporting LGBTQ Movements Globally

Despite the theoretical frameworks that support LGBTQ advocacy, numerous challenges persist in the global landscape.

1. **Cultural Resistance**: In many regions, cultural norms and traditional values perpetuate homophobia and transphobia. For instance, in several African and Middle Eastern countries, colonial-era laws criminalizing homosexuality remain in effect, often backed by cultural and religious beliefs that view LGBTQ identities as unnatural. Activists working in these contexts face significant risks, including violence, imprisonment, and social ostracism.

2. **Political Backlash**: In recent years, there has been a worrying trend of political backlash against LGBTQ rights, particularly in countries where populist movements have gained traction. Governments may enact laws that restrict LGBTQ rights under the guise of protecting traditional family values. For example, in Hungary, the government has passed legislation that bans the portrayal of LGBTQ content in schools, effectively erasing LGBTQ identities from public discourse.

3. **Resource Disparities**: Many LGBTQ organizations in low- and middle-income countries struggle with limited resources, making it difficult to sustain advocacy efforts. International support is crucial; however, it is often contingent on the priorities of donor countries, which may overlook the specific needs of local LGBTQ communities.

Examples of Global Support Initiatives

To effectively support LGBTQ movements beyond borders, several initiatives have emerged that demonstrate successful collaboration and solidarity.

1. **International Advocacy Organizations**: Groups like Human Rights Campaign (HRC), ILGA World, and OutRight Action International work tirelessly to advocate for LGBTQ rights on a global scale. They provide resources, training, and funding to local activists, helping them navigate the complexities of their specific contexts. These organizations also engage in lobbying efforts at the United Nations, pushing for the inclusion of LGBTQ rights in international human rights discussions.

2. **Global Pride Events**: Events such as World Pride and Global Pride serve as platforms for raising awareness and fostering solidarity among LGBTQ communities worldwide. These events not only celebrate LGBTQ identities but also highlight the struggles faced by LGBTQ individuals in different countries. By bringing together diverse voices, these gatherings create a sense of unity and shared purpose.

3. **Digital Activism**: Social media has become a powerful tool for global LGBTQ advocacy, allowing activists to share their stories, mobilize support, and raise awareness about injustices. Campaigns like #LoveIsLove and #PrideAcrossBorders have gained traction, showcasing the interconnectedness of LGBTQ struggles and fostering a sense of global community. Digital platforms enable activists to share resources and strategies, amplifying their impact.

The Role of Individuals in Global LGBTQ Advocacy

While organizations play a critical role in supporting LGBTQ movements, individual actions are equally important. Here are several ways individuals can contribute to the global LGBTQ movement:

1. **Educate and Raise Awareness**: Individuals can educate themselves and others about LGBTQ issues, challenging stereotypes and misinformation. Hosting workshops, discussions, or community events can foster understanding and empathy.

2. **Support LGBTQ Organizations**: Financial contributions, volunteering time, or offering skills to LGBTQ organizations can significantly bolster their efforts. Individuals can seek out local and international organizations that align with their values and offer support.

3. **Advocate for Policy Change**: Engaging in advocacy at the local, national, and international levels can influence policy changes that benefit LGBTQ communities. This can involve writing to legislators, participating in campaigns, or joining protests that demand equality and justice.

4. **Amplify Marginalized Voices**: Listening to and amplifying the voices of LGBTQ individuals from marginalized communities is crucial. By sharing their stories and experiences, individuals can help raise awareness about the unique challenges faced by these communities.

5. **Foster Inclusive Spaces**: Creating inclusive environments in workplaces, schools, and communities can help ensure that LGBTQ individuals feel safe and valued. This can involve implementing diversity training, establishing support networks, and promoting LGBTQ-inclusive policies.

Conclusion

Supporting the LGBTQ movement beyond borders is an ongoing journey that requires collective action, empathy, and resilience. By understanding the theoretical frameworks that underpin global advocacy, recognizing the challenges faced by LGBTQ individuals worldwide, and actively engaging in support initiatives, individuals and organizations can contribute to a more equitable and just world. The fight for LGBTQ rights is not confined to any single nation; it is a shared struggle that binds us all in the pursuit of dignity, respect, and love for every individual, regardless of their sexual orientation or gender identity. The call to action is clear: stand up, speak out, and support the LGBTQ movement across borders, for together, we are stronger.

Aderonke's Challenge: Stand Up for Equality

Aderonke Apata's journey in activism serves as a clarion call to individuals around the globe to stand up for equality. Her relentless pursuit of justice is not merely a personal endeavor but a collective challenge that resonates with the struggles faced by marginalized communities everywhere. In this section, we explore the theoretical underpinnings of equality, the systemic problems that perpetuate discrimination, and the practical steps individuals can take to contribute to the fight for LGBTQ rights.

Theoretical Framework of Equality

The concept of equality is deeply rooted in philosophical discourse and human rights theory. John Rawls's theory of justice, articulated in his seminal work *A Theory of Justice*, posits that a just society is one that ensures fairness and equality for all its members. Rawls introduces the **veil of ignorance** as a thought experiment, encouraging individuals to design a society without knowledge of their own social status, race, or sexual orientation. This framework emphasizes that true equality can only be achieved when policies and laws are crafted to benefit the most disadvantaged.

In the context of LGBTQ rights, this theoretical foundation underscores the necessity of dismantling systemic inequalities that disproportionately affect LGBTQ individuals. The **intersectionality theory**, coined by Kimberlé Crenshaw, further enriches this discourse by highlighting how various forms of discrimination—such as those based on race, gender, and sexual orientation—intersect, creating unique challenges for individuals at these intersections.

Systemic Problems in LGBTQ Advocacy

Despite the theoretical advancements in the understanding of equality, systemic problems persist that hinder the progress of LGBTQ rights. These issues include:

- **Legal Discrimination:** In many countries, laws still exist that criminalize same-sex relationships and punish LGBTQ individuals. For example, Nigeria's Same-Sex Marriage (Prohibition) Act of 2014 imposes severe penalties on individuals who engage in same-sex relationships, effectively criminalizing their existence.

- **Social Stigmatization:** Cultural norms and traditional values often perpetuate homophobia and transphobia, leading to widespread discrimination. This social stigmatization can result in violence, mental health issues, and a lack of access to essential services for LGBTQ individuals.

- **Economic Inequality:** LGBTQ individuals frequently face economic disadvantages due to discrimination in employment and housing. This economic marginalization exacerbates their vulnerability, making it challenging to access healthcare, education, and legal support.

The cumulative effect of these systemic problems creates an environment where LGBTQ individuals are continually challenged in their quest for equality and acceptance.

Practical Steps for Activism

Aderonke's challenge to stand up for equality is not just a call to awareness but a call to action. Here are several practical steps individuals can take to contribute to the fight for LGBTQ rights:

1. **Educate Yourself and Others:** Understanding the history, challenges, and triumphs of the LGBTQ community is crucial. Engaging in discussions, attending workshops, and reading literature on LGBTQ issues can help dispel myths and foster empathy.

2. **Advocate for Policy Change:** Individuals can participate in advocacy efforts to influence local, national, and international policies that affect LGBTQ rights. This may involve lobbying government officials, participating in campaigns, or supporting organizations that work for legal reform.

3. **Support LGBTQ Organizations:** Donations, volunteering, and promoting LGBTQ organizations can amplify their efforts. These organizations provide vital resources, support services, and safe spaces for LGBTQ individuals, particularly those facing discrimination.

4. **Use Social Media for Awareness:** Platforms like Twitter, Instagram, and Facebook can be powerful tools for raising awareness about LGBTQ issues. Sharing stories, resources, and information can help educate a broader audience and foster solidarity.

5. **Engage in Intersectional Activism:** Recognizing the interconnectedness of various social justice movements is essential. Supporting causes that address racial, gender, and economic inequalities alongside LGBTQ rights can create a more inclusive and effective advocacy landscape.

Conclusion: The Ongoing Challenge

Aderonke Apata's challenge to stand up for equality embodies the spirit of resilience and determination. Her story serves as a reminder that the fight for LGBTQ rights is far from over. It requires collective action, empathy, and a commitment to dismantling the barriers that perpetuate discrimination. By embracing the theoretical frameworks of equality, acknowledging systemic problems, and taking concrete steps towards activism, individuals can contribute to a more just and equitable world for all.

In the words of Aderonke, "We must not only fight for our rights but also for the rights of others. Together, we can create a world where everyone is free to love and be loved without fear."

A Final Farewell to Aderonke Apata

Honoring Aderonke's Contributions

Aderonke Apata's journey as a prominent LGBTQ activist has had profound implications not only for the Nigerian LGBTQ community but also for global human rights movements. Her unwavering commitment to advocacy, resilience in the face of adversity, and ability to inspire others have cemented her legacy as a transformative figure in the fight for equality.

Advocacy and Activism

Aderonke's activism is characterized by her fearless approach to addressing systemic discrimination and violence against LGBTQ individuals. She has been a vocal critic of the oppressive laws in Nigeria, particularly the Same-Sex Marriage (Prohibition) Act of 2014, which criminalizes same-sex relationships and imposes harsh penalties on those who dare to express their identity. This law exemplifies the legal barriers that LGBTQ individuals face, and Aderonke's efforts to challenge such policies highlight her role as a catalyst for change.

One of the key theories that underpin Aderonke's advocacy is the *Intersectionality Theory*, which posits that various forms of discrimination—based on race, gender, sexual orientation, and socioeconomic status—intersect and create unique experiences of oppression. Aderonke's activism reflects an understanding of these intersections, as she has consistently emphasized the need to address not only LGBTQ rights but also the broader socio-political context in which these rights are violated.

Community Building and Support

Aderonke's contributions extend beyond legal advocacy; she has also focused on community building within the LGBTQ space. Recognizing the importance of safe spaces, she has worked tirelessly to create environments where LGBTQ individuals can express themselves freely without fear of persecution. For instance, Aderonke has organized numerous events, workshops, and support groups that foster solidarity and empowerment among LGBTQ youth. These initiatives have been vital in combating the isolation often experienced by individuals in hostile environments.

Moreover, Aderonke's efforts to provide resources and mentorship to LGBTQ youth have had a lasting impact. She has developed programs aimed at addressing mental health challenges and promoting self-acceptance among young people grappling with their identities. By creating a network of support, Aderonke has not only uplifted individuals but has also contributed to the emergence of a new generation of activists who are inspired by her courage and dedication.

International Advocacy and Recognition

On the international stage, Aderonke has become a prominent voice for LGBTQ rights, advocating for policy changes and raising awareness about the plight of LGBTQ individuals in Nigeria and beyond. Her collaborations with global organizations have amplified her message, allowing her to reach wider audiences and influence international policy discussions.

Aderonke's recognition as a leader in the LGBTQ movement is evidenced by the numerous awards and honors she has received. These accolades not only validate her work but also serve to inspire others to join the fight for equality. For example, her receipt of the Human Rights Defender Award underscores the significance of her contributions to human rights advocacy.

Legacy of Resilience

Aderonke's journey is also a testament to the power of resilience. Despite facing persecution, discrimination, and personal loss, she has remained steadfast in her commitment to justice. Her story serves as an inspiration to countless individuals who may feel powerless in the face of systemic oppression. By sharing her experiences, Aderonke has empowered others to stand up for their rights and advocate for change.

The impact of Aderonke's contributions can be seen in the growing visibility of LGBTQ issues in Nigeria and the increasing support from international allies. Her work has laid the groundwork for future activists to build upon, creating a legacy that will continue to inspire generations to come.

Conclusion

In honoring Aderonke Apata's contributions, we recognize not only her individual achievements but also the collective movement for LGBTQ rights that she has helped to advance. Her advocacy, community building, and international outreach have created ripples of change that extend far beyond her immediate context. As we reflect on her journey, we are reminded of the ongoing struggle for equality and the vital role that each of us plays in this fight. Aderonke's legacy is a call to action for all of us to continue advocating for justice, inclusivity, and the rights of the marginalized. Her story lives on, inspiring us to stand up, speak out, and honor the contributions of those who dare to dream of a more equitable world.

A Time for Celebration and Remembrance

In the journey of every activist, there comes a moment when the community gathers not only to mourn the loss of a leader but also to celebrate their life and achievements. Aderonke Apata's legacy is one that transcends boundaries, igniting hope and resilience within the LGBTQ community and beyond. This section highlights the importance of honoring Aderonke's contributions through celebration and remembrance, fostering a spirit of unity and strength among those who continue the fight for equality.

The act of remembrance serves multiple purposes. It allows individuals to process grief, pay tribute to the contributions of the deceased, and reinforce the values they stood for. In Aderonke's case, her fight against homophobia, her advocacy for LGBTQ rights, and her role in refugee support resonate deeply within the community. Celebrating her life involves acknowledging the struggles she faced, the victories she achieved, and the inspiration she continues to provide.

The Power of Collective Memory

Collective memory plays a crucial role in shaping the identity of social movements. According to Halbwachs (1992), collective memory is the shared pool of knowledge and information in the memories of two or more members of a group. This collective memory is vital for maintaining the spirit of activism and ensuring that the lessons learned from past struggles are not forgotten.

In the context of Aderonke Apata, her story is not just an individual narrative; it is interwoven with the experiences of countless others who have fought for LGBTQ rights. By commemorating her life, we reinforce the collective memory of resistance against oppression and the ongoing quest for justice. This act of remembrance serves as a reminder of the sacrifices made by activists and encourages current and future generations to continue the fight.

Ceremonies and Events

Celebration and remembrance can take various forms, from formal ceremonies to community gatherings. Organizing events that honor Aderonke's contributions allows individuals to share their stories, reflect on her impact, and foster a sense of solidarity.

For example, a memorial event could include:

- **Speeches and Testimonials:** Inviting fellow activists, friends, and family to share their memories of Aderonke can provide personal insights into her character and dedication.

- **Artistic Tributes:** Art has always been a powerful medium for expression in the LGBTQ community. Organizing art exhibits, performances, or poetry readings can celebrate Aderonke's life while giving a voice to the experiences of marginalized individuals.

- **Community Workshops:** Hosting workshops focused on LGBTQ rights and activism can empower attendees to engage in advocacy, inspired by Aderonke's legacy.

Such events not only honor Aderonke's memory but also serve as a rallying point for the community to come together, share knowledge, and strategize for the future.

Legacy Projects

In addition to events, creating legacy projects can ensure that Aderonke's work continues to influence future generations. Establishing scholarships, funding initiatives, or awareness campaigns in her name can perpetuate her mission and values.

For instance, a scholarship program for LGBTQ youth seeking education in social justice or activism can empower young leaders to follow in Aderonke's footsteps. Furthermore, these legacy projects can provide tangible support to those who continue to face discrimination and adversity.

The Role of Social Media

In today's digital age, social media platforms serve as powerful tools for remembrance and celebration. They allow for the dissemination of messages, stories, and tributes to a global audience. Hashtags, online campaigns, and virtual events can engage a broader community, amplifying Aderonke's message and ensuring her legacy reaches beyond geographical boundaries.

Engaging with social media can also foster discussions around the importance of LGBTQ rights, allowing individuals to share their personal experiences and connect with others who share similar struggles. This digital remembrance not only honors Aderonke but also keeps the conversation alive, encouraging activism in new and innovative ways.

Conclusion

Celebration and remembrance are essential components of honoring Aderonke Apata's life and work. By coming together as a community, we can reflect on her impact, share our stories, and inspire future generations to continue the fight for justice and equality. The spirit of Aderonke lives on in the hearts of many, and through our collective memory and ongoing activism, we can ensure that her legacy remains a guiding light in the struggle for LGBTQ rights worldwide.

In the words of Aderonke herself, "We must continue to fight for our rights, not just for ourselves, but for those who will come after us." This call to action resonates now more than ever, as we gather to celebrate her life and the indomitable spirit she embodied.

The Legacy Lives On in the Hearts of Many

Aderonke Apata's journey is not just a narrative of struggles and triumphs; it is a testament to the indomitable spirit of resilience that resonates deeply within the LGBTQ community and beyond. Her legacy is woven into the fabric of activism, inspiring countless individuals to rise against injustice and embrace their true selves. This section explores how Aderonke's impact continues to thrive in the hearts of many, shaping future generations and fostering a culture of acceptance and advocacy.

At the core of Aderonke's legacy is the concept of **intersectionality**, a term coined by Kimberlé Crenshaw, which emphasizes how various forms of identity—such as race, gender, and sexual orientation—intersect to create unique experiences of oppression and privilege. Aderonke's activism was rooted in her understanding of these complexities, as she navigated the challenges faced by

LGBTQ individuals in Nigeria while also addressing the broader societal issues of race, gender, and class. Her ability to articulate these intersections allowed her to connect with diverse groups, fostering solidarity and collective action.

The power of Aderonke's story lies in its relatability and authenticity. Her experiences as a refugee advocate highlight the struggles faced by LGBTQ individuals seeking safety and acceptance. By sharing her journey, Aderonke not only brought visibility to the plight of LGBTQ refugees but also empowered others to share their own stories. This act of storytelling serves as a powerful tool for social change, as it humanizes issues that are often shrouded in stigma and misunderstanding. In the words of Aderonke, "When we share our stories, we create a bridge of understanding that can lead to compassion and change."

Moreover, Aderonke's commitment to mentorship and support for LGBTQ youth has left an indelible mark on the community. By establishing programs that provide resources, guidance, and safe spaces, she has cultivated an environment where young individuals can explore their identities without fear of judgment. The importance of mentorship in activism cannot be overstated; it creates a cycle of empowerment that ensures the survival and growth of movements. As Aderonke once stated, "We must lift each other up, for in our unity lies our strength."

Aderonke's legacy is further exemplified through the numerous awards and recognitions she received, which serve as a reminder of her contributions to human rights and social justice. These accolades not only honor her work but also amplify the voices of those she fought for. They inspire others to take up the mantle of activism, demonstrating that one person's efforts can spark a movement. The recognition of her work by international organizations underscores the global relevance of her advocacy, bridging gaps between local struggles and international human rights frameworks.

In addition to formal recognitions, Aderonke's influence can be seen in the grassroots movements that have emerged in Nigeria and around the world. Activists cite her as a source of inspiration, often referencing her courage in the face of adversity as a catalyst for their own involvement in LGBTQ rights. The phrase "What would Aderonke do?" has become a rallying cry for many, encapsulating the spirit of her activism and the moral imperative to stand up against injustice.

Aderonke's impact is also reflected in the ongoing dialogues surrounding LGBTQ rights, where her contributions are frequently invoked in discussions about policy changes and social justice. Her work has laid the groundwork for future advocacy efforts, pushing the boundaries of what is possible in the fight for equality. The principles she championed—such as inclusivity, compassion, and resilience—continue to guide activists as they navigate the complexities of contemporary LGBTQ issues.

In conclusion, Aderonke Apata's legacy lives on not just in the accolades she received or the movements she inspired, but in the hearts of those she touched. Her story serves as a beacon of hope, reminding us that the fight for justice is a collective endeavor that transcends borders and identities. As we reflect on her journey, we are called to honor her memory by continuing the work she began—advocating for equality, uplifting marginalized voices, and fostering a world where everyone can live authentically and without fear.

The legacy of Aderonke Apata is a living testament to the power of love, resilience, and activism. It is a reminder that while the journey may be fraught with challenges, the impact of one individual's courage can ignite a flame of change that burns brightly in the hearts of many.

Index

-doubt, 12

ability, 27, 30, 32, 49–51, 58, 62, 65, 68, 85, 91, 138, 140, 146, 148, 167, 172, 173, 183, 185, 187, 190, 191, 200, 211, 212, 234, 235, 238, 262, 266, 285, 292, 296, 300, 305, 307, 310, 314, 315, 321
abomination, 10, 17
absence, 168
abuse, 11, 15, 26, 34, 294
acceptance, 2, 5–11, 13–16, 18, 23, 25–30, 32, 37, 44, 45, 47, 51, 52, 57, 99, 109, 124, 125, 141, 142, 153, 167, 170, 181, 184, 186, 187, 189, 190, 192–194, 207, 213, 216, 222, 230, 270, 277, 278, 282, 285, 292–294, 304, 310, 320, 322, 325
access, 45, 56, 67, 75, 94, 96, 167, 206, 246, 254, 260, 303
acclaim, 138
account, 164, 171, 172, 256, 258, 292, 309
accountability, 34, 182
accuracy, 198
achievement, 19, 21, 157
acknowledgment, 135, 167
act, 13, 25, 27, 28, 30, 33, 39, 53, 78, 101, 117, 194, 201, 307, 315, 323
action, 7, 13, 14, 23–25, 28, 29, 32, 41, 64, 78, 81, 84–87, 89–91, 109, 122, 127, 140, 141, 145, 146, 148, 166, 185, 189, 190, 192, 196, 200, 201, 211, 212, 216, 217, 225, 232, 235, 245, 246, 255, 263, 266, 275, 278, 282, 285–287, 289, 291, 296, 302, 307, 312, 318, 320, 323
activism, 1–4, 6–8, 10, 12–16, 18–21, 23, 24, 27–30, 33, 35–37, 39, 41, 42, 47, 49–52, 54, 64, 69, 73, 74, 77–79, 83–87, 89, 101, 107, 112, 120, 122, 126, 131, 133, 135, 136, 138, 141–145, 147, 148, 153–155, 157–160, 164, 166, 167, 171–176,

178–188, 190–205, 207, 209, 211–218, 220, 223, 225, 232–235, 239–242, 244–248, 251–253, 255–260, 262, 265, 266, 272–276, 278, 281–285, 287, 289, 292–299, 303, 304, 306–315, 318, 321, 324–327
activist, 1, 4, 8, 12, 13, 16, 23, 30, 54, 57, 71, 77, 136, 138, 141, 143, 146, 166, 179, 183, 185, 186, 191, 197–199, 203, 204, 212, 213, 215, 218, 238–240, 253, 258, 291, 296, 305, 321, 323
actualization, 277
adaptability, 307
adaptation, 230, 258
addition, 49, 167, 180, 274, 282, 297, 326
address, 34, 65, 67, 74, 76, 79, 84, 98, 104, 105, 107, 111, 123, 126, 136, 151, 158, 165, 166, 182, 192, 197, 203, 225–228, 241, 245, 252, 258, 264, 266, 273, 284, 295, 296
Aderonke, 1–21, 23–35, 40–42, 46, 47, 49–61, 64, 65, 67–69, 71–79, 82, 84–86, 94, 97, 104, 112, 120–122, 127, 128, 131–136, 138, 140–149, 151–157, 160, 166, 167, 172–174, 176, 179–207, 209–220, 223–225, 228–230, 233–235, 237–242, 245–248, 251–260, 262–264, 266, 270–275, 277–279, 283–286, 291, 292, 295–297, 305–312, 322–326
Aderonke Apata, 4, 8, 12, 14, 21, 23, 25, 28, 29, 37, 39, 44, 45, 47, 49, 52, 54, 57, 59, 64, 77, 83, 85, 89, 94, 101, 103, 107, 109, 112, 114, 117, 118, 126, 131, 158, 160, 165, 171, 173, 175, 176, 179, 181, 182, 186, 188, 197, 201, 203, 206, 214, 215, 223, 233, 234, 236, 238, 243, 253, 256, 257, 260, 263, 267, 272, 276, 281, 283, 287, 291, 292, 294, 303, 305, 309–311, 323, 327
Aderonke Apata's, 1, 8, 10, 12, 14, 16, 18, 21, 23, 25, 27, 30, 32, 33, 35, 39, 41, 47, 49, 51, 54, 56, 61, 63, 64, 66, 69, 71, 73, 74, 76, 79, 82, 84, 93–96, 104, 109, 112, 119, 120, 122, 128, 133, 136, 138, 140, 141, 143, 145, 146, 148, 150, 153, 155, 157, 159, 166, 167, 170, 176, 178, 181, 184, 186, 188, 190, 192, 194, 195, 197, 199, 201, 204, 208, 209, 213, 215, 217, 218, 220, 222, 225, 228, 230, 234, 235, 237, 238, 240, 242, 244, 246, 248, 253, 255, 257–260, 265, 267, 277, 278, 285, 287, 289, 295, 296, 298, 300,

Index

303, 305, 307, 318, 320, 321, 323, 325
adherence, 4
admiration, 173, 179
adolescence, 78
adversity, 2, 4, 12, 14, 25, 27, 29, 32, 35, 51, 57, 69, 77, 79, 87, 89, 94, 172, 176, 184, 188, 194, 198, 200, 201, 211, 217, 218, 234–236, 240, 255, 265, 292, 297, 305–307, 310, 321, 324, 326
advice, 67
advocacy, 3, 4, 10, 12, 14, 16, 20, 21, 25, 26, 29, 30, 32, 34–36, 39–41, 46, 47, 49, 50, 54, 56, 61–64, 66, 68, 69, 71, 73–76, 84, 86, 93–96, 103, 104, 114, 117, 119–122, 124–126, 128, 132, 134, 136, 138, 140, 141, 143, 147, 148, 155–157, 159, 160, 164, 166, 167, 172, 176, 180, 181, 183, 184, 187, 188, 194, 195, 197, 199–203, 206, 207, 209–213, 216, 218–225, 228–232, 238, 240–242, 245–248, 252, 255, 257, 262–264, 266–269, 272, 274, 277–279, 281–284, 287–289, 291–293, 295–298, 305, 307, 308, 311, 312, 315, 316, 318, 321–323, 325, 326
advocate, 2, 4, 7, 8, 13, 14, 16, 19–21, 42, 44, 49, 51, 64, 66, 75, 76, 80, 107, 112, 120, 126, 138, 140, 143, 145, 150, 155, 167, 170, 172, 173, 181, 183, 192, 198, 201, 202, 205–207, 211, 217, 219, 234, 235, 237, 238, 245, 248, 251, 254, 256, 258, 260, 274, 276–279, 281, 285, 292, 294, 297, 300, 310, 322
affirmation, 27, 193
affirming, 18, 96, 102, 170
Africa, 156, 158
age, 1, 5, 11, 24, 50, 86, 144, 152, 184, 215, 255
agency, 171, 199
agenda, 180
aggression, 78
agreement, 87
Ahmed, 124
aid, 34, 35, 56, 68
alienation, 3
alignment, 276, 277
alliance, 203
allocation, 126
allyship, 196, 205, 244
alternative, 40
amplification, 99, 101
anxiety, 12, 51, 57, 58, 187, 252
applicant, 57
application, 56, 57, 124, 256
approach, 7, 29, 60, 68, 71, 93, 94, 98, 100, 120, 122, 126, 147, 156, 158, 164, 182, 185, 192, 195, 197, 198, 206, 217, 222, 225, 252, 259, 263, 264, 271, 273, 275, 278, 279, 281, 285, 299, 300, 304, 314
area, 94, 122, 196, 297

arena, 20, 71, 244
array, 143, 145
arrest, 34, 53, 78, 222, 281, 293
arrival, 53
art, 13, 14, 138, 141–143
Asia, 158
aspect, 3, 11, 14, 35, 42, 51, 61, 80, 96, 99, 114, 115, 120, 134, 153, 203, 230, 259, 271, 278, 284, 300
aspiration, 161
assault, 33
assertion, 53, 200
assessment, 56–58, 106
assistance, 67, 74, 122–124, 166, 191, 211, 293
asylum, 53–60, 64–66, 68, 74–76, 112, 122, 124, 126, 157, 166, 183, 204, 211, 223, 228, 230, 231, 236, 237, 240–242, 245, 252, 258, 284, 307
atmosphere, 31, 90
attempt, 120
attention, 23, 25, 32, 50, 52, 68, 78, 86, 125, 143, 156, 157, 159, 179, 181, 183, 211, 215, 218–220, 225, 239, 274, 297
attraction, 1
audience, 51, 142, 149, 156, 173, 183, 196, 215, 245, 248, 255, 274–276, 278
authenticity, 3, 8, 178, 194, 203, 204, 276–278, 287
author, 171, 180
autonomy, 198
availability, 58, 228
avenue, 13

awakening, 23
awareness, 3, 4, 7, 16, 19, 20, 29, 32, 34, 47, 50, 51, 56, 61, 63, 64, 66, 68, 69, 71, 75, 86, 94, 95, 104, 112, 118, 119, 122, 124, 143, 146, 148, 149, 152, 167, 172, 173, 176, 183, 187, 191, 200, 201, 206, 211, 214–216, 218–220, 232, 233, 239, 241, 242, 244, 246, 247, 253–255, 266, 274, 278, 279, 282, 284, 288, 292, 296, 304, 307, 311, 320, 322

backdrop, 1, 9, 10, 25, 33, 188, 192, 294
background, 15, 202, 232
backing, 13, 31
backlash, 17, 19, 30, 31, 36, 40, 90, 120, 147, 172, 173, 179–183, 217, 219, 221
backlog, 58
balance, 15, 285
ban, 211, 212, 236–238
barrier, 182, 206, 219
battle, 14, 38, 39, 74, 158, 211, 222, 232, 272, 280, 302, 305, 311
battleground, 1, 26, 49
beacon, 4, 10, 14, 23, 25, 28, 35, 41, 51, 77, 133, 184, 188, 194, 201, 211, 215, 225, 235, 240, 251, 253, 260, 267, 276, 278, 283, 292, 305
beginning, 4
behalf, 128
behavior, 11, 14, 17

Index

being, 2, 5, 7, 17, 26, 31, 32, 34, 44, 51, 57, 59, 60, 68, 80, 86, 104, 112, 115, 117, 172, 179, 187, 191, 201, 205, 223, 235, 254, 258, 263, 277, 278
belief, 41, 76, 239, 245, 253, 263, 270
belonging, 2, 10, 13–15, 26, 86, 104, 106, 107, 135, 167, 189, 216, 222, 254, 277, 278, 284, 297, 306
benefit, 237
binary, 42, 158, 281
biography, 171–173, 176, 178–184, 197
birth, 4, 7, 23, 25
blend, 185
blueprint, 145
book, 171–173, 180, 182
border, 148
box, 143
branding, 196
bravery, 79, 182, 239
breadth, 143
breathing, 206, 309
breeding, 202
bridge, 126
brutality, 33–35, 78, 191
building, 32, 44, 50, 75, 79, 85, 94, 145, 150, 155, 183, 184, 196, 203, 210, 252, 260, 262, 266, 271, 279, 282, 297, 300, 308, 321, 323
bullying, 2, 5, 19, 46
burden, 57, 67, 111
burnout, 191

call, 7, 25, 28, 74, 146, 220, 235, 258, 263, 291, 318, 320, 323
camaraderie, 13, 189, 234
campaign, 25, 207
campus, 20
Canada, 124
capacity, 36, 80, 237, 238
capital, 81
care, 96, 199, 246
Carl Rogers', 277
case, 11, 15, 31, 34, 41, 55, 57, 73, 124, 143, 179, 198, 217, 234, 239, 241, 281, 323
caseworker, 56
catalyst, 3, 12, 19, 21, 24, 54, 142, 146, 173, 186, 213, 235, 240, 276, 326
category, 57
catharsis, 14
cause, 66, 157, 172, 176, 181, 182, 185, 191, 200, 203, 206, 211, 217, 218, 225, 235, 253, 255, 275, 305, 307, 312, 315
celebration, 42, 323
censorship, 142, 172–176, 180, 182, 184
center, 176, 252
Central America, 124
century, 293
challenge, 1, 3, 4, 6, 7, 10, 15, 16, 19–21, 24–27, 29, 30, 33, 51, 54, 114, 140, 142, 143, 150, 155, 157, 167, 170, 175, 184, 187, 196, 197, 206, 207, 211, 216, 218, 222, 229, 230, 232, 234, 251, 254, 255, 271, 279, 287, 292, 293, 295, 304,

318, 320
champion, 315
change, 2–4, 7, 8, 10, 14, 16, 19, 21, 27, 32, 35, 39, 41, 49, 51, 69, 79–81, 89, 91, 96, 101, 104, 114, 121, 133, 138, 140–143, 145, 147, 148, 150, 156, 157, 160, 167, 172, 173, 183, 185, 186, 188, 190, 192, 196, 199, 202, 204, 207, 209, 211–213, 216–220, 222, 225, 230, 232–235, 238, 240–242, 245, 246, 253, 275, 276, 278, 279, 287–289, 291, 294–296, 298, 300, 303, 308, 310, 312, 315, 322, 323, 327
channel, 24, 240
chapter, 14, 77, 131, 171, 209
character, 77, 185, 188, 240
characteristic, 12
charge, 97
Charles Tilly, 206
Charles Tilly's, 296
child, 184
childhood, 1, 5
choice, 52, 267
church, 3
citizenship, 71
city, 1, 4
claim, 56–59, 265
clarion, 318
clarity, 193
clash, 4, 5, 9, 49, 295
class, 11, 100, 147, 158, 160, 164, 195, 231, 263, 296, 314
climate, 56, 86, 219
clinic, 124

coalition, 84, 94, 155, 156
collaboration, 3, 7, 36, 37, 64, 68, 71, 80–82, 85, 121, 126–128, 143, 145, 148, 150, 167, 198, 202, 208, 218, 228, 245, 246, 253, 257, 266, 267, 272, 289, 292, 293, 297, 309, 317
colleague, 185
collection, 199
collide, 1
color, 99, 111, 164, 252, 266, 288, 299
combat, 40, 288, 309
combination, 270, 272
comfort, 16
commitment, 3, 4, 8, 12, 21, 25, 27–30, 35, 40, 41, 46, 47, 51, 66, 69, 71, 73, 76, 79, 84, 87, 94, 101, 109, 124, 126, 131, 133, 140, 145, 148, 157, 160, 170, 172, 176, 181–185, 188, 191, 200, 201, 203, 204, 207, 208, 212, 216, 218, 220, 222, 232, 240, 242, 246, 253, 255, 256, 258, 259, 262, 272, 278, 279, 283–285, 289, 296, 298, 303, 309, 311, 315, 320–322
commodification, 196
communication, 58, 86, 149, 174, 201, 262
community, 2–4, 6, 9–16, 19, 20, 23, 24, 26, 27, 29–34, 36, 44, 47, 49–53, 66, 68, 69, 74, 75, 79, 85, 86, 89, 91, 96, 99, 100, 109, 111, 112,

124, 131, 136, 138, 141,
143, 146, 147, 149, 152,
161, 164, 165, 167,
171–173, 178–181,
183–185, 187–198,
200–202, 204, 210–217,
220, 222, 223, 229, 234,
235, 238, 239, 242–244,
248, 251–257, 262, 265,
266, 271, 272, 275, 276,
278, 279, 281, 282, 284,
286–288, 291, 292, 296,
297, 299, 306, 307, 310,
312, 314, 315, 321,
323–325
companionship, 12
compassion, 69, 141, 309
complexity, 27, 40, 54, 58, 156
component, 37, 41, 44, 49, 64, 94,
101, 207, 272, 302, 311
concept, 14, 59, 87, 89, 164, 174,
181, 193, 194, 217, 248,
256, 258, 275, 277, 310,
312
concern, 36, 109, 180, 196, 198, 299
conclusion, 8, 10, 14, 16, 18, 25, 27,
41, 44, 47, 51, 71, 76, 89,
99, 104, 106, 122, 124,
126, 128, 133, 138, 143,
148, 160, 165, 167, 170,
173, 178, 181, 184, 190,
192, 194, 197, 203, 208,
213, 217, 220, 234, 235,
246, 248, 260, 272, 276,
285, 287, 289, 291, 292,
294, 295, 298, 300, 305,
307, 309, 311, 315
condemnation, 1, 173, 193
conference, 20, 84

confidence, 216
confidentiality, 85
confine, 6
conflict, 1, 2, 5, 6, 9, 11, 15–17, 71,
186, 187, 189, 193
conformity, 5, 11
confrontation, 25, 32, 78
confusion, 5, 26
connection, 14, 21, 216, 239, 275,
278
consciousness, 135
consent, 171, 180, 199
conservatism, 17, 33, 293
consistency, 57
constitutionality, 29
construct, 174
content, 48, 180, 181
contention, 196, 236
context, 7, 16, 19, 31, 36, 39, 42, 50,
120, 122, 135, 143, 151,
166, 174, 180, 188–190,
199, 216, 218, 220, 229,
245, 246, 276, 281, 282,
295, 307, 323
continuation, 309
continuity, 9
contrast, 24
contributing, 75, 94, 99, 155, 276,
305
control, 171, 172, 181, 197
controversy, 171, 181
conversation, 172, 212, 248, 256,
273, 325
conversion, 101–104
core, 39, 197, 251, 258
cornerstone, 3, 47, 84, 89, 148, 170,
192, 278
counseling, 254
counter, 32, 100

country, 9, 10, 28, 30, 58, 124, 194, 218, 247
courage, 24, 25, 28, 30, 32, 51, 77–79, 94, 133, 157, 166, 179, 184, 215, 217, 222, 242, 291, 294, 298, 310, 311, 322, 326, 327
coverage, 32, 75, 180
crackdown, 182, 194
creation, 86, 116, 181
creativity, 91, 143
credibility, 55–57, 59, 202
credit, 185, 217
criminalization, 28, 222, 246
crisis, 6, 122
critic, 246
criticism, 179, 196
critique, 195, 196
critiqued, 195, 196
crowd, 33
crucible, 294
cry, 178, 326
culmination, 7
culture, 8, 9, 13, 34, 42, 79, 141, 142, 181, 186, 192, 196, 197, 207, 214, 272, 293, 325
curricula, 20, 244, 297
custody, 34
cycle, 12, 34, 59, 286

danger, 2, 52, 284, 304
daughter, 184
death, 53, 230, 304
debate, 195, 196
decision, 52, 56, 58, 127, 156, 171, 282
declaration, 25
deconstruction, 42
decriminalization, 29, 282
dedication, 52, 66, 76, 131, 166, 202, 212, 213, 216, 253, 285, 322
defense, 178
defiance, 24, 25, 28, 30, 78, 142, 172, 175
definition, 305
demand, 287
denial, 14, 40
deportation, 56, 75
depression, 12, 51, 58, 187, 252
depth, 143, 180, 188
desire, 1–3, 6, 7, 11, 194
despair, 12, 189
detection, 85
detention, 68
determination, 3, 6, 8, 19, 23, 25, 29, 30, 41, 94, 120, 142, 157, 182, 184, 233, 235, 272, 283, 287, 294, 305, 310, 320
development, 13, 115, 135, 157, 191, 211, 212, 216, 241, 245
deviant, 13, 174
deviation, 5, 11, 14, 193
dialect, 58
dialogue, 13, 14, 18, 31, 42, 50, 121, 122, 140, 142, 145, 146, 172, 183, 196, 197, 219, 220, 230, 247, 252, 266
dichotomy, 6, 32
difficulty, 26, 186
diffusion, 145
dignity, 14, 39, 41, 57, 68, 102, 126, 156, 170, 190, 201, 227, 232, 253, 263, 272, 295, 315, 318
diplomacy, 156
disadvantage, 164, 195, 263, 303

disappointment, 172
discomfort, 17
disconnect, 229
discourse, 69, 74, 75, 100, 121, 148, 174, 180, 181, 197, 199, 203, 220, 244–246, 282
discovery, 1, 25, 187, 192, 194
discretion, 85
discrimination, 2–4, 7, 9, 11–13, 15, 17–19, 23, 25–30, 33, 40, 42, 44, 45, 47, 51, 53, 57, 59, 60, 68, 75, 78, 81, 84, 86, 93, 94, 99, 102, 109, 115, 122, 140, 142, 147, 148, 151, 157, 158, 160, 164, 166, 167, 174, 183, 187–189, 191, 195, 198, 200, 201, 207, 211, 212, 214, 217–222, 225, 228, 230, 232, 234, 236, 238–241, 245, 246, 248, 251–255, 258, 260, 263, 265, 271, 273, 277, 281, 282, 284, 291, 293–297, 299, 303, 304, 306, 307, 310, 313, 314, 318, 320, 322, 324
discussion, 40
disdain, 2
disillusionment, 257
dismissal, 34, 230
disparity, 281
displacement, 60
dissemination, 309
dissonance, 11, 194
distance, 275
distress, 59
distrust, 85

diversity, 16, 20, 29, 114, 141, 187, 195, 212, 275, 304
doctrine, 11
document, 57
documentation, 23, 57, 59, 124
doubt, 12, 13, 194
drafting, 157
drama, 180
dream, 25, 287, 323
driving, 6, 12, 194, 233, 234
duality, 1, 5, 164, 172, 189, 293
duty, 310, 312
dynamic, 146
dynamism, 4

educate, 49, 64, 67, 231, 244, 279, 313
education, 11, 19–21, 42, 50, 96, 104, 109, 112, 114, 148, 153, 155, 167, 201, 251, 254, 272, 279, 284, 292, 304, 305, 312, 315, 324
effect, 3, 24, 68, 81, 91, 96, 192, 204, 241, 248, 278, 287, 298, 320
effectiveness, 96, 106, 109, 145, 196, 228, 229, 266, 267
efficacy, 81, 86, 308
effort, 117, 157, 289, 304, 307, 315
element, 99
eloquence, 75
embrace, 4, 6, 8–11, 14, 18, 23, 26–28, 112, 186, 188, 194, 195, 201, 235, 253, 259, 277, 278, 287, 292, 296, 309, 311, 325
emergence, 10, 23, 35, 305, 322
empathy, 30, 141, 145, 167, 185, 232, 234, 248, 275, 311,

318, 320
emphasis, 71, 201, 248, 284
empowerment, 10, 13, 19, 45, 49, 50, 109, 117, 183, 187–189, 193, 194, 201, 209, 270, 272, 276, 278, 279, 284, 286, 292, 300, 302, 308, 322
enactment, 293
encounter, 62, 105, 122, 162, 166, 223, 230, 235, 248, 281, 300
encouragement, 106, 284
endeavor, 32, 69, 228, 295, 308, 309, 312, 318
enforcement, 33
engagement, 16, 30, 96, 147, 155, 166, 178, 183, 203, 247, 253–255, 276, 315
environment, 1, 5, 6, 8, 9, 11, 15, 17, 19, 20, 23, 25–27, 33, 35, 46, 50, 57, 78, 85, 90, 99, 114, 115, 120, 155, 182, 186, 189, 192, 194, 200, 210, 216, 218, 244, 246, 248, 251, 258, 278, 284, 289, 293, 295, 296, 306, 320
equality, 7, 8, 10, 14, 23, 25, 26, 28–30, 32, 37, 39–41, 47, 49, 51, 52, 66, 69, 71, 74, 76, 77, 79, 89, 96, 99, 101, 124, 129, 131, 133, 138, 140–143, 145, 146, 148–150, 155, 157–161, 167, 170, 173, 181, 186, 190, 192, 196, 199, 200, 203, 206, 210, 211, 213, 215, 218, 220, 222, 233, 234, 239, 240, 242, 245, 246, 248, 249, 252, 253, 256, 260, 263, 265–267, 272, 276, 278, 280–285, 287–289, 292, 294–298, 300, 302–305, 309, 310, 312, 315, 318–323
equation, 13, 15, 16, 89, 93, 146, 147, 151, 171–173, 182, 183, 216, 227, 228, 245, 246, 252, 265, 270, 275, 276, 285, 286, 292, 303, 304, 313, 315
equity, 42, 96, 97, 112, 114, 246
era, 151, 258, 281, 293
escape, 31, 74
essence, 13, 89, 147, 156, 292, 294, 310, 315
establishment, 34, 42, 44, 50, 68, 96, 141, 210, 257, 279, 297
ethos, 292
Europe, 20
event, 29, 31, 32, 34, 78, 86, 141, 214, 315, 324
evidence, 56–59, 124, 230
evolution, 54, 128, 192, 197, 283, 291, 292, 294
examination, 3, 55
example, 9, 13, 20, 24, 31, 36, 48, 50, 74, 84, 96, 111, 141, 149, 164, 191, 192, 207, 217, 221, 235, 237, 239, 241, 247, 251, 257, 259, 266, 271, 274, 275, 281, 282, 284, 297, 299, 303, 307, 322, 324
exception, 6, 57, 179
exchange, 20
exclusion, 2, 5

exhibit, 106
exile, 54, 281
existence, 1, 2, 14, 25, 221
expectation, 1, 5
experience, 11, 12, 14, 17, 32, 33, 53, 59, 67, 74, 99, 111, 138, 160, 164, 181–183, 194, 205, 211, 212, 229, 235, 237, 252, 256, 258, 265, 275, 277, 282, 291, 292, 299, 303, 304
expertise, 58
exploitation, 198, 199
exploration, 3, 7, 13, 42, 199
exposure, 3, 14
expression, 14, 15, 24, 141–143, 186, 285
exterior, 5

fabric, 180, 325
face, 4, 10, 12, 14, 15, 17, 25, 27–29, 32, 35, 37, 51, 57, 58, 60, 65, 67–69, 71, 78, 79, 84, 87, 89, 90, 94, 99, 102, 115, 117, 120, 122, 124, 149, 158, 164, 174–176, 180, 181, 183, 184, 188, 189, 193, 194, 200, 201, 203, 206, 211, 212, 216–219, 221, 222, 225, 228, 230–232, 238, 240, 246, 248, 252, 255, 258, 263, 265, 277, 281, 282, 292, 293, 297, 299, 300, 303–305, 307, 310, 312, 321, 322, 324, 326
facet, 39, 170
factor, 37, 306
failing, 9, 17

faith, 3, 6, 7, 9, 15, 17, 18, 142, 187, 189, 193
family, 1, 2, 5, 6, 9, 10, 15, 24, 40, 53, 184, 186, 193, 194, 217, 277, 312
fatigue, 191
fear, 2, 6, 10–13, 17, 24, 26, 27, 31, 33–35, 42, 44, 47, 53, 54, 57, 68, 76, 78, 85, 90, 115, 120, 122, 124, 149, 156, 174, 182, 183, 185, 186, 189, 194, 219, 227, 239, 246, 248, 252, 265, 277, 285, 296, 306, 322
feeling, 5, 9, 60, 68
femininity, 11, 14, 193
feminism, 315
festival, 141
fight, 4, 7, 14, 18, 23–26, 28–30, 32, 33, 35, 37, 39–41, 47, 49, 51, 57, 59, 66, 69, 71, 74, 76, 78, 79, 84, 89, 94, 96, 99, 101, 104, 109, 112, 122, 124, 126, 128, 129, 131, 133, 138, 140, 141, 143, 145–148, 150, 156–160, 165–167, 170, 173, 174, 176, 181, 183–186, 190, 192, 194, 195, 197, 200, 201, 206, 208, 211, 216, 218, 220–222, 225, 227, 228, 230–236, 238, 240, 242, 246, 248, 252, 253, 255, 256, 259, 263, 265–267, 272, 276, 279–282, 284–287, 289, 292, 294–300, 302–305, 309, 311, 312, 315, 318,

320–324
fighting, 2, 16, 27, 73, 79, 187, 191, 220, 281
figure, 21, 45, 49, 132, 138, 140, 181, 184, 202, 233, 283, 297, 321
film, 138
finding, 14, 18, 186, 194
fire, 4, 14, 24, 78
firm, 30, 35, 103
firsthand, 2, 15, 17, 26
flame, 327
flight, 53
fluidity, 42
focus, 51, 107, 124, 133, 149, 160, 180, 196, 202, 203, 229, 244, 254, 260, 266, 271
following, 34, 84, 106, 117, 124, 133, 217, 262, 313, 315
force, 6, 29, 33, 54, 79, 91, 194, 223, 234, 235, 240, 286
forefront, 51, 211, 303, 312
form, 9, 10, 13, 27, 36, 135, 141, 172, 195, 196, 214, 293
formality, 55
formation, 50, 84, 85
forum, 203
foster, 19, 20, 30, 36, 50, 75, 107, 117, 141, 143, 150, 153, 155, 167, 170, 183, 200, 201, 204, 207, 232, 234, 244, 262, 271, 277–279, 322, 325
Foucault, 174
foundation, 6, 8, 79, 166, 208, 210, 292, 297, 298, 300
fragmentation, 89, 91
frame, 39

framework, 2, 9–11, 16, 17, 31, 41, 53, 57, 59, 75, 99, 112, 135, 147, 153, 156, 164, 174, 190, 206, 211, 219, 220, 229, 256, 258, 263, 265, 277, 281, 282, 293, 296
framing, 9, 17, 245, 295, 300
freedom, 281
friction, 148, 260
friend, 184
front, 81, 86, 144, 148, 207, 260
frustration, 182
fuel, 19, 185, 188, 251, 311
fulfillment, 277
function, 245, 272, 304
funding, 127, 143, 260, 266, 293
future, 3, 6, 8, 10, 12, 14, 16, 21, 23, 35, 42, 44, 47, 58, 74, 84, 97, 104, 106, 112, 114, 122, 124, 133, 138, 143, 145, 157, 161, 170, 183, 188, 190, 200, 206–208, 213, 215, 218, 220, 222, 230, 236, 246, 249, 253, 260, 262, 272, 283–287, 291, 292, 294, 296, 297, 305, 309, 312, 322, 324, 325

gain, 186, 188
gap, 18, 126, 174
gathering, 13, 221
gay, 68, 90, 124, 217
gender, 1, 4, 11, 14–17, 20, 21, 26, 27, 40, 42, 59, 61, 66, 68, 94, 96, 99–102, 104, 109, 111, 117, 122, 125, 126, 140, 147, 157, 158, 160,

Index

164, 192, 195, 213, 215, 216, 225, 227, 229–231, 236, 242, 252, 256, 258, 263, 273, 277, 281, 289, 294, 296, 303, 314, 318
generation, 25, 32, 35, 47, 51, 107, 117, 140, 143, 161–163, 191, 201, 216–218, 220, 248, 259, 278, 284, 292, 297, 309, 311, 322
girl, 1
globalization, 89
globe, 140, 142, 166, 173, 298, 300, 302, 303, 318
goal, 40, 41, 89, 91, 308
Gossip, 201
gossip, 201–204
government, 29, 31–34, 49, 50, 71, 75, 121, 182, 194, 219, 247, 254
grain, 184
grant, 56
grappling, 5, 13, 187, 189, 322
grief, 323
ground, 202, 239
groundwork, 4, 6, 12, 14, 24, 47, 200, 293, 322
group, 11, 34, 57, 64, 89, 156, 193, 216, 221, 234, 277, 312
growth, 27, 204, 277, 287, 305
guidance, 45, 64, 68, 104, 106, 185, 191, 216, 217, 272, 278, 279, 284
guilt, 15, 17, 193
guise, 236

hallmark, 212
hand, 167, 179, 198, 201, 202, 219, 278

harassment, 30, 33, 40, 42, 49, 52, 90, 115, 142, 219, 255, 281, 284, 293, 297, 305
hardship, 217, 240
harm, 180, 199
hatred, 12
haven, 6, 59, 234
head, 12, 29, 34, 194, 200, 306
health, 12, 19, 22, 46, 47, 51, 58, 75, 79, 86, 96, 102, 109–112, 115, 117, 141, 167, 187, 191, 193, 205, 210, 211, 228, 246, 252, 254, 255, 259, 271, 272, 297, 299, 322
healthcare, 22, 60, 94–97, 126, 167, 206, 246, 259, 260
heart, 5, 53, 253, 296
heartbeat, 1
help, 68, 79, 106, 112, 124, 126, 207, 227, 244, 252, 304
helplessness, 33
Henri Tajfel, 277
Henri Tajfel's, 11
heritage, 221
heteronormativity, 14
heterosexuality, 26
hierarchy, 266
highlight, 41, 47, 50, 59, 104, 166, 179, 185, 187, 200, 207, 212, 221, 254, 263, 284, 291, 303
history, 20, 48, 313
Hodges, 41
home, 57, 64, 67, 117, 124, 125, 166, 194, 223, 225, 228, 230, 231, 258, 311
homelessness, 97–99, 206, 260, 297
homonormativity, 256

homophobia, 2, 5, 11–13, 15, 17, 19, 23, 26, 31, 33, 57, 78, 109, 111, 120, 140, 164, 183, 189, 193, 200, 219, 234, 245, 258, 273, 277, 284, 291, 293, 299, 306, 323

homosexuality, 2, 5, 6, 9, 10, 15, 17, 26, 29, 66, 102, 151, 174, 187, 192, 193, 221, 246, 247, 281, 282, 293

honor, 5, 9, 138, 199, 292, 298, 300, 309, 323, 324, 326

hope, 4, 10, 14, 23, 25, 28, 35, 41, 51–54, 69, 77, 97, 133, 188, 190, 194, 200, 201, 211, 212, 215, 217, 220, 222, 225, 235, 240, 251, 253, 260, 267, 276, 278, 283, 292, 296, 305, 323

host, 62, 68, 142, 166, 211, 248

hostility, 11, 14, 16, 18, 60, 166, 194, 221, 255

household, 6

housing, 60, 67

human, 8, 19, 23, 29, 34, 39–41, 50, 57, 62, 64, 66, 69, 71, 109, 121, 122, 124, 126, 135, 138, 146–148, 155–158, 166, 190, 199, 200, 206, 211, 219, 220, 223, 230, 232, 236, 238, 240, 245–248, 253, 260, 263, 265, 281, 282, 285, 287, 295–297, 302, 305, 308, 311, 315, 321, 322, 326

humanity, 28, 74, 76, 146, 170, 227, 272

humiliation, 78

hurdle, 2

idea, 15, 85, 145, 172, 192, 276, 278, 312

ideal, 256

ideation, 51, 252

identity, 1–6, 8–18, 20, 21, 24, 26–28, 42, 49, 50, 53, 57, 59, 61, 66–69, 96, 99, 101, 104, 107, 109, 111, 115, 117, 122, 125, 126, 135, 140, 142, 157, 158, 164, 165, 171, 180, 184, 186–190, 192–194, 197, 202, 203, 205, 213, 215, 216, 222, 225, 227, 229, 230, 233, 234, 236, 238, 239, 242, 248, 252, 253, 258, 259, 263, 265, 275–278, 281, 289, 292, 294–296, 303, 304, 307, 314, 318

ignorance, 174

illustration, 310

image, 194

immigrant, 76, 259

immigration, 55, 58, 59, 68, 126, 252

impact, 2, 8, 12, 18–20, 26, 32, 33, 47, 49–51, 66, 73, 75, 76, 84, 86, 112, 119, 124, 131, 136, 138, 140, 142, 143, 145, 146, 149, 166–168, 173, 176, 182, 184, 186, 189, 191, 193–195, 201, 202, 206, 209, 211, 213, 215, 217, 220, 223, 228, 235, 236, 238, 240–242, 248, 252, 255, 276, 292, 293, 296–298, 300, 307, 309, 311, 322, 325, 327

imperative, 94, 119, 124, 232, 238, 267, 292, 295, 326
imperialism, 195
implementation, 96, 113, 127, 256
importance, 2, 3, 7–9, 12, 14, 16, 20, 21, 25, 27, 29, 32, 41, 42, 54, 56, 59, 68, 69, 75, 78, 81, 84–86, 89, 94, 96, 100, 102, 104, 109, 112, 116, 117, 119, 122, 124, 136, 141, 142, 157, 160, 166, 167, 170, 173, 181–183, 185, 187, 188, 190–192, 194, 195, 197, 204, 205, 207, 212, 213, 216–218, 229, 231, 235, 239, 242–244, 248, 256, 259, 260, 262, 272, 277–279, 281, 282, 284, 288, 289, 292, 295, 297, 299–301, 303, 305, 307, 308, 312, 321, 323, 325
imposition, 36, 236, 237, 293
inability, 237
incident, 11, 34, 181, 239
inclusion, 42, 75, 96, 157, 229, 245, 246
inclusivity, 20, 44, 145, 220, 228, 251–253, 256–259, 285, 297, 323
inconsistency, 57, 230
increase, 148, 275, 285, 288
independence, 293
India, 282
indifference, 34
individual, 5, 9, 34, 51, 55, 56, 58, 79, 86, 99, 101, 126, 138, 140, 142, 143, 151, 156, 167, 196, 197, 201, 206, 209, 213, 216, 232, 234, 240, 242, 252, 253, 259, 263, 283, 286, 287, 291, 292, 294, 298, 313, 317, 318, 323, 327
individuality, 1
inequality, 25, 40, 94, 164–166, 260, 303, 305, 313
influence, 1, 10, 11, 16, 19, 26, 84, 140, 142, 143, 151, 153–155, 180, 188, 189, 195, 199–201, 207, 209, 212, 217, 221, 223–225, 244, 246, 248, 258, 260, 279, 281, 283–285, 295, 322, 326
information, 24, 66, 67, 86, 144, 149, 154, 174, 198, 309
initiative, 141, 207, 217, 257
injustice, 4, 21, 79, 94, 157, 249, 297, 309, 312, 325, 326
insensitivity, 36
insight, 188, 296
inspiration, 7, 13, 30, 41, 44, 79, 184, 188, 215, 234, 236, 240, 253, 256, 278, 322, 323, 326
instance, 5, 9, 17, 25, 31, 32, 50, 68, 75, 78, 83, 86, 99, 121, 126, 140, 142, 149, 153, 155, 156, 160, 164, 175, 180, 189, 191, 195, 200, 202, 203, 207, 214, 217, 227, 228, 230, 232, 235, 237, 242, 244–246, 252, 257, 259, 260, 266, 277, 281, 295, 322, 324
institution, 3, 40, 196
integration, 56, 91, 211, 276

integrity, 196, 197
intensity, 256
intent, 171
interaction, 304
interconnectedness, 7, 21, 155, 212, 217, 263, 266, 275, 307
internalization, 12, 193
interplay, 8, 23, 39, 71, 151, 155, 179, 182, 186, 192, 292, 303, 313
interpretation, 187
intersect, 99, 147, 201, 229, 259, 281, 314
intersection, 14, 18, 59, 84, 94, 109, 138, 141, 160, 174, 176, 181, 187, 189, 203, 206, 209, 211, 213, 233, 244, 282, 291, 294–296
intersectionality, 3, 23, 27, 59, 62, 64, 67, 69, 99, 101, 122, 148, 158, 161, 164, 192, 195, 197, 200, 208, 212, 217, 222, 223, 229, 231, 242, 244, 253, 256–260, 263, 265, 267, 272, 275, 281, 283–285, 296, 297, 299, 303, 305, 314, 315
intertwining, 16
intervention, 34, 36, 71
interview, 55, 57, 184
intimacy, 9
intimidation, 5, 33
intolerance, 3, 12
intrigue, 171
introduction, 5
introspection, 204
invisibility, 117
involvement, 2, 10, 19, 74, 128, 143, 157, 166, 189, 278, 312, 326
isolation, 6, 9, 12, 19, 58, 68, 85, 147, 149, 216, 241, 248, 252, 265, 306, 322
issue, 7, 11, 16, 34, 68, 78, 117, 125, 147, 151, 200, 225, 229, 242, 247, 256, 266

jargon, 64
John Turner, 277
journalism, 197
journey, 1, 3, 4, 8, 10, 13, 14, 16, 18–21, 23, 25–28, 30, 37, 41, 45, 49, 53, 54, 56, 57, 59, 64, 66, 69, 71, 74, 77, 79, 96, 112, 125, 131, 133, 136, 138, 141, 143, 157, 166, 167, 173, 176, 178, 186–188, 190–194, 199, 201, 204, 209, 210, 213, 215, 217, 218, 220, 222, 228, 232–235, 238, 240, 253, 258, 260, 272, 277, 278, 283–285, 287, 289, 291, 292, 294, 296, 298, 300, 302, 305, 307, 308, 310, 311, 315, 318, 321–323, 325, 327
joy, 1
judgment, 2, 183, 252
Judith Butler, 167
juncture, 56
justice, 19, 20, 25, 28–30, 35, 39, 41, 42, 49, 51, 54, 62, 64, 66, 69, 71, 74, 76, 77, 96, 101, 112, 114, 122, 124, 129, 133, 138, 140, 145, 146, 148, 150, 155, 157, 164–167, 171, 173, 186,

Index

190–192, 195, 196, 200, 203, 206, 208, 212, 213, 215, 217, 218, 220–223, 225, 232–234, 236, 238–240, 242, 246–248, 251–253, 256, 258–260, 262, 263, 266, 267, 272, 276, 278, 284–286, 288, 289, 291, 292, 295, 296, 298, 300, 302, 305, 307, 309–312, 315, 318, 322–324, 326

key, 19, 67, 71, 84, 95, 115, 122, 161, 168, 215, 219, 253, 311
keynote, 84
Kimberlé Crenshaw, 59, 99, 164, 195, 217, 256, 258, 263, 265, 281, 296, 303, 314
kindness, 53
knowledge, 7, 19–21, 26, 107, 143, 149, 174, 248, 270, 324

lack, 6, 20, 34, 45, 58, 60, 61, 101, 104, 114, 124, 153, 172, 206, 211, 228, 230, 266, 284, 294
Lagos, 1, 4, 6, 12, 14, 23, 25, 34, 78, 86, 141, 188, 191, 192, 217, 221, 239, 306, 310
land, 54
landmark, 29, 282
landscape, 1, 16, 30, 35, 37, 39, 47, 49, 64, 74, 75, 85, 89, 120, 122, 124, 143, 149, 153, 166, 167, 195, 221, 232, 253, 258, 259, 272, 274, 284, 285, 291, 294–296, 309, 311, 315, 316

language, 141
law, 25, 33, 39, 58, 293
layer, 40, 193
lead, 9, 10, 15, 26, 32, 50, 51, 56, 58, 67, 89, 102, 143, 145, 149, 186, 188, 191, 193, 195, 196, 198, 213, 229–231, 235, 245, 257, 258, 260, 266, 275, 277, 296, 299, 312
leader, 4, 14, 183, 184, 322, 323
leadership, 20, 136, 138
legacy, 25, 32, 51, 66, 106, 131, 133, 140, 148, 151, 157, 166, 167, 184, 199, 201, 206–208, 213, 218, 220, 235, 242, 248, 249, 259, 271, 272, 278, 279, 285, 287, 292, 296–300, 309, 312, 321–327
legalization, 304
legislation, 46, 71, 75, 218, 254, 266, 293
lens, 17, 59, 174, 180, 193, 195, 206, 230, 231, 265, 273, 296, 300
lesbian, 26, 27, 57, 59, 164
lesson, 284
level, 23, 147, 217, 246, 253, 276, 278, 303
leverage, 23, 51, 150, 200
leveraging, 29, 124, 167, 230, 293
liberation, 258
liberty, 263
life, 3, 5, 6, 8, 10–12, 14, 18, 25, 40, 52, 58, 131, 167, 172, 179, 180, 182, 185–190, 194, 197, 202, 203, 205, 263, 291, 295, 305, 310, 323

lifeline, 12, 47, 279
lifetime, 4
light, 34, 120, 171, 184, 188, 201, 220, 285
likelihood, 16, 58
limbo, 58
lineage, 9
listening, 192
litigation, 39
living, 14, 206, 222, 292, 309, 327
lobbying, 34, 46, 75, 120–122, 231, 245, 254
location, 111
loneliness, 5
look, 206, 285, 292, 309
loss, 322, 323
love, 5, 7, 12, 18, 25, 39–41, 51, 156, 184, 186, 187, 292, 318, 327

mainstream, 18, 196, 266
maintenance, 42, 116
making, 9, 30, 31, 56–58, 64, 67, 127, 146, 156, 167, 182, 188, 219, 222, 229, 247, 260, 278, 280, 295
male, 17
man, 1, 9, 68, 124, 217
Mancur Olson's, 312
manifest, 59, 142, 147, 164, 256
manner, 193
mantle, 272, 326
march, 29, 32
marginalization, 13, 15, 26, 99, 311
Maria, 124
mark, 71, 143, 199, 311
Mark Jordan, 193
marriage, 9, 39–41, 149, 167, 196, 260, 266, 304

marrying, 39
Martin Seligman, 235
masculinity, 14, 193
material, 172
matter, 71, 109, 119, 126, 157, 185, 227
means, 10, 14, 19, 21, 53, 93, 229, 276, 279
media, 23, 24, 29, 30, 32, 34, 47–50, 64, 67, 68, 75, 86, 94, 121, 140, 144, 145, 149, 152, 154, 155, 167, 176, 180, 181, 183, 196, 203, 214, 215, 217–219, 239, 255, 274, 277, 293, 305, 325
member, 11, 14, 53, 156, 192
membership, 57
memory, 323, 324
mentee, 185
mentoring, 216, 297
mentorship, 47, 105, 106, 185, 191, 201, 207, 216, 217, 235, 259, 272, 278, 284, 322
message, 78, 96, 138, 142, 147, 156, 181, 196, 202, 218, 255, 274, 287, 309, 322
messaging, 86
metropolis, 1, 4
Michel Foucault's, 174
midst, 2, 15
migration, 54, 166, 238, 252
mind, 185
mindset, 235
Ming Yusuf, 180
minority, 102, 256
misalignment, 229
misinformation, 153, 198, 202, 305
misrepresentation, 182
mission, 117, 141, 197, 203

Index

mix, 33, 171
mob, 221
mobilization, 24, 47, 190, 279, 282, 300, 309
model, 102, 207, 287, 307
modernity, 1
moment, 11, 23, 78, 323
momentum, 51
morality, 17
mother, 184
motivator, 218
movement, 3, 7, 14, 18, 21, 23, 25, 30, 41, 42, 51, 66, 71, 74, 76, 77, 85–87, 89, 101, 129, 132, 133, 135, 136, 138, 140, 142, 143, 148, 150, 156, 158, 160, 161, 164, 165, 167, 181, 182, 185, 190, 196, 197, 199, 201, 204, 206, 213, 218, 220, 242, 244, 256–259, 267, 271, 274, 278, 279, 282, 285, 289, 293, 294, 296–298, 304, 309, 312, 315, 317, 318, 322, 323, 326
multitude, 275
music, 5, 13, 141
myriad, 57, 62, 125, 220, 223

narrative, 5, 9–11, 23, 26, 27, 30, 50, 54, 57, 74, 79, 131, 142, 157, 167, 171–175, 178–181, 183, 188, 190, 196–198, 200, 202, 211, 213, 233–235, 248, 275, 276, 291, 292, 307, 323, 325
nation, 16, 49, 267, 289, 318

national, 29, 51, 148, 176, 236, 245, 253, 315
nationality, 57, 236
nature, 25, 32, 40, 54, 73, 76, 77, 86, 127, 164, 172, 180, 195, 231, 245, 252, 260, 267, 277, 292, 296, 302
necessity, 39, 123, 164, 247, 256, 257, 260, 267, 292, 308, 315
need, 2, 3, 16, 22, 25, 32–34, 39, 54, 58, 60, 68, 69, 75, 76, 93, 94, 112, 124, 166, 167, 173, 181, 183, 187, 197, 212, 217, 221, 228, 232, 237, 241, 245–247, 251, 259, 268, 274, 277, 279, 281, 282, 284, 291, 295, 297, 305, 306
neocolonialism, 36
net, 191, 307
network, 2, 12, 14, 20, 49, 128, 138, 143, 145, 187, 216, 248, 322
networking, 32, 82, 85
New Zealand, 84
newfound, 7, 26, 305
Nigeria, 1–10, 13–17, 19–21, 23–26, 29–33, 35–39, 41, 42, 47, 49–59, 66, 69, 74, 78, 85, 86, 90, 93, 94, 120–122, 128, 132, 138, 140–143, 146, 149, 153, 155, 159, 167, 172, 173, 175, 179–184, 186–196, 200, 201, 203, 207, 209–211, 213–222, 228, 229, 233–235, 237, 239, 240, 244, 247, 248, 254,

255, 258, 259, 266, 267,
273–275, 277, 278, 281,
283, 284, 291–298, 304,
306, 310, 311, 322, 326
norm, 5, 11, 14
north, 16
notion, 5, 18, 211, 235, 236
notoriety, 202
number, 205

obligation, 9, 124
obstacle, 238
odyssey, 215
officer, 57
on, 5, 8, 10, 12, 13, 15, 18–21, 23,
25, 29, 32, 34, 40, 41,
49–54, 56–61, 69, 71, 73,
74, 79, 83–86, 93, 95, 99,
107, 117, 119–122, 124,
125, 128, 133, 136, 140,
141, 143, 145, 148, 149,
151, 153, 155–158, 160,
161, 164, 166–168,
171–173, 176, 180,
182–184, 186–191,
193–196, 198–205, 209,
211–213, 215–220,
223–225, 228–230, 236,
238, 240, 242, 244–248,
251, 252, 254–258, 260,
262, 266, 271, 274, 278,
283, 284, 289, 291–294,
296, 298–300, 305, 306,
311–313, 315, 321, 323
one, 5, 8, 28, 33, 41, 71, 79, 87, 99,
133, 142, 146, 179, 182,
184, 187, 188, 194, 198,
201, 205, 210, 217, 222,
240, 242, 258, 259, 267,
275–278, 289, 292, 298,
304, 307, 315, 323, 326,
327
openness, 79, 214
opinion, 26, 57, 140, 153–155, 218
opponent, 101
opportunity, 47, 55, 99, 106, 124,
172, 179, 227, 245, 287
opposition, 32, 141, 147, 239
oppression, 1, 3, 7, 12, 23, 25, 27,
30, 35, 59, 76, 79, 89, 141,
144, 164, 165, 167, 172,
193, 200, 229, 232, 256,
258–260, 265–267, 279,
286, 289, 296, 303, 322,
323
optimism, 235
ordeal, 54
organization, 13, 24, 29, 30, 124,
218
organizing, 19, 27, 29, 30, 34, 86,
90, 141, 189, 200, 214,
216, 218, 239, 251, 253,
279, 292, 293, 309
orientation, 6, 9, 12, 15, 17, 20, 21,
26, 35, 54, 55, 57, 60, 61,
66, 68, 96, 99, 101, 104,
109, 117, 122, 124–126,
140, 157, 158, 164, 193,
213, 215, 216, 225, 227,
229, 230, 236, 242, 252,
258, 263, 277, 289, 294,
296, 314, 318
ostracism, 2, 5, 9, 11, 15, 17, 26, 50,
85, 221, 222
other, 2, 26, 34, 41, 96, 128, 142,
143, 150, 155–157, 167,
174, 202, 212, 217, 225,
240, 241, 252, 262, 266,

269, 284, 286, 303, 307
out, 7, 18, 71, 124, 176, 185, 194,
    217, 237, 297, 318, 323
outcome, 56, 58
outlook, 234
outreach, 86, 323
overlap, 281, 314
oversight, 195
ownership, 171, 181, 183

pain, 1, 4, 12, 23, 24, 27, 187, 212,
    235
pandemic, 22, 149, 206
part, 2, 7, 26, 66, 78, 143, 156, 180,
    200, 201, 223, 235, 251,
    287, 315
participation, 13, 78, 82, 90, 175,
    214, 245, 247, 271, 274,
    297, 307, 312
partnership, 40
passage, 212
passersby, 141
passion, 2, 4, 7, 8, 13, 52, 75, 185,
    191, 208, 242
path, 3, 8, 28, 85, 151, 190, 193,
    215, 217, 220, 283, 305
patient, 96
Paulo Freire's, 279
pedagogy, 112, 114, 279
people, 5, 20, 46, 49, 185, 252, 259,
    266, 299, 322
perception, 29, 94, 121, 153,
    180–182, 201, 203, 221
performance, 19
period, 58, 203
permission, 198
persecution, 9, 13, 24, 25, 53–57,
    59, 61, 64, 66, 71, 75, 76,
    84, 85, 117, 122, 124, 125,
    128, 149, 155, 156, 166,
    176, 182, 194, 201, 204,
    223, 225, 227, 228, 230,
    232, 233, 236, 237, 247,
    248, 252, 253, 258, 291,
    295, 296, 304, 311, 322
perseverance, 212, 282
persistence, 94, 281
person, 47, 99, 201, 263, 265, 326
personal, 7, 9, 11, 14, 16, 19, 21, 23,
    24, 26–28, 30, 31, 34, 54,
    57, 71, 75, 78, 86, 101,
    109, 131, 141, 146, 154,
    167, 171–174, 178, 180,
    181, 184, 186–192, 194,
    196, 197, 200–204, 209,
    211–215, 222, 232–235,
    239, 240, 247, 248,
    275–278, 281, 287, 291,
    294, 295, 305, 307, 311,
    313, 318, 322, 325
perspective, 3, 20, 27, 40, 102, 122,
    158, 191, 195, 198, 231,
    263, 281, 282
phenomenon, 180, 193, 256
philosophy, 135
phrase, 326
picture, 184
pillar, 28, 312
place, 6, 12–14, 27, 140, 194, 248,
    265
planning, 30, 31
platform, 14, 15, 18, 24, 32, 47, 82,
    142, 143, 148, 155, 172,
    179, 182–184, 203, 211,
    214, 216, 219, 244
plausibility, 57
play, 26, 50, 104, 106, 107, 115, 141,
    145, 167, 198, 208, 289,

                    293, 304, 312, 315, 317
playground, 1
plight, 50, 54, 61, 67, 71, 75, 78, 86,
                    117, 125, 159, 176, 183,
                    211, 218, 225, 233, 239,
                    241, 252, 274, 278, 296,
                    307, 311, 322
poetry, 13, 141
point, 11, 25, 52, 182, 236, 324
police, 31, 33–35, 52, 57, 78, 191,
                    297
policy, 20, 46, 64, 75, 84, 96, 109,
                    120–122, 136, 140, 147,
                    155, 166, 167, 201, 206,
                    211, 212, 225, 228, 229,
                    231, 232, 237, 241, 245,
                    247, 248, 253, 274, 288,
                    289, 307, 322
pool, 260
population, 16, 74, 76, 126, 201,
                    227, 230
portion, 16, 64
portrayal, 153, 167, 172, 180, 182
position, 203, 239
possibility, 18, 59
post, 27, 195
potential, 18, 24, 31, 36, 37, 49, 50,
                    57, 80, 81, 85, 121, 122,
                    141, 150, 162, 172, 180,
                    182, 194, 198, 199, 229,
                    236, 260
poverty, 222
power, 2, 4, 6, 10, 12, 19, 24, 25,
                    27–29, 32, 34, 41, 47,
                    49–51, 66, 68, 77, 79, 83,
                    89, 91, 101, 104, 117, 122,
                    128, 142, 143, 145, 150,
                    155, 157, 167, 173, 174,
                    176, 180, 181, 185, 188,

                    190, 195, 198, 201, 207,
                    211, 213, 225, 233, 234,
                    239, 240, 242, 246, 247,
                    253, 255, 257, 276, 277,
                    282, 287, 289, 292, 296,
                    307, 322, 327
practice, 101, 102, 285
praise, 195
precedent, 157, 285
prejudice, 60, 270, 304
preparation, 58
presence, 51, 140, 152, 157, 167,
                    215, 216, 221, 274, 277
pressure, 1, 5, 9–11, 14, 32, 34, 57,
                    121, 148, 156, 185, 186,
                    219, 247
pride, 31, 32, 50, 112, 194, 217
principle, 89, 192, 256, 260, 271,
                    276, 312
priority, 167
privacy, 197, 199
privilege, 229
problem, 34, 228
process, 53–60, 64, 66, 68, 74, 76,
                    126, 193, 194, 198, 204,
                    230, 237, 240, 242, 245,
                    258, 284, 301, 304, 305,
                    307, 323
product, 286
professional, 31
program, 257, 324
progress, 41, 151, 156, 158, 165,
                    167, 181, 182, 194, 206,
                    210, 222, 248, 263, 268,
                    280, 282, 287, 293, 319
project, 127
promotion, 112, 114
proof, 57
proportion, 227

prospect, 53
protection, 34, 56, 59, 126, 166, 211, 221, 228, 230–232, 236, 248, 258, 284
protest, 33, 78, 239, 266
provision, 47, 122
public, 5, 26, 29, 30, 34, 41, 50, 56, 61, 64, 67, 68, 75, 76, 94, 121, 136, 140–143, 153–155, 172, 174, 179–182, 184, 197, 201–203, 214, 216, 218, 220, 221, 232, 246, 248, 251, 254, 277, 279, 304
publication, 171, 176
purpose, 27, 36, 91, 135, 235, 293, 305
pursuit, 21, 54, 71, 74, 76, 77, 122, 167, 192, 219, 247, 260, 276, 291, 298, 310, 318
push, 94, 121, 156, 167, 288, 308
pushback, 142

quality, 77, 185
queer, 13, 39, 60, 99, 141, 142, 175, 186, 216, 232, 258, 277, 281
quest, 14, 16, 30, 41, 66, 85, 171, 187, 188, 267, 280, 320, 323
question, 3, 7
questioning, 6, 33, 40, 60, 68, 237
quo, 7, 10, 24, 32, 42, 142, 180, 200, 206, 218, 255, 292, 295

race, 27, 57, 59, 100, 111, 147, 158, 160, 164, 195, 229, 231, 244, 256, 258, 263, 273, 296, 303, 314

racism, 111, 164, 258, 299
raid, 31
rainbow, 32
raising, 4, 20, 32, 34, 51, 66, 71, 75, 95, 104, 119, 146, 183, 218, 220, 241, 244, 246, 247, 253, 274, 278, 279, 282, 284, 322
rally, 86
rallying, 24, 178, 182, 239, 324, 326
range, 99
rationale, 236
reach, 156, 191, 228, 305, 322
reaction, 172, 179, 182
reality, 9–12, 33, 59, 161, 187, 194
realization, 26, 183, 193, 235
realm, 24, 85, 87, 126, 164, 183, 197, 201, 232, 236, 245, 256, 275, 276, 298
rebellion, 4, 7, 10, 23–25
receipt, 140, 322
reception, 53, 172, 179–182
recognition, 26, 39, 41, 75, 89, 101, 112, 126, 131, 135, 136, 138, 140, 173, 182, 195, 222, 228, 247, 282, 288, 289, 322, 326
reconciliation, 18
reconsideration, 194
recourse, 34, 221
reference, 17
reflection, 51, 181, 188, 197, 206, 258
reform, 25, 39, 84, 93, 209, 218–220, 232, 247
refuge, 12, 15, 53, 54, 56, 59, 64, 204, 225, 236, 297
refugee, 8, 53, 60, 61, 66–69, 74–76, 84, 117–119, 122, 124,

126, 166, 167, 179–181,
198, 205, 211, 213,
223–225, 227, 228,
230–232, 241, 245, 248,
258, 277, 295, 323
regime, 24
region, 71, 304
rejection, 1, 2, 6, 8, 10, 15, 17, 24,
25, 28, 34, 55, 78, 109,
186, 187, 194, 216, 252,
277, 285, 310
relationship, 9, 16, 186, 246, 294
release, 171, 176, 179, 182, 183
relevance, 326
relief, 13
religion, 3, 16, 18, 57, 189, 293, 295
reluctance, 277
remembrance, 323, 325
reminder, 11, 21, 25, 30, 53, 54, 57,
59, 69, 76, 84, 140, 157,
173, 178, 181, 188, 190,
194, 207, 208, 212, 213,
216, 235, 242, 259, 292,
295, 298, 308, 311, 320,
324, 326, 327
repeal, 25, 246
report, 34, 68, 299
representation, 14, 20, 29, 34, 58,
124, 141, 142, 155,
167–171, 178, 180, 181,
198, 217, 230, 244, 276,
278, 303, 304
representative, 165, 281
repression, 31, 86, 90, 91, 182, 189,
281, 282
reputation, 9, 180
requirement, 57
resilience, 4, 8, 10, 12, 13, 16, 23, 27,
29, 30, 32, 39, 41, 50, 51,
53, 54, 57, 59, 66, 69, 74,
75, 77–79, 91, 94, 107,
109, 112, 122, 133, 141,
152, 166, 167, 172, 173,
176, 180–182, 184–191,
193, 194, 198, 200, 201,
203, 204, 211–215, 217,
220, 222, 233–235,
238–240, 247, 248, 253,
255, 256, 260, 265, 272,
276–278, 283, 285, 287,
291, 294, 296, 297, 299,
303, 305–308, 310, 311,
318, 320–323, 325, 327
resistance, 7, 10, 13, 15, 16, 34, 42,
49, 78, 114, 120, 141, 142,
156, 172, 214, 219, 220,
312, 323
resolution, 157
resolve, 2, 23, 33, 57, 86, 90, 235,
297
resource, 126, 300
respect, 32, 42, 68, 94, 96, 114, 199,
219, 222, 262, 263, 304,
318
response, 10, 33, 34, 69, 117, 127,
142, 172, 176, 178, 179,
181, 182, 197, 200, 202,
203, 220, 266, 296, 315
responsibility, 289, 309, 312, 313,
315
result, 58, 230, 255, 282, 284
retaliation, 149
retribution, 12
return, 59
rhetoric, 18
rhythm, 4
ridicule, 2
rift, 9, 266

Index 353

right, 19, 39, 40, 76, 109, 122, 156, 171, 197, 212, 236, 263
ripple, 24, 68, 96, 192, 241, 248, 278, 287, 298
rise, 76, 292, 325
risk, 12, 196, 199, 281, 297
road, 41, 51, 74
roadmap, 235
role, 3, 4, 6, 9, 12, 13, 15, 16, 26, 29, 32, 35, 47, 49, 50, 67, 72, 86, 94, 104, 106, 107, 111, 115, 128, 136, 140, 141, 143, 145, 148, 155–157, 160, 167, 181, 183, 187, 191–193, 200, 205, 208, 216, 218, 235, 244, 246, 278, 282–285, 289, 294, 303, 304, 307, 312, 315, 317, 323
room, 9, 14, 193
ruling, 41

s, 1–16, 18–21, 23–30, 32–35, 39, 41, 42, 46, 47, 49–61, 63, 64, 66, 68, 69, 71, 73–79, 82, 84, 93–96, 101, 104, 109, 112, 119–122, 128, 131–133, 136, 138, 140–143, 145–148, 150, 153–157, 159, 160, 166, 167, 170–176, 178–218, 220, 222–225, 228–230, 233–235, 237–242, 244–248, 251–255, 257–260, 263–267, 270–272, 275–279, 283–285, 287, 289, 291, 292, 295–300, 303, 305–312, 318, 320–327

safety, 12, 24, 30, 31, 59, 62, 64, 66, 124, 125, 191, 227, 230–232, 235, 281, 297, 307
sanctuary, 2, 12, 26, 67, 189
satisfaction, 96
scale, 21, 23, 25, 50, 54, 71, 73, 84, 140, 145, 148, 157, 172, 183, 191, 209, 230, 240, 245, 246, 248, 274, 283, 315
scandal, 180
scapegoat, 219
scholar, 258, 303
scholarship, 324
school, 2, 5, 11
score, 15
scorn, 5
scripture, 3, 18
scrutiny, 57, 179, 184, 196, 197, 201, 202, 237
search, 64, 230
secrecy, 85
section, 1, 21, 26, 37, 42, 47, 54, 61, 71, 80, 82, 87, 89, 99, 112, 120, 122, 136, 138, 141, 148, 158, 173, 179, 182, 195, 199, 216, 223, 228, 230, 240, 253, 256, 267, 280, 283, 298, 300, 302, 310, 312, 315, 318, 323, 325
security, 36, 227, 236, 263
self, 1, 8, 9, 11–15, 25–28, 135, 186, 187, 189, 192–194, 197, 202, 216, 276–278, 285, 322
semblance, 24
sensationalism, 180

sense, 1–3, 5, 10–16, 20, 23, 26, 27, 31–33, 36, 49–51, 57, 79, 85, 86, 91, 104, 106, 107, 135, 144, 149, 157, 167, 174, 181, 183, 187, 189, 192–194, 200, 204, 216, 217, 235, 246, 254, 275, 277, 278, 284, 292, 293, 297, 306, 307, 312
sensitivity, 60, 68, 198, 228, 229, 237
sentiment, 56, 76, 184
series, 206, 218
session, 156
set, 5, 59, 236, 284, 287
setback, 293
setting, 180
sex, 20, 25, 31, 39, 41, 85, 120, 156, 189, 200, 218, 219, 230, 258, 282, 293, 296, 304, 306
sexism, 258
sexuality, 6, 13, 16, 18, 27, 42, 59, 100, 158, 186, 187, 189, 193, 244, 256, 281
shame, 5, 9, 13, 15, 17, 193, 194
shape, 5, 33, 74, 84, 99, 106, 142, 166, 180, 199, 218, 229, 242, 272, 292, 294
share, 13, 24, 48–51, 67, 75, 80, 82, 86, 142, 144, 148–150, 152, 155, 167, 183, 185, 187, 204, 210, 214, 215, 244, 245, 248, 253, 257, 266, 274, 276, 278, 284, 305, 324, 325
sharing, 20, 29, 34, 35, 69, 71, 75, 79, 81, 86, 101, 112, 126, 128, 142, 149, 155, 181, 188, 190, 191, 200, 211, 214, 216, 217, 234, 235, 241, 247, 248, 255, 272, 277, 278, 284, 289, 295, 307, 322
shelter, 99
shift, 27, 50, 94, 103, 121, 155, 196, 220, 259
significance, 82, 127, 135, 138, 148, 167, 178, 190, 286, 322
silence, 9, 11–13, 34, 52, 173, 176, 194, 213–215
silencing, 213
sin, 17
sister, 184
situation, 71, 85
skepticism, 60, 147
slacktivism, 49
society, 4, 6, 8, 10–12, 14–17, 20, 21, 24, 26, 29, 37, 42, 49, 52, 56, 76, 81, 94, 101, 104, 106, 109, 120, 121, 124, 126, 142, 155, 170, 180, 181, 186–189, 192, 193, 195, 202, 213, 216, 217, 219, 220, 227, 252, 253, 265, 267, 276, 293, 311, 313, 315
socio, 30, 109, 111, 195, 218–220, 256, 258, 273, 281, 284
solace, 2, 6, 12–14, 18, 26, 68, 187, 191, 193, 306
solidarity, 2, 3, 7, 13, 14, 16, 29, 32, 36, 37, 39, 50, 54, 69, 71, 75, 79, 84–87, 89, 91, 126, 140, 141, 144–146, 148–150, 157, 161, 165, 167, 176, 181, 183, 185, 189–191, 200, 201, 204, 207, 212, 217, 234, 242,

Index

244, 248, 252, 254, 266, 267, 271, 277, 279, 285, 289, 292, 295, 299, 300, 302, 305, 307–309, 311, 312, 315, 317, 322
source, 4, 12, 16, 30, 184, 187, 191, 193, 202, 234, 236, 326
south, 16
South Africa, 41, 304
space, 6, 13, 14, 27, 32, 185, 187, 278, 321
speaker, 146
speaking, 71, 75, 140, 142, 146–148, 214, 218, 248, 251, 277
spectacle, 196
specter, 201
spectrum, 26, 27, 82, 252, 256
speculation, 201–204
speech, 84, 174
sphere, 180, 214
spirit, 1, 8, 23, 25, 30, 57, 77, 84, 140, 176, 190, 212, 236, 256, 260, 265, 287, 309–312, 320, 323, 325, 326
spirituality, 187, 193
square, 286
stability, 62
stage, 83, 220, 248, 322
stance, 17, 50, 52, 78, 121, 196, 219, 247
stand, 4, 28, 29, 35, 79, 103, 104, 184, 188, 212, 218, 249, 289, 292, 305, 309, 318, 320, 322, 323, 326
standing, 12, 27, 29, 30, 194, 312
state, 34, 87, 280, 281
statement, 147, 182

status, 7, 10, 15, 24, 32, 42, 59, 111, 124, 142, 180, 181, 200, 206, 218, 229, 252, 255, 256, 258, 292, 295, 303
step, 24, 53, 64, 222
stigma, 2, 6, 9, 12, 13, 26, 31, 34, 45, 51, 61, 75, 85, 102, 120, 174, 200, 213, 216, 219, 222, 230, 241, 246, 248, 251, 255, 277, 281, 296, 303, 307
stigmatization, 9, 94
storm, 176
story, 10, 16, 21, 25, 27, 28, 30, 35, 51, 53, 57, 58, 68, 75, 86, 96, 124, 133, 142, 148, 157, 171–173, 178, 179, 181, 182, 185, 188–190, 194, 195, 198, 199, 205, 208, 212–217, 222, 233, 235, 240–242, 247, 253, 272, 274–278, 287, 291, 292, 295–297, 307–309, 320, 322, 323
storyteller, 275
storytelling, 29, 53, 64, 120, 142, 155, 167, 171, 173, 178, 181, 183, 190, 198, 207, 248, 276, 307
strain, 58, 205
strategy, 32, 126, 181, 185, 230, 248
street, 4
strength, 4, 6, 8, 12, 13, 27, 30, 85, 148, 183, 188, 189, 191, 193, 198, 212, 228, 239, 265, 286, 305–307, 311, 315, 323
strengthening, 183
stress, 58, 102, 111, 191, 256, 305

struggle, 2, 6–11, 14–16, 23, 25, 27, 30, 32, 33, 37, 39, 66, 68, 69, 71, 85, 89, 91, 94, 96, 99, 131, 140, 143, 158, 167, 170, 172, 181–183, 186–190, 192, 193, 198, 200, 205, 209, 211, 213, 215, 222, 240, 242, 258, 267, 271, 272, 280–282, 285, 287, 289, 293–296, 302, 305, 311, 312, 318, 323
student, 19
study, 143
subject, 171, 197, 198
substance, 180
success, 85, 96, 145, 196, 216, 235
suffering, 58
summary, 12, 59, 140, 145, 199, 201, 291
support, 6, 13, 16, 18, 22, 24–26, 29, 31, 32, 34–37, 41, 42, 45, 46, 49–53, 56–60, 64, 66–69, 74, 75, 78, 79, 85–87, 89, 104–107, 112, 120, 122, 124–128, 143, 144, 146, 149, 152, 161–163, 166, 173, 179, 183, 185, 187, 189–194, 200, 202–204, 207, 210, 211, 215, 216, 219, 225–228, 230, 232–234, 239, 241, 242, 245, 248, 252, 253, 255, 257–259, 265, 266, 270–272, 274, 275, 278, 279, 284, 286, 289, 292, 293, 295, 296, 299, 303, 306, 307, 309, 315–318, 322–324

suppression, 173–176, 182
surveillance, 86, 149
survival, 53
sword, 179, 201
symbol, 141, 201, 214, 296
synergy, 80
Syria, 71
system, 19, 20, 34, 58, 64–66, 156, 211, 221, 258, 306

t, 185
taboo, 5, 213
tactic, 33
tailoring, 227
tale, 74, 131, 234
tapestry, 1, 4, 7, 124, 186, 188, 201, 260
target, 52
task, 53, 55, 57, 121, 221
team, 29, 31, 141
technology, 24, 86, 91, 255, 309
television, 155
temptation, 198
tenacity, 303
tendency, 256, 266
tension, 6, 9, 171, 186, 197
term, 164, 195, 256, 281
terrain, 201
testament, 8, 10, 16, 18, 23, 25, 27, 30, 32, 33, 51, 66, 77, 84, 117, 122, 138, 140, 145, 167, 176, 185, 188, 189, 194, 200, 206, 212, 234, 240, 246, 253, 255, 258, 265, 287, 291, 292, 294, 296, 305, 310, 322, 325, 327
testimony, 241
the Middle East, 156

the United Kingdom, 53, 54, 56, 57, 59, 74, 223, 241, 258, 267, 284, 295, 307
the United States, 41, 124
theater, 141
theme, 2, 6, 176, 184, 185, 291
theory, 11, 27, 33, 39, 40, 42, 62, 85, 99, 102, 122, 135, 142, 143, 145, 158, 164, 180, 190, 195, 200, 206, 216, 217, 223, 238, 244, 256, 263, 265, 267, 275, 279, 281, 285, 296, 303, 308, 312, 315
therapy, 101–104
thinking, 7, 234
thought, 20
thread, 188
threat, 13, 24, 31, 32, 78, 142, 187, 222
time, 11, 13, 149, 181, 182, 184, 222, 315
today, 151, 294
tokenism, 196
toll, 52, 58, 187, 191, 235
tomorrow, 294
tool, 7, 14, 21, 24, 34, 47, 49, 50, 107, 141, 144, 152, 167, 183, 196, 211, 215, 240, 247, 274, 307
topic, 203
torch, 218, 287
traction, 34, 282
tradition, 1
traditionalist, 180
training, 36, 68, 96, 126
trait, 79, 238
trajectory, 285

transformation, 10, 184, 190, 196, 213, 305
transgender, 34, 124, 217, 252, 282, 288, 303
transition, 26, 258
transparency, 182, 203
transphobia, 109, 284
trauma, 27, 33, 34, 60, 67, 109, 191, 198, 254, 305
travel, 147, 211, 212, 236–238
treatment, 126, 205, 242, 251
tribute, 323
triumph, 28, 131, 133, 188, 190, 193, 234, 236, 247, 278
trust, 85
truth, 24, 28, 176, 192, 198, 287
truthfulness, 199
turmoil, 15, 64, 186, 193
turning, 11, 25, 52, 54

Uganda, 242
UK, 53, 55, 59, 60, 68, 75, 204, 233, 240, 257, 258, 284
umbrella, 147
uncertainty, 31, 58, 59
undercurrent, 5
underpinning, 80
understanding, 1–3, 5–8, 11, 12, 14, 17–20, 27, 30, 40, 42, 44, 45, 61, 78, 99, 101, 102, 109, 111, 112, 117, 141, 142, 153, 158, 160, 164, 165, 167, 170, 184, 186–189, 192, 199, 217, 230–232, 237, 243, 244, 248, 256, 259, 260, 267, 272, 275, 276, 278, 281, 284, 297, 300, 304–306, 309, 313, 318, 319

undertaking, 28
union, 9
unity, 6, 78, 89, 214, 286, 315, 323
universality, 195
university, 20, 184
upbringing, 5, 6, 8, 14, 187
uplift, 202, 260
urgency, 5, 23, 51, 211, 245, 246
use, 19, 23, 48, 51, 86, 143, 196, 285

vacuum, 10, 314
validation, 135, 196
validity, 101
variety, 281
victim, 34
victimization, 34, 198, 231
view, 9, 27, 142, 195, 206, 221
violation, 40, 171, 263
violence, 2, 7, 10, 17, 24, 28, 31–34, 40, 42, 47, 50, 52–55, 57, 78, 85, 86, 90, 102, 115, 141, 142, 149, 156–158, 174, 185, 187, 191, 200, 211, 214, 218, 219, 221, 222, 225, 230, 234, 236, 248, 252, 254, 263, 265, 271, 281, 282, 284, 288, 293, 296, 297, 304, 310
visa, 147
visibility, 2, 14, 24, 25, 30, 32, 39, 78, 94, 121, 141, 143, 147, 148, 155, 167–170, 172, 182, 183, 188, 196, 200, 213, 215–217, 228, 239, 241, 245, 248, 276, 278, 282, 292, 293, 303, 311, 322
vision, 76, 263–265

voice, 8, 30, 47, 49, 54, 69, 71, 76, 79, 84, 155, 173, 175, 191, 198, 200, 289, 307, 322
vulnerability, 67, 204, 232

waiting, 58
wake, 176, 183
warmth, 5
way, 10, 16, 81, 104, 122, 157, 160, 215, 222, 253, 257, 260, 278, 307
wealth, 162
web, 53, 99
weight, 5, 14, 58, 187
well, 26, 44, 51, 80, 86, 104, 112, 115, 117, 122, 179, 187, 191, 195, 239, 254, 277, 310–312
wellbeing, 271, 272
Wellington, 84
wellness, 112
whirlwind, 176
whitewashing, 256
whole, 197
willingness, 167, 197, 262, 307
woman, 17, 27, 34, 124, 175, 186, 216, 217, 258, 277, 296, 303
work, 8, 12, 29, 32, 44, 47, 50, 52, 61, 64, 66, 68, 69, 74, 76, 90, 94, 96, 99, 104, 112, 114, 119, 120, 124, 126, 128, 133, 138, 140–143, 145, 148, 150, 155–157, 161, 165–167, 170, 173, 180, 182, 185, 197, 200–203, 209–211, 213, 217–220, 222, 223, 225, 229–231, 237, 238,

240–242, 246, 248, 251–255, 257, 259, 260, 266, 267, 277, 278, 283, 284, 289, 292, 295, 297, 303, 305, 308, 311, 322, 326

world, 2, 6, 7, 10, 11, 18, 20, 23, 25, 28, 30, 43, 45, 54, 64, 71, 74, 76, 107, 140, 142, 146, 158, 166, 167, 171, 172, 180, 188, 192, 194, 208, 223, 234, 235, 238, 240, 256, 260, 263, 265, 278, 280, 287, 292, 298, 302, 307, 311, 315, 318, 321, 323, 326

worth, 8, 28, 126, 193

worthlessness, 12

youth, 20, 45–47, 49, 104–109, 112, 115–117, 185, 192, 200, 207, 216, 217, 252, 253, 259, 278, 297, 299, 322, 324

zealotry, 33

Milton Keynes UK
Ingram Content Group UK Ltd.
UKHW051143031124
450424UK00019B/1236